A HISTORY OF POLICE AND MASCULINITIES, 1700–2010

This unique collection brings together leading international scholars to explore how ideologies about masculinities have shaped police culture, policy and institutional organization from the eighteenth century to the present day.

It addresses an under-researched area of historical inquiry, providing the first in-depth study of how gender ideologies have shaped law enforcement and civic governance under 'old' and 'new' police models, tracing links, continuities and changes between them. The book opens up scholarly understanding of the ways in which policing reflected, sustained, embodied and enforced ideas of masculinities in historic and modern contexts, as well as how conceptions of masculinities were, and continue to be, interpreted through representations of the police in various forms of print and popular culture.

The research covers the UK, Europe, Australia and America and explores police typologies in different international and institutional contexts, using varied approaches, sources and interpretive frameworks drawn from historical and criminological traditions.

This book will be essential reading for academics, students, and those interested in gender, culture, police and criminal justice history as well as police practitioners.

David G. Barrie is lecturer in British history at The University of Western Australia. His research interests include crime and punishment in eighteenth- and nineteenth-century Scotland. He is author of *Police in the Age of Improvement: Police Development and the Civic Tradition in Scotland, 1775–1865* (Willan, 2008), which was awarded 'best first book' in Scottish history by the international committee of the Frank Watson Book Prize. He has published widely on Scottish policing in leading international journals.

Susan Broomhall is Winthrop Professor in history at The University of Western Australia. Her research focuses on early modern gender history. Most recently she is editor (with Jacqueline Van Gent) of *Governing Masculinities in the Early Modern Period: Regulating Selves and Others* (Ashgate, 2011) and author (with Jennifer Spinks) of *Early Modern Women in the Low Countries: Feminising Sources and Interpretations of the Past* (Ashgate, 2011).

A HISTORY OF POLICE AND MASCULINITIES, 1700–2010

Edited by David G. Barrie and Susan Broomhall

 Routledge
Taylor & Francis Group

LONDON AND NEW YORK

First published 2012
by Routledge
2 Park Square, Milton Park, Abingdon, Oxon, OX14 4RN

Simultaneously published in the USA and Canada
by Routledge
711 Third Avenue, New York, NY 10017

*Routledge is an imprint of the Taylor & Francis Group, an informa
business*

British Library Cataloguing in Publication Data
A catalogue record for this book is available from the British Library

Library of Congress Cataloging in Publication Data
A history of police and masculinities, 1700-2010 / edited by David G.
Barrie and Susan Broomhall.
p. cm.
ISBN 978-0-415-67129-3 (hbk.) — ISBN 978-0-415-69661-6 (pbk.)
1. Police—History. 2. Police—Social aspects. 3. Masculinity. I. Barrie,
David G. II. Broomhall, Susan.
HV7903.H57 2012
363.209–dc23
2011027696

ISBN: 978–0–415–67129–3 hbk
ISBN: 978–0–415–69661–6 pbk
ISBN: 978–0–203–14142–7 ebk

Typeset in Times New Roman by Prepress Projects, Perth, UK

CONTENTS

ILLUSTRATIONS

Figures

Table

CONTRIBUTORS

David G. Barrie is Lecturer in British history at The University of Western Australia. His research interests include crime and punishment in eighteenth- and nineteenth-century Scotland. He is author of *Police in the Age of Improvement: Police Development and the Civic Tradition in Scotland, 1775–1865* (Willan Publishing, 2008). He has published widely on Scottish policing, governance and civil society and is currently writing a monograph (with Susan Broomhall) entitled *Police Courts in Nineteenth-Century Scotland: Crime, Community and Control* (contracted to Ashgate).

Susan Broomhall is Winthrop Professor in history at The University of Western Australia. Her research focuses on early modern gender history. Most recently, she is editor (with Jacqueline Van Gent) of *Governing Masculinities in the Early Modern Period: Regulating Selves and Others* (Ashgate, 2011) and author (with Jennifer Spinks) of *Early Modern Women in the Low Countries: Feminising Sources and Interpretations of the Past* (Ashgate, 2011). She is currently writing a monograph (with David G. Barrie) entitled *Police Courts in Nineteenth-Century Scotland: Crime, Community and Control* (contracted to Ashgate).

Francis Dodsworth is a Research Fellow in the ESRC Centre for Research on Socio-Cultural Change (CRESC) at The Open University, UK, where he is also a member of the International Centre for Comparative Criminological Research. His work explores the history of security in the modern British city since c. 1700. He has also published on the histories of government and commercial architecture, and non-conformist religion.

David Garrioch is Professor of History at Monash University, Australia. He has written on neighbourhood, class and policing in eighteenth-century Paris, on early modern European towns and on the Enlightenment. His most recent book is *The Making of Revolutionary Paris* (University of California Press, 2002). Current projects include a study of Protestants and religious toleration in eighteenth-century Paris, and a history of religious confraternities in Paris before the French Revolution.

Joanne Klein is Professor of History at Boise State University, Idaho, USA. Her publications include *Invisible Men: the Secret Lives of Police Constables in Liverpool, Manchester and Birmingham, 1900–1939* (Liverpool University Press, 2010), ' "Moving On,' Men and the Changing Character of Interwar Working-Class Neighborhoods: from the Files of the Manchester and Liverpool City Police', *Journal of Social History*, vol. 38, no. 2 (2004) and 'Irregular Marriages: Unorthodox Working-Class Domestic Life in Liverpool, Birmingham and Manchester', *Journal of Family History*, vol. 30, no. 2 (2005). Her research focuses on the everyday lives of British police constables and working-class society.

Matthew McCormack is Senior Lecturer in History at the University of Northampton, UK. He works on masculinity in 'public' contexts in eighteenth-century England. His publications include *The Independent Man: Citizenship and Gender Politics in Georgian England* (Manchester University Press, 2005) and, as editor, *Public Men: Masculinity and Politics in Modern Britain* (Palgrave Macmillan, 2007). He is currently working on an AHRC-funded project 'Soldiers and Soldiering in Britain, 1750–1815' and is completing a book on the Georgian militia.

Simona Mori is Associate Professor of the History of Political Institutions and Early Modern European History at the University of Bergamo, Italy. She works on the Italian States between the eighteenth and nineteenth centuries, with an emphasis on central and local government and on the development of policing. She is presently investigating nineteenth-century professional literature about the Italian police. Her publications include *Il Ducato di Mantova nell'età delle riforme (1736–1784): Governo, amministrazione e finanze* (Firenze, 1998). On policing she published in *Società e storia* and *Acta Histriae*, and contributed with chapters to L. Antonielli (ed.), *Polizia, ordine pubblico e crimine fra città e campagna: un confronto comparativo* (Soveria Mannelli, 2010), to L. Antonielli (ed.), *La polizia del lavoro: il definirsi di un ambito di controllo* (Soveria Mannelli, in press) and to the conference proceedings S. Mori and L. Tedoldi (eds), *Forme e pratiche di polizia del territorio nell'Ottocento preunitario* (Soveria Mannelli, in press).

Gerda W. Ray teaches History of Crime and Justice and other courses at the University of Missouri, St. Louis, USA. She received her PhD from the University of California, Berkeley and has also taught at Wesleyan University in Middletown, Connecticut. She is currently working on the commodification of immigrant imprisonment in the USA.

Guy Reel is Associate Professor of Mass Communication at Winthrop University in Rock Hill, South Carolina, USA. A former newspaper reporter and editor for The Commercial Appeal of Memphis, Tennessee, Reel teaches journalism and mass communication and has written extensively about issues in journalism and communication history. He is author of *The National Police Gazette and the Making of the Modern American Man, 1879–1906* (Palgrave Macmillan, 2006), a study of portrayed masculinities in nineteenth-century tabloids. He received his PhD from Ohio University, his master's from the University of Memphis and his undergraduate degree from the University of Tennessee.

Haia Shpayer-Makov earned a PhD in history from the University of London, UK, and currently teaches British and European history at the University of Haifa, Israel. Her earlier research focused on the anarchist movement in Britain. In the past two decades she has concentrated on the history of policing in Britain. Author of *The Making of a Policeman: A Social History of a Labour Force in Metropolitan London* (Ashgate, 2002), *The Ascent of the Detective: Police Sleuths in Victorian and Edwardian England* (Oxford University Press, 2011) and co-editor with Professor Clive Emsley of *Police Detectives in History, 1750–1950* (Ashgate, 2006), she has also published extensively in leading scholarly journals.

Marisa Silvestri is a Senior Lecturer in Criminology at London South Bank University, UK, and a senior member of the Crime Reduction and Community Safety Research Group. Her research and publications have focused on the broad area of gender and criminal justice. In addition to various articles and reports, she has written *Women in Charge: Gender: Policing and Leadership* (Willan Publishing, 2002) and (with C. Dowey-Crowther) *Gender and Crime* (Sage, 2008).

Dean Wilson is Associate Professor of Criminology and Criminal Justice at Plymouth University, UK, and was formerly a Senior Lecturer in Criminology at Monash University, Melbourne, Australia. Dean's research interests include histories of policing, surveillance and contemporary policing. He is author of *The Beat: Policing a Victorian City* (Circa Press, 2006) and co-editor (with C. Norris) of *Surveillance, Crime and Social Control* (Ashgate, 2006) and has published widely in edited collections and leading journals.

ACKNOWLEDGEMENTS

This volume has developed in collaboration with a wide range of individuals and support networks beyond the contributors and it is a pleasure to thank them here. We acknowledge the financial support of a University of Western Australia Research Development Award (reference number 12104406).

We acknowledge the work of Iain Hutchison, Joanne McEwan and Kate Riley for their research and editing assistance. We thank the teams at Willan and Routledge for their enthusiasm, support and professional contributions to making the volume a success. A debt of gratitude is owed to the contributors to the collection. It has been a pleasure working with them and we appreciate their willingness to engage with the project. We also thank the anonymous reviewers whose insights added much to the clarity of ideas developed in the collection. Similarly, a great debt is owed to previous scholars in the field whose work has laid the conceptual frameworks on which this study builds.

Sue thanks David for his patience and his careful attention to both the big picture and the fine details of the volume. She also thanks Tim, Fionn and Cai, who, in their own way, remind her of the bigger picture and the finer details of life. David thanks Sue for her perceptive insights and for convincing him of the possibilities that such a collection offered. He also thanks his gorgeous nephew, Oliver, for being such a joyful 'distraction' and apologises for the collection's limited focus on just one type of 'man in uniform'. The history of Postman Pat and masculinities is still to be written!

INTRODUCTION

Susan Broomhall and David G. Barrie

This collection explores how ideologies about masculinity have shaped police culture, practice, policy and institutional organization from the eighteenth century to the present day.[1] It aims to open up scholarly understanding of the ways in which policing reflected, sustained, embodied and enforced ideas of masculinity in historic and modern contexts, as well as how conceptions of masculinity were, and continue to be, interpreted through representations of the police in various forms of print and popular culture. The contributors explore police systems in different international and institutional contexts, using varied approaches, sources and interpretive frameworks drawn from historical and criminological traditions. As a whole, the collection identifies significant changes to the circumstances in which notions of masculinity were forged as well as enacted over this period, and also highlights how masculine characteristics have been sustained in new police models, ideas and practices that have emerged to meet changing situations and contexts.

Policing provides an excellent case study of how conceptions of masculinity have been constructed and applied over the last 300 years. Police institutions not only incorporate changing models of male authority, but also are closely inter-twined with the distribution and operation of power in society. One form of power is the assumption of authority and control over oneself and others,[2] and one way in which this has been formalized in societies is through modes of policing. As the chapters in this collection suggest, ideals, representations and enactments of masculinity in policing not only occur through the formation of power, but also are shaped in part *through* an understanding of the relationship of varied social identities and behaviours to power and authority. Moreover, the analysis of police policy – that is, the determination of how policing was to be conducted and carried out, who was to be surveyed and the limits of police supervision and control – provides insight into other historicized models of male and female behaviour, such as those of individuals who were considered subordinate, weak, dependent, criminal and threatening.

Historicizing police masculinities

In exploring the above issues, the chapters in this collection contribute to an under-researched area of historical inquiry. Although criminologists have conducted much research in recent years on the importance of gender and masculinity in shaping police culture, their main focus has understandably centred on modern policing.[3] The gendered representation of the police in the modern media – both in journalism and in fictional entertainment – has also been studied,[4] as have the implications of gender ideologies on the carriage of justice and notions of those policed.[5] Moreover, the importance of masculinity, or male values, in shaping modern policing has been stressed in a number of studies,[6] with scholars recognizing that policing and police culture are strongly linked to gender ideologies.[7] A conclusion that has persisted from early scholarly work posits that the masculine culture of the police, its 'machismo', relates to the nature of police tasks; that is, it stems from 'the combination of danger and authority'[8] as 'police work consists of coping with problems in which force may have to be used.'[9] As Frances Heidensohn has pointed out, this conclusion rests on a number of assumptions about the relationship between force, physique, men, authority and danger. It assumes that '*coercion* requires *force* which *implies physique and* hence policing by *men*.'[10]

A further consistent feature, we would add, of the current analyses of gender and policing is a dearth of broad-scale historical work that could help trace the ways in which gender ideologies shift, change, adapt and map to new circumstances, new policing tasks and new policing personnel, as the institution itself changes conceptually over time.[11] To date, limited attention has been given to the historical contexts from which gendered notions of policing cultures have evolved.[12] What work has been done highlights the gendered nature of police work and the policeman as a public servant,[13] the important role ideas about gendered identities played in the construction of police authority,[14] and how officers and detectives epitomized national characteristics of manhood.[15] Attention has also focused on the ways in which violence[16] and images of manliness helped to contest and assert police legitimacy,[17] and how an 'authoritarian personality' has impacted upon the construction of the police as a labour force and as a profession.[18] Furthermore, a series of studies has examined the experience of police personnel, placing the policeman and policewoman at the heart of such investigations.[19] In particular, the role of the first female police officers in England (appointed during the First World War in response to labour shortages) has been the focus of a number of historical studies.[20]

However, scholars have given significantly more attention to the influence of gender on crime, people and criminal justice systems than on policing. A particular focus of inquiry has been the experience of women before the law, as they were morally policed in Victorian society,[21] in the social structures of convict colonies,[22] and especially in their treatment as perpetrators and victims of violent crimes.[23] The performance of normative masculinities in legal proceedings, meanwhile, has been studied in such domains as criminal and family law,[24] the criminal trial,[25] connections between culture, crime and criminal justice systems,[26] sentencing[27] and violence within households.[28] But much more attention needs to be given to the influence gender had on policing in historical contexts – especially the ways in which the ideas about masculinity have shaped how the police monitored and regulated criminal and social behaviours.

The historical studies that have been carried out on policing are immensely valuable in their own right, but they tend to focus on a particular period and rarely put masculinity at the centre of historical inquiry. Although these works have helped increase knowledge of the practice of gender ideologies in policing in different historical settings, what remains to be done is to relate these to each other and to use them as the building blocks for a new phase of analysis that explores and explains how conceptions of masculinity within the police have evolved over time and in different international contexts. This collection seeks to address this by focusing on the concepts, representations and practices of masculinity in policing, as these have been performed within both the institution and the communities policed. In doing so, we are able to identify those aspects of masculinity that have remained relatively steady since the eighteenth century, and those where its contours have altered over time.

Theorizing police masculinities

In order to analyse masculinities within policing, it is first important to establish what is meant by the term. We understand masculinity, first, as a concept that can be historicized, thus shifting and changing from the eighteenth century to the present day. Second, we view it as both a lived and an imagined principle, exploring here the tensions between representations and realities. Third, we understand it as meaning different things to different social groups at any given historical period.

One particular presentation and practice of masculinity that has been widely reported as being visible within modern police culture is 'hegemonic masculinity'. According to Nigel Fielding, this is the 'dominant form of masculinity as constructed in relation to (and therefore dependent on) femininities and subordinated, marginalized masculinities'.[29] Many studies have examined the way in which hegemonic masculinity exerts influence on (typically negative) behaviours within the institution. In particular, how this culture has been experienced by women both as personnel and as part of the community with whom the police interact has been the focus of important recent investigations.[30]

As a result of this groundwork, scholars are now beginning to offer a more nuanced interpretation of hegemonic masculinity within the police. In exploring policewomen in senior management and leadership positions, Silvestri, for example, argues that different cultures which carry different ideas about gender, masculinity and policing operate within police institutions. These have a different impact on women and offer women varied opportunities to influence them.[31] Other scholars have also critiqued the notion of hegemonic masculinity in relation to crime and policing. They argue that it implies too stable a notion. It lacks, they maintain, the sense of action (and anxiety) with which the practices and behaviours of masculinity must be 'achieved' by the men who engage with policing from different social perspectives.[32] The experiences of both women and men, these scholars argue, are affected by diverse masculine cultures in policing, not just a dominant one.

Likewise, the chapters gathered in this collection highlight multiple understandings and expressions of masculinity operating through policing. They tease out the particular forms and models of masculinity that operate or are represented in different contexts, groups and status, and which are enacted in different forms of police behaviour. The authors emphasize distinctions such as ethnicity, class, religion, age, health and sexuality as important elements in the determination of codes of masculine conduct and identities. Indeed, it is clear that, in some contexts, gender ideologies were not necessarily the most powerful influence on developments in policing.[33] However, as Toril Moi has argued, gender is 'always a socially *variable* entity, one which carries different amounts of symbolic capital in different contexts'.[34] The collection thus examines the complex relationships between social forces at different periods. These range from the visible importance of class in shaping expectations of policing and policed masculinities in early nineteenth-century Britain, to the influence of race for US policing particularly.[35] Indeed, in comparing some of the chapters' findings, it seems that race was a more explicit force in shaping masculinities in the latter environment than unexamined assumptions about indigenous and non-white inhabitants in Victorian Australia – whose reference points remained firmly the British metropolis.[36] Similarly, as Mori's study of police culture in nineteenth-century Italy reveals (Chapter 4), Catholic theology brought profound influence to bear on the model of a caritative, local policeman, whilst implicit assumptions about heterosexuality and marital status determined the male police officer's capacity for self-governance and supervision of households beyond his own.

The collection, therefore, offers a nuanced vision of the complex hierarchies and differences in the ideals, representations and practices of masculinity across classes, professional duties within the police force, and in comparison with those who were policed. The authors have drawn out precise meanings of masculinity in their case studies, clarifying the producers and the practitioners of certain forms of masculinity, and the implications of these models for police practice. By tracing the history of police over three centuries, the collection reveals the powerful continuity of a key masculine model that is physical, active and based in solidarity and fraternity of the rank-and-file officer. This persists, the collection reveals, alongside the emergence of other models of masculinity, such as the rise of intellectual masculinity of the detective or the competitive leader in the modern management era, which have emerged as policing has developed new positions and hierarchies. These models have been both reflected in, and produced through, the institution, personnel and policy of the police, in complex and often mutually reinforcing ways.

Conceptualizing masculinity in policing models

Between the eighteenth century and the present day, the organization, nature, function and purpose of policing experienced landmark developments. In the late eighteenth and nineteenth centuries, these included the construction of powerful, modern bureaucratic police organizations under hierarchical command structures, the employment of full-time, uniformed policemen, and the greater regulation of those to be surveyed. These initiatives were later followed by the introduction of detectives and female police officers – albeit after many years of resistance and opposition in certain circles, including within the police institution itself.[37] As is explored below, some of these developments heralded a smooth transition in assumptions about manhood, yet others necessitated re-conceptualization of male behaviour (both for practitioners and those policed) and prompted new forms of police masculinity to emerge.

In older, traditional English police histories, London's Metropolitan Police – established by Sir Robert Peel in 1829 – is perceived to be the pioneer of modern policing.[38] According to this interpretation, the policemen who took to the streets in that year not only were a marked improvement on the old, decrepit night watch-men who hitherto had failed to maintain law and order, they also set the standard against which future policemen were measured. Indeed, according to this view, the principles and practices by which the Metropolitan Police were governed were to become the prototype for liberal countries throughout the world and an example of how the need for law enforcement could be reconciled with the need for liberty. As Ascoli, in his study of the Metropolitan Police, noted: 'it is an indisputable fact that for 150 years the . . . [Metropolitan Police] . . . has become the model for every other democratic society and the envy of less fortunate people'.[39]

However, the extent to which the 1829 Metropolitan Police Act was a water-shed in policing has been challenged in recent years. Studies not only have pointed to considerable innovation in law enforcement prior to 1829,[40] but also have revealed that the 'new' police were largely based on the underlying principles of eighteenth-century neo-classical governance[41] and suffered from the same prob-lems and weaknesses as the 'old' 'police'.[42] Yet despite this, the concept of the 'old' and 'new' police model has remained a powerful one in English police histo-riography – especially when it comes to determining the parameters of historical inquiry. Although there have been some notable exceptions,[43] the tendency among historians has been to look at policing practices in these models in isolation from one another. Similarly, the belief that the Metropolitan Police was the world's most imitated model continues to be popular in academic circles. Although his-torians have also stressed the role of indigenous influences in shaping colonial, Scottish, European and American policing structures,[44] it is still widely claimed that the Metropolitan model was the most favoured of all urban, civilian policing structures in nineteenth-century Europe[45] and the standard against which rural forces in England were measured.[46]

However, European and colonial police systems studied in this collection developed different trajectories, the former often characterized by multiple organizational models in accordance with their changing political systems, and colonial experiences generally by more stable institutional models. Furthermore, developments did not occur in isolation. It is clear that models of policing in France, Italy and England developed in relation to each other: the French example being revered and condemned in equal measure among the English in the late eighteenth century, as McCormack notes (Chapter 2); French policing literature forming a basis for Italian instructional texts, as Mori observes (Chapter 4); and colonial environments being profoundly influenced by European examples, as Wilson demonstrates (Chapter 7).[47]

Importantly, as the chapters in this collection highlight, much of the gender ideology of older forms of law enforcement and policing of civil society was carried through almost seamlessly to new police systems and organizations in France, England, Scotland, Italy and colonial environments. All the models examined, at every period, demonstrate a deep and abiding connection between masculine identity and community control through policing. Policing the urban environment was one dimension of civic activities in which participation was an attractive expression of masculine political power[48] – and one established on an ideal of civil society that Carole Pateman has suggested was constituted as a masculine order.[49] These were long-held values and relationships whose continued promotion helped to establish policing by consent. McCormack's chapter, for example, focuses attention on how police reformers in England developed a police institution whose power was informed by civic ideals of governance but also embedded characteristics of martial masculinity. Indeed, no matter which model is under scrutiny in this collection, presentations and practices of masculine characteristics (and indeed, often a particular set of characteristics: paternal, householderly, emotionally detached and physically capable) have served as a foundation for the legitimacy of governance over others.

We suggest, therefore, that, in historical studies of policing that take gender as a key focus of analysis, conceptualizations of 'old' and 'new' police models cannot be sustained. All historic models of policing have linked their justification and practice of power and control over communities to concepts of masculinity. Moreover, we contend that policing's intimate relationship with masculinity has significant implications for the historian's understanding of international police typologies. Rather than holding up the Metropolitan model as being the template for modern policing practices as many studies have done, we stress the importance of different models in shaping international institutional policing structures and practices – models that were shaped by conceptions of masculinity and which have been subject to change in different historical and geographical settings, as the chapters presented here reveal.[50] The collection, therefore, contends that the growing trend in police historiography towards comparing international police typologies needs to take account not just of institutional structures, practices and indigenous cultures,[51] but also of the underlining gendered assumptions that are embedded within them and the contexts that produced them.

Representations of masculinities and/in policing

A critical part of the analysis in this collection examines how masculinities were represented, expressed and indeed fashioned in a range of sources, ranging from police handbooks, memoirs and internal correspondence to contemporary forms of media. The authors show that the representation of models of police masculinity in these varied forms has been ubiquitous and often a critical support to its maintenance.

First, the police institution's ideals of appropriate male conduct for officers, and its expectations of those to be policed, have been embedded in institutionally produced documentation such as policy and regulations, police manuals and handbooks for officers. Police manuals, in particular, sought to promote the institution's cultural values by defining and constructing boundaries concerning police behaviour. These texts blossomed from the early nineteenth century and became a key source for institutional self-representation, one that many of the authors of this collection explore for constructions of masculinities. The increasing frequency with which such texts were published was the product of the efforts of both governments and senior police officials to develop policing as a full-time, highly disciplined profession.

However, many of these sources also served a broader function. The concept of 'cultural hegemony', as developed by Italian writer and political theorist Antonio Gramsci, is often associated with the view that the police are an institutional branch of the coercive state, but it is equally significant for analysing police sources as cultural products that promote and uphold dominant ideologies and mould public opinion.[52] The sources produced by police institutions aimed to legitimize police presence in communities and were thus targeted to a wider public. Improvements in literacy, the expansion in print culture and the rise of new media forms across our period allowed the police's growing preoccupation with public image to be demonstrated in manuals and contemporary reports that became prolific from the mid-nineteenth century, as Mori observes. These sources provide important evidence for how senior officials represented the police institution as well as how they wanted the public to see them, with implications for understanding the connections between the legitimacy of the police and notions of masculinity. Indeed, this pre-occupation with public image is potentially of particular significance in understanding how communities that were initially hostile to the introduction of the police came to be reconciled – or, at least, less opposed – to the advent of a policed society.[53]

Second, models of police masculinity have been imbibed and disseminated by memoirs, letters, speeches and writings of practising and retired personnel. Internal correspondence of the police, as examined by Garrioch for late eighteenth-century France and Ray for mid-twentieth-century America, reveals understandings, expectations and practices of masculinity at work (Chapters 1 and 10 respectively). During the nineteenth century, a growing body of retired police officers, not simply the institution's governing men, began to publish memoirs of their experiences in the force, as chapters by Dodsworth (Chapter 5), Shpayer-Makov (Chapter 6), Klein (Chapter 9) and Mori demonstrate. In many ways, these reflected the masculine identities fostered in official representations, but they also exposed distinctions between the police ideals for officer interaction with the general public and those internal models of masculinity shared and practised among policemen. In addition, both published and personal writings have offered criticism of official representations of police masculinity, especially as they were experienced by those who perceived themselves as belonging to marginal groups. Recent personal reflections by former police officers, for example, have shed light on the challenges that masculine culture posed for women[54] and homosexuals in the police.[55] In another way, publications such as the English journal *The Police Review* were intended for the internal dissemination, education and improvement of the rank and file. These journals could act as an outlet for the expressions of officer grievances about their treatment by both offenders and the legal system and were especially significant as they expressed complaints that could not be articulated to the wider public. They provided an internal environment that could express some of the frustrations of the institution's lower-ranking participants without challenging the status quo.

Third, models of police masculinity have been reinforced, as well as challenged, by contemporary media of the day. Since the early nineteenth century at least, investigative and popular journalism has been influential in judging, reinforcing and shaping the idea, and ideals, of police masculinity. For many, factual and fictional representations of the police in the press and crime literature were the main influences on how they viewed not just the police, but also crime and the criminal justice system as a whole.[56] Print media, through reporting and visual representations, have at times ridiculed the masculinity of constables, as Reel demonstrates (Chapter 8). Other chapters in the collection observe, however, the close and supportive relationship between the media and the police, institutions that were both controlled by men of fairly high social standing and with shared ideas about the characteristics of masculinity required for community governance. Broomhall and Barrie (Chapter 3), for instance, argue that nineteenth-century Scottish journals tended to endorse the masculinity performed by police judges in their interactions with others. Over the past 300 years, the press has certainly critiqued specific aspects and events of policing,[57] but it has rarely (if ever) challenged the idea that policing is a male practice. Indeed, by not explicitly questioning this, it could be argued that the media have in fact reinforced the connection between masculinity and policing.

Importantly, the sources used here also highlight important distinctions between appropriate manly conduct imagined and articulated in handbooks, memoirs and media, on the one hand, and the practice of masculine behaviours shown in police action, responses to crime, and justice proceedings, on the other. A bourgeois ideal of chivalric conduct towards the weak was consistently evoked from the early nineteenth through to the early twentieth centuries, as chapters by Dodsworth, Mori and Klein show. Yet this held little sway in the face of working-class female offenders in the early Victorian courtroom, as Broomhall and Barrie reveal. Some source types were inflected with expectations and actual practice. Police policies, as Wilson argues, responded to male policing behaviours considered aberrant by emphasizing expectations. Memoirs of the kind analysed by Dodsworth and Mori saw policing work selectively recalled at least in part to reflect favourable models of manhood for the author, his colleagues and sometimes also for his criminal opponents. Occasionally, those facets of masculinity that were revealed, even in the middle-class media that shared the values of the police hierarchy, were ones that blurred the distinctions between the putative rougher masculinity of the policed, and respectable notions of manly behaviour of the police magistrates and officers.

Some works, such as fictional texts, offered a new representation of manly police conduct. Reel's study of early twentieth-century sources shows how print journalism could validate male householders' interest in cheap crime periodicals by constructing such reading as part of a neighbourhood policing role. In another way, Sherlock Holmes looms large as the most well-known exemplar of a new agent of law enforcement, giving status to a type of police labour founded on intellectual endeavour. This was a model that appealed to detectives, whose emerging position required placement in the conceptual hierarchy of police masculinities. Popular fictions then as now went on to shape detectives' identity as men of power, as Shpayer-Makov's chapter shows, even if actual detecting practices (and indeed personnel) were somewhat different. As Robert Reiner has argued of modern fictional representations of the police on television, this form of entertainment is nonetheless 'not innocent of profound ideological effects in the images it constructs and conveys'.[58] Neither were the representations of the literary fictions and images that were produced by those beyond the police institution.

Performances I: hierarchy and masculinities within the police force

As a plethora of criminology studies have convincingly shown, police institutions comprise a variety of sub-cultures.[59] Although a number of unifying character-istics can be found in police organizations, criminologists have identified many cultural differences, variations and nuances within and between different police sectors and personnel. Often, these are closely aligned to internal hierarchical structures and ranks and can vary over time. It is therefore important, as Janet Foster points out, to explore and convey these nuances rather than presenting police culture 'as if it is singular, monolithic and unchanging'.[60]

In this section of the introduction, we explore the diverse performances of masculinity that comprise, create and sustain hierarchies within police institutions. Collectively, the chapters show that different sectors of the police institution have developed and enacted different models of masculinity. We explore these in three distinct groups: as patrol officers, as detectives and as senior management. This section argues that these differing performances or models of masculinity operate in relation to each other, and hold different values in terms of what is expected of them and as they are expressed. They have been shaped in relation to policing tasks and functions, as well as in relation to the class and gender of their personnel. Finally, these models, as we shall explore, are susceptible to change over time in differing ways.

Men of the street

As Robert Reiner has argued, an understanding of how police officers view themselves, the society they live in and the role they play in it – 'cop culture' – is crucial to understanding the function and purpose of policing.[61] Although recognizing that variant 'subcultures' often exist within police forces, Reiner contends that 'police forces in modern liberal democracies . . . face similar basic pressures that shape a distinctive and characteristic culture'.[62] This, he suggests, consists of a 'subtle and complex intermingling' of a police officer's sense of purpose and a thirst for action-orientated behaviour, as well as pragmatism, solidarity and authority. Other scholars have claimed that machismo, prejudice and intolerance are facets of rank-and-file police culture (a view that has a number of critics), whilst some point more specifically to the importance of class, race and gender in shaping the many sub-cultures that exist among low-ranking officers.[63]

The overwhelming majority of these studies have focused on modern-day policing. However, as Paul Lawrence has pointed out, an awareness of 'cop culture' is just as important to criminal justice historians as it is for criminologists. Yet it has not received anywhere near the same level of attention in historical studies as it has in modern ones.[64] With a few notable exceptions,[65] historical investigations (at least in an English context) have tended to focus on detectives rather than on police officers and in most cases have ascribed only a minor role at best to the importance of masculinity in shaping police experiences and representations (see next sub-section).

What relevant work has been carried out in an historical context has tended to emphasize 'physicality' and 'toughness' as being defining characteristics of the officer on the beat.[66] This should hardly come as a surprise, as, unlike other public servants, police officers have always been able to deploy legitimate use of reasonable force in the exercise of their duties.[67] They are the state's chief instrument in appropriating violence within a specific territory, as Max Weber has argued.[68] Although instruction manuals and senior police officials emphasize civility, discipline and self-restraint, historical studies have shown that beat policemen often exercised their own notion of masculinity when it came to violence – a rougher masculinity more akin to that of the working-class neighbourhoods from which they were drawn. As Emsley, Clapson and Brogden have shown, police-men in England in the nineteenth and early twentieth centuries often relied upon strength and aggression to establish authority and reputation in the districts they patrolled.[69] There was a rationale to this. Many working-class communities were hostile to the police and assaults on officers were common.[70] Moreover, in inter-war Glasgow, police violence was often a response to sectarian violence, as Davies has explored.[71] Thus, a policeman's capacity to use physical force was not only essential to his manly reputation within certain areas; it was essential to his personal safety.

However, the use of aggression was also important to a policeman's reputa-tion among fellow officers. In some cases, an officer's masculinity was defined according to the beats he patrolled – with the toughest officers walking the rough-est and most demanding beats.[72] Despite the rhetoric to the contrary that emanated from senior officers, police violence was often tolerated within the service as part of the 'civilising process' as long as it was directed at working-class communities, not the respectable classes,[73] and did not exceed what was perceived to have been an undefined acceptable level. Although rarely condoning such behaviour, senior officers often turned a blind eye if it served to discipline the communities that the police were instructed to control.

Some of the chapters in this collection also emphasize the importance of physicality in shaping the masculinity of police officers on the beat. Some police memoirs, for instance, suggested that it could be an additional sign of the police-man's manliness if, despite the disadvantage of his weaponry, he was rarely overcome. A similar pre-occupation with portraying a 'hard man' image was also a feature of French police memoirs in the late nineteenth and early twen-tieth centuries, as Lawrence has shown.[74] However, the collection also reveals the importance of different markers of masculinity within low-ranking police officers in history. The models that the rank-and-file constables, officers, *sbirri* or *commissaires* created among themselves bear many similarities to modern police organizations – with their defining characteristics being typically fraternal, collegial, heterosexual and soldierly. But the chapters also highlight the role of local circumstance and setting in shaping the importance and evolution of these characteristics within different policing structures.

In his chapter, McCormack shows the efforts that were taken to distinguish English police officers structurally and politically from the model of soldiers of the late eighteenth century. Yet, as other authors in the collection also point out, police officers were largely drawn from the same working-class and less educated communities as soldiers. Moreover, in terms of their gender identity, policemen retained many of the characteristics valued in the contemporary model of mascu-linity present in the culture of foot soldiers, including sexual prowess, excessive alcohol consumption and fraternal bonding.[75] The performance of this masculinity has typically been for internal consumption; that is, for fellow officers. Indeed, it has operated in distinction to the performance of masculinity that officers were expected to present to the general public whom they served. To understand these two contrasting masculinities that lower-ranking officers performed, we must examine the behaviour expected of officers in their relationships with the public and its consequences for the masculine identity they performed within the institution.

Access to weapons has been a key part of the symbolic creation of power for lower-ranking police officers who interacted directly with the public. However, these weapons have typically been distinct, explicitly so, from those used by soldiers. The police on mainland Britain, for instance, traditionally carried batons, not swords or firearms, and Italian civilian officers wielded sidearms less impressive than their military counterparts, the *carabinieri*. Moreover, as the collection shows, police personnel have commonly perceived the over-use of weapons to be cowardly or a sign of weakness. Dodsworth, for example, notes that the internal police publication, *The Police Review*, was highly critical of officers who resorted to excessive violence, although it expected that policemen who used only moderate violence, which could leave them vulnerable on the streets, would be supported by senior police officials and magistrates.

Scholars have also often identified that lower-ranking police personnel have operated in a heterosexual culture. Whether it was sleeping with prostitutes, displaying macho or chauvinistic behaviour in front of female officers or ostracizing homosexuals within their own force, there has historically been a strong heterosexual undertone embedded within policing organizations.[76] The chapters in this collection show that this culture served a variety of purposes. The need to chastise and ultimately dismiss police officers for fraternizing with female prostitutes helped associate higher-ranking officers with superior male control, whilst also helping to validate to rank-and-file colleagues and those beyond the institution an alternative physical masculine identity based on sexual achievement. Yet control of sexuality could also function to raise men within a hierarchy of masculinities. Indeed, some of the chapters reveal that demonstration of sexual as well as other forms of self-governance has been a prerequisite for progression to higher offices within some police systems. By contrast, in Italy, marriage distinguished the civilian police from the celibate *carabinieri*. As Mori argues, one model of manhood emphasized the need for proximity to, and experience in, family and household relations, the other the intense vocational and self-sacrificing model of the priesthood.

The existence of such models of masculinity within rank and file to some extent reflected the cultural and social backgrounds from which policemen were drawn. However, it is also possible that such masculine cultures operated because of the very strong subordination of the police constable by those higher up the institutional hierarchy. The bodily, speech, sexual and gustatory habits of lower-ranking police officers have always been heavily controlled by their superiors. Indeed, even police officers' access to marriage has been the subject of institutional determination.[77] For Wilson's subordinated constables, marriage appeared to be deemed the marker of full adult respectable status for men. The right to marry was thus carefully controlled for those whom the police institution wanted to keep in submission to senior officers.

The interdependence of lower-ranking officers also seems a critical factor in this overt and physical performance of masculinity, at least for their own internal audience. As officers have frequently worked in pairs or in a team environment on the streets, their need to rely on each other has been significant. We should not overlook either that policing has traditionally been poorly remunerated and challenging work in which turnover rates among the rank and file were often very high. Yet the interdependence of their activities has required a level of trust in colleagues; trust that has been commonly forged in hyper-masculine contexts – drinking and heterosexual behaviours particularly – which have enabled the development of a shared identity, just as it was for the not-fully-adult apprentices and journeymen of the early modern period.[78] This interdependence has also functioned as a form of subordination, because police officers have not had complete independence of action (unlike detectives, a factor that gave the latter an immediately distinct masculine status). The uniform has likewise been a sign of strength for the police institution as a group, symbolic of its wider force and power. However, it has provided the policeman little individuality, a characteristic that was the hallmark of a certain, middle-class form of masculinity which reflected his right to individual self-determination and identity. Although the uniformed police officers' strength in numbers has conveyed the masculine power of the institution to the communities it has policed, it has left the individual policeman a rather weak and subordinated, external presentation of masculine identity. As A. Wynter perceptively, and rather poignantly, wrote in the *Quarterly Review* in 1856, the policeman on the beat 'is an institution rather than a man'.[79]

The fact that rank-and-file police officers have been subordinated in terms of institutional power (distinct from the power they exercise over the wider community) has had significant implications for their expression and performance of masculinity. It has, we argue, resulted in their masculinity being overt in its display within the institution and perhaps beyond. Moreover, although the existence of different sub-cultures and notions of masculinity have existed within this sector of the police organization, rank-and-file officers in different historical settings have nonetheless shared a number of salient characteristics. Indeed, the chapters in this collection suggest that few changes can be discerned to some of the more common characteristics associated with the masculinity of the officers on the beat identified in this sub-section.[80] We contend that this is one of the more stable masculine identities within policing, as the essential causes of it are inherent in the officers' position and function in the hierarchical organization of the police institution, which have altered little over the past 300 years.

Detecting manhood

A number of chapters in this collection examine the development of the detective as a masculine presence within the police institution. Neglected for many years by historians in favour of the uniformed officers who walked the streets, the detective has recently become subject to increased historical inquiry.[81] Early scholarly attention focused on eighteenth-century 'thief takers' and the development of organized detection in the shape of London's famous Bow Street Runners,[82] but more recently historians have examined how press reports,[83] Hollywood media genres,[84] scientific advances,[85] popular fiction and the memoirs of former officers have reflected, shaped and reinforced detective images and stereotypes.[86] Most of these have looked at the male detective, although in recent years the female detective's interaction with professional, gender and class identities has also been examined.[87]

This growing fascination with the detective in history has been partly conditioned by the availability of a bourgeoning volume of print and visual sources. From the late nineteenth century, the detective autobiography effectively became a literary genre of its own, such was the penchant among former officers for self-representation. Indeed, detectives were more likely than police officers, or other occupational groups, to write about and publish recollections of their professional lives.[88] As Shpayer-Makov has argued in an earlier publication, the impetus behind this growing concern with self-representation among detectives in nineteenth- and early twentieth-century London stemmed from a desire to rectify the distorted fictional and unflattering detective image that had become popular in literary works. To redress the balance, detective memoirs projected a glamorous, romantic, appealing image of intelligent, highly skilled, self-made men, which in all likelihood served to enhance the public's perception of Scotland Yard. Similarly, detectives have been shown to have endured a reciprocal, and at times uneasy, relationship with the press in late Victorian and Edwardian England. Sometimes critical, sometimes supportive, the press, nonetheless, ultimately proved to be 'instrumental in ending the public's opposition to the existence of plain clothes officers, and later in entrenching a positive image of them as protectors of society and of the empire'.[89]

Yet, despite increasing scholarly interest in the relationship between the public and the self-image of the detective, much more attention needs to be devoted both to the role of masculinity in shaping detective identities, and to how media genres have reflected, negotiated and influenced ideas about detective masculinity.[90] What strides have been made on these topics have been primarily in the fields of criminology[91] and film and media studies.[92] Philippa Gates's pioneering research into the relationship between Hollywood detective films and masculinity over the course of the twentieth century has been immensely valuable in showing how representations of detectives have shifted and evolved over time in line with broader social and cultural change, whilst continuing to be underpinned by a specific form of American masculinity that is defined by manliness, perseverance and heroism.[93] But there is certainly scope to extend historical inquiry over a longer time period, to different contexts and through different media and sources. Indeed, broadening the scope of historical inquiry is especially important in light of detectives' introduction and increasing importance within the police service from the late Victorian period. As this collection reveals, the employment of detectives had significant implications for the police service as a whole, not least as it required a re-evaluation of the status of other personnel in the police hierarchy, and at times their performance of masculinity.

As Reel explores in Chapter 8, the model of masculinity presented by the 'loner' detective in America at the turn of the twentieth century served to emasculate the uniformed, rank-and-file officer who was tightly embedded in an institutional hierarchy. In contrast to his uniformed colleague, the detective was portrayed as one who rejected all forms of dependence and also control. Contemporary sources highlighted his physical independence: he was imagined to be physically self-reliant and tough in a fight, for he worked alone. This idea of the detective's visible autonomy was reflected in practice by his 'right' to plain clothes. The literary detective was also depicted as a renegade: the demarcation from a form of criminal was at times dangerously close. Indeed, at times, the boundaries between whether the detective was a formal law enforcer or law unto himself seemed far from clear. This complicated position partly arose from the fact that many detective services were not originally part of the police, but rather were conducted by private agencies. In this respect, there were similarities between the representation of detectives in early twentieth-century America and the representation of detectives in post-revolutionary Paris, nineteenth-century France and twentieth-century Victoria: detectives in the last three settings were often recruited from the ranks of ex-convicts, which initially damaged their self-image, as other studies have shown.[94]

In an anthropological vein, fictional texts of the nineteenth century cast the detective as an observer of people, not among them. However, as Shpayer-Makov demonstrates, some private agencies found that women and boys were useful detectives precisely because they could fit into the communities they were observing, not stand apart from them. That the police institution lagged behind private agencies in the employment of women in such roles is suggestive of the degree to which masculinity was foundational to the legitimacy, authority and identity of policing work. As a literary type epitomized by Sherlock Holmes, the detective's expertise was a rational, scientific one, lacking or even perhaps eschewing emotional engagement. There were similarities here with experiences in Australia and New Zealand, where scientific advances and new technologies in the early twentieth century gave rise to the image of the detective as a technocrat who relied less on intimate personal knowledge of the criminal underworld and more on depersonalized modern practices.[95] Yet Shpayer-Makov's evidence suggests that those who were more emotional, supple and subtle might have been more productive in the field. In such ways, an ideal of masculine behaviour has been more appealing for the police than the reality of characteristics that were beneficial to detecting work.

Indeed, a conclusion from the analyses in this collection, we contend, is that the popular imagination and representations of the masculinities of the manly detective have dominated the realities of detectives' work and their subjectivity as men. Although recent studies have shown that there were often competing representations available,[96] male detectives, it seems, selectively embraced the positive expressions of male identity and masculine attributes offered to them in fiction. The form of masculinity presented for the detective in literary texts has been so attractive that it appears to have merged with the historical performance of masculinities by detectives themselves, mirroring a similar conclusion Lawrence came to for memoirs of French and English policemen in the late nineteenth and early twentieth centuries.[97] Representation and performance have converged to produce an appealing image of male identity that the institution as a whole has been keen to embrace and which for the most part has been promoted by a supportive press.[98]

Leading and managing men

As a number of recent investigations have highlighted, women in the last few decades have risen up through police ranks to fill senior positions within the police hierarchy.[99] However, those who have succeeded in doing so are very much in the minority.[100] Police management continues to be dominated by men – leaving senior female officers, according to Silvestri, feeling outnumbered and isolated.[101] In this sub-section we examine the challenges that the changing nature of police work has posed for male police leaders, specifically in relation to how it has impacted upon their masculinity. We contend that the performance of police leaders' masculinity is one that has seen explicit change over our period, as their roles and responsibilities have been adapted and as they have responded, it seems, to wider public discourses. However, in arguing this, we recognize that it is not easy to ascertain whether these changes represent a shift in how governance of others and leadership are understood as gendered concepts, or whether they are merely subtle re-interpretations and presentations of old values that map onto new circumstances.

Just as there has never existed one dominant or consistent form of police masculinity, neither has there been a single, homogeneous police leader. As Bryman has pointed out, there are a range of definitions for what constitutes 'police leadership'.[102] Often, it is taken to mean 'the process of influencing the activities of an organised group toward achievement'.[103] The nature of police leadership – and the diffusion of power within police organizations – has differed and changed in various international and regional settings in the last 300 years. Police leadership has been determined not only by the type of police model and its relationship to the central and local state, but also by the level of autonomy that senior officers have enjoyed in relation to the elected (and sometimes unelected) officials who oversee them.[104] Police governance has always been characterized by external and internal leaders – the former often as representatives of the national or local state under whose authority officers act, and the latter as senior-ranking officers for whom policing is their profession.[105]

In the last few centuries there has been a change in the balance of power in this relationship. In the eighteenth and nineteenth centuries, elected, and in some cases appointed, police commissioners managed and sometimes undertook policing tasks within their respective wards – often with the assistance of a senior police officer who was appointed by, and subservient to, them.[106] Although senior officers enjoyed limited autonomy regarding day-to-day policing issues, commissioners managed the key policing issues at a committee level. However, over the course of the nineteenth century senior police officials in the United Kingdom and beyond acquired greater autonomy.[107] As with other institutions, power and authority were increasingly embedded in bureaucratic structures within police organizations themselves.[108] Both became more and more linked to knowledge, expertise and experience.[109] As a consequence, senior police officials within the internal structure of police organizations became more readily identifiable as police leaders, even though elected representatives have continued to exert considerable influence over police affairs in many liberal democracies.[110]

Although the police leader has always been distinctly differentiated from the rank and file, the nature of this differentiation has also altered over the past 300 years. In the early nineteenth century, high property qualifications ensured that police commissioners in the United Kingdom were overwhelmingly drawn from middle-class backgrounds.[111] As a result, the masculinity of the police commissioner was largely structured and defined by his middle-class origins and ideals, which distinguished him from the working-class recruits who comprised the rank and file.[112] Yet, from fairly early in their histories, police forces in England, as Klein notes, filled their senior internal officer positions from the ranks. Work experience combined with education was therefore established as another valid pathway to police leadership. Today, the modern internal police leader must now be able to understand their experiences on the street. The male police leader ostensibly derives his authority to lead not from his social background, but rather from experience and education. Like the rank and file, he too must prove his legitimacy to police others by display of masculine behaviours. This includes its own forms of physical performance, such as exhaustion from overwork, in which bodily failure is a positive marker of devotion to duty, as Silvestri argues (Chapter 11). High visibility and successful overwork are indicative of the male physical stamina of the new 'smart macho' police leader. In such ways, it appears that the institution's long-held commitment to a vocational model for men remains firm but finds new forms in the modern police.

Distinct from the commonalities of male experience that bind men of the rank and file, police leadership has forged a divergent model of highly competitive individualism. This has included the experimental humanitarian activities of police chiefs in late eighteenth-century Paris, such as de Sartine and Lenoir, who established wet-nursing, money-lending and venereal disease treatment agencies under their personal leadership, as Garrioch explores. Also, in the early nineteenth century, the development and analysis of statistical information introduced the possibility of quantitative measurements of success for police leaders.[113] Indeed, there has been a long history of competition between different towns over perceptions of order, judged through crime returns and public reports.[114] The widespread dissemination of such information through the contemporary media from the mid-nineteenth century has opened the judgement of police leadership to a broad public. Senior managers have been thus defined by the production of quantifiable 'outputs', creating a masculinity defined by results-driven achievement that is pinpointed to one individual as leader.

However, the police leader has never acted in isolation. Then, as now, the activities of those subordinated are pivotal to the identities of men governing the institution. Wilson's chapter shows the intense regulation of discipline required of the constable's body. A pre-occupation with internal discipline was to a large extent conditioned by the problems of ill-discipline, drunkenness and high turnover rates that characterized especially the nineteenth-century police forces. As a number of studies have shown, the 'Making of a Policeman', to quote Shpayer-Makov's apt phrase, was far from easy and senior police officials faced many problems in attempting to mould the ideal policeman.[115] The disciplining of the rank and file speaks not just to the need for mastery over the constabulary to subordinate them, but also to the way in which subordinated masculinities within policing have created the manhood of managers within the institutional hierarchy. The masculine status of senior police officials has been dependent on their ability to 'control their own household'. Male police leaders are judged as men, with the potential to be shamed or rendered honourable, by individuals over whom they must assert control. Senior men in the police institution are not therefore in control of their own masculine status, but are, too, dependent on others in the institutional hierarchy. The interdependency of police masculinities has been an important feature of its history.

The performance of governing masculinity within the police institution has certainly changed its face over the past 300 years. New criteria for validating achievement and access to power have been accepted, from education to experience and from independent, individual decision making to collaborative and consultative approaches. Yet the organizational structure of the institution and the dynamics between men that this produces continue to underpin presentations of police leaders as men. For example, the interdependency of male performance remains critical to the institution's hierarchy and legitimacy. Likewise, police leaders have found new forms in which to demonstrate devotion to duty as a sign of their physical, intellectual and moral strength. Yet however overtly leadership styles have altered, especially in the modern era, the conceptual connection between leadership and authority of policing on the one hand and masculinity on the other has not yet been uncoupled.

In summary, then, we argue that masculinities performed by personnel at different levels of the police institution both underpin and are also produced by the institutional hierarchy of the police. In saying this, it is vital to distinguish the performance of male power from the practice of institutional power. Those rank-and-file officers who perform the most overt presentations of manliness for each other hold the least institutional power, while those senior managers whose leadership styles within the organization display the collaborative, consultative and adaptive approaches perceived as feminine are those who wield the most institutional power. Whether this suggests that police power is changing towards a more gender-neutral model, or simply that senior men have less need to assert their masculinity in overt ways because it is embedded in their position of power, requires further research. But in terms of the management style and practice of senior police officials, it appears as though traditional gender boundaries are becoming a little more blurred, even though this is not fully recognized in the gender composition of high-ranking positions.

Performances II: the masculinity of the police institution in the community

In this section we explore another arena in which masculinity is presented and performed by police: that is, in its relation to the wider community beyond the organizational hierarchy. This presentation of masculinity has been forged in relation to two particular groups whom we examine in turn: the criminal and the wider, governed community.

Masculinizing criminality

The masculinity of the policed has always been conceived in relationship with the enforcer. Each has shaped the other. The gender identity ascribed to those deemed criminal is therefore a critical facet in the production of police masculinities. In the early nineteenth century, it was the mysterious otherworld of crime that was evoked, especially in media sources and memoirs. In this scenario, the policeman braved the 'wilds' as something akin to contemporary European missionaries. He was, as Robert Storch has famously argued, a 'Domestic Missionary' charged with visiting working-class communities in order to impose control and discipline onto the sprawling industrial masses.[116] His purpose, apparently, was also to save criminals from themselves. According to this representation, a disempowered male and female criminal class sat ready to be rescued by a police father figure. As Chapters 3 and 4 show, this vision can be discerned in media representations of Scottish police court work and early nineteenth-century police manuals in Italy. Those who committed criminal acts were distant from but redeemable for the world of (middle-class) civilization.

This missionary view was typically reported from the outside and from those above the criminal class being described. A closely related representation examined by Dodsworth occurred when police officers themselves entered the literary discourse. The texts that they produced peeled back the layers of grime to reveal the criminal underworld for a fascinated middle-class readership. Criminals had names and stories to tell. Practised with an intellectual eye, these 'rational' analyses of criminal specimens connected closely to the emergent anthropological and sociological turn in understandings of criminality.

The rise of statistical analyses by the mid-nineteenth century turned criminals into quantitative data, rendering them little more than numbers and patterns without individual subjectivity.[117] However, the development of criminality as a scholarly field by the later nineteenth century created first a model of hardened and recidivist individuals (with links to the science of phrenology), and then the personas of 'tough men' criminals and the criminal (male) mastermind. The last two models, discussed by Shpayer-Makov, Mori and Reel, became types who raised the status of police officers and detectives, by giving them worthy adversaries. Fighting crime became a war between men.

There were similarities here with the police's relationship with youth gangs. As Andrew Davies's investigations into masculinity and gang culture in late Victorian Manchester and Salford have revealed, police constables viewed young male gang members as a challenge to their authority on the streets and deliberately targeted them in order to enhance their own reputation for toughness.[118] However, female gang members were not viewed in the same light. Police officers and magistrates 'seem to have shared a broader Victorian perception of women as more malleable creatures than men'.[119] Unlike the male gang member, the female threatened the masculinity of the constable only in so far as she diverted his attention away from the 'manly' pursuit of dealing with real (male) offenders.

There was little place for the female criminal; she could not be a worthy foe of the policeman. The female criminal could be cast as a victim who needed saving, if she was repentant, as Mori, Broomhall and Barrie and Dodsworth discuss. But what of those who were unrepentant – did they lose their rights to police respect and protection? The position of the female criminal was complex and ambiguous, and problematic for policemen. They could not deal man-to-man with her, and her mere presence was potentially effeminizing to the officers who were required to interact with her.[120] In some ways, this was resolved by the police institution first allowing women helpers to assist male officers and then by formally recruiting female officers, as Klein, Shpayer-Makov and Silvestri explore.[121] Isolating interaction with women from standard male policing work prevented female offenders from reducing police officers' status as men. Indeed, as Louise Jackson has argued in an earlier publication, the successful assimilation of female officers into police forces in England prior to 1970 was determined by their capacity to maintain an ethos of difference based on femininity.[122] Thus, far from the introduction of female officers symbolizing progress in terms of gender integration and equality within the police institution, as some studies have implied,[123] gender expectations were instrumental to women's participation and role in twentieth-century policing. Moreover, Jackson's argument that female officers developed a distinct feminine identity through professional policing resonates with the findings of a number of the chapters in the collection, with female officers fulfilling a social welfare function and taking on a specialist role in dealing with women and children.

Likewise, for much of the nineteenth century, juvenile criminals who committed petty larcenies were not perceived by the police to be true adversaries as they were not fully mature and did not threaten the policeman's control of the streets in the same ways as adult males or male youth gangs (although teenage boys were a sizeable group of offenders). This was especially the case for female delinquents.[124] Although much police time was taken up with juvenile delinquency in the first half of the nineteenth century, the legislative reforms that sought to remove juveniles from the higher courts in England from the mid-nineteenth century somewhat downgraded how they came to be viewed by the police.[125] The subsequent introduction of industrial and ragged schools helped to separate many young people from various aspects of the legal system. The police continued to interact with juvenile offenders by apprehending them and bringing them to court, but the transition helped create the impression that the policeman's main role was to deal with harder, more serious criminals, and reformatories with minor young offenders. Indeed, as Jackson points out, public concern with the growth of juvenile delinquency and child neglect during the First World War increased the demand for women police officers.[126] The development of social work as a discipline of (university) training enabled the separation of some aspects of such police work, but the challenges faced by modern forces to conceptualize their community liaison roles in a manly guise indicates the persistence of underlying assumptions about what both policing and masculinity entail.[127]

The wider community

Police masculinities have also been developed through relationships with others in the community who create and imbibe the representations as well as the practices of the police. They have been important interlocutors in institutional transitions, making judgements to which police masculinities respond and adapt.

As mentioned previously, the police institution worked to legitimize its activities in communities by promoting an image of discipline and respect. These formed part of the masculine values of governing men. As Broomhall and Barrie show, chivalry epitomized the middle-class ideals of police leaders and magistrates in nineteenth-century Scottish summary courts. These were, and continue to be, the same qualities advocated for officers as they served their communities, as Mori and Klein demonstrate for nineteenth-century Italy and twentieth-century England respectively. At times, however, these expectations were far removed from actual practice. The chapters in this collection reveal police forces that were extremely concerned both with their own image and with establishing high levels of internal discipline and professionalism – both of which had important implications for community relations.

Moreover, the collection also highlights the highly supportive relationship that became established between certain men and the police institution. This relationship was beneficial to their identities as men, as mutually reinforcing and dependent forms of male power. As the eighteenth-century police chief Lenoir reflected in his memoirs, policing depended on every master exercising discipline over those workers under his control. White men in the United States could expect the police to legitimize their authority over non-whites. Likewise, nineteenth-century Italian and Scottish middle-class householders were expected to support the police in their activities, who in return by and large reinforced their own authority behind closed doors and protected their vision of community and commercial interests. Thus, as Reel and Dodsworth argue, such acts as reading police fictions could function to validate the masculinity of community men. In this guise, reading 'penny trash' was far from being a trivial pleasure – it could be re-cast as part of their householder duties to be aware of what dangers were present in order to better protect their communities.

Thus, this 'external' model of masculinity, which has been performed by police in their work with the general public and with offenders specifically, has been a fairly unified one that serves to represent the institution as a whole. It has been characterized ostensibly by Christian chivalric values of controlled and potential force held under firm control, of services of care, loyalty and sacrifice to communities, and of protection for the poor, the weak and the defenceless. It is a vision of an institution that has been produced according to ideals about masculinity held by the governing elite, and promulgated through official documentation intended for internal consumption, such as handbooks, as well as external audiences through publicly available reports and briefings. It has, in addition, been largely supported and seconded through media and other powerful representational forces controlled by men who have shared these values.

Conclusion

Together, the new analyses gathered in this collection offer a range of conclusions. At the level of ideals and especially conceptualization of policing as a practice, we suggest that there is a strong narrative of continuity. Policing has been firmly embedded with notions of masculinity. This has not in itself changed markedly over the period, even if the specific characteristics of masculinity have altered over time. Representations of police masculinities articulated in handbooks, memoirs, art and media have always played a key role in maintaining ideas generated by, and practices conducted by, the institution, generally supporting but also occasionally challenging them. It is in terms of police practices that the most evidence of concrete changes that have implications for performances of masculinity can be discerned: in the tasks performed as policing; in how they are understood as policing; in who conducts the policing; and in the changing considerations extended to those who are to be policed. The chapters in this collection demonstrate many adaptations and nuances of masculine behaviour that is presented to external communities, but they also highlight the continued importance for policemen at varied levels in the institution to validate their status as men through differentiated values and practices. The need for this continued internal enactment of gender identity points to the deep and abiding relationship of power to masculinity within policing.

It is inescapable how strongly policing – as a kind of power – in all forms and aspects is gendered male. This is certainly a strong continuity. However, perhaps it is also true to say that this conceptualization of policing as a male activity has been changing in practice for longer than scholars have generally recognized. This is indeed what an historical analysis over the long term can help to reveal. For, as we have seen, women and boys were recognized as useful detectives in the nineteenth century, 'women's' social working styles were brought in from the 1930s, and today a 'feminine' collegial and collaborative style of management is considered an established model of police leadership.

This may seem small progress in breaking the hegemonic mould, especially as there is considerable subtlety in how different aspects, forms and models of masculinity reassert themselves in new situations and contexts to address both internal and external changes (in ideas and in practices), and which themselves make changes to ideas and practices. Nonetheless, it will be fruitful for historians to examine more closely those fissures and points of tension that have allowed these new perspectives and skills to find their rightful place in the broader sets of knowledge and practices that policing requires. Such moments either create or stem from the recognition that policing is as much about the domestic as the commercial domain, about the local and the broader contexts in which the police are situated. Policing requires understanding of the communities of which it is at once part protector, part protagonist and part oppressor. Indeed, the existence of these fissure points highlights the fact that communities comprising men and women can and do change over time. They can evolve to appreciate that diversity rather the sameness of perspective can be a strength and not a weakness to a unified organization; an organization for which association with physicality is still at the heart of its everyday moniker as 'the force'.

Notes

1 As the collection draws on different disciplines and covers a broad time span in different international contexts, it has not been possible to list in full all relevant studies. Key international studies have been cited, but preference has been given to those focusing on the United Kingdom as these reflect the research backgrounds of the editors in this area of criminal justice history.

2 For more on the relationship between power and masculinity in a slightly earlier period than this collection is concerned with, see Susan Broomhall and Jacqueline Van Gent (eds), *Governing Masculinities in the Early Modern Period: Regulating Selves and Others*, Aldershot: Ashgate, 2011.

3 See, for instance, Louise Westmarland, *Gender and Policing: Sex, Power and Police Culture*, Cullompton: Willan, 2002; Marisa Silvestri, *Women in Charge: Policing, Gender and Leadership*, Cullompton: Willan, 2003; M. Young, *An Inside Job: Policing and Police Culture in Britain*, Oxford: Oxford University Press, 1991; Joseph Balkin, 'Why Policemen Don't Like Policewomen', *Journal of Police Science and Administration*, 1988, vol. 16, no. 1, pp. 29–38; and A. Prokos and I. Padavic, '"There Oughtta Be a Law against Bitches": Masculinity Lessons in Police Academy Training', *Gender, Work and Organization*, 2002, vol. 9, pp. 439–59.

4 For interesting studies on the media in a criminological context, see, for instance, M. Maguire, R. Morgan and R. Reiner, *Media Made Criminality: The Representation of Crime in the Mass Media*, Oxford: Oxford University Press, 2007; Robert Reiner, 'Media, Crime, Law and Order', *Scottish Journal of Criminal Justice Studies*, 2006, vol. 12, pp. 5–21; R. Reiner and T. Newburn, *Policing and the Media*, Cullompton: Willan, 2003; and Frank Leishman and Paul Mason, *Policing and the Media: Facts, Fictions and Factions*, Cullompton: Willan, 2003.

5 There has been an abundance of literature published on the impact of gender ideology on the workings of criminal justice systems in the last few years, much of which is cited in this introduction. Useful studies not cited elsewhere in this collection are Dierdre Palk, *Gender, Crime and Judicial Discretion, 1780–1830*, Woodbridge: Boydell Press, 2006; and Sandra Walklate, *Gender, Crime, and Criminal Justice*, Cullompton: Willan, 2004.

6 H. Toch, *Peacekeeping, Police, Prison and Violence*, Lexington, MA: Lexington Books, 1976, p. 44; Frances Heidensohn, *Women in Control? The Role of Women in Law Enforcement*, Oxford: Clarendon Press, 1992, p. 202; Dorothy Moses Schultz, *From Social Worker to Crime Fighter: Women in United States Municipal Policing*, Westport, CT: Praeger, 1995, p. 7; and J. Brown, 'Women in Policing: A Comparative Research Perspective', *International Journal of the Sociology of Law*, 1998, vol. 25, pp. 1–19 (p. 13).

7 See, for instance, Robert Reiner, *The Politics of the Police*, 2nd edn, Hemel Hempstead: Harvester Wheatsheaf, 1992; Frances Heidensohn, 'Gender and Policing', in Tim Newburn (ed.), *Handbook of Policing*, Cullompton: Willan, 2003, pp. 556–77; P. Rawlings, 'The View of Policing: A History', *Policing and Society*, 1995, vol. 5, pp. 129–49; and J. Chan, *Changing Police Culture: Policing in Multicultural Society*, Cambridge: Cambridge University Press, 1997.

8 J. Skolnick, *Justice without Trial*, New York: Wiley, 1966, p. 44.

9 E. Bittner, *Aspects of Police Work*, Boston: North Eastern University Press, 1990, p. 256.

10 Heidensohn, *Women in Control*, p. 73, original emphasis, cited in Jennifer Brown and Frances Heidensohn, *Gender and Policing: Comparative Perspectives*, Houndmills: Macmillan, 2000, p. 29. The last few footnotes and discussion of this section are a recap from this work.

11 Marisa Silvestri has observed that organizational processes of change have been viewed by scholars largely in gender-neutral terms and suggests that these may be better understood themselves as gendered processes. Silvestri, *Women in Charge*, p. 16.

12 A few rare exceptions are Francis Dodsworth, 'Masculinity as Governance: Police, Public Service and the Embodiment of Authority, c. 1700–1850', in Matthew McCormack (ed.), *Public Men: Masculinity and Politics in Modern Britain*, Basingstoke: Palgrave Macmillan, 2007, pp. 33–53; Susan Broomhall and David G. Barrie, 'The Changing of the Guard: Policing and Masculinity in Enlightenment Scotland', *Parergon: Journal of the Australian and New Zealand Association for Medieval and Early Modern Studies*, 2011, vol. 28, no. 1, pp. 65–90; and Harry Daley, *This Small Cloud: A Personal Memoir*, London: Weidenfeld and Nicolson, 1987.

13 For a recent publication on the lives of constables in England in the early twentieth century, see Joanne Klein, *Invisible Men: The Secret Lives of Police Constables in Liverpool, Manchester, and Birmingham, 1900–1939*, Liverpool: Liverpool University Press, 2010. See also Carolyn Steedman, *Policing the Victorian Community: The Formation of English Provincial Police Forces, 1856–80*, London: Routledge, 1984, which examines the role of gender in shaping the concept of the policeman as a public servant in Victorian England; Barbara Weinberger, *The Best Police in the World: An Oral History of English Policing*, Aldershot: Scolar Press, 1995, which examines the gendered nature of everyday policing in the inter-war years; and Louise Jackson, *Women Police: Gender, Welfare and Surveillance in the Twentieth Century*,

Manchester: Manchester University Press, 2006, which provides the first comprehensive academic history of policewomen's experiences in Britain. For an interesting comparison between police constables and firefighters see Shane Ewen, 'Managing Police Constables and Firefighters: Uniformed Public Services in English Cities, c. 1870–1930', *International Review of Social History*, 2006, vol. 51, pp. 41–57.

14 Dodsworth, for instance, argues that close ties between police and masculinities were not simply indicative of the physical demands of a dangerous occupation, but were also the product of 'a longstanding link between a certain vision of manly independence and public, civil authority in British political discourse'. Dodsworth, 'Masculinities as Governance', p. 33. Although not concerned specifically with masculinities, W. Miller, *Cops and Bobbies: Police Authority in New York and London, 1830–1870*, 2nd edn, Ohio: Columbus, 1999, argues that police authority was constructed by employing officers who embodied dominant values of authority.

15 Haia Shpayer-Makov, 'Explaining the Rise and Success of Detective Memoirs in History', in Clive Emsley and Haia Shpayer-Makov (eds), *Police Detectives in History, 1750–1950*, Aldershot: Ashgate, 2006, pp. 103–34.

16 A number of historical studies make brief reference to the importance of violence and physicality in shaping the masculinity of policemen. These are outlined at various points below. Among the most detailed investigations are Clive Emsley, *The English and Violence since 1750*, London: Hambledon Continuum, 2005, pp. 132–6; and Mark Clapson and Clive Emsley, 'Street, Beat and Respectability: The Culture and Self-Image of the Late Victorian and Edwardian Urban Policeman', in Louis A. Knafla (ed.), *Policing and War in Europe*, Criminal Justice History, vol. 16, Westport, CT: Greenwood Press, 2002, pp. 107–31.

17 Gerda W. Ray, 'Cossack to Trooper: Manliness, Police Reform, and the State', *Journal of Social History*, 1995, vol. 28, no. 3, pp. 565–86.

18 Clive Emsley, 'The Policeman as a Worker: A Comparative Survey, c. 1800–1940', *International Review of Social History*, 2000, vol. 45, no. 1, pp. 89–110; and Haia Shpayer-Makov, *The Making of a Policeman: A Social History of a Labour Force in Metropolitan London, 1829–1914*, Aldershot: Ashgate, 2002.

19 Clive Emsley and Mark Clapson, 'Recruiting the English Policeman, c. 1840–1940', *Policing and Society*, 1994, vol. 3, pp. 269–86 and David Taylor, 'The Standard of Living of Career Policemen in Victorian England: The Evidence of a Provincial Borough Force', *Criminal Justice History*, 1991, vol. 12, pp. 107–31. For a study of police wives, see Barbara Weinberger, 'A Policewife's Life Is Not a Happy One: Police Wives in the 1930s and 1940s', *Oral History*, 1999, vol. 21, pp. 46–53.

20 R. M. Douglas, *Feminist Freikorps: The British Voluntary Women Police, 1914–1940*, London: Praeger, 1999; Mary S. Allen, *The Pioneer Policewoman*, London: Chatto & Windus, 1925; and Angela Woollacott, *On Her Their Lives Depend: Munitions Workers in the Great War*, Berkeley: University of California Press, 1994. Other interesting studies that take a broader view of women's experiences include Schultz, *From Social Worker to Crime Fighter*; J. Appier, *The Sexual Politics of Law Enforcement and the LAPD*, Philadelphia: Temple University Press, 1998; J. Lock, *The British Policewoman: Her Story*, London: Hale, 1979; and Allan T. Duffin, *History in Blue: 160 Years of Women Police, Sheriffs, Detectives, and State Troopers*, Workingham: Kaplan, 2010.

21 Stefan Petrow, *Policing Morals: The Metropolitan Police and the Home Office 1870–1914*, Oxford: Clarendon Press, 1994.

22 For a recent example, see Kirsty Reid, *Gender, Crime and Empire: Convicts, Settlers and the State in Early Colonial Australia*, Manchester: Manchester University Press, 2007.

23 There is a growing volume of historical literature on women and violent crime, infanticide, domestic violence and child abuse, which is too extensive to list here. See, for instance, Anne-Marie Kilday, *Women and Violent Crime in Enlightenment Scotland*, Woodbridge: Boydell Press, 2007.

24 See, for example, James W. Messerschmidt, *Masculinities and Crime: Critique and Reconceptualization of Theory*, Lanham, MD: Rowman & Littlefield, 1993; Richard Collier, *Masculinities, Law and the Family*, London: Routledge, 1995; P. Carlen and T. Jefferson (eds), 'Special Issue: Masculinities and Crime', *British Journal of Criminology*, 1996, vol. 33, no. 6; and Cynthia Lee, *Murder and the Reasonable Man: Passion and Fear in the Criminal Courtroom*, New York: New York University Press, 2003.

25 E. Cohen, *Talk on the Wilde Side: Towards a Genealogy of a Discourse of Male Sexualities*, London: Routledge, 1993; and Angus McLaren, *The Trials of Masculinities: Policing Sexual Boundaries, 1870–1930*, Chicago: University of Chicago Press, 1997, explore the criminal trial as an arena in which normative masculinities were debated, challenged and reinforced in late Victorian Britain. For other studies on masculinity and the courts, see Derek Neal, 'Suits Make the Man: Masculinity in Two English Law Courts, c. 1500', *Canadian Journal of History/Annales canadiennes d'histoire*, 2002, vol. XXXVII, pp. 1–22; Rachel G. Fuchs, 'Magistrates and Mothers, Paternity and Property in Nineteenth-Century French Courts', *Crime, Histoire & Sociétés/Crime, History & Societies*, 2009, vol. 13, no 2, pp. 13–26; and Patrizia Guarnieri, 'Men Committing Female Crime: Infanticide, Family and Honor in Italy, 1890–1981', *Crime, Histoire & Sociétés/Crime, History & Societies*, 2009, vol. 13, no. 3, pp. 41–54.

26 Martin J. Wiener, *Men of Blood: Violence, Manliness and Criminal Justice in Victorian England*, Cambridge: Cambridge University Press, 2004, explores the cultural basis behind shifting legal and court practices towards violence. For more on sexual violence, see J. Walkowitz, *City of Dreadful Delight. Narratives of Sexual Danger in Late-Victorian London*, Chicago: University of Chicago Press, 1992; and S. D'Cruze, *Crimes of Outrage. Sex, Violence and Victorian Working Women*, London: UCL Press, 1998. For the development of new notions of masculinity over the eighteenth century and its impact on violence, see Robert B. Shoemaker, *Gender in English Society 1650–1850: The Emergence of Separate Spheres*, London: Longman, 1998; and Robert B. Shoemaker, 'The Taming of the Duel: Masculinity, Honour and Ritual Violence in London, 1660–1800', *The Historical Journal*, 2002, vol. 45, no. 3, pp. 525–45.

27 For the influence of gender on sentencing patterns, see B. Godrey, S. Farrall and S. Karstedt, 'Explaining Gendered Sentencing Patterns for Violent Men and Women in the Late Victorian and Edwardian Period', *British Journal of Criminology*, 2005, vol. 45, no. 5, pp. 696–720.

28 Elizabeth Foyster, *Marital Violence: An English Family History, 1660–1857*, Cambridge: Cambridge University Press, 2005.

29 N. Fielding, 'Cop Canteen Culture', in T. Newburn and E. A. Stanko (eds), *Just Boys Doing Business? Men, Masculinities and Crime*, London: Routledge, 1994, pp. 163–84, p. 47.

30 See, for example, Brown and Heidensohn, *Gender and Policing*, and Westmarland, *Gender and Policing*.

31 Silvestri, *Women in Charge*.

32 Messerschmidt, *Masculinities and Crime*, pp. 80–1.

33 See, for example, Jeff Hearn and David L. Collinson, 'Theorizing Unities and Differences between Men and between Masculinities', in Harry Brod and Michael Kaufman (eds), *Theorizing Masculinities*, Thousand Oaks, CA: Sage, 1994, pp. 97–118.

34 Toril Moi, *What Is a Woman? And Other Essays*, Oxford: Oxford University Press, 2001, p. 291.

35 Other studies that emphasize the importance of race in shaping the development of American policing include Dwight Watson, *Race and the Houston Police Department, 1930–1990: A Change Did Come*, Texas: Texas and A&M University Press, 2005;

and H. M. Henry, *Police Control of the Slave in South Carolina*, New York: Negro University Press, 1968.

36 The extent to which the English and Irish police models influenced policing practices and structures has been fairly extensively researched in recent years. See, for instance, Mark Finnane, 'A "New Police" in Australia', in Tim Newburn (ed.), *Policing: Key Readings*, Cullompton: Willan, 2005, pp. 48–68; and Stefan Petrow, 'The English Model? Policing in Late Nineteenth Century Tasmania', in B. S. Godfrey and G. Dunstall (eds), *Crime and Empire 1840–1940: Criminal Justice in Local and Global Context*, Cullompton: Willan, 2005, pp. 121–34. English and Irish influence on the early development of policing in America has also been identified. See Miller, *Cops and Bobbies*; and E. H. Monkkonen, *Police in Urban America, 1860–1920*, Cambridge: Cambridge University Press, 1981. Critics of this view include Patrick V. Murphy, 'The Development of Urban Police', *Current History*, 1976, vol. 70, pp. 245–8; and Hubert Williams and Patrick V. Murphy, 'The Evolving Strategy of Policing: A Minority View', *Perspectives on Policing*, 1990, vol. 13, pp. 1–16.

37 For good overviews and case studies of police histories in the countries with which this collection is concerned (and which have not already been cited), see Clive Emsley, *The English Police: A Political and Social History*, London: Longman, 2006; Clive Emsley, *Crime, Police, & Penal Policy: European Experiences 1750–1940*, Oxford: Oxford University Press, 2007; David Taylor, *Policing the Victorian Town: The Development of the Police in Middlesbrough c. 1840–1914*, Basingstoke: Palgrave Macmillan, 2002; David Philips and Robert D. Storch, *Policing Provincial England, 1829–56: The Politics of Reform*, London: Leicester University Press, 1999; S. H. Palmer, *Police and Protest in England and Ireland, 1780–1850*, Cambridge: Cambridge University Press, 1988; David G. Barrie, *Police in the Age of Improvement: Police Development and the Civic Tradition in Scotland, 1775–1865*, Cullompton: Willan, 2008; Clive Emsley, *Gendarmes and the State in Nineteenth-Century Europe*, Oxford: Oxford University Press, 1999; Jean-Marc Berliere, *Le monde des polices en France*, Brussels: Complexe, 1996; Alan Williams, *The Police of Paris, 1718–1789*, Baton Rouge: Louisiana State University Press, 1979; P. Napoli, *Naissance de la police moderne*, Paris: La Découverte, 2003; John A. Davis, *Conflict and Control: Law and Order in Nineteenth-Century Italy*, London: Macmillan, 1988; Robert C. Wardman and Thomas Allison, *To Protect and to Serve: A History of Police in America*, Englewood Cliffs, NJ: Prentice Hall, 2004; Mark Finnane (ed.), *Policing in Australia: Historical Perspectives*, Kensington: New South Wales University Press, 1987; and Mark Finnane, *Police and Government: Histories of Policing in Australia*, Oxford: Oxford University Press, 1994. For a recent overview of the early development of policing in Europe, see Catherine Denys, 'The Development of Police Forces in Urban Europe in the Eighteenth Century', *Journal of Urban History*, 2010, vol. 36, no. 3, pp. 332–44.

38 Prominent in this school are Charles Reith, *British Police and the Democratic Ideal*, Oxford: Oxford University Press, 1943; T. A. Critchley, *A History of Police in England and Wales, 900–1966*, London: Constable, 1967; D. Ascoli, *The Queen's Peace: The Origins and Development of the Metropolitan Police, 1829–1979*, London: D. Hamilton, 1979; and L. Radzinowicz, *A History of English Criminal Law and Its Administration from 1750*, vols 3 and 4, London: Stevens, 1968.

39 Ascoli, *The Queen's Peace*, p. 3. For an overview of contrasting schools of thought, see D. Taylor, *The New Police in Nineteenth-Century England: Crime, Conflict and Control*, Manchester: Manchester University Press, 1997.

40 Ruth Paley, ' "An Imperfect, Inadequate and Wretched System?" Policing London before Peel', *Criminal Justice History*, 1989, vol. 10, pp. 95–130; E. A. Reynolds, *Before the Bobbies: The Night Watch and Police Reform in Metropolitan London, 1720–1830*, Stanford, CA: Stanford University Press, 1998; and R. D. Storch, 'Policing Rural Southern England before the Police: Opinion and Practice, 1830–56',

in D. Hay and F. Snyder (eds), *Policing and Prosecution in Britain, 1750–1850*, Oxford: Clarendon Press, 1989, pp. 211–66.

41 Francis M. Dodsworth, ' "Civic" Police and the Condition of Liberty: The Rationality of Governance in Eighteenth-Century England', in *Social History*, 2004, vol. 29. no. 2, pp. 199–216.

42 Emsley, *The English Police*, pp. 24–64; and J. Styles, 'The Emergence of Police: Explaining Police Reform in Eighteenth-Century and Nineteenth-Century England', *British Journal of Criminology*, 1987, vol. 27, no. 1, pp. 18–21.

43 See, for example, Philips and Storch, *Policing Provincial England.*

44 See the works cited in note 36 plus David G. Barrie, 'A Typology of British Police: Locating the Scottish Municipal Police Model in Its British Context, 1800–1835', *British Journal of Criminology*, 2010, vol. 50, no. 2, pp. 259–77.

45 Emsley, *Crime, Police, & Penal Policy*, argues that the Metropolitan model was the most influential in Europe, pp. 246–66.

46 Philips and Storch, *Policing Provincial England*, argue that after 1829 the Metropolitan Police made policing arrangements in rural England appear backward, pp. 6 and 45–6.

47 This supports the conclusion of Clive Emsley that European countries, states and cities looked at each other's policing models. *Crime, Police, & Penal Policy, passim.*

48 See, for example, G. J. Barker-Benfield, *The Culture of Sensibility: Sex and Society in Eighteenth-Century Britain*, Chicago: Chicago University Press, 1992, pp. 104–53; Philip Carter, *Men and the Emergence of Polite Society, Britain 1660–1800*, London: Longman, 2001; and David G. Barrie, 'Police in Civil Society: Police, Enlightenment and Civic Virtue in Scotland, 1780–1833', *Urban History*, 2010, vol. 37, no. 1, pp. 45–65.

49 See, for example, Carole Pateman, *The Disorder of Women: Democracy, Feminism and Political Theory*, Cambridge: Polity Press, 1989, pp. 33–57.

50 For a critique of Metropolitan's influence on policing in Scotland, see the forthcoming article by David G. Barrie, 'Anglicisation and Autonomy: Scottish Policing, Governance and the State, 1833 to 1885', *Law and History Review*, 2012 (to be published in vol. 30).

51 Clive Emsley, 'A Typology of Nineteenth-Century Police', *Crime, Histoire & Sociétés/Crime, History & Societies,* 1999, vol. 3, pp. 29–44; and Barrie, 'A Typology of British Police', pp. 259–77.

52 Antonio Gramsci, *Prison Notebooks*, vol. 1, with Joseph A. Buttigieg, New York: Columbia University Press, 1992. For how his theories have been interpreted, see Thomas R. Bates, 'Gramsci and the Theory of Hegemony', *Journal of the History of Ideas*, 1975, vol. 36, no. 2, pp. 351–66; K. A. F. Crehan, *Gramsci, Culture and Anthropology*, Berkeley: University of California Press, 2002; T. J. Jackson Lears, 'The Concept of Cultural Hegemony: Problems and Possibilities', *The American Historical Review*, 1985, vol. 90, no. 3, pp. 567–93; and Max Travers, *Understanding Law and Society*, New York, Routledge, 2010, p. 72.

53 For opposition to the police, see the classic study by R. D. Storch, ' "The Plague of Blue Locusts": Police Reform and Popular Resistance in Northern England, 1840–57', *International Review of Social History*, 1975, vol. XX, pp. 61–90.

54 L. Wyles, *A Woman at Scotland Yard: Reflections on the Struggles and Achievements of Thirty Years in the Metropolitan Police*, London: Faber and Faber, 1952; and Daley, *This Small Cloud.*

55 Susan L. Miller, Kay B. Forest and Nancy C. Jurik, 'Diversity in Blue: Lesbian and Gay Police Officers in a Masculine Occupation', *Men and Masculinities*, 2003, vol. 5, no. 4, pp. 355–85.

56 See, for instance, Robert B. Shoemaker, 'Print Culture and the Creation of Public Knowledge about Crime in Eighteenth-Century London', in Paul Knepper, Jonathan Doak and Joanna Shapland (eds), *Urban Crime Prevention, Surveillance and Restorative Justice: Effects of Social Technologies*, Boca Raton, FL: CRC Press, 2009, pp. 1–21; David Lemmings and Claire Walker (eds), *Moral Panics, the Media and*

the Law in Early Modern England, Basingstoke: Palgrave Macmillan, 2009; P. King, 'Newspaper Reporting and Attitudes to Crime and Justice in Late-Eighteenth and Early-Nineteenth-Century London', *Continuity and Change*, 2007, vol. 1, pp. 73–112; Martin J. Wiener, 'Convicted Murderers and the Victorian Press: Condemnation vs. Sympathy', *Crimes and Misdemeanours*, 2007, vol. 1, no. 2, pp. 110–25; P. Williams and J. Dickinson, 'The Relationship between Newspaper Crime Reporting and Crime', *British Journal of Criminology*, 1993, vol. 33, pp. 33–56; and Leishman and Mason, *Policing and the Media.*

57 L. Perry Curtis, *Jack the Ripper and the London Press*, New Haven, CT: Yale University Press, 2001.

58 R. Reiner, 'The Dialectics of Dixon: The Changing Image of the TV Cop', in M. Stephens and S. Becker (eds), *Police Force, Police Service: Care and Control in Britain*, London, Macmillan, 1994, p. 18.

59 The criminological literature is too extensive to list in full. For a good overview, see Janet Foster, 'Police Cultures', in Newburn, *Handbook of Policing*, pp. 196–227.

60 Ibid., p. 196.

61 Robert Reiner, *The Politics of the Police,* 3rd edn, Oxford: Oxford University Press, 2000, p. 85. See also P. A. J. Waddington, 'Police (Canteen) Sub-Culture: An Appreciation', *British Journal of Criminology*, 1999, vol. 39, no. 2, pp. 286–309.

62 Reiner, *The Politics of the Police*, p. 86. Next sentence quoted from p. 90.

63 For a good overview of criminological literature on these topics, see the collection of chapters in Newburn, *Handbook of Policing.*

64 Paul Lawrence, ' "Scoundrels and Scallywags, and Some Honest Men . . .": Memoirs and Self-Image of French and English c. 1870–1939', in Barry Godfrey, Clive Emsley and Graeme Dunstall (eds), *Comparative Histories of Crime*, Cullompton: Willan, 2003, pp. 125–44 (p. 125).

65 See, for instance, ibid.; Taylor, *Policing the Victorian Town*; Clapson and Emsley, 'Street, Beat and Respectability', pp. 107–31; and Shpayer-Makov, *The Making of a Policeman, passim.*

66 The main historical studies which deal with the relationship between the police and masculinity are listed in the following notes contained within this sub-section, although most make only fleeting reference to masculinity *per se.*

67 Emsley, *The English and Violence*, p. 132.

68 Max Weber, *The Theory of Social and Economic Organisation*, edited and introduced by Talcott Parsons, London: Collier-Macmillan, 1964, p. 156. Similarly, David H. Bayley, *Patterns of Policing: A Comparative International Analysis*, New Brunswick, NJ: Rutgers University Press, 1985, pp. 7–13, argues that the use of physical force is one of the key defining features of the modern police. For a critique, which claims that the police rarely resort to force, see Jean-Paul Brodeur, 'Police et Coercition', *Revue française de Sociologie*, 1994, vol. 35, pp. 457–85.

69 Clive Emsley, ' "The Thump of Wood on a Swede Turnip": Police Violence in Nineteenth-Century England', *Criminal Justice History*, 1985, vol. 6, pp. 125–49; Emsley, *The English and Violence*, pp. 135–6; Clive Emsley, *The Great British Bobby: A History of British Policing from the 18th Century to the Present*, London: Quercus, 2009, pp. 144–76; Clapson and Emsley, 'Street, Beat and Respectability', pp. 107–31; and Mike Brogden, *On the Mersey Beat*, Oxford: Oxford University Press, 1991.

70 The most recent overviews on this are David Taylor, *Hooligans, Harlots, and Hangmen: Crime and Punishment in Victorian Britain*, Santa Barbara, CA: Praeger, 2010, pp. 133–9; and Taylor, *Policing the Victorian Town*, pp. 88–9, 119, 177–9.

71 Andrew Davies, 'Sectarian Violence and Police Violence in Glasgow during the 1930s', in R. Bessel and C. Emsley (eds), *Patterns of Provocation*, Oxford: Berghahn Books, 2000, pp. 41–62. For the police's role in dealing with gang culture in inter-war Glasgow, see Andrew Davies, 'Street Gangs, Crime and Policing in Glasgow during the 1930s: The Case of the Beehive Boys', *Social History*, 1998, vol. 23, no. 3, pp. 251–67.

72 Emsley, *The English and Violence*, p. 136.

73 Ibid., p. 146.

74 Lawrence, ' "Scoundrels and Scallywags" ', pp. 125–44.

75 For models of masculinity within soldiers, see Matthew McCormack, 'Citizenship, Nationhood and Masculinity in the Affair of the Hanoverian Soldier, 1756', *The Historical Journal*, 2006, vol. 49, no. 4, pp. 971–93; and Matthew McCormack, 'The New Militia: Gender, Politics and War in 1750s Britain', *Gender and History*, 2007, vol. 19, no. 3, pp. 483–500.

76 For instance, police officers fraternizing with prostitutes and drinking on duty were some of the main challenges that nineteenth-century police commissioners and chief constables faced in trying to instil discipline among the rank and file. Taylor, *Policing the Victorian Town*, *passim*.

77 See also Emsley, *The Great British Bobby*, *passim*; and Taylor, *Hooligans, Harlots, and Hangmen*, p. 129.

78 Foster, 'Police Cultures', pp. 196–227; and M.E. Wiesner, '*Wandervogels* and Women: Journeymen's Concepts of Masculinity in Early Modern Germany', *Journal of Social History*, 1991, vol. 24, no. 4, pp. 767–82.

79 A. Wynter, 'The Police and Thieves', *Quarterly Review*, 1856, vol. XCIX, pp. 160–200 (p. 171).

80 There have, admittedly, been changes in how many of the ideals played out in practice – not least in terms of police violence, which has almost certainly declined along with violence in society in the last 300 years. See, for instance, Emsley, *The English and Violence*, *passim*.

81 See, for example, the collection of chapters in Emsley and Shpayer-Makov, *Police Detectives in History*; Haia Shpayer-Makov, 'Becoming a Police Detective in Victorian and Edwardian London', *Policing and Society*, 2004, vol. 14, no. 3, pp. 250–68; John Beattie, 'Garrow and the Detectives: Lawyers and Policemen at the Old Bailey in the Late Eighteenth Century', *Crime, Histoire & Sociétés/Crime, History & Societies*, 2007, vol. 11, no. 2, pp. 2–23; and David Cox, *A Certain Share of Low Cunning: A History of the Bow Street Runners, 1792–1839*, Cullompton: Willan, 2010. There are also a couple of major new publications on the detective in England in the eighteenth and nineteenth centuries: Haia Shpayer-Makov, *The Ascent of the Detective Police Sleuths in Victorian and Edwardian England*, Oxford: Oxford University Press, 2011; and J. M. Beattie, *The First English Detectives: The Bow Street Runners and the Policing of London, 1750–1840*, Oxford: Oxford University Press, 2012.

82 See, for instance, J. M. Beattie, *Policing and Punishment in London, 1660–1750: Urban Crime and the Limits of Terror*, 2001, Oxford: Oxford University Press, pp. 226–58; R. Paley, 'Thief-Takers in London in the Age of the McDaniel Gang, c. 1745–54', in Douglas Hay and Francis Snyder (eds), *Policing and Prosecution in Britain, 1750–1850*, Oxford: Oxford University Press, 1989, pp. 301–41; and Douglas Hay, 'Using the Criminal Law, 1750–1850: Policing, Private Prosecution, and the State', in Hay and Snyder (eds), *Policing and Prosecution in Britain*, pp. 16–25. More recent studies include J. M. Beattie, 'Early Detection: The Bow Street Runners in Late Eighteenth-Century London', in Emsley and Shpayer-Makov, *Police Detectives in History*, pp. 15–32.

83 Haia Shpayer-Makov, 'Journalists and Police Detectives in Victorian and Edwardian England: An Uneasy Reciprocal Relationship', *Journal of Social History*, 2009, vol. 42, no. 4, pp. 963–87; and Haia Shpayer-Makov, 'From Menace to Celebrity: The English Police Detective and the Press, c. 1842–1914', *Historical Research*, 2010, vol. 83, no. 222, pp. 672–92.

84 Philippa Gates, *Detecting Men: Masculinity and the Hollywood Detective Film*, New York: State University of New York Press, 2006.

85 Dean Wilson and Mark Finnane, 'From Sleuths to Technicians? Changing Images of the Detective in Victoria', in Emsley and Shpayer-Makov, *Police Detectives in History*, pp. 135–56.

86 See, for example, Shpayer-Makov, 'Explaining the Rise and Success of Detective Memoirs in History'.
87 Louise A. Jackson, 'The Unusual Case of "Mrs Sherlock": Memoir, Identity and the "Real" Woman Private Detective in Twentieth-Century Britain', *Gender & History*, 2003, vol. 15, no. 1, pp. 108–34.
88 Shpayer-Makov, 'Explaining the Rise and Success of Detective Memoirs in History', p. 103.
89 Shpayer-Makov, 'Journalists and Police Detectives in Victorian and Edwardian England', p. 980.
90 For work that has been carried out in an historical context, see, for instance, Gates, *Detecting Men*, *passim*; and Shpayer-Makov, *The Making of a Policeman*, *passim*.
91 See, for instance, Robert Reiner, 'Keystone to Kojak: The Hollywood Cop', in Philip Davies and Brian Neve (eds), *Cinema, Politics, and Society in America*, paperback reprint, 2nd edn, 1985, Manchester: Manchester University Press, pp. 195–220.
92 See, for instance, Brenton J. Malin, 'Viral Manhood: Niche Marketing, Hard-Boiled Detectives and the Economics of Masculinity', *Media Culture Society*, 2010, vol. 32, pp. 373–90 (p. 373); and Philippa Gates, 'Always a Partner in Crime: Black Masculinity in the Hollywood Detective Film', *Journal of Popular Film and Television*, 2004, vol. 32, no. 1, pp. 20–9.
93 Gates, *Detecting Men*. See also Philippa Gates, 'Detectives', in Michael S. Kimmel and Amy Aronson (eds), *Men and Masculinities: A Social, Cultural and Historical Encyclopaedia*, vol. 1, 2004, California: ABC-CLIO, p. 218.
94 Howard G. Brown, 'Tips, Traps and Tropes: Catching Thieves in Post-Revolutionary Paris', in Emsley and Shpayer-Makov (eds), *Police Detectives in History*, pp. 33–60; Clive Emsley, 'From Ex-Con to Expert: The Police Detective in Nineteenth-Century France', in Emsley and Shpayer-Makov, *Police Detectives in History*, pp. 61–78; and Wilson and Finnane, 'From Sleuths to Technicians?'.
95 Wilson and Finnane, 'From Sleuths to Technicians?'; and Graeme Dunstall, 'Local "Demons" in New Zealand Policing, c. 1900–55', in Emsley and Shpayer-Makov, *Police Detectives in History*, pp. 157–82. Both studies, however, question the extent to which the image was matched by reality.
96 See, for instance, Shpayer-Makov, 'Journalists and Police Detectives in Victorian and Edwardian England'.
97 Lawrence, ' "Scoundrels and Scallywags" ', p. 140.
98 Shpayer-Makov, 'From Menace to Celebrity'.
99 Silvestri, *Women in Charge*; and Marion E. Gold, *Top Cops: Profiles of Women in Command*, Chicago: Brittany, 1999.
100 For recent studies of rank-and-file policewomen in modern America, see S. E. Martin, *Breaking and Entering*, Berkeley: University of California Press, 1980; Sandra K. Wells and Betty L. Alt, *Police Women: Life with the Badge*, Westport, CT: Praeger, 1995; and Adam Eisenberg, *A Different Shade of Blue: How Women Changed the Face of Police Work*, Lake Forrest, CA: Behler, 2009.
101 Silvestri, *Women in Charge*; and Heidensohn, 'Gender and Policing', p. 574.
102 A. Bryman, *Leadership and Organisations*, London: Routledge & Kegan Paul, 1986, p. 1.
103 C. F. Rauch and O. Behling, 'Functionalism: Basis for an Alternate Approach to the Study of Leadership', in J. G. Hunt (ed.), *Leaders and Managers: International Perspectives on Managerial Behaviour and Leadership*, New York: Pergamon, 1984, p. 46. Reiner, in surveying chief constables in England in 1991, identified four 'ideal types' of chief officer – the Baron, the Bobby, the Boss and the Bureaucrat. R. Reiner, *Chief Constables: Bobbies, Bosses or Bureaucrats?* Oxford: Oxford University Press, 1991, pp. 6, 301–8.
104 For an overview of recent developments in modern day police leadership in England, see Matt Long, 'Leadership and Performance Management', in Newburn, *Handbook of Policing*, pp. 628–54.

105 For an investigation of this relationship in Australia, see Finnane, *Police and Government*, pp. 7–51.

106 Barrie, *Police in the Age of Improvement*, *passim*.

107 For more on this, see Barrie, 'Anglicisation and Autonomy'.

108 This was, in part, due to an ideological backlash against the desirability of having short-term elected representatives oversee important policing decisions for which they were not fully qualified.

109 This diffusion of power from the centre to local police institutions and to full-time officers was in keeping with Foucault's notion of 'governmentality' in that it was a de-centralized model of governance that was not limited to state politics alone. M. Foucault, 'Governmentality', translated by Rosi Braidotti and revised by Colin Gordon, in Graham Burchell, Colin Gordon and Peter Miller (eds), *The Foucault Effect: Studies in Governmentality*, Chicago: Chicago University Press, 1996, pp. 87–104. For an elaboration of this concept, see M. Dean, *Governmentality: Power and Rule in Modern Society*, London: Sage, 1999. For a critique, see Thomas Lemke, 'Foucault, Governmentality, and Critique', *Rethinking Marxism*, 2002, vol. 14, no. 3, pp. 49–64.

110 For the increasing power and influence of police constables in the United Kingdom, see M. Brogden, *The Police: Autonomy and Consent*, London: Academic Press, 1982.

111 Paul Langford, *Public Life and the Propertied Englishman 1689–1798*, Oxford: Clarendon Press, 1991, pp. 234–6; and J. Prest, *Liberty and Locality: Parliament, Permissive Legislation, and Ratepayers' Democracies in the Nineteenth Century*, Oxford: Clarendon Press, 1990, p. 189.

112 Barrie, *Police in the Age of Improvement*, pp. 131–9.

113 For criminal returns and police in nineteenth-century England, see Clive Emsley, *Crime and Society in England, 1750–1900*, 2nd edn, London: Longman, 1996, *passim*; V. A. C. Gatrell, 'The Decline of Theft and Violence in Victorian and Edwardian England', in V. A. C. Gatrell, B. Lenman and G. Parker (eds), *Crime and the Law: The Social History of Crime in Western Europe since 1500*, London: Europa, 1980, pp. 238–337; and V. A. C. Gatrell, 'Crime, Authority and the Policeman-State', in F. M. L. Thompson (ed.), *The Cambridge Social History*, vol. 3, Cambridge: Cambridge University Press, 1990, pp. 243–310.

114 For the politicization of crime statistics in England and Wales, see Howard Taylor, 'The Politics of the Rising Crime Statistics of England and Wales, 1914–1960', *Crime, Histoire & Sociétés/Crime, History & Societies*, 1998, vol. 2, no. 1, pp. 5–28.

115 Shpayer-Makov, *The Making of a Policeman*. See also Steedman, *Policing the Victorian Community*, pp. 65–156.

116 R. D. Storch, 'The Policeman as Domestic Missionary: Urban Discipline and Popular Culture in Northern England, 1850–80', *Journal of Social History*, 1976, vol. 9, pp. 481–509.

117 For more on the rise of criminal statistics and the ways in which they were manipulated by government in England and Wales, see Chris A. Williams, 'Counting Crimes or Counting People: Some Implications of Mid-Nineteenth-Century British Police Returns', *Crime, Histoire & Sociétés/Crime, History & Societies*, 2000, vol. 4, no. 2, pp. 77–93; and Robert M. Morris, 'Lies, Damned Lies and Criminal Statistics: Reinterpreting the Criminal Statistics in England and Wales', *Crime, Histoire & Sociétés/Crime, History & Societies*, 2001, vol. 5, no. 1, pp. 111–27.

118 Andrew Davies, ' "These Viragoes are No Less Cruel than the Lads": Young Women, Gangs and Violence in Late Victorian Manchester and Salford', *British Journal of Criminology*, 1999, vol. 39, no. 1, pp. 72–89 (p.76).

119 Davies, ' "These Viragoes are No Less Cruel than the Lads" ', p. 72. See also Andrew Davies, 'Youth Gangs and Late Victorian Society', in Barry Goldson (ed.), *Youth in Crisis? 'Gangs', Territoriality and Violence*, Basingstoke: Routledge, 2011, pp. 38–54; Andrew Davies, *The Gangs of Manchester*, Preston: Milo Books, 2008; and Andrew

Davies, 'Youth Gangs, Masculinity and Violence in Late Victorian Manchester and Salford', *Journal of Social History*, 1998, vol. 32, no. 2, pp. 349–69.
120 Jackson, *Women Police.*
121 Further works on this include Emsley, *The Great British Bobby*, pp. 177–201; and Klein, *Invisible Men*, pp. 222–47.
122 Jackson, *Women Police.* See also Louise A. Jackson, 'Care or Control? The Metropolitan Police and Child Welfare, 1919–1969', *The Historical Journal*, 2003, vol. 46, no. 3, pp. 623–48.
123 Philippa Levine, ' "Walking the Streets in a Way No Decent Woman Should": Women Police in World War I', *Journal of Modern History*, 1994, vol. 66, pp. 34–78; and John Carrier, *The Campaign for the Employment of Women as Police Officers*, Aldershot: Ashgate, 1988.
124 For the influence of gender in shaping various aspects of the workings of criminal justice systems' treatment of juvenile delinquents, see M. Cain (ed.), *Growing Up Good: Policing the Behaviour of Girls in Europe*, London: Sage, 1989; and L. Mahood, 'The "Vicious" Girl and the "Street-Corner" Boy: Sexuality and the Gendered Delinquent in the Scottish Child-Saving Movement, 1850–1940', *Journal of the History of Sexuality*, 1994, vol. 4, pp. 549–78.
125 Heather Shore, *Artful Dodgers: Youth and Crime in Early Nineteenth-Century London*, Woodbridge: Boydell Press, 1999; and Peter King, 'The Rise of Juvenile Delinquency in England 1780–1840: Changing Patterns of Perception and Prosecution', *Past and Present*, 1998, no. 160, pp. 116–66. For the 'invention' of the juvenile delinquent in nineteenth-century Europe, see Heather Shore, ' "Inventing" the Juvenile Delinquent in Nineteenth-Century Europe', in Godfrey, Emsley and Dunstall, *Comparative Histories of Crime*, pp. 110–24.
126 Jackson, *Women Police.*
127 For more on modern community policing, see Nick Tilley, 'Community Policing, Problem-Orientated Policing and Intelligence-Led Policing', in Newburn, *Handbook of Policing,* pp. 311–39; and Daniel Donnelly, 'Policing the Scottish Community', in Daniel Donnelly and Kenneth Scott (eds), *Policing Scotland*, Cullompton: Willan, 2005, pp. 130–56.

1

THE PATERNAL GOVERNMENT OF MEN

The self-image and action of the Paris police in the eighteenth century[1]

David Garrioch

The police of Paris were a point of reference for rulers and reformers across eighteenth-century Europe. In England they were generally a symbol of despotism, symptomatic of the evils of absolute monarchy. In other parts of Europe they represented, for some, a model of how a large city could be administered, whereas for others they offered simply a well-known comparison. The prominence of the Paris example was in part due to the remarkable four-volume treatise on policing written by Nicolas Delamare, one of the *commissaires* working in the French capital. Delamare's work represented an ideal and a programme, though it has often been used, by contemporaries and by historians, as a description of the actual operation of the Paris police.[2] He took for granted, as did most people at the time and many writers since, that the relationship between government and people was a paternalistic one, but no one has looked closely at the way this metaphor was used or at the effect it had on the nature of policing. This chapter looks at the three-way relationship between the ideal of paternal government, the accompanying ideas about masculinity and the way that the police of Paris operated in the eighteenth century. It suggests that, although the broad overall understanding of policing as a manifestation of the patriarchal rule of the king changed little from the late seventeenth to the late eighteenth century, the significant shifts in images of fatherhood that occurred during this period did have an impact both on the way the relationship was imagined and on the way the Paris police worked. At the same time, shifts in wider ideals of masculinity also influenced the way that individual officers operated and thought about their role.

The police of the French capital was very different, in both form and function, from a modern police force. In the seventeenth century it was shared between the municipality, various seigneurial and ecclesiastical jurisdictions, the local royal courts (the Châtelet) and the magistrates of the Parlement, whose jurisdiction extended beyond Paris to much of France. A major reorganization took place in the 1660s when the new position of Lieutenant-General of Police was created, one of many changes that extended royal authority during Louis XIV's rule. It consolidated in the hands of a single individual, named by the king and reporting both to him and to the Parlement, many functions previously undertaken by other authorities, although in many respects the precise division of roles was only to be clarified over the following century.[3] The new Lieutenant-General was to work primarily with an existing group of forty-eight *commissaires* who were responsible for particular areas of the city. Although their title makes them sound like contemporary police officers, in fact they were nothing of the sort, and policing was only part of their role. They were office holders, which meant that they purchased their positions (as a doctor today might buy a medical practice) and could not be removed without compensation. Like many groups in Old Regime France, they formed a small corporation, in theory independent and self-governing, with their own rooms, library and elected representatives who spoke on their behalf. They were not paid a salary, but earned their income from the various tasks they undertook, particularly from civil functions such as hearing witnesses in civil law cases and – most lucrative of all – placing seals on deceased estates so that nothing could be removed before a full inventory could be drawn up. Yet they were also broadly responsible for public order. They had no subordinates reporting to them and could rarely make use of physical force. Nor did they normally make arrests or undertake any of the criminal investigations we associate with the police, although they did draw up reports on crimes and interview witnesses, and they also interrogated suspects and were empowered to imprison or release them. At the same time, they had a range of other responsibilities that included many aspects of what we would call city administration. These roles were often shared with elected officials, with municipal officers (nominally elected but in practice chosen by the Crown) and with other royal authorities, although increasingly it was the *commissaires* who did the work of checking weights and measures, overseeing street lighting and the collection of rubbish, and taking measures related to public health and morality. Yet here, curiously, they had no direct powers of enforcement, instead reporting infringements to the police court, which decided on a conviction.[4]

Across the eighteenth century, in practice, the *commissaires* became subordinates of the police chief. A succession of royal edicts confided new tasks to them, under his supervision, and they spent more and more of their time on police work. Successive Lieutenants-General used both their personal authority and financial incentives to win obedience, and gradually the *commissaires* became a key element in a larger machine. They worked increasingly closely with a corps of twenty inspectors, created in the early eighteenth century, who reported exclusively to the Lieutenant-General. It was the inspectors who, by the late eighteenth century, were undertaking investigations and carrying out arrests, while also sharing with the *commissaires* particular duties such as the surveillance of markets, of prostitution and of gaming houses. Unfortunately, only fragmentary records of their activity have survived.[5]

The third key element within the Paris police structure, alongside the *commissaires* and the inspectors, was the city guard, a semi-military group that was reorganized progressively to make it, by the late eighteenth century, a fairly effective front-line force. It developed out of, and alongside, the old city watch, but was removed from municipal to police control. Divided into small patrols stationed in different parts of the city, it arrested people suspected of criminal activity, both on its own initiative and at the request of the citizens, and took them to a *commissaire* who would decide whether to release them or lock them up. But the city guard was not directly subordinate either to the inspectors or to the *commissaires*, taking its orders from its own commander and from the Lieutenants-General.[6]

The police was thus a disparate grouping, with no clear hierarchy. Both its role and its personnel evolved across the eighteenth century, so generalization is difficult, but the story is essentially one of growing centralization, consolidation and streamlining. An increasingly efficient bureaucracy developed in the offices of the Lieutenant-General, who became in many ways the de facto administrator of the city. It was these very wide powers, and particularly his ability (and willingness) to order arrests in the king's name, together with the deployment of city guards organized on military lines that made the Paris police a byword for despotism in some circles.[7] Yet it always had to negotiate with other authorities, particularly the Parlement and the municipality, sometimes working smoothly alongside them and sometimes conflicting with them over jurisdiction. There were parts of the city where the police had no authority and the privileges of particular social and occupational groups also greatly limited its powers.

As will already be clear, policing in eighteenth-century France had a wider sense than in most Western societies today. It was understood as almost equivalent to government. In 1758, for example, Emer de Vattel's *Le droit des gens* suggested that 'policing represents the attention that the Prince and the Magistrates give to maintaining social order. Wise ordinances should prescribe everything that best ensures public security, utility, and convenience.'[8] For Nicolas Des Essarts in 1786, it was 'the science of governing men, in order to benefit them, the art of making them as happy as possible and as far as they can be in the general interest of society'.[9]

Policing, as both theorists and practitioners understood it, thus extended far beyond law enforcement. 'It consists', wrote the Paris police officer Jean-Baptiste Charles Lemaire in 1770, in a famous description supposedly requested by the Empress of Austria,

> in maintaining good order, looking after and seeing to the common needs of the citizens, in preventing everything that could trouble the peace and tranquillity which is their right, in prescribing the rules that they must follow and obliging them to observe them; in maintaining surveillance over all those whose conduct . . . can be prejudicial to others, arresting, correcting and suppressing abuses and disorder; in preventing crime . . . ; in removing from society those who will only harm it; in offering to all citizens . . . an exact

and prompt justice; and in providing them with the assistance and protection which they can reasonably expect.[10]

This description was in fact a normative claim rather than a reality, but for many writers it was the police of Paris who most closely realized this ideal. A late eighteenth-century dictionary, defining 'police', recalled the mission given to the second Lieutenant-General, in 1697: 'the King, Monsieur, expects you to provide safety, cleanliness, cheapness'. 'In effect', comments the author of the article, 'these three items cover everything to do with policing.'[11]

Successive police chiefs interpreted these instructions in slightly different ways, but more and more broadly. From the late seventeenth century onwards, public safety extended to banning firearms and restricting other weapons, installing and progressively improving street lighting, inspecting and later removing large shop signs that might fall on people's heads and, for the same reason, forbidding the inhabitants of upper floors from keeping plant pots and other objects on their window ledges. A vast number of police regulations aimed to improve public morality, attempting to restrict prostitution (especially around churches), remove beggars from the streets and prevent gambling and public drunkenness. Measures were taken against those who wore swords without being entitled by their rank to do so, and in the early years of the eighteenth century a major campaign was launched against 'sodomites'.[12] Other ordinances aimed to 'civilize' the city by banning public brawling, verbal abuse and other forms of turbulent behaviour. Attempts were made to clean up the streets by forbidding people to empty chamber pots out of their windows and deposit refuse in the streets, and industrial waste and even noise were increasingly regulated. Still other ordinances fixed opening hours, controlled weights and measures and capped the prices of necessities. Traffic became a growing preoccupation of the Paris police, leading to measures to prevent artisans from working in the middle of the street, limit street stalls to particular places and reduce their size and ultimately reform building regulations so that streets and intersections were wider.[13] Most of these things were not regulated by laws enforceable in the ordinary criminal courts, and infringements of police regulations – detected in the course of patrols, as a result of denunciations or through specific police campaigns – were prosecuted summarily in a court presided over by the Lieutenant-General himself.

This all-embracing understanding of policing rested firmly on a patriarchal concept of government. 'The ruler', wrote Vattel, 'through wise policing, accustoms the people to order and obedience; he preserves tranquillity, peace, and concord among the Citizens.'[14] These were, in the eighteenth century, the duties of a good father towards his own household, and the image of the king as father was a well-established one. Jurists had long described the kingdom as a family, in which the ruler occupied the place of the father, exercising his God-given authority for the benefit of his subjects. This was rooted in history, asserted the early eighteenth-century legal writer Jean Domat, as 'the paternal authority of the first head, whose children and descendants composed this people, was in his person a power of government'.[15] The same imagery made its way into political discourse: France was, the magistrates of the Paris Parlement told the young Louis XV, 'a family of which you are the father and the master all together'.[16] Sermons conveyed the same message. 'A kingdom', pronounced one preacher, was like 'a large family whose members are linked to its head and dependent on him.'[17] And as in a family, it was a two-way relationship. The father ruled in the interests of all and the wife, children and servants owed him obedience and respect. So too in the kingdom, where the ruler 'policed' and the people had the same filial responsibility towards him.

The king was, under God, the father of all, but the social order was held intact by a great chain of patriarchal authority. The kingdom was composed of many families, each ruled by a father with his own 'policing' responsibilities. Montesquieu had argued that in a republic the influence of paternal authority within individual families was absolutely indispensable because of the weakness of central authority, whereas in a monarchy it was less vital.[18] Nevertheless, as the former Lieutenant-General Lenoir reflected in his memoirs, 'the exercise of ordinary policing depended in part on the internal discipline that masters exercised over their journeymen, workers, and apprentices'.[19] At moments of crisis the authorities expected this discipline to be exercised strictly; immediately after the riots of May 1775, the Lieutenant-General instructed the *commissaires* to warn all the inhabitants of their quarters to keep at home all their workers and servants, 'being responsible for the misdemeanours they might commit . . . You will give the same warning to all building contractors and foremen of workshops.'[20]

But there were, in practice, many people who did not belong to a natural family, and others who rebelled against this just authority. In these cases, the role of the police was to reinforce the chain, stepping in where links were weak or missing. Because the paternal authority exercised by employers was of such importance in the social order, the police were quick to reinforce it when workers rebelled. The *commissaire* Thierry peremptorily summoned an apprentice who had left his master and warned him to return or face imprisonment. Another apprentice, a pastry cook, spent two weeks in jail when he refused to return to his master's shop, and the police released him only when his employer agreed that he had been punished enough; they were reinforcing his authority, not supplanting it. A journeyman printer faced the same fate, he was warned in 1777, if he did not faithfully fulfil his duties in the print shop where he worked.[21]

Workers who did not have masters, such as errand boys and labourers on the ports and in the streets and markets, were considered to be like orphans and were therefore placed directly under the paternal guidance of the police.[22] A police inspector supervised the workers in the central market, and many other independent workers were required to register with the police. Hawkers and cab drivers, for example, were given a numbered badge that they were supposed to display at all times. So were authorized beggars. Water carriers, who delivered water in buckets to those prepared to buy it, were assigned by the *commissaires* to a particular supply point, usually one of the many fountains that were scattered around the city. In 1767 a short-lived and incomplete attempt was made to register all workers not attached to a guild.[23]

The police, as servants of the king, were an extension of his paternal authority, and this was reflected in the way they thought about and behaved towards those they dealt with. Their attitude was strongly determined by the rank and occupation of each individual, recalcitrants of higher status requiring the involvement of a higher paternal authority, but ordinary working people were unabashedly treated like children, who should obey without question.[24] The *commissaire* Fontaine informed the Lieutenant-General that he had twice ordered a woman whose fruit stall was blocking the street to move it to a wide section further along, but she had not done so. 'I do not know what is sustaining her in this disobedience.'[25] On another occasion he complained of the 'dangerous insubordination' of a lodging-house keeper who had dared to talk back: 'fear rather than reason keeps them in line. It is therefore necessary that they respect the *commissaire* who is their primary judge.'[26] It was common, too, for the *commissaires* to act like schoolmasters in sorting out disputes between people in their jurisdiction, ordering the aggressors to behave themselves. 'Sieur LeBorgne will lodge Monsieur Thiemet this evening', read a note to a hotel keeper in 1780, 'and will come tomorrow at 11 to the *commissaire* Hugues, rue Neuve Saint-Eustache, to sort out the issue that divides them, he will be sure to attend without fail.'[27] The expectation of obedience was backed up by the threat of punishment. The stall keeper mentioned by the *commissaire* Fontaine was arrested and brought before him, 'so that I can punish her for her disobedience, or show her mercy a third time, depending on the circumstances'. The police chief agreed that, although it was up to the *commissaire* to decide, he thought the woman should be sent to prison.[28] Such decisions were subject to judicial review by the Lieutenant-General, but even a few days in an eighteenth-century prison was a significant summary punishment.

One can see here a reflection of the distinction made in French judicial theory between law and police regulation, often blurred because both were often in the hands of the same individuals. The law was set out in written texts and subject to judicial review, whereas policing was a flexible exercise of direct monarchical power in response to immediate and local circumstances. As Montesquieu noted:

> in policing, it is the magistrate who punishes, rather than the law: in dealing with crime, it is the law that punishes, rather than the magistrate. . . . The actions of the police are prompt, and concern everyday matters: major punishments are therefore not appropriate.[29]

The same idea was taken up, with a harsher twist, by Mirabeau senior – father of the future revolutionary – in his influential book *L'Ami des hommes*: 'true Policing, Policing worthy of a great Prince, of the Father of the people, of God's anointed One, consists less in punishing crimes than in stifling the seeds of vice by encouraging and germinating those of virtue'.[30] In a reprise of this notion, Louis XVI's minister Vergennes wrote in 1781 that 'there are a host of cases where the king, as a consequence of his paternal kindness, intervenes to correct so that justice does not need to punish'.[31] The Paris police did exactly this in response to a host of minor misdemeanours. In 1752, for example, the inspector of police Dumont, then the *commissaire* Grimperel, rebuked two barbers who, having worked for a master in the rue Saint-Lazare and got to know his clients, set up their own shop in the immediate vicinity. This was forbidden by guild rules that were reinforced by police by-laws, and could have been prosecuted through the courts, but the police chose to short circuit the process by simply warning the two young men to move elsewhere. They took similar action to stop a man who was working, with no qualifications, as a surgeon – presumably he was bleeding people, the main task undertaken by barber-surgeons.[32] Complaints against neighbours sometimes led to similar action, when by-laws were being infringed. In 1784 the police chief instructed the *commissaire* Ninnin to take action against some laundrywomen who hung their washing on long poles that extended in front of their neighbours' windows, blocking the light. He was to tell them to shorten their poles, or face a fine in the police court.[33]

Domestic violence and marital debauchery offer another example in which the law was not involved, as neither was a criminal matter. A wife could bring a civil case against her husband on the grounds that her life or dowry was at risk, but to do this she needed financial resources and support from the Crown prosecutor, as a married woman could not initiate legal proceedings without her husband's permission. In cases of extreme violence or neglect, the police were prepared to use the king's paternal power because the men concerned had rendered themselves unworthy to exercise patriarchal authority.[34] They therefore took action against husbands like Paul Bourdeaux, a journeyman watchmaker who beat his wife, abandoned her periodically and left her for long periods without financial support.[35] Again in 1772 the Lieutenant-General wrote to the *commissaire* Trudon, instructing him to 'severely reprimand' the tailor Schwipps 'and order him, from me, to leave his wife alone, on pain of arrest. You will be so good as to inform me of his response.'[36] Although the paternal, protective role of the police is clear in this example, it should be stressed that it was a last resort: the police were very reluctant to interfere with patriarchal authority.

The preventative 'correction' that Vergennes referred to had developed, during the eighteenth century, into the notorious system of *lettres de cachet* – orders supposedly bearing the king's signature – well documented by Arlette Farge and Michel Foucault. Because of the centrality of the family to eighteenth-century conceptions of the social and political order, behaviour that imperilled family integrity and honour was considered a threat to society. Most often, given the importance of sexual 'purity' in female reputation, it was women who were punished. In 1751, a tinker named LaBussière complained to the Lieutenant-General that his wife was misbehaving and that their daughter looked like following in her mother's footsteps. The neighbours confirmed that, while the husband was away at work, often overnight, rumours about his wife's infidelity were rife. She was duly imprisoned 'by order of the King'.[37] Imprisonment in such cases generally lasted until the Lieutenant-General decided to terminate it, or if the husband was paying for her board until he requested her release. Having a wife locked up did not seem to reflect on a man's reputation; rather, scandal and dishonour arose from her behaviour, and recourse to the police was viewed as a legitimate way for him to reinforce his authority. Daughters were subject to the same discipline, and many parents requested the incarceration of girls who had become unmanageable.[38]

Women were the most common targets of this action, but young men who ran off the rails and whose parents were no longer able to control them were also punished. The police confined Jean Hannen in a monastery for four months – 'by order of the King' – when he was seventeen. Three years later, as 'he has not stopped getting drunk, frequenting soldiers and prostitutes and places of ill repute', his parents requested that he be locked up again, this time in a prison.[39] Jeanne Menage requested a second term of imprisonment for her son, who refused to work. Other petitions from parents accuse sons of stealing from them, of spend-thrift, drunken or debauched behaviour, and of general disobedience.[40]

As in these examples, it was generally the families themselves who requested police action when ordinary parental authority was lacking or inadequate. It is clear that women saw themselves as playing a key role in family governance, but the police were unlikely to intervene without the father's involvement, unless he was clearly incapable. The conspicuous exception was when widows were strug-gling to raise children alone and where the police therefore stepped in as a direct replacement for the father or husband.[41] But the same principle applied when a man grossly neglected his patriarchal responsibilities, as in the case of extreme domestic violence or debauchery mentioned above, or when a father did not keep his own children in line. Catherine and Marianne Bouillerot, both in their teens, had lost their mother young and their father was a bad sort. The girls 'swear like real soldiers, are without religion and do no work, following the example that their father has given them'. The police officer concluded that as 'the father is not capable of having them instructed; therefore I think it is just and charitable to put them into prison'.[42] In the early years of the century, men who too overtly raised their children as Protestants were also sometimes considered to fall into this category. 'It seems to me severe to remove their children from the arms of a mother and a father', reads a police report of 1727, once again expressing official reluctance to interfere with paternal authority, 'but in a case like this one it seems to me that it is good use of authority to save a soul for God by placing this girl in the New Catholic convent'.[43] Such men were also failing in their patriarchal duty and in the interests of social order – as defined by an intolerant state – the police once again felt obliged to intervene.

Arbitrary arrests by *lettre de cachet* were carried out with growing frequency from the 1730s onwards, and used in a widening range of circumstances. For example, in 1751 the Hennequin family requested that action be taken against a young man named Desnoyers after he seduced their twenty-one-year-old daugh-ter. As he was a gambler, they would not consent to him marrying her, but he would not leave her alone, so they asked that he be sent into exile, presumably in the Caribbean colonies.[44] The increasingly arbitrary use of police authority in this way came under overt attack in the 1780s by those such as Mirabeau, and, more discreetly, from within government ranks, by Malesherbes.[45] Perhaps anticipating such criticism, in 1776 Lieutenant-General Lenoir gave the *commissaires* careful instructions on the distinction between 'justice' and 'administration', drawing on the difference mentioned above between the role of the courts in enforcing the law and that of the police in maintaining social order. Justice, he wrote, was slow and measured, but applied the letter of the law. 'Administration', on the other hand, 'must move promptly to prevent crime, and by a beneficent foresight protect society from disorder and save the honour of families that would be compromised when the law obliges the courts to condemn.'[46] Lenoir gave the example of a son under the age of twenty-five who had begun to develop spendthrift and debauched habits. Here, he explained, there was nothing criminal, but there was a serious threat to the family whose reputation might be damaged, and it was appropriate for the police to assist. In a similar way, if a husband had cause to complain of the behaviour of his wife, an 'administrative' intervention was justifiable, as the law did not permit a husband to seek separation from his wife unless he could prove that she had committed adultery. But it was quite different, he warned, when a wife accused her husband, because the law allowed her to request separation of life or of property if he mistreated her or squandered her dowry. The only exception here was if she did not have the resources to take legal action and her life was at risk.

Lenoir's instructions should not be taken simply as a straightforward description of the way policing worked. On the one hand, in separating 'administrative' measures from judicial ones he was affirming the independence of a police structure that chafed under oversight by the magistrates of the Parlement.[47] On the other, he was attempting to reform a system that was, in his view, being used too freely. We do not know how far his instructions were followed. In the 1780s the police were still investigating petitions from wives against their husbands, as the *commissaire* LeRat intervened to order a cobbler to move out of the conjugal home and not to mistreat his wife or even speak to her in future. Nor did this concern only poor households, as in another case the wife offered to pay her husband's board if the police agreed to lock him up.[48] More consistent with Lenoir's instructions was the action taken by the *commissaire* Ninnin in 1784. Investigating a complaint by the Baron du Wavre against his wife, the *commissaire* declined to make a firm judgement on the issue but did suggest:

> something that appears to me to be worthwhile . . . which is to remove from under her control a daughter who will receive only bad counsel from her [mother] . . . and to place her in a convent where she will learn honesty and religious principles.[49]

This was precisely the kind of action, in the interests of the girl and of society, that Lenoir was advocating. In all of these instances, the fatherly concern exercised by the police (in the ruler's name) justified going beyond mere enforcement of the law and seeking to prevent not only crime but also anything that might endanger social order and conventional morality.

This idea was not new: it had been used in the seventeenth century by magistrates in the different Paris courts – the Parlement and the Châtelet – who spoke of their role in supporting the 'natural' authority of male heads of households, of employers and of the leaders of the guilds. But across the eighteenth century, ideals of fatherhood and of paternal authority shifted markedly, and this had a significant impact on the role and self-understanding of the police. The ideal father, as we can observe him in literature, art and the writing of moralists, went from being a distant and authoritarian figure to being a far more tender and sensitive one. Sparing the rod was no longer seen to mean spoiling the child, and paternal harshness was increasingly condemned. The good father followed his heart and – like Julie's father in Jean-Jacques Rousseau's novel *Julie, ou la nouvelle Héloïse* – was more likely to win the trust and obedience of his children through persuasion and affection than through discipline. As ideal family relationships in general came to be represented as more sentimental, model fathers become gentler, more sensitive and virtuous, more interested in the education and the well-being of their children.[50]

The image of the king as father of his people was inevitably affected by these changes. It legitimized criticism of 'despotic' behaviour or of any policy that could be seen as contrary to the interests of the people as a whole. The king was no longer justified in defending the interests of his dynasty if these did not coincide with the welfare of what many writers were beginning to call 'the nation'. Like the good father, the king had to win the obedience and love of his people through demonstrating his concern for them, not by force or punishment or appeals to divine right.[51] This was the rhetoric mobilized by the magistrates of the *parlements* when they warned that, if he continued to ignore their claims, the French, 'far from seeing in their ruler a father whom they love', would 'only discern in him a master whom they fear'.[52] Even pro-monarchical imagery began to endorse this shift, with depictions of the ruler emphasizing his enlightened benevolence rather than his military prowess or power. Equestrian statues disappeared, and Louis XVI was often portrayed distributing alms, moved by the sufferings of the poor.[53] In 1788 he became enormously popular when he appeared to be conforming to the image of the tender father, responding to the distress and the desires of his people by summoning the Estates-General.[54]

In turn, these changing images of the father-king influenced the way the police saw their own role. The *commissaire* Lemaire, describing the Paris police in 1770, insisted that their duty was 'to do as much general good as possible', recognizing human fallibility and aiming 'to return [men] to their duty more by warnings, gentle and salutary corrections . . . than by the weight of excessive rigour'.[55] Like other defenders of absolutism, the police continued to emphasize royal authority and the duties of subjects to obey, but, unlike their early eighteenth-century predecessors who had been largely indifferent to public opinion, increasingly they perceived their role as one of public service. The language of 'public service' was gaining currency both in administrative circles and in public discourse more broadly, and we can see it taking on a new meaning.[56] In 1762, when de Sartine instructed the *commissaires* 'to avoid everything that could slow down or disturb the service', he was presumably using the term to mean the service of the king or of the state. In 1780, when Lenoir wrote of 'the public service, which is the most necessary and the most elevated of your functions', the phrase was more ambiguous; he may still have been thinking of the work of administration performed by those with a public office.[57] The shift is clear, however, in a document prepared by one of the *commissaires* in 1784, on behalf of his colleagues, affirming that their principal ambition was 'to become increasingly useful to Society and to merit the consideration of the public'.[58] I have suggested elsewhere that this was a response not only to pressure from the Lieutenants-General but also to demand from the Paris middle classes and even from sections of the working population – male and female – who increasingly made use of the services of the police and subtly influenced their operation.[59] The fact that the *commissaires* were using such arguments to claim greater authority and status does not negate their significance. The police were justifying their action in new ways and had almost certainly internalized something of this enlightened sense of mission, one that was consistent with the new ways of thinking about paternal duty.

In his memoirs, Lieutenant-General Lenoir defined the chief concerns of the police as 'public order, the safety of individuals, and the good of humanity'.[60] Written during the French Revolution, this was partly self-justification, yet his actions when in power, like those of his immediate predecessor de Sartine, suggest that it was how both men had seen their role. De Sartine had established a wet-nursing agency that enabled poor parents to find a disease-free wet nurse at reasonable cost. This was designed to reduce infant mortality (and hence increase the population of France), and also to counter the indebtedness among poor families that saw fathers put into prison at the demand of their creditors. Both de Sartine and Lenoir sponsored experiments to improve the quality and abundance of bread, and Lenoir used police funds to establish a free clinic to treat venereal disease. He was also one of the key movers in creating the Mont-de-Piété, the government-run pawnbroker that lent small sums of money at reasonable rates of interest. It assisted the poor by providing cheap credit, thus saving them from rapacious moneylenders. These were only a few of the humanitarian activities initiated by successive police chiefs and they are evidence of a new approach to policing. It continued to be about maintaining social order and authority – to Lenoir, both were entirely compatible with humanitarian concern. But alongside punitive measures went a new emphasis on service to society, a manifestation of the ruler's fatherly concern but sometimes simply a benefit in itself.[61]

Recent work has shown that in the 1770s and 1780s the police of Paris, as in other cities across Europe, were engaged in much internal discussion about their role.[62] This was part of wider Enlightenment debates over the nature of government, authority and the mutual rights and responsibilities of rulers and their subjects. The many documents discussing the proper workings of the police were partly prompted by attacks on traditional paternalist arguments, but they also demonstrate the appearance of a new conception of policing as part of the changed relationship between the monarch and his people.[63] If, as Frederick II of Prussia put it, the ruler was 'the first servant of the state', accountable to his fellow citizens, then the agencies he employed were equally in the service of the public.[64] This was largely rhetoric, but the power of language to effect change is indicated – as I have suggested above – by the growing number of humanitarian initiatives that were related to public order and to the maintenance of royal authority only within the new ideology of the benevolent father-king.

Broader changes in conceptions of masculinity, not solely those concerning the ideal father, equally had a bearing on conceptions of policing. They helped to determine both the kind of action that the police and a wider public considered legitimate, and to shape the relationships between individual police officers and those with whom they came into contact. The growing literature on early modern masculinities has led to a general reinterpretation of the 'civilizing process' as a gendered phenomenon, suggesting that, although in practice there was always a variety of masculinities, defined by status and to some degree by individual pref-erence, in a general sense the aggressive military virtues that had characterized the aristocratic gentleman until the sixteenth century were being replaced by an emphasis on self-control and bodily discipline. By the eighteenth century, civility, politeness and humanity were the hallmarks of the gentleman (now including the middle classes), and birth was of less value unless accompanied by appropriate bearing. By the end of the century, sensibility was also part of the model.[65]

These changes were inseparable from some of the most vigorous debates of the time: on the nature of 'civilization' and 'civil society', on the proper role of the nobility, on the virtues of commercial society and – perhaps above all – on luxury. Eighteenth-century concerns about excessive luxury were partly about manliness, reflecting concern about the 'feminizing' effects of excessive comfort and of Court life, and, in the writings of Rousseau and his many disciples, of urban life in general.[66] Given the definition of 'policing' as the government of cities, this had a direct bearing on understandings of the police role. It accentu-ated parental concern about the temptations of urban life and the 'debauchery' of young men, and increased demand from families, across a surprisingly wide social range stretching from the nobility to the working classes, for the police to intervene, in the interests both of the family and of society as a whole.[67]

The impact of changing conceptions of masculinity on the image of the ideal *commissaire* is harder to grasp. As we have seen, respect and obedience were central to their role, and these depended in part on their ability to project a par-ticular kind of male persona. This was partly guaranteed by a difference of rank between them and the majority of the people they dealt with; although we do not know very much about their social origins, it is clear that the *commissaires* were educated bourgeois men. They had the manners, vocabulary and physical presence that such individuals learned from tutors and picked up from their family environment. Other traits of the 'gentleman', personal dignity, gravity and self-control, tact and a sound grasp of social niceties, were certainly also requirements of the job, although they were largely taken for granted and rarely discussed. Excessive sensibility, however, was certainly not part of the job description and would have been a handicap.

But the *commissaires* needed more if they were to function effectively as police officers. Part of their authority came from their dress, something that marked social status far more effectively in the eighteenth century than today. Over their bourgeois costume they wore the long black robes of their office, similar to those of judges in court. In 1762, Lieutenant-General de Sartine wrote to remind them of the necessity of wearing their robes, even when accompanied by other officers, as neglecting to do so 'can give rise to a lack of respect for them and to difficulties which can have consequences contrary to security and to subordination'.[68] On a later occasion when the streets were so full of muddy snow that some of the *commissaires* were leaving their robes at home, the Lieutenant-General wrote to say that if they did this, particularly when visiting parts of the city where people did not know them, they should be accompanied by a soldier 'so that their person should command respect'.[69] They also seem routinely to have worn wigs, a mark of rank and dignity.

But if it was the office that thus commanded respect, it was vital that the right kind of man occupy that office. 'The choice of individuals for this delicate position is of the greatest importance; a greedy or corrupt *commissaire* can produce a host of small, unnoticed evils', suggested Louis-Sébastien Mercier.[70] Robinet's *Dictionnaire universel* suggested that 'the more the *commissaires* are able, honest, prudent, disinterested, the better run the Police will be', and this was very much the message conveyed by successive Lieutenants-General and occasionally by other magistrates.[71] They insisted that police officials be available to the public at all times. The *commissaires* had to be attentive to every detail of process, never cut corners, always be aware of the possibility of injustice if they made a decision without checking all the facts first. 'I am persuaded', wrote the magistrate responsible for criminal matters in the Châtelet courts, 'of the zeal that drives you, for the benefit of Justice.'[72] Those who met these expectations were rewarded with commendations, extra pay and promotion.[73] Any hint of negligence, on the other hand, led to reprimands and to threats to 'withdraw my confidence' from the offenders. In 1779 Lieutenant-General Lenoir issued a stern warning that the *commissaires*' clerks were not to act on behalf of their employers, and were certainly not permitted to order the imprisonment of people brought in by the city watch. He had also heard that some *commissaires* had refused to go down to the river when drowning people were rescued. This, he said, was 'contrary to duty and even to humanity'.[74] The police chiefs were particularly on the watch for any hint of bribe taking, cupidity or collusion between different elements of the police. On learning that the *commissaire* Roland had accepted payment from a number of stall keepers to whom he had given places next to the police headquarters, de Sartine wrote crisply: 'I would be very grateful to know on what grounds you felt this sum was due to you.' The care Roland devoted to explaining himself is clear from his taking the trouble to write a rough draft first![75]

Many of these letters testify to the *commissaires*' appetite for honour and status, both as individuals and as a group. In one letter sent to all of them, de Sartine took the unusual step of naming four of their number who had been at fault, threatening further action if a reprimand was not sufficient. His successor was usually more positive, but appealed to the same instincts: 'I am busy attempting to make your role more distinguished', he wrote to the inspectors in 1782, at the same time reminding them that those who were not scrupulous in their duties would not be paid.[76] Looking back later, Lenoir felt that his efforts had been successful. Writing of the *commissaires*, he claimed that '48 individuals of equal worth will not be found again'.[77] And although critics of the police, particularly after 1789, accused the *commissaires* of cupidity, their archives offer many examples of people actively seeking their assistance as conciliators, even depositing money with them for safe keeping.[78]

All of this testifies to a growing professionalization, among the *commissaires* in particular, although there are also hints of it among the inspectors. It is often difficult to distinguish from the more traditional defence of a corporate group, for both the *commissaires* and the inspectors formed a 'company', like the trade guilds or other groups in eighteenth-century society. But this emerging form of professional identity was characterized, as we have seen, by an emphasis on a more abstract form of public service and on the personal qualities of the members. It paralleled that of other groups such as the surgeons and the barristers, who insisted on better qualifications and higher ethical standards that would improve the reputation and the honourability of the entire group. In the late eighteenth century the *commissaires* proposed a system of self-policing, with any breaches they committed to be judged and punished by a committee of their peers.[79] In one sense this was not new. A model of the perfect magistrate had existed for at least two centuries, emphasizing personal integrity and morality, strong Catholic values and incorruptibility in the service of the king. Given the aspirations of the *commissaires* to be treated as judges, they readily adopted elements of this masculine ideal. They were, furthermore, confronted with some of the same issues as the magistrates of the sixteenth-century Parlement, as they were increasingly expected to enforce the law even when those before them were of higher rank.[80] The model of the man of principle and integrity assisted them to overcome the difficulty of dealing with nobles who breached police regulations, although such situations still required great tact – 'circumspection' was the term used by de Sartine in 1768 – and often the direct support of the Lieutenant-General.[81] In reality, of course, the personal qualities of the *commissaires* varied greatly. There is circumstantial evidence, nevertheless, that in the later part of the eighteenth century their formal qualifications were improved, as most had law degrees.[82] The proliferation of projects and attempts to define (or redefine) policing in the 1770s and 1780s is itself evidence of a changing self-awareness. Lemaire's document of 1770, already mentioned more than once, placed the *commissaires* at the heart of the entire mechanism: 'the exercise and ordinary duties of policing, in Paris, are entirely confided to the *commissaires* . . . The laws determining their functions give them, in order to carry them out, a power similar to that [of the Lieutenant-General].'[83] This was an exaggeration and a claim to status, but one that influenced their assiduity and their sense of professionalism.

The paternal model of policing evolved as ideals of masculinity were shifting across the eighteenth century. Even though much of the language remained the same, new understandings of fatherhood transformed the way the good king was imagined, as a far more benevolent, less distant and less self-interested figure. This meant that the policing undertaken in the name of paternal rule was also seen in new ways. In its ideal form, it was presented, in public commentary and in both internal and public documents produced by the police themselves, less as a prop to kingly glory and as a force for maintaining the rigid hierarchy on which absolutism depended, and more as a service to 'the public' and to 'society'. This was an important shift, although, as will be apparent from the examples I have given, it did not in any way make policing less concerned to defend social order. As for the *philosophes* themselves, both 'society' and 'the public' were understood as comprising educated people, and the mass of the population was seen as incapable of reason, needing to be directed.[84] But this was nevertheless a new, more inclusive social order, premised less on privilege and tradition and more on enlightened rationality. Public service, as now understood, was designed not only to maintain the health of the social body, but also to be both prophylactic and philanthropic; it should not simply respond to problems but should forestall them, and – in the spirit of the Enlightenment – it should work to improve society. Such tasks, in turn, required a new kind of policeman, someone who was able to use his position for the public good. In order to do this he had to be a man of integrity and civic virtue, displaying personal discipline so as to deserve public respect, authoritarian when circumstances required it, yet not unnecessarily harsh and never vindictive, always motivated by benevolence and working in the public interest.

The French Revolution was to transform both thinking about policing and ideals of masculinity. It did not do so immediately, for paternal imagery continued to be used throughout the period of the Constituent Assembly from 1789 to 1791. As late as January 1791, for example, when the pro-revolutionary parish clergy of Saint-Médard swore the oath in acceptance of the Civil Constitution of the Clergy, the parish priest made a speech urging the people to have confidence in 'the paternal care of the virtuous men' of the Paris Municipal Council.[85] But such language was becoming outdated as a more egalitarian concept of rights gained acceptance; in what Lynn Hunt has termed 'the family romance of the French Revolution', the nation's sons had come of age, rejecting paternal authority both metaphorically and, practically, through legal reform.[86] The Paris population had already rejected the Old Regime system of policing, driving the Lieutenant-General into exile in 1789, and most preventative policing, particularly the discredited *lettres de cachet*, was discarded. The *commissaires* were initially retained as enforcers of urban by-laws, under close and often mistrustful surveillance by the local lawyers and wealthy merchants who led the new revolutionary districts, men of similar social status to their own. But in 1791 the old system was replaced entirely, the functions of the *commissaires* being divided between two new officials, neither of whom enjoyed the same discretionary judicial authority. Revolutionary policing required new qualities: a commitment to the rule of law and to the new, more egalitarian society that was being created, and after 1792 also loyalty to the Republic.

Yet in some respects these developments were an extension of those in the final years of the absolute monarchy. The growing commitment of the Paris police to the new masculine values of benevolence and humanitarian concern, of personal and institutional integrity and of civic virtue prefigured the ideology of the early Revolution. Although we should not underestimate the authoritarian tendencies of most members of the police, some of them could and did readily embrace the new values; after 1791, no fewer than five of the former *commissaires* became revolutionary justices of the peace.[87]

Notes

1 I am grateful to Barbara Caine, Susan Broomhall and David Barrie for their comments on this chapter.
2 N. Delamare, *Traité de la police*, 4 vols, Paris: Michel Brunet, 1705–38; N. Dyonet, 'Le *commissaire* Delamare et son *Traité de la police* (1639–1723)', in C. Dolan (ed.), *Entre justice et justiciables. Les auxiliaires de la justice du Moyen Âge au XXe siècle*, Québec: Presses de l'Université Laval, 2005, pp. 101–19; and S. L. Kaplan and V. Milliot, 'La police de Paris, une "révolution permanente"? Du *commissaire* Lemaire au lieutenant de police Lenoir, les tribulations du *Mémoire sur l'administration de la police* (1770–1792)', in C. Denys, B. Marin and V. Milliot (eds), *Réformer la police. Les mémoires policiers en Europe au XVIIIe siècle*, Rennes: Presses Universitaires de Rennes, 2009, pp. 69–115, p. 69. On Paris as a model, see Alan Williams, *The Police of Paris, 1718–1789*, Baton Rouge: Louisiana State University Press, 1979, p. xvi; and P. Napoli, *Naissance de la police moderne*, Paris: La Découverte, 2003, p. 28.
3 P. Piasenza, 'Opinion publique, identité des institutions, "absolutisme". Le problème de la légalité à Paris entre le XVIIe et le XVIIIe siècle', *Revue historique*, 1993, vol. 290, pp. 97–142.
4 For general surveys, see M. Chassaigne, *La Lieutenance générale de police de Paris*, Paris: A. Rousseau, 1906; F. E. Ghoul, *La police parisienne dans la seconde moitié du XVIIIe siècle (1760–1785)*, 2 vols, Tunis: Université de Tunis, 1995; and A. Williams, *The Police of Paris*. On the *commissaires*, see S. L. Kaplan, 'Note sur les *commissaires* de police de Paris au XVIIIe siècle', *Revue d'histoire moderne et contemporaine*, 1981, vol. 28, p. 669–86; D. Garrioch, 'The People of Paris and their Police in the Eighteenth Century: Reflections on the Introduction of a "Modern" Police Force', *European History Quarterly*, 1994, vol. 24, pp. 511–35; V. Milliot, 'Le métier de *commissaire*: bon juge et "mauvais" policier? (Paris, XVIIIe siècle)', in Dolan, *Entre justice et justiciables*, pp. 121–36; and J.-M. Berlière, 'Du magistrat de quartier au policier spécialisé: Pierre Chénon, *commissaire* du quartier du Louvre (1751–1791)', in J.-M. Berlière, C. Denys, D. Kalifa and V. Milliot (eds), *Métiers de police. Être policier en Europe, XVIIIe–XXe siècle*, Rennes: Presses Universitaires de Rennes, 2008, pp. 315–31.
5 Garrioch, 'The People of Paris'.
6 J. Chagniot, 'Le guet et la garde de Paris à la fin de l'ancien régime', *Revue d'histoire moderne et contemporaine*, 1973, vol. 20, pp. 58–71.

7 On arbitrary arrests, see A. Farge and M. Foucault, *Le désordre des familles. Lettres de cachet des Archives de Bastille*, Paris: Gallimard Julliard, 1982; and C. Quétel, *De par le Roy. Essai sur les lettres de cachet*, Paris: Privat, 1981.

8 E. de Vattel, *Le droit des gens ou Principes de la loi naturelle appliqués à la conduite et aux affaires des nations et des souverains*, 2 vols, London: Droz, 1758, vol. 1, p. 165. All translations are mine unless otherwise indicated.

9 N. T. Des Essarts, *Dictionnaire universel de la police*, 7 vols, Paris, 1786–9, cited in P. Peveri, 'Les *Principes généraux* du major de Bar ou la police illuminée, 1772', in V. Milliot (ed.), *Les Mémoires policiers, 1750–1850. Écritures et pratiques policières du Siècle des Lumières au Second Empire*, Rennes: Presses Universitaires de Rennes, 2006, pp. 197–217 (p. 215).

10 A. Gazier, 'La police de Paris en 1770. Mémoire inédit composé par ordre de G. de Sartine sur la demande de Marie-Thérèse', *Mémoires de la Société de l'Histoire de Paris et de l'Ile-de-France*, 1878, vol. 5, pp. 1–131 (p. 28).

11 J.-B. R. Robinet, *Dictionnaire universel des sciences morale, économique, politique et diplomatique; ou Bibliotheque de l'homme-d'état et du citoyen*, 30 vols, London: Les librairies associés, 1777–83, vol. 26, p. 451.

12 J. Merrick, 'Sodomitical Inclinations in Early Eighteenth-Century Paris', *Eighteenth-Century Studies*, 1997, vol. 30, pp. 289–95.

13 J. Chagniot, *Paris et l'armée au XVIIIe siècle*, Paris: Economica, 1985, pp. 60–3; Piasenza, 'Opinion publique'; and P. Piasenza, *Polizia e città. Strategie d'ordine, conflitti e rivolte a Parigi tra sei e settecento*, Bologna: Il Mulino, 1990, pp. 101–70; Williams, *Police of Paris*, pp. 189–277.

14 Vattel, *Le droit des gens*, vol. 1, p. 165.

15 J. Domat, *Les Lois civiles dans leur ordre naturel*, Paris, 1713, quoted in J. Merrick, 'Fathers and Kings: Patriarchalism and Absolutism in Eighteenth-Century French Politics', *Studies on Voltaire and the Eighteenth Century*, 1993, vol. 308, pp. 281–303 (p. 289) (Merrick's translation).

16 J. Merrick, 'Patriarchalism and Constitutionalism in Eighteenth-Century Parlementary Discourse', *Studies in Eighteenth Century Culture*, 1991, vol. 20, pp. 317–30 (p. 319).

17 Louis Bourdaloue, quoted in Merrick, 'Fathers and Kings', p. 288 (Merrick's translation). See also F. Cosandey and R. Descimon, *L'absolutisme en France. Histoire et historiographie*, Paris: Le Seuil, 2002, pp. 265–7.

18 C.-L. de Secondat, baron de Montesquieu, *De l'esprit des lois*, Geneva: Barrillot, 1748, Book V, ch. VII.

19 Bibliothèque municipale, Orléans (henceforth BMO), MS 1422, fol. 637. Lenoir's memoirs have now been published, with a superb introduction, but too late to be taken into account in this chapter: V. Milliot, *Un policier des Lumières, suivi de Mémoires de J.C.P. Lenoir, ancien lieutenant général de police de Paris écrits en pays étrangers dans les années 1790 et suivantes*, Paris: Champ Vallon, 2011.

20 Archives nationales, Paris, Y13728, Albert to *commissaire* Gillet, 5 May 1775. All manuscript references are to the Archives nationales unless otherwise indicated.

21 Y11267A, Lenoir to *commissaire* Thierry, 21 August 1776, and accompanying notes. Y12830, Lenoir to *commissaire* Dupuy, 4 July 1777.

22 BMO MS 1422, fol. 637.

23 Y13764, 22 July 1757, for arrest of unauthorized hawker. Y12830, Lenoir to *commissaires*, 19 August 1780. Y13377, Berryer to *commissaire* Grimperel, 1752. Y9508. See V. Milliot, 'Jean-Charles-Pierre Lenoir (1732–1807), lieutenant-général de police de Paris (1774–1785): ses "mémoires" et une idée de la police des Lumières', *Mélanges de l'École française de Rome, Italie et Méditerranée*, 2003, vol. 115, p. 801.

24 This idea of 'the people' is not commented on by D. Cohen, *La Nature du peuple. Les formes de l'imaginaire social (XVIIIe–XXIe siècles)*, Paris: Champ Vallon, 2010, but is consistent with the view she describes, that they had no rationality and no independent will.

25 Y13163, Fontaine to Lenoir, 10 July 1777.
26 Y13163, undated draft letter to [Lieutenant-General], c. 1778.
27 Y11037, 13 March 1781. 'Sieur' was a less distinguished title than 'Monsieur'. For further examples see Y12597, 31 December 1752; Williams, *Police of Paris*, p. 122.
28 Y13163, Fontaine to Lenoir, 10 July 1777; Lenoir to Fontaine, 18 July 1777. For another example of 'disobedience' see Y15114A, de Sartine to *commissaire* Trudon, 29 December 1770.
29 de Secondat, *Spirit of the Laws*, Book XXVI, ch. XXIV. On the development and uses of this idea see Napoli, *Naissance*, pp. 45–7, 57–63.
30 V. Riqueti, marquis de Mirabeau, *L'Ami des hommes*, Avignon: Hérissant, 1757, quoted in Napoli, *Naissance*, p. 62.
31 Quoted in Farge and Foucault, *Le désordre des familles*, p. 354. Montesquieu's words are quoted in Lemaire's 1770 description of the Paris police: Gazier, 'La police de Paris', p. 8.
32 Y13377, complaint of 30 May 1752; report of 16 June; Berryer to Grimperel, 21 June; Berryer to Grimperel, n.d. [April 1752].
33 Y15114B, 3 May 1784. This and other files referred to contain many other examples.
34 Farge and Foucault, *Le désordre des familles*, pp. 95–124.
35 Bibliothèque de l'Arsenal (henceforth Arsenal) MS 11131, fols 430–8, dossier Bourdeaux (1731–2).
36 Y15114A, de Sartine to *commissaire* Trudon, 26 February 1772. For other examples, see Farge and Foucault, *Le désordre des familles*, pp. 95–124.
37 Arsenal MS 11751, fols 59–66 (1751). For another example see Y13377, petition of Pierre Billant and Marguerite LeClerc (1752).
38 Farge and Foucault, *Le désordre des familles*, p. 33, and for specific examples, pp. 49–94.
39 Arsenal MS 11286, fols 54–57 (1734–7).
40 Y13377 (June 1752). For further examples, see Farge and Foucault, *Le désordre des familles*, pp. 174–201.
41 Farge and Foucault, *Le désordre des familles*, pp. 289–96.
42 Arsenal MS 11040, fols 2–25 (1729), quotations fols 20, 13.
43 Arsenal MS 10975, fol. 254. For another example see Arsenal MS 11028, dossier Soulier (1718–28).
44 Arsenal MS 11751, fol. 20, n.d. [1751].
45 H.-G. Riqueti, comte de Mirabeau, *Des lettres de cachet et des prisons d'état*, Hamburg, 1782; G. A. Kelly, 'The Political Thought of Lamoignon de Malesherbes', *Political Theory*, 1979, vol. 7, p. 497; and Quétel, *De par le Roy*.
46 Y13728, Lenoir to *commissaires*, 3 August 1776.
47 Piasenza, 'Opinion publique', *passim*.
48 Y15114B, undated petition from Marguerite Bequaire [1786]; report of inspector Noel, 6 March 1786. See also Y11037, undated petition [1780].
49 Y15114B, n.d. [1784].
50 C. Duncan, 'Fallen Fathers: Images of Authority in Pre-Revolutionary French Art', *Art History*, 1981, vol. 4, pp. 194–200; and L. Hunt, *The Family Romance of the French Revolution*, Berkeley: University of California Press, 1992, pp. 21–8.
51 Duncan, 'Fallen Fathers', p. 187–8; Hunt, *Family Romance*, pp. 18–20.
52 Remonstrances of the Paris Parlement, quoted in Merrick, 'Fathers and Kings', p. 294.
53 Hunt, *Family Romance*, p. 20; J. Merrick, 'Politics on Pedestals: Royal Monuments in Eighteenth-Century France', *French History*, 1991, vol. 5, pp. 234–64; and D. Roche, *France in the Enlightenment*, Cambridge, MA: Harvard University Press, 1998 (first published Paris, 1993), pp. 271–3.
54 J. Markoff, 'Images du roi au début de la Révolution', in M. Vovelle (ed.), *L'image de la Révolution française*, Paris: Pergamon, 1989, vol. 1, pp. 237–45.
55 Gazier, 'La police de Paris', p. 27.

56 Piasenza, 'Opinion publique', p. 130; D. Margairaz, 'L'invention du "service public": entre "changement matériel" et "contrainte de nommer"', *Revue d'histoire moderne et contemporaine*, 2005, vol. 52, no. 3, pp. 10–32 (esp. p. 12).

57 Y13728, de Sartine to *commissaires*, 9 March 1762; Y12830, Lenoir to *commissaires*, 27 December 1780. See also Williams, *Police of Paris*, pp. 159–60.

58 Y15114B, 'mémoire', discussed by the *commissaires* 1 December 1784.

59 Garrioch, 'People of Paris', p. 526. See also Kaplan and Milliot, 'La police de Paris', pp. 98–103.

60 BMO MS 1422, p. 701.

61 For more detail see D. Garrioch, 'The Police of Paris as Enlightened Social Reformers', *Eighteenth-Century Life*, 1992, vol. 16, pp. 43–59; and V. Milliot, 'Qu'est-ce qu'une police éclairée? La police "amélioratrice" selon Jean-Charles Pierre Lenoir, lieutenant-général à Paris (1775–1785)', *Dix-huitième siècle*, 2005, vol. 37, pp. 117–30.

62 Denys, Marin and Milliot, *Réformer la police*; V. Milliot, *Les Mémoires policiers*.

63 Kaplan and Milliot, 'La police de Paris', pp. 74–5.

64 Frederick II, *Essay on Forms of Government* (1777), in I. Kramnick (ed.), *The Portable Enlightenment Reader*, New York: Penguin, 1995, p. 458 (Kramnick's translation).

65 C. E. Forth, *Masculinity in the Modern West: Gender, Civilization and the Body*, Basingstoke: Palgrave Macmillan, 2008, pp. 22–32; A. C. Vila, 'Elite Masculinities in Eighteenth-Century France', in Christopher E. Forth and Bertrand Taithe (eds), *French Masculinities: History, Culture and Politics*, Basingstoke: Palgrave Macmillan, 2007, pp. 15–30; and T. Hitchcock and M. Cohen (eds), *English Masculinities, 1660–1800*, London: Longman, 1999.

66 Forth, *Masculinity*, pp. 32–40.

67 On those who went to the *commissaires* see Garrioch, *Neighbourhood and Community*, Cambridge: Cambridge University Press, 1986, esp. chs 1, 8.

68 Y11949, 27 January 1762.

69 Y13728, 10 February 1784.

70 L.-S. Mercier, *Tableau de Paris*, nouvelle édition, 12 vols, Amsterdam: 1782–8, vol. 9, p. 129.

71 Robinet, *Dictionnaire universel*, p. 452.

72 Y12830, procureur du roi to *commissaires*, n.d. [1779].

73 Kaplan, 'Note sur les *commissaires*', p. 674.

74 Y13728, de Sartine to *commissaires*, 7 October 1764. Y12830, Lenoir to *commissaires*, 11 March and 10 April 1779. Y13728, Lenoir to *commissaires*, 8 October 1779. See also letter of 22 January 1777 and second, undated letter soon after.

75 Y12830, 30 November 1765, and draft reply. For other 'abuses' see Y12830, 28 August 1779, 27 December 1780.

76 Y12830, 7 September 1782.

77 Williams, *Police of Paris*, pp. 122–3.

78 The negative image was particularly shaped by P. Manuel, *La police de Paris dévoilée, par l'un des administrateurs de 1789*, Paris: Garnéry, Treuttel & Boffe, Year II, although for accusations made early in the century see S. L. Kaplan, *The Bakers of Paris and the Bread Question, 1700–1775*, Durham, NC: Duke University Press, 1996, pp. 531–2. For examples of trust involving different *commissaires*, see Y14484, 1 April 1789; Y15117, 20 February and 10 September 1788; Y15402, 11 July 1788.

79 T. Gelfand, *Professionalizing Modern Medicine: Paris Surgeons and Medical Science and Institutions in the Eighteenth Century*, Westport, CT: Greenwood Press, 1980; V. Milliot, 'Écrire pour policer: les "mémoires" policiers, 1750–1850', in Milliot (ed.), *Les Mémoires policiers*, pp. 15–41 (pp. 36–7); L. Brockliss and C. Jones, *The Medical World of Early Modern France*, Oxford: Oxford University Press, 1997, ch. 9; D. A. Bell, *Lawyers and Citizens: The Making of a Political Elite in Old Regime France*, New York: Oxford University Press, 1994, pp. 51–66; and Kaplan, 'Note sur les *commissaires*', p. 675.

80 C. Kaiser, 'Les cours souveraines au XVIe siècle: morale et Contre-Réforme', *Annales: ESC*, 1982, vol. 37, pp. 15–31.
81 Y12830, 5 October 1768.
82 Berlière et al., 'Métiers de police', p. 321; Milliot, 'Le métier de *commissaire*', pp. 132–3.
83 Gazier, 'La police de Paris', p. 42.
84 H. Chisick, *The Limits of Reform in the Enlightenment: Attitudes towards the Education of the Lower Classes in France*, Princeton, NJ: Princeton University Press, 1981.
85 Bibliothèque nationale de France, BnF Ld4 3207 'Paroisse St-Médard de Paris. Prestation de serment par le clergé de cette paroisse, le Dimanche 9 janvier 1791'.
86 Hunt, *Family Romance*, esp. pp. 40–52.
87 Milliot, 'Le métier de *commissaire*', p. 136, n. 41.

2

'A SPECIES OF CIVIL SOLDIER'

Masculinity, policing and the military in 1780s England[1]

Matthew McCormack

On 2 June 1780, the Protestant Association led by Lord George Gordon marched upon Westminster to exert pressure on parliament to repeal an act granting civil rights to Roman Catholics. What started as an orderly procession descended into mob violence that quickly spread throughout the city, subjecting London to a week of anarchy. This was quelled only when the military was called in, suppressing the rioting with bloody force and killing 285 civilians. The Gordon Riots were unique in their scale, but in many ways typified the Georgian state's vulnerability to mob violence and its heavy-handed response to it. The English aversion to standing armies and centralized state power ensured that there was no national police force in a modern sense; but disorder often exceeded the limited capabilities of the civil power and so, paradoxically, there was frequent recourse to the military. As we will see, after the Gordon Riots many contemporaries looked back with horror at the alternatives of mob violence or military suppression, and contemplated a reform of the police. Debating the issue in parliament, Lord Shelburne famously noted that 'it must be evident that the Police of Westminster is an imperfect, inadequate and wretched system'. He concluded: 'Recollect what the Police of France is. Examine its good but do not be blind to its evil.' The mention of the French police shocked the other Lords, who associated it with the worst excesses of centralized and militarized state power. This prompted the Duke of Northumberland to leap to the defence of the city authorities: 'if the House would give themselves the trouble to enquire into the characters of many of the gentlemen now in the commission for Westminster they would find the greatest part of them very liberal-minded, honest worthy men'.[2]

This exchange goes to the heart of the English debate on law enforcement, revolving as it has for three centuries around issues of national character, professionalism, militarism and masculinity. To this day, the 'Great British bobby' is supposed to embody the civil qualities of politeness, restraint and public service.[3]

This is in implied contrast to the more martial masculinity of the continental *gendarme* (literally 'man of arms'). The French police that so troubled the Duke of Northumberland was considered to be highly statist and highly militarized: it was involved in activities such as government surveillance, was structured along military lines, was largely staffed by former soldiers and was answerable to the ministry of war.[4] In the nineteenth century, the English policeman was also contrasted with the Prussian *schutzmann* – who has been described as 'a bureaucrat-soldier'[5] – and the American patrolman. Wilbur Miller has compared the formation of police services in New York and London in the nineteenth century and has argued that, although the cop came from a similarly civil tradition to the bobby, the different context of New York meant that he was impolite, unrestrained and heavily armed.[6] This work suggests that notions of the policeman have historically depended upon their society, political culture and nation-state.

Thinking about the personal qualities of the policeman also indicates the importance of masculinity in this context. Police work is largely performed by men, requires physical attributes such as strength and stature, and is associated with a cluster of masculine qualities such as authority, decisiveness and courage. On the other hand, Francis Dodsworth has argued that there is nothing 'natural' about the link between policing and masculinity. In his work on the origins of the New Police, he demonstrates that the bobby drew upon older ideas of the constable, which embodied gendered political and social ideologies; the masculinity of the English policeman is therefore historically and contextually specific, and this has implications for the type of authority that he exercises.[7]

This chapter will similarly adopt a gendered perspective in order to explore an episode in the Georgian debate on policing, but will focus in particular on the role of militarism in the image of the policeman. The standard account of English policing argues that it developed along purely civil lines, based upon a consensual respect for law and aversion to military despotism; the civil and military powers are kept scrupulously separate, the latter being called on to support the former only in exceptional and regrettable circumstances; and the product of all this is a policeman who enjoys the respect of his community, is free from political interference and, crucially, is unarmed. Arguably, though, this creates a false opposition between the civil and the military, the citizen and the soldier. As Clive Emsley has noted, it is a myth that the English policeman did not carry arms in the nineteenth century, given that some units were armed with cutlasses and pistols, and even the fabled truncheon could prove 'a formidable weapon'.[8] Moreover, in the eighteenth century the citizen and the soldier were never truly separate. On the one hand, the military were routinely involved in police duties, and, on the other, civilians were routinely involved in the military. During the Gordon Riots, county militia regiments and volunteer associations composed of civilians worked alongside the regular troops in putting down the disturbances and conducting patrols, searches and arrests. Within the Georgian state, military volunteering and policing were informed by essentially the same ideas about the duties beholden on the amateur male citizen. Furthermore, in practice these duties fell to similar classes of men, as their exacting demands were accommodated by parallel systems of substitution that involved paying men of lower rank. In the debate that followed the Gordon Riots, this was not lost on a host of commentators whose proposals for police reform were built upon the ideal of the citizen-soldier.

The backgrounds of these writers on police reform are instructive. Sir Bernard Turner and Sir William Blizard were active in military associations and Sir William Jones and Granville Sharp were enthusiasts for militia reform. All were active in city politics and some were serving aldermen: Blizard, Jones and Sharp were known for their involvement in radical politics and all would have regarded themselves as 'patriots' politically. Furthermore, several of the authors were active philanthropists, notably Jonas Hanway. This blend of paramilitarism, radicalism and moralism all informed their response to the Gordon Riots and their subsequent polemics for police reform. These pamphlets subscribed to a common worldview, which was highly gendered in both its diagnosis and its cure. The Gordon Riots confirmed their view that the roots of disorder lay in moral corruption and that a form of 'police' was essential to the survival of the state, but that it could be accomplished only by virtuous, martial, independent men. Furthermore, all of these pamphlets resisted foreign innovations and instead sought to adapt indigenous ancient practices. They were drawn in particular to the police institutions of the constabulary and the watch, and the military institutions of the militia and the volunteer association, and considered how their best features might be combined. The answer to police reform therefore lay not in a purely civil system, nor in perceived military despotism, but somewhere in the middle: in the ideal of the masculine citizen-soldier.

Policing and militarism

In order to understand the role of the citizen-soldier in these debates on policing, it is important to put them in the context of the British state. Georgian political culture emphasized the liberties of the individual in opposition to the power of the state: centralization, officeholding and a standing army threatened to increase the size and power of the executive, and should therefore be kept to a minimum; in their place the citizen was expected to take responsibility for the administration and security of his community. David Philips identifies this ethos with 'the gentry' and argues that voluntary service was the price that they paid for their class power, but political historians have more recently argued that this 'Country' politics was a common culture that could be appropriated by 'the freeborn Englishman' more widely.[9] 'Citizenship' was not a consistent legal category in the eighteenth century, but symbolically the citizen was the male head of household, possessed of property, a stake in his community and (probably) the parliamentary franchise. This was therefore a classical political culture that evaluated the male citizen in highly gendered moral terms, in terms of his independence, his patriarchal responsibility and his civic virtue.[10] All of this had implications in practice for both policing and the military, and I will examine each of these in turn.

The English state had long relied upon the activities of local amateurs. Michael Braddick argues that it is essential to explore the institutions and personnel of county and parish governance if we are to understand the early modern state, as a wide range of political, legal and military functions in the localities were carried out by unpaid gentlemen.[11] This continued to be the case in the eighteenth century, which celebrated the civic virtue of local office.[12] Professionalization was resisted on the negative grounds of hostility to the growth of the state and taxation, and the positive grounds that local government was supposed to be participatory, a matter of obligation rather than vocation.[13] A 1782 proposal for reforming the London militia and watch argued not for professionalization, but rather relied upon the 'Spirit, Generosity, and Honor of . . . the Gentlemen of *London*', who would naturally offer their services rather than 'put their fellow Citizens to any unnecessary Expence'.[14] In reality, however, the duties were increasingly beyond the willingness and capacity of those on whom they fell. Viscount Barrington, for example, privately lamented in 1768 the difficulties of appointing magistrates in Middlesex: 'If persons properly qualified will not serve gratis they should be paid in some shape or other.'[15] The ideal that offices would be shared by volunteering, rotation or ballot did not always work in practice. Systems of fines and substitutions maintained the fiction of gentry service, when in reality the duties were increasingly being performed by paid functionaries of a lower social rank.

This was particularly true when it came to institutions of law and policing. It is worth emphasizing that Englishmen in the eighteenth century did not use the term 'police' in the way that we do today: it was a condition rather than an institution, which encompassed 'all matters affecting the survival and well-being of the state (*polis*)'.[16] One of the few commentators of the 1780s who used the term systematically was Jonas Hanway, whose tracts on the 'defects of police' included topics such as irreligion, vagrancy, emigration, luxury, lotteries and adultery. These were all sources of 'effeminacy', moral corruptions that threatened to undermine the body politic, as the masculine virtue of the citizenry was central to its integrity; within this classical worldview, 'police' had a political importance as well as a governmental one. He acknowledged that the 'word *police* is not universally intelligible'[17] and felt the need to counter the complaint 'that the nature of our constitution will not admit of a *police*'.[18] This is because the term had French connotations: '*la police*' connoted French-style despotism and militarism, and encompassed a range of political activities such as spying that went well beyond the English remit of legitimate policing.[19] Clive Emsley has argued that this political hostility to the military and state power long frustrated the cause of police reform.[20]

It certainly moulded English attitudes towards the institutions and personnel of law enforcement. The English gentleman's hostility to standing armies resulted in a reliance upon citizen-soldiers, which they then had to organize, so ironically these same men had overlapping civil and military responsibilities. Power in the counties was wielded by the Lords Lieutenant, who had responsibility for raising the militia as well as administering the law. The day-to-day business of the latter fell on the sheriff, a demanding and unpaid role that was understandably held for only a year. He also had responsibility for raising the *posse comitatus*, literally 'the power of the county', an ancient convention whereby any male between the ages of sixteen and sixty was liable to assist in the apprehension of felons. The *posse* could also be raised for defence, as it had been in the northern counties during the 1715 Jacobite rebellion.[21] We will see that its dual policing and military functions appealed to the police reformers of the 1780s.

Beneath the shrievalty was the magistracy, who staffed the county bench and oversaw parish officers. Magistrates had a key role in the interface between the civil and the military powers, particularly when it came to riot control. The Riot Act of 1715 empowered the military to use lethal force against a crowd with indemnity once a magistrate had read the proclamation and an hour had elapsed. This did not supersede the obligation on soldier and citizen alike to prevent riots, or the right to use force against felons, but in practice the military refused to act without it.[22] The limited early response to the Gordon Riots was less a result of lack of troops and more because of a lack of magistrates, as they disappeared in fear of reprisals. On the fourth day of the riots, the Secretary at War explained that it was the duty of troops 'to act only under the Authority of the Civil Magistrate'. As he wrote in frustration to Lord Stormont: 'If, therefore, the Civil Magistrate . . . refuses to act, I leave it to your Lordship to judge in how defenceless and how disgraceful a situation the military are left.'[23] Philips argues that criticism of the magistracy after the Gordon Riots was borne of elite disdain for the capital's 'trading justices', men of low rank who took the position to enrich themselves rather than from a sense of responsibility.[24] But dissatisfaction with magistrates was not limited to individuals in the critiques of the 1780s, which instead concerned policing systems and their ability to cope with riots.

At the local level was the constable, an ancient office that was central to the ideology and practice of policing. High constables were supposedly drawn from the gentry, but what had once been an honour was increasingly becoming an onerous administrative job.[25] They oversaw the petty constables, who were drawn from the householders and in a sense were their democratic representatives: posts were held for a year and holders were elected or rotated. When a male householder could or would not serve, or when the householder was a woman, a substitute could be hired with the 'fine' imposed. Beattie argues that there was:

> a major shift away from men in the solidly middling ranks of the City's inhabitants who held the post for a year as an aspect of their sense of civic duty and towards men of lower rank and wealth, many of whom it seems right to assume did it as a way of supporting themselves.[26]

Nevertheless, exacting requirements were placed upon substitutes to ensure that they were broadly of the same class and gender. Constables were supposed to be the social equal of their fellow citizens, and to be literate and propertied. A police reformer in the 1770s argued that property qualifications ensured that constables were 'honest, sober and conscientious'.[27] As Dodsworth has shown, they were supposed to embody physical as well as moral masculine qualities: the New Police's requirements for the strength, height and appearance of constables merely codified earlier ideals.[28] These soldierly requirements are all the more comprehensible given their key role in civil defence. In times of riot, the constable was the first line of defence (assisted by special constables sworn in for the occasion), and should military assistance be called in then they would be expected to work alongside soldiers.[29] In addition, they had responsibility for billeting soldiers and for raising the militia: constables drew up the lists of men liable to serve, organized the ballot, swore in recruits, arranged substitutes, advertised exercises and administered the parish relief to which militiamen's families were entitled.[30] Constables' exemption from the militia ballot was not so much to distance them from the military, as an acknowledgement of the crucial role that they played in administering it.

In urban areas, the constabulary was supplemented by the watch. The 1285 Statute of Winchester required towns and boroughs to provide a body of men on the streets after dark.[31] In theory it was the householders' obligation to provide a night watch, but these were systematically substituted to the extent that it became a lowly paid role, and by the eighteenth century they tended to be paid from a central fund rather than fines. Beattie notes that, whereas 'constables, however poor, were householders, watchmen were more likely to be lodgers'.[32] Nevertheless, watchmen were carefully selected, with a preference for former soldiers who were tall, fit, under forty years of age and of good character.[33] Watchmen had traditionally been armed with halberds, a spear with an axe blade, the weapon of the drill sergeant. By the mid-eighteenth century they had been replaced by the lantern and staff, which were more suited to their increasingly mobile role, but they would still be expected to use the military halberd for riot control and on ceremonial occasions.[34] Indeed, Hanway regarded watchmen as a 'species of *civil soldier*' and we will see how reformers in the 1780s sought to remodel the watch along military lines.[35]

Militarism and policing

If the civil was involved in the military, then the reverse was also true. Throughout the eighteenth century, the army and militia were regularly involved in police duties. Besides riot control, these included fire-fighting, guarding key buildings and working for the excise; the last required a military response as gangs of smugglers were heavily armed.[36] Attitudes to the military were also informed by the civil: the same anti-militarism that frustrated police reform similarly stunted the army. The 'standing army' was the great bugbear in British politics, based upon memories of the civil war, perceptions of continental militarism and a fundamental distrust of executive power. The army was therefore a very sensitive issue politically, and soldiers were pointedly marched out of town during elections and assizes so as not to interfere in the civil process. Parliament annually made its point that the military was subordinate to it by grudgingly passing the Mutiny Act, replete with restrictions and for one year only. In particular, it tightly circumscribed the army's legal position: as we have seen in relation to riot control, the army's role was limited, jealously monitored and dependent upon direction from legal personnel. The regular soldier's anomalous legal position – being subject to a different set of laws from free citizens – was one of many reasons why Georgians held him in such contempt.[37]

Given Britain's reliance on its military, the complacency of this anti-militarism is striking. The received wisdom on the backbenches, however, was that there was no need for a large army, as the beloved navy would defend the coasts and patriotic citizens would overawe anyone who dared to invade. Just as civilian men were expected to provide their own policing, so they were expected to act in their country's defence. The citizen was required by ancient laws such as the Statute of Winchester to keep up a proficiency in arms and to associate and intervene in order to restore the king's peace. Granville Sharp reasoned that if men were anciently obliged to be able to use a long bow, why not *require the exercise of ALL MEN in the use of the present fashionable weapons, the musquet and bayonet*?[38] It is striking that Georgians so routinely returned to these common law principles when discussing policing and home defence. The notion of the *posse comitatus* features prominently in Sir William Jones's writings on police reform[39] and continued to be influential: it informed plans to prevent invasion in the 1790s and to deal with riots in the 1810s and even 1830s.[40]

The obligation of the citizen to provide for the nation's defence was embodied in the institution of the militia. The militia was the 'constitutional force', which had pride of place in opposition Whig ideology as it celebrated the manly independence, martial valour and civic virtue of the patriotic citizen. It was safer than a standing army as it was not the tool of a would-be despot, but was rather an expression of the people's power. The militia in the first half of the eighteenth century was the remnant of an early modern institution that relied upon the patriarchal leadership of the gentry to keep up regiments. In practice it had fallen into disrepair, so the renewed threat of invasion at the beginning of the Seven Years' War presented an opportunity for reform. The 'New Militia' had been justified in parliament and the press in terms of masculine citizen-soldiering, evoking the image of the patriotic householder who would wish to defend his own.[41] In practice, however, it was very different to its predecessor as it switched the obligation from the wealth of the gentry to the labour of the common man: all adult men were balloted from a new national census of military manpower, but anyone who could afford it bought themselves out so service fell overwhelmingly on the lower classes. Attempts by constables to draw up lists of recruits were therefore greeted with some of the worst rioting of the century.[42] Protesters at Hexham in 1761 argued that 'what common men desire is men of estates to hire men for the militia as they were formerly; being very fit that they who have lands should hire men to maintain them'. The protest turned into a riot and an existing militia regiment was called in to restore order. Fifty civilians and one soldier were killed, showing how involving the military in police actions could lead to a massacre.[43] In general, the New Militia resembled the regular army: it shared the same uniforms, weaponry, encampments and regulations. Its critics like Granville Sharp argued that it 'savour[ed] too much of a *standing army*' and turned civilians into '*mere soldiers*', and urged a return to the true values of citizen-soldiering.[44]

Nevertheless, the militia retained its ideological appeal among many gentlemen, not least because it confirmed their position as governing men. As in the Old, the New Militia was expected to be officered by the propertied, who would naturally possess martial gentility and provide social leadership for the local regiments. The property qualifications for militia commissions paralleled those for civil offices: £300 in land was usually required to be a major or a JP, respectively.[45] Serving in the militia or magistracy carried social prestige and a sense of public duty, and connoted similar masculine virtues. Hanway judged that a JP should possess 'probity, candour and courage': 'Every one who has read of real heroism, will find it consisted in deeds of valour, in preserving a fellow-citizen, securing the disturbers of the peace, and invaders of the property of their neighbours.'[46] In theory, the masculine ideal of the militiaman paralleled that of the constable. Rather than a professional, he was a man from the community who was performing a duty of citizenship, and was motivated by a desire to defend his own. As a proponent of the militia argued, militiamen should 'fight not for Pay but for *Property*; for their *Families*; for their *Religion*, and *Liberties*'.[47] In practice, this realistically applied only to officers, and the rank and file socially resembled the watch more than the constabulary. But it is striking how systems of property qualification and substitution operated similarly in both spheres, in order to recruit appropriate men for their places within hierarchical institutions.

After its re-establishment in 1757, the militia was regularly involved in riot duty. Because the militia was not permitted to be marched out of the kingdom, and because Britain never experienced invasion in this period, it was virtually the only active duty they saw. Indeed, the militia was embodied full time only during wartime when the regular army was deployed abroad, and it was usually in wartime that rioting occurred, in response to its increased demands on enlistment, taxation and food supply. Several county militia regiments were called into London during the Gordon Riots as they were stationed in the south-east in anticipation of invasion. Their service earned the praise of Londoners, who far preferred the idea of rural citizen-soldiers on their streets to the alternative of contemptible, despotic regulars. Edward Gibbon, for example, lauded the Northumberland Militia, which arrived tired after a twenty-five-mile march, but immediately set to work defending the Bank of England: 'Colonel Holroyd was all night in Holborn among the flames with the Northumberland Militia, and performed very bold and active service.'[48] Whilst in London these regiments conducted regular patrols. The 2nd Regiment of the West Riding of Yorkshire Militia, for example, took the following circular route: 'From Museum, through Great Russell Street, Oxford St., St Giles's, part of Drury Lane, Holborn, Grey's Inn Lane to the Turnpike in

Constitution Row, King's Road, Bedford Street, Red Lyon Square, Bloomsbury to the Museum.'[49] We also have a comprehensive account of the Northamptonshire Militia's patrols from a captain's order book.[50] These street patrols with their regular route, high visibility and preventative purpose strongly resemble the 'beat' of a constable.

Militiamen were not the only citizen-soldiers involved in putting down the Gordon Riots. Existing military associations such as the London Military Foot Association (LMFA) and the Honourable Artillery Company were active throughout the riots, and were supplemented by new volunteer associations that sprang up all over the city during and after the disturbances. Sir William Blizard was one such citizen-volunteer: he described the LMFA as an association composed of 'gentlemen of character and property'. Formed to combat invasion, in practice he recalled that their role was '*in supporting the civil power in the maintaining of* PEACE *and* ORDER'.[51] Another former member, Sir Bernard Turner, proudly recalled that their service in the summer of 1780 was consistent with 'what each Individual of that Corps owed to himself as a Gentleman, a Soldier, and a Citizen'.[52] Both Blizard and Turner were notable police reformers who drew upon their experiences of June 1780 in proposing schemes of policing for London. Indeed, accounts by former volunteers suggest that they conceived of their role as being essentially a police one: the mobs consisted of 'thieves of every species' rather than insurrectionists as such.[53] The LMFA also performed more standard police roles during and after the riots.[54] These included conducting patrols, night watches, searching houses, accompanying peace officers and 'the apprehension of thieves and other bad men'.[55] We can see this in Blizard's first-hand account of one such patrol during the riots:

> We were twice on duty, attended by peace-officers, particularly two who have been long employed in the mysteries of thief-taking. One of our detachments visited *Chick Lane, Field Lane, Black-boy Alley*, and some other such places. From the first-named, we escorted persons to prison. These places constitute a kind of separate town or district, calculated for the reception of the darkest and most dangerous enemies to society, and in which, when pursued for the commission of crimes, they easily conceal themselves.[56]

Blizard included this account in his polemic for police reform. In its emphases on criminal classes and districts, 'dangerous enemies to society' and the 'mysteries' of current police methods, it parallels other police reform writings from the period.[57]

The Gordon Riots therefore give us a snapshot of the variety of military and policing methods that could be deployed against rioters in the eighteenth century. Hanway compared the records of the constables, regular soldiers and military volunteers during the riots. Tellingly, he rather damned the second with faint praise, while lauding the other two in strikingly similar terms:

We have at length demonstrated good sense, and valour in domestic duty, by a corps of constables, chosen men of principle: let us call them by the honourable name of *volunteer police guards*. Our soldiery in general have behaved with the utmost propriety, and we owe them thanks for what they have, and what they have not done. The *London Association* is also entitled to every mark of gratitude and applause. As this corps is bound by ties of *loyalty, knowledge of the frame of our happy constitution, filial and parental love,* to defend each other, their wives and children, and their neighbour; it may be hoped this fraternity (let us drop the word association) will give itself such laws, as may secure its virtuous constancy.[58]

Whereas he can only bring himself to commend *regular* soldiers for what 'they have not done', the *citizen-soldiers* are praised to the skies, and in terms that underline their fraternal and familial masculinities. If regular soldiers were expected to be bachelors, citizen-soldiers could reach the apogee of manliness as husbands, fathers and householders – and would draw their superior motivation from this. The citizen-soldier therefore had a key role to play in the Georgian state, and was compatible with parallel ideals and practices in the justice system. It is comprehensible that this emotive masculine ideal should have held such an appeal for police reformers.

The debate of the 1780s

The Gordon Riots prompted an intense debate about the state of policing in London. We began with Shelburne's comments in the Lords, condemning the present system of police and commending that of France. A year later in the Commons, Sheridan condemned the 'defective state of the magistracy' and called for an enquiry; in 1785, Pitt sought a thorough reform of policing in the capital.[59] Equally important was a flurry of pamphlets by police reformers in the half-decade that followed the riots. This chapter will conclude by exploring this debate, and in particular the role that it proposes for citizen-soldiers in schemes of policing.

Historians used to take this debate seriously: Sir Leon Radzinowicz devoted several chapters to it in his monumental *History of the English Criminal Law* of the 1950s and 1960s. In recent decades, police historians have instead attempted to understand the practice of the Old Police on its own terms but, in the process, these critiques of the 1780s have been neglected. There are various possible reasons for this. First, in emphasizing that changes originated in actual practice on the ground, revisionists serve to downplay the influence of eighteenth-century reformers,[60] and even of the intellectual context in general.[61] Second, this 'bottom-up' and localized approach serves to re-emphasize the civil character of English police development, so the 'obsession with militias' in these pamphlets does not fit the story.[62] Third, in emphasizing broad continuities, the impact of dramatic events like the Gordon Riots is downplayed.[63] More recently, however, these debates have come back into fashion, as historians such as Dodsworth have tried to rehabilitate the influence of neo-classical political ideologies upon Georgian ideas and practices of governance.[64] It is worth analysing these pamphlets in detail, in order to establish why their arguments should have struck a chord at this often-neglected phase in the history of English policing.

First, the worldview of these writers was fundamentally a moral one. They combined Christian and classical concepts to argue that individual morality had a bearing on national strength: on the one hand, man was sinful and this would bring God's judgement on the state; and on the other, man was corruptible and this would undermine the health and viability of the polity.[65] Hanway therefore combined philanthropy and patriotism – notably in schemes such as the Marine Society, which trained orphans for the fleet[66] – and his interest in policing was no different in this respect. His 1775 tract *The Defects of Police* argued that Britons 'have been, for some years, in an *undisciplined state*' of crime, immorality and irreligion. 'In every rank, folly predominates: if our superiors lose their taste for what is great and manly, the *correction* by a well-regulated *police* will be neglected, and the foundations of government undermined, and require some further props.'[67] The need for such a 'prop' was confirmed by his experience of June 1780, so he reissued the tract with a substantial preface reflecting on the riots and how they might be prevented in future. He praised the police actions of the various volunteer military associations, and as such proposed 'a plan of mutual defence, on the principles of *common courage* and *activity*'. His plan brought together '*civil, military*, and *ecclesiastical*' elements, and hoped that '*reformation* should take place in the *morals* of the people' as a result.[68] Other pamphlets had a similar emphasis on morality. Blizard insisted that criminals should be punished, '*not to destroy, but to save*', by 'calling back the corrupted members of society to a sense of social duties'.[69]

All of these pamphlets proposed voluntary action on the part of the male citizen, emphasizing that policing one's own community was both a right and a duty of citizenship. Sir William Jones was a noted radical and emphasized the libertarian implications of this in *An Inquiry into the Legal Mode of Suppressing Riots* (1782). For Jones, the use of standing armies against crowds was illegal and a threat to liberty. It was also unnecessary, as 'the law doth permit and command *every subject of this realm* to arm himself and use his arms with effect for the suppression of tumults'. Ancient institutions like the *posse* should therefore be revived, which would mean the army would never have to be used in this way.[70] Granville Sharp takes a very similar line, arguing that ancient statutes indefeasibly enshrine 'the *natural right* of every individual to repel force with force, in defence of himself and his property'. 'The late unhappy tumults prove', he argued, 'that these principles of the English constitution are as *necessary* to be enforced *at present as ever they were*.' Sharp saw this not as an onerous obligation, but as empowering: voluntary associations should elect their officers and employ the ancient terminology of Anglo-Saxon parish democracy.[71]

In calling upon the male citizen to act in this way, these writers appealed to his masculine qualities and motivations. Blizard urged that policing was 'the duty of every man' and appealed to their 'courage, calmness, and fortitude'. He also tugged at heartstrings, appealing to a patriarch's supposedly natural sense of protectiveness towards women and children: if citizens had to be spurred to action, then Georgians invariably had recourse to sentiment.[72] Turner concludes his tract with an emotional plea to the citizens of London:

> If you will remain Deaf to the calls of self-preservation – if you are so familiarized to the idea of Ruin and Slavery, as to think any Trouble too great, to oppose them – if neither your Feelings, as Britons, as Citizens, or as Friends to Society will rouse you – if the Protection of our most excellent Constitution, as established at the glorious Revolution to yourselves and Posterity, is a matter of Indifference – if these things can be, but for a moment in the Metropolis of the British Empire, *Alas! our Ruin is Inevitable!*[73]

His emotive appeal to feeling, shame, patriotism, posterity and emancipation was calculated to motivate the Georgian man.

The various plans that these authors proposed were not homogeneous. Jones's was localized and individualist, whereby propertied men provided their own arms,[74] whereas others proposed national or city-wide institutions with formal regulations. But all of the schemes were based, to differing degrees, upon combining the functions of the militia and watch. Hanway proposed the formation of a 'police guard', which would take over the duties of the watch and constabulary, and provide an 'auxiliary force' in times of riot or invasion.[75] As we have seen, Sharp was critical of the present New Militia, and instead sought the formation of a 'National Militia' for civil defence:

> As the sole purpose of *Military Associations* is the support of the *Civil Magistrate* . . . it is necessary that each associated company be formed, upon principles as opposite to those of *standing armies* (valour and good discipline excepted) as can possibly be devised.

Such militiamen would be part-time, so they would not lose their civilian occupations or characters, and could associate as neighbours to prevent crime and organize a watch.[76] As its title relates, Turner proposed a comprehensive *Plan for Rendering the Militia of London Useful and Respectable, and for Raising an Effective and Regulated Watch* (1782). Essentially he sought to merge the two organizations. On the one hand, this underlined the civil character of the militia: 'THE MILITIA is a Force, which naturally offers itself to a cautious Patriot, on any Emergency that exceeds the Controul usually exerted by the Civil Power.' On the other hand, it militarized the watch: like modern police forces, they were to be subjected to a military regime of drilling, inspection and discipline, and organized in a hierarchical fashion along military lines. The institution would be divided into forty-eight companies with regular 'beats' around the city, and recruits would have to be 'stout active Men, of good Characters, and Soldier like Appearance and Ability'.[77]

The visual appearance of these new solider-policemen preoccupied the authors, who wrote at length about their uniforms. Hanway emphasized the importance of uniform, both for how his police guards were perceived and also for how they conducted themselves:

> A military force derives part of its awful appearance from dress: and it will be generally found, that an uniform adds to the courage of the men, possessing the honourable occupation of a soldier, creates a stronger mutual confidence, and prevents confusion where numbers appear.

In an age when military dress was often criticized for its foppery, however, he insisted that 'this *police guard* should prefer a graver deportment, and not use cockades, or any military distinction'. He cited the example of a parish volunteer association from the Gordon Riots, who wore 'a plain blue light frock' to distinguish them from redcoats and to signal their essentially civil purpose.[78] Turner, by contrast, prescribed different uniforms for militia and watch duties. Whereas militia duties would be performed in a standard military uniform, when on watch they would wear 'a good strong Fairnought Great Coat, and a strong Uniform Cap, made to resist the Weather and the blow of a Stick'. Besides these practical considerations, Turner was keen that the public should know whether the men in question were performing military or civil duties – literally, what hat they were wearing. The visibility of the police was very important, both so that they could prevent crime and also so that they could not be accused of being spies, one of the key objections to the French police. Turner insisted that every recruit should have a number displayed on his uniform, so that they would be clearly distinguishable and individually accountable.[79] These considerations would continue to be important in the formation of the New Police half a century later.[80]

In the short term these plans apparently came to nothing. Most of the local military associations formed during and after the Gordon Riots folded after a matter of weeks. Turner's and Blizard's plans were submitted to the City authorities for consideration but were rejected.[81] Pitt's 1785 proposal for stipendiary magistrates and constables foundered on traditional fears of militarism, professionalism and centralization – and on the self-interest of the City.[82] These schemes were not without influence, however; after all, most police reform bills failed, but they still offer historians an insight into the ideas of their times. Arguably, the passage of the 1785 Bill was mishandled and a 'more limited measure' might have got through.[83] Moreover, its principles were adopted wholesale in the Dublin Police Act of 1786,[84] and historians have long recognized the influence of Ireland's militarized policing upon Peel's conception of the New Police.[85] It would be simplistic therefore to suggest that these plans of the 1780s failed because they were 'militaristic', and therefore should be ignored.[86]

The importance of the citizen-soldier in the eighteenth century, and the overlaps between the civil and the military spheres, meant that a particular form of militarism has always had a place in the English police tradition. Police historians who try to rehabilitate the Old Police tend to downplay the importance of these paramilitary reformers of the 1780s, but their critiques were far from being utopian schemes, detached from the everyday practice of policing; rather, they were grounded in the realities of the Georgian state and the immediate experience of the Gordon Riots. Ironically, we have to return to older Whiggish accounts in order to see these debates taken seriously. Adding masculinity to the picture helps us to identify the emotive ideals of citizenship and martiality in these discourses, and also to comprehend how political ideologies come to be embodied in practice. In current debates about militarized police methods in Britain, therefore, it would be complacent to assume that its police tradition has historically been an entirely civil one.[87] Rather, it is essential to locate the strain of martial masculinity within the cherished ideal of the citizen-constable itself.

Notes

1 I would like to thank Drew Gray and Francis Dodsworth for their help with this project.
2 Quoted in C. Hibbert, *King Mob: The Story of George Gordon and the Riots of 1780*, London: Longman, 1958, pp. 64–5.
3 C. Emsley, *The Great British Bobby: A History of British Policing from 1829 to the Present*, London: Quercus, 2009.
4 C. Emsley, *Policing and its Context, 1750–1870*, Basingstoke: Macmillan, 1983; and C. Emsley and B. Weinberger, 'Introduction' to *Policing Western Europe: Politics, Professionalism and Public Order 1850–1940*, London: Greenwood, 1991.
5 H. Reinke, ' "Armed as if for War": the State, the Military and the Professionalism of the Prussian Police in Imperial Germany', in Emsley and Weinberger (eds), *Policing Western Europe*, p. 55.
6 W. Miller, *Cops and Bobbies: Police Authority in New York and London 1830–1870*, Chicago: Chicago University Press, 1977, p. ix.
7 F. Dodsworth, 'Masculinity as Governance: Police, Public Service and the Embodiment of Authority, c. 1700–1800', in M. McCormack (ed.), *Public Men: Masculinity and Politics in Modern Britain*, Basingstoke: Palgrave Macmillan, 2007.
8 C. Emsley, 'Arms and the Victorian Policeman', *History Today*, 1984, vol. 34, no. 11, pp. 37–42, p. 38.
9 D. Philips, ' "A New Engine of Power and Authority": The Institutionalization of Law-Enforcement in England 1780–1830', in V. Gatrell, B. Lenman and G. Parker (eds), *Crime and the Law: The Social History of Crime in Western Europe since 1500*, London: Europa, 1980, p. 160; and K. Wilson, *The Sense of the People: Politics, Culture and Imperialism in England, 1715–1785*, Cambridge: Cambridge University Press, 1995.
10 M. McCormack, *The Independent Man: Citizenship and Gender Politics in Georgian England*, Manchester: Manchester University Press, 2005.
11 M. Braddick, *State Formation in Early Modern England c. 1550–1700*, Cambridge: Cambridge University Press, 2000, p. 1.
12 L. Colley, ' "What Is to Be Expected of the People?" Civic Virtue and the Common Man in England, 1700–1760', in G. Schochet (ed.), *Politics, Politeness and Patriotism*, Washington: Folger Institute, 1993.

13 F. Dodsworth, '"Civic" Police and the Condition of Liberty: The Rationality of Governance in Eighteenth-Century England', *Social History*, 2004, vol. 29, no. 2, pp. 199–216 (p. 204).

14 B. Turner, *A Plan for Rendering the Militia of London Useful and Respectable, and for Raising an Effective and Well-Regulated Watch, Without Subjecting the Citizens to Additional Taxes or the Interposition of Parliament*, London, 1782, p. 48. Italics in all quotations original.

15 W. Barrington to T. Bradshaw (12 October 1768): T. Hayter (ed.), *An Eighteenth-Century Secretary at War: The Papers of William, Viscount Barrington*, London: Bodley Head, 1988, p. 262.

16 C. Emsley, *The English Police: A Political and Social History*, Hemel Hempstead: Harvester, 1991, p. 3.

17 J. Hanway, *The Defects of Police, the Cause of Immorality, and the Continual Robberies Committed, Particularly in and about the Metropolis*, London, 1785, p. xx.

18 J. Hanway, *The Citizen's Monitor: Shewing the Necessity of a Salutary Police, Executed by Resolute and Judicious Magistrates, Assisted by the Pious Labours of Zealous Clergymen, For the Preservation of the Lives and Property of the People, and the Happy Existence of the State*, London, 1780, p. iii. This work is essentially a reprint of *Defects of Police*, but with a new preface that draws lessons from the Gordon Riots.

19 F. Dodsworth, 'The Idea of Police in Eighteenth-Century England: Discipline, Reformation, Superintendance, c. 1780–1800', *Journal of the History of Ideas*, 2008, vol. 69, no. 4, pp. 583–605 (p. 594).

20 Emsley, *Policing and its Context*, p. 21.

21 J. Oates, 'Responses in the North of England to the Jacobite Rebellion of 1715', *Northern History*, 2006, vol. 43, no. 1, pp. 77–95 (pp. 81–2).

22 T. Hayter, *The Army and the Crowd in Mid-Georgian England*, Basingstoke: Macmillan, 1978, p. 35.

23 Quoted in J. P. de Castro, *The Gordon Riots*, London: Oxford University Press, 1926, p. 72.

24 Philips, 'New Engine', p. 163.

25 Emsley, *Policing in its Context*, p. 24.

26 J. M. Beattie, *Policing and Punishment in London, 1660–1750*, Oxford: Oxford University Press, 2001, p. 134.

27 Quoted in E. Reynolds, 'Sir John Fielding, Sir Charles Whitworth and the Westminster Night Watch Act, 1770–1775', in L. Knaffa (ed.), *Policing and War in Europe*, Greenwood: London, 2002, p. 10.

28 Dodsworth, 'Masculinity as Governance', pp. 47–8.

29 Hayter, *Army and the Crowd*, p. 169; Beattie, *Policing and Punishment*, p. 128.

30 The whole range of the constables' duties relating to the militia are referred to in the records of the parish of St Peter's in Cambridge: Cambridge University Library MS Doc. 3971, fols 1–21.

31 E. Reynolds, *Before the Bobbies: The Night Watch and Police Reform in Metropolitan London 1720–1830*, Basingstoke: Macmillan, 1998, p. 9.

32 Beattie, *Policing and Punishment*, p. 205.

33 Emsley, *Policing in its Context*, pp. 25–6.

34 Beattie, *Policing and Punishment*, pp. 128, 181.

35 Hanway, *The Citizen's Monitor*, p. xiii.

36 Hayter, *Army and the Crowd*, pp. 220–1.

37 Philips, 'New Engine', pp. 160–1; M. McCormack, 'Citizenship, Nationhood and Masculinity in the Affair of the Hanoverian Soldier, 1756', *The Historical Journal*, 2006, vol. 49, no. 4, pp. 971–93 (pp. 984–5).

38 G. Sharp, *Tracts Concerning the Ancient and Only True Legal Means of National Defence, by a Free Militia*, London, 1781, p. 15.

39 W. Jones, *An Inquiry into the Legal Mode of Suppressing Riots. With a Constitutional Plan of Future Defence*, London, 1782, p. 11.
40 L. Radzinowicz, *A History of the English Criminal Law and its Administration from 1750*, London: Stevens, 1968, vol. 4, pp. 105–7.
41 M. McCormack, 'The New Militia: War, Politics and Gender in 1750s Britain', *Gender and History*, 2007, vol. 19, no. 3, pp. 483–500.
42 J. R. Western, *The English Militia in the Eighteenth Century: The Story of a Political Issue, 1660–1802*, London: Routledge, 1965, pp. 290–6.
43 T. Corfe, *Riot: The Hexham Militia Riot, 1761*, Hexham: Hexham Community Partnership, 2004, quotation from a contemporary handbill at p. 28.
44 Sharp, *Tracts*, p. 59.
45 P. Langford, *Public Life and the Propertied Englishman 1689–1798*, Oxford: Oxford University Press, 1991, pp. 296–7.
46 Hanway, *Citizen's Monitor*, p. viii.
47 C. Sackville, *A Treatise Concerning the Militia*, Dublin, 1752, p. 11.
48 Quoted in de Castro, *Gordon Riots*, p. 130.
49 London Metropolitan Archives, ACC/1264/001, 'Disposition of the Patroles in and about London during the Late Riots, Beginning of June 1780'.
50 Northamptonshire Record Office: Capell Brooke, vol. 162, 'The Order Book of Captian Supple'.
51 W. Blizard, *Desultory Reflections on Police: With an Essay on the Means of Preventing Crimes and Amending Criminals*, London, 1785, pp. v, vi.
52 Turner, *Plan*, p. 40.
53 Quoted in de Castro, *Gordon Riots*, p. 144. This contradicts Elaine Reynolds's argument that crime and public order were regarded as being separate issues in this period: *Before the Bobbies*, p. 31
54 Radzinowicz, *History of the English Criminal Law*, vol. 3, pp. 102–3.
55 Blizard, *Desultory Reflections*, p. 1. For an account of the LMFA on patrol, see Hanway, *Citizen's Monitor*, pp. xvi–xviii.
56 Blizard, *Desultory Reflections*, p. 30.
57 C. Emsley, *The English Police: A Political and Social History*, 2nd edn, London: Longman, 1996, pp. 17–18.
58 Hanway, *Citizen's Monitor*, p. xii.
59 Radzinowicz, *History of the English Criminal Law*, vol. 3, p. 91.
60 R. Paley, ' "An Imperfect, Inadequate and Wretched System"? Policing London Before Peel', *Criminal Justice History*, 1989, vol. 10, pp. 95–130; and D. Gray, *Crime, Prosecution and Social Relations: The Summary Courts of the City of London in the Late Eighteenth Century*, Basingstoke: Palgrave, 2009, pp. 35–6.
61 Beattie argues that changes in the criminal justice system 'were accompanied by very little public discussion': *Policing and Punishment*, p. 5.
62 A. Harris, *Policing the City: Crime and Legal Authority in London, 1780–1840*, Columbus: Ohio State University Press, 2004, p. 40.
63 The riots barely merit a page in Harris's *Policing the City* (p. 40); and Reynolds's *Before the Bobbies* (pp. 59–60).
64 Dodsworth, 'Masculinity as Governance'; 'Civic Police'; and 'Idea of Police'. See also C. Emsley, *Crime, Police and Penal Policy: European Experiences 1750–1940*, Oxford: Oxford University Press, 2007, p. 42.
65 F. Dodsworth, 'Police and the Prevention of Crime: Commerce, Temptation and the Corruption of the Body Politic, from Fielding to Colquhoun', *British Journal of Criminology*, 2007, vol. 47, pp. 439–54.
66 Colley, 'What is to be Expected', p. 206.
67 Hanway, *Defects of Police*, pp. 1, 4.
68 Hanway, *Citizen's Monitor*, pp. xxi, xxv.
69 Blizard, *Desultory Reflections*, p. 35.

70 Jones, *Inquiry*, p. 32.
71 Sharp, *Tracts*, pp. 9, 24, 74–5.
72 Blizard, *Desultory Reflections*, pp. 11, 7, 48–9.
73 Turner, *Plan*, p. 79.
74 Jones, *Inquiry*, p. 37.
75 Hanway, *Citizen's Monitor*, p. xvi.
76 Sharp, *Tracts*, pp. 73, 77, 80–3.
77 Turner, *Plan*, pp. 1, 14, 16–19.
78 Hanway, *Citizen's Monitor*, pp. xxiii–xxiv, xxvi.
79 Turner, *Plan*, pp. 14, 52–3.
80 B. Weinberger, 'Are the Police Professionals? An Historical Account of the British Police Institution', in Emsley and Weinberger (eds), *Policing Western Europe*, p. 79.
81 Blizard, *Desultory Reflections*, p. 57; and Harris, *Policing the City*, p. 40.
82 Emsley, *Policing in its Context*, p. 28; and Philips, 'New Engine', pp. 165–8.
83 Reynolds, *Before the Bobbies*, p. 75.
84 S. Palmer, *Police and Protest in England and Ireland 1780–1850*, Cambridge: Cambridge University Press, 1988, pp. 92–104.
85 Philips, 'New Engine', p. 184; Emsley, *The English Police*, pp. 20, 24.
86 Harris, *Policing the City*, p. 40.
87 J. Kelly and K. Fraser, 'England riots: what could the police do to stop the disorder?', BBC News website, 9 August 2011: http://www.bbc.co.uk/news/magazine-14459127 (accessed 13 October 2011).

3

MAKING MEN

Media, magistrates and the representation of masculinity in Scottish police courts, 1800–35

Susan Broomhall and David G. Barrie

In this chapter, we examine the practices and ideologies expressed in the police courts of Scotland and their media representation in the first half of the nineteenth century. These courts, established in Scotland's largest urban centres in the early nineteenth century, were the principal places of summary jurisdiction in terms of the sheer number of cases they handled.[1] Whether for non-payment of police rates, breaching local by-laws, committing criminal acts or seeking legal redress and advice, urban inhabitants were most likely to be brought before these courts, potentially giving them greater impact on the lives of ordinary people than the much more widely studied higher courts. In its first month of sitting in August of 1805, the Edinburgh Police Court dealt with over 300 cases, as diverse as from petty theft, trespassing and assault, to keeping mischievous dogs, running improper shows and riding dangerously in the streets.[2] By 1835, it was dealing with up to ninety-eight cases per working day and over 6,000 cases per year.[3]

Scholars have increasingly examined the influence of gender ideologies in shaping criminal trials, prosecutions and sentencing patterns, in civilizing unruly behaviour, impacting on long-term trends in violence between men, and classifying domestic violence as a specific category of offence.[4] We argue that the police court environment reflected and developed the views of its middle-class male personnel such as magistrates, judges and police superintendents. It also included those of police officers who, though of lower status, were expected to enforce the values of their superiors, even if, in doing so, their own moral conduct sometimes fell below what was expected of those in positions of authority and power.[5] However, as other scholars have recognized, the space of the police court was interactive, and the process and practice of the law was negotiated between court participants from a wide range of circumstances as offenders and witnesses.[6] We view police courts as spaces in which competing notions, ideas and identities were negotiated between legal participants (albeit with differing capacity to impose their views). The courts brought into interaction men and women of differing social status, whose ideologies of manhood could be in conflict with each other. We argue that police court personnel upheld police policies regarding legitimate and unacceptable male (and female) behaviour whilst also applying cultural rules about different class, religious and ethnic variations in their expectations of men. At the same time, communities and individuals brought forth offences to police courts that they interpreted as transgressing acceptable male behaviour. But interestingly, the chapter reveals that neither magistrates nor the media that represented court interactions expected lower-class men and women who appeared in court to achieve consistently those ideals and practices of middle-class masculinity to which they were expected to aspire.

The influence of the media on eighteenth- and nineteenth-century court proceedings has received growing scholarly attention, especially its role in creating moral panics that influenced structures of law and governance.[7] This chapter likewise examines how ideals and practices of masculinity were infracted by diverse social identities as the courts were presented in the media. More specifically, it analyses the role of media reporting on the way that ideals of masculinity were conveyed and enforced in the Scottish police courts in their first decades of operation. The chapter reveals how the court auditory and the press acted as forms of respondents and points of commentary on cases and their meanings, including their interpretations of masculine ideals and expectations. It is argued that the media produced by the middle classes both reflected and created different notions of masculinity that were found within police courts and operated as instruments of its control.

The sources examined here have not formed the subject of detailed analysis, yet they illuminate summary proceedings in a rich, qualitative manner, ideal for assessing these questions that most other, more quantitative police records cannot. These are *Police Reports of Cases Tried before the Glasgow, Gorbals and Calton Police Courts* (1829) and *The Police Intelligencer or Life in Edinburgh* (1831–2).[8] Published with a middle-class readership in mind, these reports give lucid, sometimes amusing and sometimes disturbing descriptions of selected cases, often accompanied with a moralistic social commentary. In addition, we include comparative cases explored in independent pamphlets and newspaper sources from other urban centres.

To date, these sources have been used by historians of crime for the information they provide about police court cases in the 1820s and 1830s,[9] but they have not been explored as a distinct genre of court and crime reporting. A survey of nineteenth-century periodicals indicates that publications such as these, devoted solely to the reporting of the police courts, appeared only in the period 1828–33 for Glasgow and Edinburgh, and uniquely from 1841 to 1851 in Dundee.[10] During the late 1820s, short-lived series of these periodicals appeared under at least seven different titles. Some were likely continuations of others, their lifespan and title changes reflecting their status as unstamped publications liable to be prosecuted by the Stamp Office.[11] Their publication appeared to vary from daily to twice weekly and weekly. After this period of concentrated periodicals devoted to the police courts, at least twelve journals nationwide included information from the police courts specifically between 1834 and 1900. A further fifteen or so presented police intelligence, reports and other news from police cases, including police court proceedings, in amongst other staples of nineteenth-century periodicals such as short stories, poetry, political news, theatrical reviews and shipping and market information.

These periodicals reported extracts from courtroom dialogue that supported their authors' views and/or were perceived to be of interest to their readership. Certainly, they recorded the colourful details of speeches, events and characters where these occurred in the court. Although we cannot be sure that their presentations represent the full spectrum of courtroom positions, it seems unlikely that the quotes of statements made in court could have been fabricated without disciplinary action – perhaps especially regarding the speech of the police magistrates and officers. The publications analysed here were printed without official licensing from the Stamp Office, but their intentions do not appear to be politically radical as were some of the other forms of unstamped publications. Although, as Wiener has pointed out, the sensational and journalistic turn in criminal reporting through cheap prints, seeking big sales for dramatic stories, must surely have influenced court coverage in the press over the century,[12] these particular publications provide very little detail in general about any one case and appear rather as, at times, a rather prosaic list of some of the weekly cases before the court. They did not report all cases before the court and are therefore not used in a quantitative capacity as representative of the entirety of court business. As John Brownlie, the author of the 1829 *Police Reports*, writes for one week: 'No case of importance till the 13*th*'.[13] What is useful, therefore, is precisely what such journals perceived to be of interest to their readership and how these were presented.

Brownlie justified his publication of the business of the police court as primarily instructive and frequently emphasized drink as a major cause of criminality. He acknowledged the 'risk of injuring the feelings of the unfortunate. Keeping in view this principle, the author trusts that these Reports, while they may have the effect of wounding some, they may have the tendency of warning others.'[14]

The privacy of courtroom participants' affairs was thus to be sacrificed to the greater public good, but, as we shall see, Mr Brownlie's application of this principle was governed by middle-class notions of masculine virtue and respectability. The Edinburgh *Police Intelligencer* displayed a more overt tendency towards inflammatory reporting, a distinct curiosity about the 'way others live' and definite moralizing. Its particular method of using nicknames for many of the lower-status court participants promoted a kind of proto-Dickensian fictionalization of the lives of defenders and victims, distancing them for the readership and making them as much a subject of fiction and anthropological investigation as fellow inhabitants of a shared urban environment.[15]

Normative male anti-social behaviour

Growing revulsion towards violence as a defining characteristic of nineteenth-century middle-class manly conduct and dispute resolution has been acknowledged by scholars.[16] They have argued that control displayed by professional and mercantile men of the middle class of their bodies and their passions was a sign of their ability and entitlement to govern, reflected in shifting and increasing regulation of their sexual conduct, their manners and civility as recommended by eighteenth- and nineteenth-century commentators.[17] Martin J. Weiner has argued that these ideas were reflected in courts criminalizing and punishing male violence with more severity, although his examples tend to be for more severe forms of violence than those encountered in police courts. Violence brought to police courts was that which fiscals deemed did not warrant more than two months' imprisonment, which was the maximum length of sentence police courts could impose. As a result, the violent offences that were prosecuted in police courts tended to be less serious, such as common assault and disorderly and aggressive conduct, and tended to exclude serious assault, such as violent sexual assault, grievous bodily harm and battery with intent to rob. Anti-social behaviour by men, such as drunkenness, violence and property damage, represented a substantial proportion of police court cases. As Table 3.1 shows, the most common offences prosecuted in police courts between 1833 and 1835 were breach of the peace/drunk and disorderly conduct, assault, theft and breach of police regulations.[18] Much of the business of the police court was concerned with seeking to promote order, re-shape behaviour and control public space, subjecting urban populations to higher levels of discipline and surveillance.[19]

Such offences were regular and plentiful in press reports. However, in terms of how they were reported by the press, they do not appear to receive any particular admonition by judges, nor indeed did the media itself make explicit commentary on the propensity of men generally to violence. Nonetheless, both the media and the courts themselves revealed a great deal of their assumptions of appropriate and expected behaviour of men at various social, economic and professional levels. In some cases, it appears that the courts and media anticipated some degree of violence as normative behaviour for labouring men, and for men of particular ethnic backgrounds, most particularly when their victims were other men. Polite conduct might have been expected for achievement of middle-class masculinity by the early nineteenth century, but professional and mercantile men of the magistracy and the media still assumed that displays of physical strength symbolized manliness for those perceived to be of lower status. Media interest in such cases did not critique explicitly violence *per se* as a detrimental characteristic of masculinity, but focused instead on the causes of such events, their scale or repercussions. For example, when in April 1832 a male complainer came to Edinburgh Police Court to seek redress for his assault, which had caused a black eye, the *Intelligencer* remarked upon the complainant's misunderstanding of the police court's ability to prosecute his case:

TABLE 3.1 Police court offences, 1833–5 inclusive

Burgh	Breach of the peace	Assault	Theft	Fraud	Breach of police regulations	Vagrancy	Rape	Exposing children	Other	Total
Glasgow	1,689	247	1,566	116	N.L.	165	N.L.	N.L.	N.L.	3,783[d]
Edinburgh[a]	1,855	1,114[b]	1,141	169	1,096	273	5	1	574	6,228
Paisley	464	1,156	601	135	3,175	253	2	2	4	5,792
Dundee	N.L.	2,018	481	N.L.	715	462	N.L.	N.L.	5	3,681
Greenock	1,049	711	416	40	402	N.L.	N.L.	2	176	2,796
Perth	1,009	259	187	[c]	355	N.L.	N.L.	N.L.	N.L.	1,810
Aberdeen	168	334	249	11	15	N.L.	N.L.	N.L.	22	799

Source: collated from data recorded in 'Fourth Report by Her Majesty's Law Commissioners, Scotland, 1839'.

N.L., not listed.

Notes

a All of the returns for Edinburgh relate only to 1835.

b The assault returns for Edinburgh were broken down as thus: assault and wounding to the danger of life (15), breaches of the peace accompanied with assault (520) and complaints, at the instance of private parties, for assaults (579).

c Theft and frauds listed together.

d Only those cases deemed to be crimes were categorized under a specific offence and recorded in the Glasgow returns (totalling 3,783 out of the 16,109 offences before the court). The majority of cases that were brought before the Glasgow Police Court were not categorized.

The complainer being asked by the Magistrate if he had any witnesses, replied that he had three, viz: a brother flesher, himself, and a black eye. The Magistrate said as his eye was not a competent witness, there was only one besides the complainer, it would therefore be necessary to try the case upon a public charge, otherwise it would not prove. A public charge being made out, the charge was proved, and the defender was required to give caution. The complainer was recommended by the Magistrate to look for damages in a civil court.[20]

Although the court upheld the principle that such an assault was to be condemned and punished, the press made little comment of such a crime among men, presenting it rather neutrally (and thereby implying that it was normal, or unsurprising, behaviour).

Where violence was deemed excessive, it rendered men sub-human in their loss of rational function as humans and of requisite self-control that defined male status. In March 1832, the *Intelligencer* reported on James Fraser, whose violent behaviour in reclaiming a debt from his brother-in-law led him to appear before Bailie Anderson in Edinburgh Police Court. As the *Intelligencer* described him, Fraser presented:

the nearest resemblance of a wild beast we have ever seen, and who, moreover, possesses such Herculean strength, that he has received the merited appelation of Sir James the Lion . . . He was in a furious state, more like a wild beast or madman than a person possessed of his rational senses.[21]

This was not a man, but something closer to a beast, whose nomenclature rendered him less than human, frightening but almost comic too. The *Intelligencer* provided a similar presentation of another man who appeared in the Edinburgh Sheriff Court, in April 1832, accused of a 'shameful attack' on a woman, assaults on two men and assault on a police officer. This man, the *Intelligencer* reported, was a 'herculean fellow, who may be justly designated a Goliah[sic] of Gath'. This man attempted to dissociate his actions from his rational self, having 'nothing to say but that he was as drunk as the d-l at the time. He might have done what was said, but he was not answerable for the deeds done in the body.'[22] But his vulgar vocabulary, reported in titillating effacement, did little to impress Bailie Crichton. This 'representative of Rob Roy' was fined a substantial ten pounds or would be confined for sixty days.

On other occasions, violent behaviour appeared almost to be expected among some groups of men as part of their private dispute resolution, and its regulation was also assumed to come from within these communities without formal interaction with the law. A 'pack' of Irish men in the Edinburgh Police Court in 1832 were treated in the press as men indistinguishable from each other, and the complaint of the fellow Irishman Forbes of assault and theft by this group was dismissively labelled 'curious'. The media appeared to suggest that, as he numbered among the city's Irish, Forbes had a greater honour to stick with his fellow countrymen than to press charges for such an offence beyond the jurisdiction of his compatriots.[23]

> The parties appeared all to be Irish. Masonic signs, winks, nods, illustrations, and scientific precognitions were dealt about in handfuls at the small charge of a half-penny. Judy, poor fellow, got clear off at the bar. The pack was restored, large as life, and the case was dismissed in favour of the defenders.[24]

The *Intelligencer* both ridiculed the internal arrangements of the Irish, yet also expressed surprise that redress might be sought through the formal court structure beyond them. That this was not expected may perhaps also be suggested by the dismissal in court of the complaint itself. The media's reporting of the case implied that Forbes was unmanly to seek the support of the law, and that, for Irish men, honour was to be found in private dispute resolution among themselves.[25]

This was by no means an isolated or local interpretation of Irish men and their predisposition for violence. The *Aberdeen Journal* reported in the following terms in 1833 on one violent dispute between two Irish men that brought them before the local police court for assault: 'One night last week, two Irishmen, bearing the elegant Milesian names of Duffie and McGurrachan, happened to differ in opinion with respect to the important subject of a repeal of the Union.'[26] Disputes between Irish men in particular were treated as being of some different and separate kind of violence from those of other men, the origins of which could not be seriously political or necessitate further understanding or inquiry. The media, it seems, found less to remark upon with regard to fighting between men of the same (labouring) class or (Irish) ethnicity, and ridiculed rather than condemned them.

Violence thus took on different meanings in the courts when it was carried out by different kinds of men, implying that magistrates and media had differentiated views of violence as an aspect of masculinity for their varied male clientele. The press particularly could express surprise at unexpected sentences or prosecutions for men perceived to be of a superior social standing. In September 1831, the *Intelligencer* reported the appearance of William Crawford, 'a classical taught student in the Gilmerton University', before Bailie Morton in the Edinburgh Police Court. Crawford, who appeared 'dressed in the common garb of the students belonging to that eminent college', was charged with being drunk and disorderly and assaulting the officer who had tried to arrest him. His conduct was noted as particularly brutal, and the magistrate, 'after expressing his determination to punish such brutal conduct, to be an example to others from committing similar offences', sentenced the defender to sixty days' confinement in Bridewell. Although in practice this sentence represented the maximum that could be imposed in the police court, and therefore demonstrated how seriously magistrates viewed assaults on policemen and symbols of civic authority, the *Intelligencer's* representation of the case reflected a different response. Certainly it showed that Crawford had not expected such treatment, adding ironically: 'The heroic Gilmertonian scratched his head, and looked rather dumfoundered [sic] at receiving this unexpected sentence.'[27] Given the acknowledged violence of his offence, the reporting position of the *Intelligencer* was one of unusually mild criticism. Significantly, such a case appears to highlight distinction between police and media responses. Although both the magistracy and the media spoke for the middle-class respectable man, differences borne of their differing professional concerns can thus be discerned. That the violent attack was directed against a police officer would seem crucial in shaping the response of the police magistrate, which was more harsh than that of the media who reported upon it.

Magistrates took a fairly dim view of the few middle-class men who came before them. The direction of police policy may have been biased against the working-class population of the city in the sense that police resources were largely directed at regulating working-class culture and behaviour,[28] but, within the courts, the infrequent middle-class man who came before the judge could expect a frosty reception. He had, after all, failed to uphold the respectable status that should keep him from the court. Thus, when three men of the Regiment, including a certain 'Captain J_____' whose name was not to be revealed to the public, appeared before the Glasgow Police Court in August 1829, charged with breaking a street lamp with two colleagues, Brownlie in his *Police Reports* betrayed a more sympathetic interpretation of the affair than that of the court.[29] Although ideologies between magistrates and the press might have been similar, this did not necessarily influence how the former administered law. A key determinant for the magistrate's handling of this proceeding appeared to be the fact that the men did not admit their guilt, leading the judge to insist: 'If you are guilty, please to say so, you are surely men of honour.'[30] However, when they refused, claiming that they had wished only to light their 'segars' from the street light, it would be the evidence of an eyewitness that convicted them. Bailie McLellan bestowed the full fine of five pounds on the Captain, although a lesser fine on his two accomplices. Brownlie concluded that 'the prisoners left the office, no doubt considerably chagrined at the result of their evening's amusement'. Here, it is unclear if the more significant crime was one of honour, rather than the initial property damage that had brought the men to court. Bailie McLellan also tied the issue directly to a middle-class model of masculinity that held public bodily decorum in high regard: 'As for the smoking of segars on the streets, he declared it to be a very filthy practice, which he and his brother Magistrates were determined to put an end to, a practice directly contrary to good breeding, and decency.'[31] McLellan's remarks suggest that the Captain and his colleagues were expected to act in accordance with the ideals of middle-class masculine governance; that their redemption might yet be possible was offered by Brownlie's decision not to print the three convicted offenders' names.

In general, the court was outwardly consistent in admonishing personal and property violence; it took violence between men seriously in the sense that it heard, investigated, fined and imprisoned those brought before it. Of course, a wide range of practical factors contributed to how police magistrates decided to administer the law, such as men's ability to pay, how crowded local jails were and the number of dependents a man had. The social identities of the perpetrator and victim were, however, critical. Even how these financial issues were judged both responded to, and impacted on, how different notions of masculinity played out in court practice. The interpretation of violence in the court and especially its presentation in the media highlighted how meanings of violence and assault could vary as they were inflected with different expectations of masculinity and their perpetrators' different possibilities for redemption. Weiner has argued that displays of physical violence became less acceptable as symbols of respectable masculinity, indicated by the increasing penalization of male violence over the nineteenth century. Although the evidence of the police court shows enforcement designed to prioritize such ideals, media commentaries and court outcomes both suggested that these ideals be achievable only by civilized men and gentlemen of the middle class, or those aspiring to this ideal. The presentation of male anti-social behaviour in the media appeared fairly disinterested when the drunkenness, violence and damage were committed by men of the lower classes or particular ethnic groups. The press assumed rather than condemned such acts among these latter men, and it was rather the punishment of middle-class men and youths whose anti-social behaviour could be cast as pranks and high jinks that was deemed both noteworthy and shameful to court journalists.

The role of vulnerability in shaping gentlemanly behaviour

If the generic violence between men of the same class, especially the labouring classes, appeared unremarkable to the media reporting on the police courts, this was not so of violence perpetrated on those perceived to be vulnerable. Male violence could be deemed non-normative by police courts and their press when it was inflicted on those perceived to be less than their equal. A schoolmaster who appeared before the Glasgow Police Court in 1829, charged with excessively beating a schoolboy in his care, was not only fined but also received a stern rebuke considered worthy of note in the weekly circular of police court cases: 'this conduct, said the worthy Magistrate, was truly shameful, and unlike a person of his appearance, *looking forward to the church*'.[32] The shame was partly that it was a man of his class, station and persuasion losing his temper as much as the unequal status of his victim. 'This case excited great sensation in court', wrote Brownlie of the auditory.

Likewise, other men in similar positions of authority could not be condoned for rough behaviour towards the vulnerable. In August 1831, a 'Serjeant belonging to the light company, on the recruiting service', was charged with being drunk and disorderly and striking two young women on the High Street in Edinburgh. Admitting he was drunk, the magistrate 'informed him that his being intoxicated was no extenuation of his guilt; on the contrary, he (the Magistrate) rather considered it an aggravation'.[33] Fining him a guinea, there was little sympathy for his personal weakness, especially when it threatened those who such public officials were intended to protect.

Police officers were expected to embrace the core values of a masculinity distinct to the upper echelons of society – an ideal of masculinity that reflected more the ancient office of constable than the eighteenth-century night watchman or city guard.[34] Despite being drawn predominantly from the poorer and labouring sections of society, constables were to divorce themselves from the rougher elements of working-class masculinity by demonstration of self-control. Thus, in August 1831, two police officers were fined by the Edinburgh Police Court for handling a young boy too roughly.[35] Control of self, in theory a first step to control of others, entitled officers to governing status just as it had for elite men in previous generations. But although bodily self-control of officers was important, their bodies and behaviour were also deemed necessary of middle-class supervision. Police officers featured among those who were brought to court for excessive violence. A police officer charged with being drunk and disorderly and assaulting a 'decent girl' with his baton was brought before the Edinburgh Police Court in October 1832.[36] The magistrate, Robert Ritchie, with the agreement of the superintendent, insisted upon his immediate dismissal and imposed a fine of two pounds or fourteen days in the Lock-up House, opining 'that the appearance of this night guardian would have a very bad impression on those who saw him'. For the sake of public confidence in police officers, discipline had to be maintained. Police officer bodies were to be exemplars of middle-class masculine conduct for the wider community.[37]

Some women also attempted to use the police court as a means of protecting themselves, even if, in doing so, they, like men, demonstrated that they did not understand the intricacies of the legal system with which they were interacting. In September 1831, the young wife of a lace weaver complained to Bailie Morton in the Edinburgh Police Court that 'she had been married only eight months, and that she was quite sick with matrimony. The usage she had experienced during that short interval was so harsh, that she was determined if possible to obtain a separation between them.'[38] The *Intelligencer* portrayed Morton as sympathetic, informing her 'that the Police Court was not competent to give her redress by separation; but should the charge be proved, he would be bound under a heavy penalty to keep the peace towards her'. When the case had been heard, Morton indeed insisted that the husband provide a substantial ten-pound caution, a symbolic but meaningful form of protection that he could offer.

In a recent publication, Annmarie Hughes has claimed that domestic violence in the period 1850–1950 was often not taken seriously by either the Scottish legal system or the press, with both showing considerable mercy towards abusive husbands.[39] Far from a re-definition of masculinity effecting a growing revulsion towards such violence, as Weiner claims for England, Hughes contends that there was 'considerable opposition to new conceptions of masculinity' within the Scottish legal system and media.[40] Moreover, she argues that the extension of summary justice during this period 'guaranteed that violent men could find themselves shielded from the harsher sanctions the High Court could enforce',[41] while the press offered little discursive condemnation of domestic assault.[42]

This is an important study that should caution against overstating the extent to which changing conceptions of masculinity impacted on behaviour and the workings of the criminal justice system. However, it also needs to be recognized that the extension of summary justice in police courts was extremely significant in effecting a far larger number of prosecutions of cases of domestic violence than hitherto had been prosecuted in the High Courts. The evidence produced by Anna Clark suggests that police courts in the first half of the nineteenth century were attempting to curb such behaviour. Her analysis reveals that in a nine-month period during 1835 and 1836, eighty-one cases of domestic violence came before the Gorbals Police Court – approximately two per week.[43] Although a relatively small number – and in all likelihood just the tip of the iceberg of the total – it nonetheless suggests that police courts did not view all domestic violence cases as being outside their legal domain. Indeed, throughout the country as a whole, police courts in the mid-nineteenth century are likely to have prosecuted far more domestic violence cases in a typical day than the High Courts had done in a typical year before the rise of summary justice.[44]

Significantly, the qualitative evidence uncovered in this study for the first half of the nineteenth century suggests that there were important social nuances in terms of both how masculinity was conceived and how domestic violence was dealt with, and represented, in police courts and the media. Violent behaviour among the working class was perceived by magistrates and the media as being run of the mill and thus was rarely worthy of comment or condemnation. However, magistrates and the media showed more sympathy towards women who fulfilled middle-class values of femininity and were extremely critical of middle-class male abusers. For such men, discursive condemnation centred on the fact that they had transgressed the acceptable boundaries of middle-class male propriety and masculine self-control. Although providing only an insight into the cases that the press deemed worthy of reporting, the examples below reveal that there were complex factors at work in terms of how the courts and the media dealt with and reported cases of domestic violence, much of which centred on social class and the differing conceptions of masculinity that underpinned it.

A case in the Perth Police Court in 1823, for instance, reveals that both the severity of an assault and the extent of community support that victims received could play an important part in influencing the response of magistrates and the media.[45] The fact that such a case could be brought to court – and was deemed worthy of being reported in the media – suggests that people had standards of masculine conduct and knew when these had been transgressed (even if not every victim was in a position to seek legal redress and protection).[46] The case was prosecuted before magistrates only three weeks after the couple were married. The woman had been supported by neighbours, 'who, shocked at the usage she had received', had felt themselves called upon to bring the matter under the notice of the police. 'The Sitting Magistrate declared it to be the most aggravated case of the kind that had ever come under his observation', sentencing the perpetrator to sixty days' imprisonment.[47] In this case, the neighbourly support for the evidence provided by the abused wife was significant in determining the judgement, but it is important to note that neighbours' ability to uphold an understanding of appropriate masculine conduct could be successful only if it matched that held by police officials who would prosecute the case in court on their behalf.

However, on occasion, it was possible for police court officials to establish a position on appropriate masculine behaviour that was not held (or at least willingly articulated) by the victims themselves. In this way, the court structure acted in defence of the better interests of the vulnerable. It was in this context that John Gilvray's second appearance before the Edinburgh Police Court in September 1831 was deemed noteworthy for the *Intelligencer*. He had struck his wife with a pair of tongs on the face as well as other parts of her body, prompting Bailie Morton to remark that 'he seldom had heard of such a wanton, cruel and ferocious attack':

> Although the charge was clearly made out against the barbarous perpetrator, not only by satisfactory evidence, but also by peculiar demonstration, too visible on the sensitive organ of the poor sufferer; yet she denied that he caused her wounds, and seemed to wish that he should be forgiven.[48]

It is possible that Gilvray's wife was considering her long-term economic and social future with and without her husband in making her stance. Nonetheless, the magistrate was unwilling to let the case go, and Gilvray was sentenced to thirty days' confinement to the Bridewell (it is possible that the lesser than maximal sentence was in partial recognition of his wife's views). In such cases as these, the courts operated as Davis has observed for London summary courts, as 'a system of poor man's justice' that would offer advice, direction and support to the lower orders, encourage them to use the law for protection and, ultimately, ensure their acceptance both of it and the social order.[49] The *Intelligencer* portrayed this case as an example of the court acting as the protector of the vulnerable, representing through its actions the chivalric code of gentlemanly conduct.

When in 1832 the *Intelligencer* reported on a case before the Edinburgh Sheriff Court, it was the court auditory who came to the fore as a participant in the courtroom dialogues concerning masculinity. A young woman was brought to court charged with violence upon her brother, after she hit him on the head with a bottle. As the case unfolded, it was revealed that their mother had recently died and that her daughter had refused to let go of the body. Her brother received the blow to his head in the course of prying away her fingers. Although it was clear that the woman had inflicted the injuries, the criticism in this case fell on the young man involved for pursuing the case through the court. The sheriff justified his dismissal of the case, having ascertained that the poor girl had some time ago been in confinement, . . . [and] remarking that he had no doubt but that the defender had at the time she had committed the assault been labouring under temporary delirium, and she was therefore not responsible for her actions.

Significantly, the *Intelligencer* followed by reporting: 'This decision seemed to give universal satisfaction to the auditory, who set up a general murmur at the cruel and unfeeling conduct of the brother towards his unfortunate sister.'[50]

Some victims did not appear to think male violence towards them was inappropriate, or at least professed such opinions in court. When in September 1832 a wife was called to testify to the violence committed on her by her husband, she insisted that she was not injured (although she admitted that it was she who had called for the police). The *Intelligencer* reported the husband's audible instruction to his wife – "Margaret, dinna say ony thing against me!' – and perceived it as the cause of her insistence: 'Margaret, taking the advice of her lord and master, declared that she was not in the least hurt.' When the sheriff insisted that she tell the court what happened, she responded: 'We'el, I'll tell the truth, he only gied me a wee bit dad on the mouth.' The focus of the *Intelligencer's* interest here appeared to be that the wife did not see her treatment by her husband as violence.[51] This is not intended to imply that women necessarily had different standards of masculine conduct but rather that the press and the court felt that they were not capable of making their men better themselves; that is, they needed the help of middle-class officials to raise up their men to better standards of behaviour.

Sometimes the media showed some of the complexity of individuals' decision-making processes more clearly. When John McDonach appeared before the Glasgow Police Court in July 1829, charged with being drunk and disorderly and striking his wife, Brownlie reported that, despite her two black eyes and the evidence of the watchmen, which supported the offence, his wife was willing not only to take him back but also to support him and their family if he would keep the peace towards her.[52] Bailie McLellan, the *Police Reports* recorded, said:

this was a most distressing case, and he was sure, that there was not a person in court, who did not sympathize. We have before us a well-doing virtuous woman, joined with a cruel husband, – a woman willing to do well, provided she is allowed peace and quietness, and I am sure, said he, from the modesty of this woman, matters must have gone a great length before she complained.

This indicated much about his expectations of good femininity, constituted by her perseverance, modesty, forbearance in the face of male violence and unreasonable action:

your conduct, sir; has been brutal; your wife, whom you are bound to cherish; and protect by the laws of God and man, has been barbarously used by you, by her appearance this day at the bar, shows your hands have not been idle. Now sir, you cannot be permitted, to use this poor woman in this way any longer, a curb must be put on your temper; it is a great deal on her part, to maintain an idle fellow like you, and your young family; and you ought to be proud, sir, to have such a well-doing wife; none but a brute would act in the way you have done towards her.

But these were precisely the qualities that made her worthy of middle-class men's protection. She was the archetypal domestic 'angel':

The court is bound and will protect her, but the course we are to pursue, is a matter of doubt and prudence. If, says Bailie, I inflict a fine, it will just be robbing this poor woman, and her helpless family.

Bailie McLellan thus dismissed the case as a first offence, threatening McDonach that he would be sent to the Bridewell for a repeat of the violence. 'Bailie McLellan was much affected with the case, and could scarcely restrain his feelings.' The show of feeling towards a helpless, *good* woman as appropriate conduct was shown through the exemplar of upstanding masculinity, Bailie McLellan. Moreover, Browlie determined that McDonach no longer had a right to anonymity. Just as he failed to uphold the middle-class values of protection towards his wife, he lost his right to that class's protection of his own honour and respectability.

The fact that some men could be deemed particularly noteworthy of *excessive* violence suggests that some level of violence among such men was perceived normal. One of the demarcations of excess was when it had led to what was commonly referred to in courts and media reports as 'the effusion of blood'. In England, it would not be until 1853 that Parliament passed an Act for the Better Prevention and Punishment of Aggravated Assaults on Women and Children.[53] In Scotland, assault charges were codified under police burgh legislation in 1862, but without specific reference to domestic violence.[54] Indeed, an assault by a husband on his wife was not recorded separately as a specific category of crime in Scottish criminal returns until the 1898 Criminal Evidence (Scotland) Act determined that a wife could be a credible witness.[55] One case of assault brought before the court in Edinburgh in April 1832 involved an assault by a man on his 'fancy wife' who was noted as barely sixteen. The magistrate, Bailie Crichton, was reported by the *Intelligencer* as saying that:

the assault was one of a very disgraceful nature. The defender not being satisfied with kicking her on the face, but even at the same time that the blood was flowing from her, he had the brutality to kick and strike her a second time.[56]

The offender was given ten days' confinement and a caution of five pounds, with Crichton adding: 'There is scarcely any case so common that comes before the court as that of men for assaulting their wives.'[57]

Although the courts were condemnatory in almost every case of domestic violence reported in the journals – although by no means every case with which they
dealt, as Hughes has shown for the second half of the century – this did not mean
that there were no distinctions to be made between the men who committed such
acts. These can best be seen through the press, as it represented and interpreted
such cases differently. In October 1832, a master glazier was brought to court
after threatening to stab his wife, a 'well dressed respectable looking woman',
reported the *Intelligencer*.[58] The media here identified the problematic nature of
the inappropriateness of his social status:

> The defender, who has every appearance of being a well doing citizen, seemed
> to feel very forcibly the awkwardness of the situation in which he was placed
> . . . The Magistrate, after animadverting [sic] on the mad like actions of the
> defender, and having admonished him as he valued his own respectability
> and safety, to be on his guard against such dangerous conduct, ordered him
> to give caution in £20.

The fact that the press did not report magistrates as equally fearful for the reputa-
tions of men of working-class status suggests that there were different ideals, or
that the press was helping to create them. Men aspiring to the ideals of middle-
class respectability had to learn to constrain their emotions and their physical
strengths, whereas men of the labouring classes were not assumed to have lasting
capability for such control, and were thus rarely condemned by the court or the
press for failing to achieve it.

Women who pursued cases against such men, however, did indicate that violence upon them was not acceptable, and these views were generally upheld by
the court, even if middle-class men – even the court officials – did not expect
men of lower social status to remain compliant to such ideals in the future. For
example, in August 1831, George Paterson appeared before the Edinburgh Police
Court charged with assaulting his 'fancy wife' Jean Johnstone. The *Intelligencer*
elected to refer to Johnstone by her nickname 'Yankie' and Paterson was reputed
to be 'a well known black guard', rendering them both caricature tropes for
middle-class readers. Although Paterson admitted the charge and was ordered to
pay a ten-shilling fine, it was the magistrate's remarks that conveyed most clearly
his perception of the ability of men of the lower status to control their violence.
Johnstone explained to Bailie Anderson that she had pulled Paterson by the tail of
his coat in order to drag him home when he turned and knocked her head against
the wall:

> Magistrate (to Yankie) – What business had you with him? Are you any rela-
> tion to him?
> Yankie – He's my lad!
> Magistrate – You will make a happy couple, no doubt![59]

This interchange seems to suggest that Paterson's violence, when situated in a domestic context, was morally different from one in which he had not known her; that she needed to explain her actions in relation to his violence. Moreover, by laughing at their domestic situation, Anderson implicitly assumed that the violence would continue. Elizabeth Foyster has suggested that, by the nineteenth century, domestic violence became for middle-class social commentators a problem of the working class.[60] Changes in legislation therefore were created in a context of condemnation but also with the assumption that working-class men required law to regulate and reform their normative behaviour.[61] In this case, there was no call for Paterson to consider his respectability; as a 'black guard' he was not given the credit of having any to lose. The *Intelligencer*, by adopting nicknames even when it knew and acknowledged the real names of offenders and their victims, rendered these citizens of the city as caricatures for its readers. They became almost fictional, displaced from the real world of the middle-class readership, distanced from them both in crimes and in their needs.

The media also played an important role in deciding the boundaries of middle-class respectability in its selective anonymity. Some men were no longer afforded the privilege of widespread public privacy when their offences were deemed by the press to be excessive. Andrew Neilson, a master tailor, appeared before Bailie Morton in the Edinburgh Police Court in August 1831, on his fourth charge of domestic violence towards his wife. The *Intelligencer* framed the case by remarking upon the wife's demeanour: 'a woman who has all the appearance of being sober, quiet, and industrious'.[62] There was, it implied, no provocation for his offences here, although its use of the phrase 'all the appearance' also suggested that it may not be possible to know the complete picture and there was always a slight possibility that a woman was somehow to blame. To complete the picture of this man's crimes, his children were brought to court to attest to his guilt.

> At that two of the daughters of the infatuated man gave evidence against their own father. To day a fine boy about fifteen years of age had the same painful duty to perform, with the tears trickling down his cheeks, he recounted many acts of his unnatural conduct towards his mother.

The *Intelligencer* placed heavier value on the son's testimony than that of the daughters. A man's word – even a young man's against another – was, in this case, suggested as the strongest evidence of the father's guilt. That the son's word was protecting his mother and sisters in a way that the father had *unnaturally* failed to do showed him as the archetype of the man that the middle class would have liked to see itself producing. Although the sentence that the magistrate gave out was among the harshest possible, consisting of sixty days' confinement in Bridewell, half the time to be fed on bread and water, the *Intelligencer* did not bother its readers with details of the magistrate's denunciation of such a crime. The content of the magistrate's 'few observations on the defender's conduct' was evidently not deemed by the paper to be sufficiently noteworthy to be reproduced.

On the other hand, a man who appeared before the Aberdeen Police Court in May 1833, charged with biting a woman in the course of a disagreement, severely wounding her arm, was ridiculed by the media: 'charged with exercising the functions of the canine species, and biting a woman!' Reduced to an animalistic state, he was shamed in principle and yet in practice his personal honour was protected by the paper's decision not to reveal his name, a stance that it did not extend to all the court's clients, male or female. 'Out of pity, we do not give his name, nor any more particulars.'[63] In this instance, he was so much less than a man that to give his name would be doubly shaming. Other men, especially those of the working classes, who 'merely' committed assault, were not extended such a courtesy by the media, thereby implying that there were few issues of shame and honour to be respected for working-class men.

Violent behaviour by men towards animals was as much a subject of contemporary criticism as that towards women or children. One magistrate even appeared as a witness in a case of animal cruelty in the Police Sheriff's Court of Edinburgh in 1831: 'Baillie Anderson, who, in several instances, has shewn anxiety to punish those hard hearted fellows who are cruel to beasts of burden, appeared as a witness against the defender.'[64] The Aberdeen apothecary William Alexander, who appeared in that city's police court for pouring turpentine into a dog's eyes, ears and nose because it would not leave his shop, was given a relatively harsh sentence of a three-guinea fine or sixty days' imprisonment. Even harsher words followed from Baillie Clark:

> a more disgraceful and dastardly piece of cruelty had never come before that Court. Of all animals the dog had the strongest claim on kindly treatment from all persons of common humanity, in respect of his fidelity and may useful qualities; but in this case this useful beast had been tortured with an ingenuity wholly unprecedented, and which made any man of feeling to shudder . . . observing that he did not envy the character for humanity, which he had that day earned before so many witnesses.[65]

Men – even a middle-class educated professional – who had been reduced to the bestial, especially in such a calculating way, were afforded no cover of anonymity by the *Aberdeen Journal*.

Sometimes it was the police court officials themselves who could display anti-social behaviour. Here, too, however, there were distinctions between the mercantile and professional men who made up the magistracy and the artisanal or labouring status of men who became the police force's officers. Emotional outbursts by magistrates were generally interpreted as signs of good behaviour by the press, showing feelings of compassion that a gentleman – literally a civilized, gentle man – ought to have towards the vulnerable. In a case of attempted indecent behaviour towards a child brought before the Glasgow Police Court in August 1829, Bailie McLellan is reported as losing his temper. John Fraser, a shoemaker, had attempted to 'violate the chastity' of twelve-year-old Catherine Melrose by offering her fourpence before he had been stopped by a watchman who considered that 'he was carrying matters too far':[66]

> Bailie McLellan, contrary to his usual custom, rose from his chair, and addressing the prisoner, said: 'I am at a loss, at a great loss, to find words to describe your case; a man you are not, but a brute. What you think of yourself? You wretch, have you any feeling? Look, at that child, and think where you now are!

McLellan's publicized loss of his 'usual' decorum was no slight in the way it was presented by the media. This was instead a sign of his gentlemanly status – that he had feelings for such matters, and could pick and choose when to lose his temper.

Through charges, admonitions, fines and imprisonment, the practice of the police court condemned men for their perceived inability to contain their physical strength or show restraint, or loss of rationality – factors that were crucial in establishing the superiority of men over women of all classes. Moreover, they were particularly critical in demarcating the boundaries of middle-class masculinity from those men of inferior status. In her study of the nineteenth-century London police courts, Jennifer S. Davis has argued that 'Crucial to the courts' popularity was magistrates' willingness to fulfil' working-class expectations of what they thought was the just application of legal power; this they did 'even if by doing so they might find themselves, at times, endorsing behaviour and values at odds with those acceptable to the propertied classes or representatives of the state'.[67] Although this may have been true in relation to other offences, when it came to judgements of masculinity, magistrates' own positions were secured by their maintenance and enactment of strict class-based gender demarcations between men.

The media was important here in reinforcing these boundaries, in articulating some aspects that the courts could not explicitly, even if their comments, actions and decisions reflected similarly differentiated masculine ideals and expectations. Certainly, the police courts were important in asserting the supremacy of middle-class values, by attempting to curb the violent tendencies that they perceived as normative for the sort of working-class men who appeared in police courts or for failed middle-class aspirants, particularly through hefty fines and imprisonments. Yet, through throwaway jibes and public commentary, both they and the media appeared to undermine the possibility of redemption and change for these violent men of lower status, and displayed no expectations of their capacity for long-term 'improvement' towards middle-class masculine values. These were values that for the middle-class press and the police court personnel (including its middle-class aspirant police officers) demarcated the line of respectability and of their own authority, which such men of lower status should strive towards, but were unlikely to achieve.

Patriarchs and heads of household

As John Tosh has observed, by the mid-nineteenth century, civic men argued that the ever-growing industrialized city presented dangers from which women were to be shielded in the domestic domain.[68] At the level of the labouring classes, the financial reality that all members of the household needed to contribute to breadwinning may have been more acute than at other social levels. Nevertheless, it is clear that police courts, through the voices of magistrates and the logic of the sentences that they obtained, upheld the principle that men were the expected heads of household with responsibility for providing for women and children within them. What was deemed noteworthy for comment from court judges, audiences and media was when men were beaten by women, or did not seem to be in control of their households. What was at stake in such exchanges was the extent of the court's powers to intervene in men's (and which sort of men's) control of the household.

In the early years of the Edinburgh Police Court's operation, through a particularly hostile exchange of printed pamphlets, a middle-class man challenged the right of officers to enter his home and control the activities that occurred under his roof. In 1807, George Thomson had published *anonymously* a short pamphlet in which he complained publicly and particularly of police incivility of the manner in which they instructed him to cease the dancing and music at a private family party in his household: '[Serjeant] Murray told me, in the rudest manner, that if it was continued after TEN, he would return with a party, and carry me and my friends to the watch-house!'[69] There ensued a printed letter from the original complainant who lived below the household, defending the police action and attesting to the noise that their dancing created: 'and from their weight, I can safely say that they were not all children'.[70] Thomson retaliated, focusing on the intrusion of the police in his domain:

> Is the peace of the city to be promoted by the odious intrusion of those officers to regulate our domestic pleasures? . . . . This is Police-law with a vengeance. What a blessed system it will be for us all, in the intercourse of social life, to have those agreeable Counsellors, the Police Officers, ever at our elbows, to caution us against making noise, and to teach us to join trembling with our mirth![71]

The case threw into sharp relief the needs of the individual householder and those of the community who were to be represented by the police officers.[72] Whereas Thomson saw the case as about interference in his masculine domain, the police court continued to insist on its right to control noise pollution for the wider community's good.

Yet in other ways the court and its media could be sympathetic to the needs of certain men who were attentive to their household responsibilities. A man who was brought to the same court for vagrancy and begging revealed in court that 'he was at one time a respectable merchant in the city of Glasgow'. The *Intelligencer* wrote sympathetically:

> The defender produced a large parcel of retired bills and receipts, which he said had passed through his hands during his mercantile transactions. He further stated that he was at one time worth a number of thousand pounds, – that he was now greatly reduced, and had a wife and six children under five years of age.[73]

This man demanded a right to sympathy because, at first glance, he had a wife and children whom he wished to protect and provide for but also he was once among the middling men who formed the basis of the magistracy. His name was not revealed to the reading public, unlike other beggars who were commonly ridiculed and referred to by their names and nicknames. Even the court responded kindly to him: 'The poor fellow was dismissed with certification.' In this case, efforts were made to preserve his dignity by both the court and the media, and the man's attempt to provide for his family and household – even by begging – was treated sympathetically and leniently.

These were values of masculinity that were also upheld by the court for other men, and presented almost favourably by the court reporters. For example, in September 1832, sixteen-year-old Ralf Mitchell was brought before Bailie George Small at Edinburgh Police Court charged with theft. However, Darling, the police patrol, reported to the court that he had 'visited the family, and found the mother and four children in a state of the greatest privation. The children were crying for bread, and in a state of nudity.' When the mother and children attested to these facts after having been summoned before the court, the magistrate 'humanely ordered them immediate relief' and 'dismissed the poor fellow, who had been forced to commit the breach of the law through dire necessity'. His was not a crime, according to the *Police Intelligencer*, but rather a 'breach of the law'. This representation of Mitchell's case by the media seemed to imply that those whose stricken circumstances explained their crimes might be extended the hand of charity, but this appeared far from the usual way in which cases concerning young boys accused of theft were presented. Perhaps Mitchell was extended favourable coverage because his youthful action was explicitly framed by the court personnel as protecting a mother and siblings as a good householder should. The majority of thefts before the court were almost certainly the product of similar hardship but their circumstances had not been revealed in court in this way. The police reporter periodicals suggest in many cases that police magistrates were cautious to condemn children to a life of almost certain crime by exacting heavy penalties or jail terms for minor and first offences, but few received such sympathetic presentation in their pages as Mitchell. His behaviour modelled an aspect of the kind of man, like the humane magistrate presiding over the court, that he could yet become – not a thief but a protector of the vulnerable.[74]

In March 1832, a man was brought to the Edinburgh Police Court charged with striking his sixteen-year-old daughter. The *Intelligencer* revealed that she had recently married another man without his knowledge and consent.[75]

> Magistrate (to the defender) – Did you strike your daughter, sir?
> Defender – To be sure I did. I think a father has a right to chastise his child.
> Magistrate – You had no right whatever to strike any man's wife, although she is your daughter.

The case having been proved, the man was required to provide a caution, but it seems that what was at stake was less the right of a man to hit a woman, but *who* had the right to strike her. The magistrate's comment, at least as it was reported by the *Intelligencer*, was not a critique of violence *per se* towards women, but of one man's use of another's property and domain.

The inappropriate balance of household gender relations was a frequent cause for police court cases and commentary. As Bailie Crichton once commented in a case of domestic violence before the court: 'There is scarcely any case so common that comes before the court as that of men for assaulting their wives, nor any so uncommon as women for striking their husbands.'[76] That very day, Crichton had sat in judgement on the case of a 'decent looking woman' charged with abusing and assaulting her husband, 'a sturdy sootyman'. The husband claimed that his wife demanded all his money; she argued that he drank it if she did not. Crichton concluded that there was fault on both sides and the case was dismissed.[77] Female violence towards a husband could not be condoned, but neither could a deficient head of the household, especially as the burden of looking after dependents would fall upon local funds.

A woman charged with assault on her son-in-law was more roundly chastised, it seems, by Bailie Paterson in the Glasgow Police Court in August 1829: 'it appears you are a rebellious old lady, you must find good, and sufficient caution to keep the peace towards your son-in-law, if he will not work, it is improper in an old duchess like you, to strike him'.[78] A woman's violence to a man was, it seems, unquestionably wrong, even though the magistrate was implicitly critical of the man's behaviour in acknowledging her perceived frustration about his unwillingness to work. Brownlie, however, had no hesitation in describing the man in no uncertain terms as 'a soft easy good-for-nothing man'.

By contrast to the manifold discussion afforded to male violence and anti-social behaviour, male extramarital heterosexual practices received very little attention in the media, perhaps in part due to a reluctance to publicise offences deemed morally ambiguous. Aberrant male sexual practices were punished only indirectly in the police court – through prosecutions for prostitution, brothel keeping or, rarely, offences such as the *attempted* sexual act with a child.[79]

Only rarely were men – as the clients of prostitutes – ever involved in police court cases relating to sexual acts. When this did occur, married men were without fail admonished by judges for their actions. In one unusual case, it was clear that the magistrate was stunned by the pursuit in the Glasgow Police Court by an anonymous 'married man of rather superior appearance' of a prostitute who he claimed had stolen two shillings from him:

> Magistrate: 'Do you really wish to persevere in your case.'
> Accuser: 'I do.'
> Magistrate: 'you must give proof.'
> Accuser: 'I have none. I will swear she took the money.'
> Prisoner: 'Deed, Bailie, I have two shillings of his, but he gave it to me as a present, and he kens himsel what for.'
> Magistrate: 'you say you are married'.
> Accuser: 'I am.'
> Magistrate: 'have you a family.'
> Accuser: 'I have.'
> Magistrate: 'do you really not think shame of yourself, look at that woman, and consider where you are now . . .'[80]

For the magistrate, this case revolved around the respectability of the man, although it is clear that the man in question evidently did not perceive that his pursuit lessened his claims to status. Rather, he insisted on the truth of his evidence; that is, he assumed that his word *as a gentleman* would weigh in his favour against the woman concerned. That the politics of anonymity were a privilege of higher status which was meaningful to contemporaries is established by the writer's closing remarks on the case that function as a personal commentary, and highlight the role of such journals as instruments of the public morality and indeed propose them as a tool of law: 'This accuser's name will be inserted if ever he again appears on a similar charge.'

Progressively, the work of police officers invaded male householders' perceived entitlements to authority in the household domain, but this did not come without challenge. The police court was the place in which many of these challenges, from noise pollution to domestic violence, were explored and determined and these encroachments validated. Yet, even if the relationship between different men for access to this household space was changing, it did not shift the assumed right of men to govern the household *per se*. Media reporting of courtroom comments appears to suggest that women who encroached male authority were chastised, even if the men they were disciplining were themselves failed providers or patriarchs. Neighbours could intervene in intra-household affairs, but they could have their views of appropriate masculine conduct recognized only if police officers and then the court itself accepted the same position.

The limits of gentlemanly conduct

For all their proposed gallantry towards the vulnerable and 'decent' in society, and women in particular, it is evident that the media reporting on the police court included only certain women in this description. Women too could be violent, and often displayed conduct that confounded judges and the press as 'unwomanly' in their expectations of feminine behaviour. Gentlemanly conduct in practice did not extend courtesies of civility to many of the police court's female participants, in either the courtroom or its media. These women were not perceived as vulnerable, they were rarely silent and their speech seemed to equate for their middle-class would-be protectors with an ability for self-protection. If working-class men were seen as separate but other, their womenfolk were fair game for slurs and derision.

When Mrs Charlotte Feathers appeared in the Edinburgh Police Court in October 1831 accused of assault, the *Intelligencer* remarked: 'Feathers, whose soft, light, and warm name, whose demure looks and affected modesty was quite enough even to deceive a judge, hang [sic] down her head and simpered out her statement of the case.'[81] The *Intelligencer* gave little thought, it seems, to her right to protection within the court or beyond it. As we have already seen, the authors of the *Intelligencer* in particular delighted in referring to working-class court participants by their reputed nicknames. This was particularly noticeable with the police court's female clientele. Thus, 'Mary Martin an African Black, who says she was born in Fife, and has resided in Edinburgh for the last twelve years, but better known by the name of Blackie, and Margaret Campbell, alias spunkie, alias Craw' were reported for their appearance in August 1831. The *Intelligencer* continued to use those nicknames for the women, rather than their actual names, for the rest of its description of the case:

> Blackie – She ca'd me a black B___! and I cried craw, craw!
> Superintendent (to Blackie) – You are much more like a craw than her.

Although both women were later dismissed of the charges of fighting with each other, the tone of this presentation was one of ridicule at two silly, squabbling poor women:

> Witnesses being called in, the Magistrate found it difficult to decide which of the craws were most to blame; but as the public did not seem to have been much disturbed by the crow fight, he was pleased to dismiss the case, without caging the craws.[82]

This appeared in the press (and in the court, it seems) as little more than amusement for the readers, rather than as a matter of real women's lives and legitimate social tensions.

Women's shortly cropped hair was frequently implied in the press as a sign of guilt, as it denoted a previous stay in the Bridewell. When Bell Boyd appeared in the Edinburgh Police Court charged with breaking window panes, the *Intelligencer* opined: 'Poor Bell complains that her hair is never allowed to grow longer than the Bridewell crop, and we believe never will, until she gives up her evil ways and mends her manners.'[83] There was no assumption of her innocence here, nor protection of her rights to anonymity. Another such interchange revealed through the *Intelligencer* occurred when Rachel Stewart 'whose wax doll face is partially covered with a perfusion of awburn ringlets' was brought to Edinburgh Police Court charged with stealing. As with a number of cases, the court officials mocked women's vanity as a persuasive argument to prevent their further offences:

> Magistrate – If you do not take care of yourself you will lose your beautiful curls!
> Superintendent – O sir, these curls are false; she has been in Bridewell!
> Stewart – They are not false, it's my own hair.[84]

Both the judge and the superintendent openly made fun of her appearance, and implied a hidden reality of her guilt that they could detect – despite her protests of innocence. When her accuser failed to appear, Stewart was dismissed, but what claims she had to a good reputation – in court and through the media – had been destroyed nonetheless.

In April 1832, the *Intelligencer* introduced the appearance of Catherine Sutherland in the court for theft by describing her as 'a randy Highland woman', 'endowed with such volocity [sic] of tongue, that on a former occasion while before the Court for disorderly conduct, her tongue went with such rapidity, that the Magistrate observed he never till now believed the possibility of perpetual movement'.[85] It seems that neither the authors of the *Intelligencer* nor the police court personnel saw such statements and jibes at the female offenders' expense as constitutive of any loss of gentlemanly behaviour on their part. Indeed, it was not uncommon for magistrates to comment particularly on women's speech in the courtroom. The *Intelligencer* described another case in August 1831 in which a crockery merchant and his wife, a 'thin scranky Irishwoman', were presented in court for being drunk and disorderly. The woman's 'gift of gab or velocity of togue [sic] so annoyed the Court, that it was with the greatest difficulty they could get her to be silent for a single moment' the *Intelligencer* reported, causing Bailie Anderson to remark: 'Your tongue goes like the pendulum of a clock! Will you not hold your tongue?'[86] Irishwomen were particularly reported by the press with unruly speech that gained them only the scorn of court personnel. In August 1822, Bailie Anderson had reprimanded another Irish woman accused of attempting to stab a police officer, Francis McGarrgal.

> After McGarrgal had given his evidence, the female Hibernian thus addressed the bench – 'Oh, dear, don't believe him – sure, now, you would not believe any thing that a Policeman says.'
> Magistrate – Hold your tongue: I want none of your advice, I am inclined to think by your conduct that you are a very bad character.[87]

It was rare to find such statements made to or about the court's male clientele in their presence.[88] Middle-class masculinity required judges and media to protect vulnerable women when they were perceived to be good, but this conduct did not extend to working-class women who were deemed bad. They could be publicly chastised, ignored or ridiculed in both court and the media.

Both the *Police Reports* and the *Intelligencer* reported the court personnel ridiculing women of the lower classes but the latter periodical appeared to attribute special attention to women's nicknames. Whether or not these women committed the offences of which they were accused it is noticeable that they were not afforded the protection of gentlemanly conduct by magistrates or the media in their public interactions. They were frequently called by nicknames even when their names were known, their speech and appearance were ridiculed and their honour publicly besmirched. Vulnerable women who were quiet, docile and often insistent that their male partners should not be charged with violent crimes were those to whom the court and the media were willing to extend the courtesy of chivalric conduct. These women inhabited or conformed to middle-class values of femininity. Ironically, in lecturing men to care better for their wives, magistrates and media were asking them to conduct themselves in a way towards working-class women that they were often not prepared to do themselves.

Conclusions

In practice, the court punished men when they failed to meet middle-class standards of masculine behaviour and behaved in such a way that it was deemed to constitute a breach of police or common law, but the way in which cases were examined and commented upon in the court and media suggested different expectations of different kinds of men. Most significantly, through their comments and judgements, it was clear that magistrates and media did not expect men of the lower classes who appeared in the court to achieve the constraints required of middle-class masculine conduct on a regular and sustained basis, even though they metered out punishments for each individual infraction as it occurred. Indeed, the separation and reinforcement of separate expectations of behaviour for men of differing social and ethnic groupings was what gave magistrates and media their moral superiority and held them in supposed authority over other men. By the latter half of the nineteenth century, these men would number among those who were re-cast as 'habitual criminals' – a way of explaining their repeated behaviour that uncoupled it from the general possibility of improvement of their class.[89]

However, their views should not obscure the fact that people of perceived lower status could and did report behaviour that they perceived to be aberrant to police officers, indicating that they had their own standards of masculine conduct that can be revealed through prosecutions in the police courts. Moreover, the evidence of the press often presented particularly women of lower status who appeared in court attempting to impose their views as forceful interlocutors. But this did not render them more successful in achieving their ends, as this behaviour reinforced to media and magistrates the extent to which they were at odd with middle-class expectations of private, civilized and quiet femininity. In doing so, these journals reinforced a distinct middle-class femininity, whilst using working-class women's behaviour as evidence of the brutality, masculinity and alterity of working-class culture generally. If masculinities were in part defined by relationships to the opposite sex, the press and police court personnel's own actions with regard to working-class women implied that it was a case of do as I say, not as I do.

These distinctions between types and expectations of men (and women) held by police court personnel were reflected, and indeed more openly expressed, in the media surrounding cases. Here, the mechanism of anonymity was used by its middle-class authors as a moral signifier, an instrument of public or social law and a way of delineating between those men deemed deserving of the right to middle-class respectability and those not. The intimate lives, hopes and aspirations of the court's poorer clientele were rarely given the same respect as other participants – especially as naming them must have surely limited their opportunities for future self-improvement. The press was well aware of its power and influence in choosing to name, shame and cast judgements on the lives of others.

Moreover, it was not just the way that the courts and media meted out judgement on the behaviour of men that conveyed their values and ideas of masculinity. Police, press and personnel inhabited and expressed the same values of the middle classes in their speech and actions. If the record of courtroom dialogue is to be believed, superintendents and police officers could play an important role in contextualizing cases for magistrates, and did not hesitate to add their own moralizing, pejorative or other asides. The role of the auditory was also important, as the press demonstrated how their laughter or compassion might affect judgements (as well as what influenced their own reactions to cases). Thus, through their actions and commentary, the magistracy, superintendents, police officers, auditory and authors of the press enacted their own values of middle-class masculinity, as protectors of the weak (whether the young, the animal or particular women) and as legitimate intruders in the households of 'lesser' or 'aberrant' men. In the process, they even helped to mould the limits of gentlemanly conduct.

Notes

1 For the little work that has been carried out on police courts in Scotland, see Lindsay Farmer, *Criminal Law, Tradition and Legal Order. Crime and the Genius of Scots Law, 1747 to the Present*, Cambridge: Cambridge University Press, 1997, pp. 67, 69, 71–3, 76–7, 85, 109; and M. A. Crowther, 'Crime, Prosecution and Mercy: English Influence and Scottish Practice in the Early Nineteenth Century', in S. J. Connolly (ed.), *Kingdoms United? Great Britain and Ireland since 1500: Integration and Diversity*, Dublin: Four Courts Press, 1999, pp. 225–38. For examples of analysis of summary courts beyond Scotland, especially London, see Jennifer S. Davis, 'A Poor Man's System of Justice? The London Police Courts in the Second Half of the Nineteenth Century', *The Historical Journal*, 1984, vol. 27, no. 2, pp. 309–35; and Drew D. Gray, *Crime, Prosecution and Social Relations: The Summary Court of the City of London in the late Eighteenth Century*, Basingstoke: Palgrave, 2009.
2 *Edinburgh Advertiser,* 27 August 1805.
3 'Fourth Report by Her Majesty's Law Commissioners, Scotland, 1839', *British Parliamentary Papers*, 1840 [241], p. 332.

4 The list is too long to cite in full. See, for instance, Angus McLaren, *The Trials of Masculinities: Policing Sexual Boundaries, 1870–1930*, Chicago: University of Chicago Press, 1997; B. Godfrey, S. Farrall and S. Karstedt, 'Explaining Gendered Sentencing Patterns for Violent Men and Women in the Late-Victorian and Edwardian Period', *British Journal of Criminology*, 2005, vol. 45, no. 5, pp. 696–720; Martin J. Wiener, *Men of Blood: Violence, Manliness and Criminal Justice in Victorian England*, Cambridge: Cambridge University Press, 2004; Robert B. Shoemaker, 'Male Honour and the Decline of Public Violence in Eighteenth-Century London', *Social History*, 2001, vol. 26, no. 2, pp. 190–208; Anne-Marie Kilday, *Women and Violent Crime in Enlightenment Scotland*, Woodbridge: Boydell Press, 2007; and Anne-Marie Kilday, 'Desperate Measures or Cruel Intensions: Infanticide in Britain', in Anne-Marie Kilday and David Nash (eds), *Histories of Crime: Britain 1600–2000*, Basingstoke: Palgrave Macmillan, 2010, pp. 60–79.

5 See David G. Barrie and Susan Broomhall, 'Policing Bodies in Urban Scotland, 1780–1850', in Susan Broomhall and Jacqueline Van Gent (eds) *Governing Masculinities in the Early Modern Period: Regulating Selves and Others*, Aldershot: Ashgate, 2011, pp. 262–82.

6 Peter King, 'The Summary Courts and Social Relations in Eighteenth-Century England', *Past and Present*, 2004, vol. 183, no. 1, pp. 125–72; Drew Gray, 'The People's Courts? Summary Justice and Social Relations in the City of London, c. 1760–1800', *Family and Community History*, 2008, vol. 11, no. 1, pp. 7–15.

7 Among the most recent additions to this literature are Judith Rowbotham and Kim Stevenson (eds), *Behaving Badly: Social Panic and Moral Outrage – Victorian and Modern Parallels*, Aldershot: Ashgate, 2003; Judith Rowbotham and Kim Stevenson (eds), *Criminal Conversations: Victorian Crimes, Social Panic, and Moral Outrage*, Columbus: Ohio State University Press, 2005; and David Lemmings and Claire Walker (eds), *Moral Panics, the Media and the Law in Early Modern England*, Basingstoke: Palgrave Macmillan, 2009.

8 Mitchell Library, Glasgow, G/364.1, John Brownlie, Writer, *Police Reports of Causes tried before the Justices of Peace, and the Glasgow, Gorbals and Calton Police Courts, from 18th July, till 3rd October* (Glasgow: G. Greig, Forbes & Owen; Aitken J. & Co., 1829); and Edinburgh Central Library (E.C.L.), YHV 8198 42900, *The Police Intelligencer, or Life in Edinburgh*, Edinburgh: Forbes and Kay (1831) Forbes and Co. (1831–1832).

9 Philippe Chassaigne, *Ville et Violence: Tensions et conflits dans la Grande-Bretagne victorienne (1840–1914)*, Paris: Presses de l'Université Paris-Sorbonne, 2005; and Anna Clark, *The Struggle for the Breeches: Gender and the Making of the British Working Class*, Berkeley: University of California Press, 1995.

10 Based on analysis of John S. North (ed.), *The Waterloo Directory of Scottish Newspapers and Periodicals, 1800–1900*, 2 vols, Waterloo, ON: North Waterloo Academic Press, 1989 (dates of publication as listed in North's survey). For Glasgow, these are *Brownlie's Police Reports*, Glasgow, 1829; *Police Reports, Causes tried in the City of Glasgow and Suburbs*, July–October 1829; for Edinburgh, C. Torrop (ed.), *Report of the Interesting Proceedings in the Police Court*, Edinburgh: G. Greig, February 1829–November 1831; *The Police Intelligencer, or Life in Edinburgh*, August 1831–June 1832; *Police Recorder*, Edinburgh, Printer: Forbes and Co., September–October 1832; *Life in Edinburgh, Police Intelligencer and Dramatic Review*, Edinburgh, Printer: Sanderson, May 1833–1833; and for Dundee, *The Dundee Police Gazette or Weekly Reporter*, Dundee: Jas. Lowe, October 1841–*c.* 1851.

11 On the period of unstamped periodicals, see Joel H. Wiener, *The War of the Unstamped: The Movement to Repeal the British Newspaper Tax, 1830–1836*, Ithaca, NY: Cornell University Press, 1969.

12 M. J. Wiener, 'The Victorian Criminalization of Men', in P. Spierenburg (ed.), *Men and Violence: Gender, Honor and Rituals in Modern Europe and America*, Columbus: Ohio State University Press, 1998, pp. 197–212 (p. 207).

13 *Police Reports*, 6 July 1829, p. 11.
14 Ibid., p. 1.
15 Similar arguments have been made for nineteenth-century fiction and social commentators by Deborah Epstein Nord, 'The Social Explorer as Anthropologist: Victorian Travellers among the Urban Poor', in W. Sharp and L. Wallock (eds), *Visions of the Modern City: Essays in History, Art, and Literature*, Baltimore, Johns Hopkins University Press, 1987, pp. 122–34; and James Buzard, *Disorienting Fiction: The Autoethnographic Work of Nineteenth Century British Novels*, Princeton, NJ: Princeton University Press, 2005. For a slightly later period than ours, see David Taylor, 'Beyond the Bounds of Respectable Society: The "Dangerous Classes" in Victorian and Edwardian England', in Rowbotham and Stevenson, *Criminal Conversations*, pp. 3–22.
16 Wiener, *Men of Blood*; Judith Walkowitz, *City of Dreadful Delight: Narratives of Sexual Danger in Late-Victorian London*, Chicago: University of Chicago Press, 1992; Shani D'Cruze, *Crimes of Outrage: Sex, Violence and Victorian Working Women*, London: UCL Press, 1998; and Robert B. Shoemaker, 'The Taming of the Duel: Masculinity, Honour and Ritual Violence in London, 1660–1800', *The Historical Journal*, 2002, vol. 45, no. 3, pp. 525–45.
17 E. Foyster, *Manhood in Early Modern England: Honour, Sex, and Marriage*, New York: Longman, 1999; P. Carter, *Men and the Emergence of Polite Society, Britain 1660–1800*, London: Longman, 2001; Shoemaker, 'Male Honour and the Decline of Popular Violence'; Wiener, *Men of Blood*; J. Carter Wood, 'A Useful Savagery: The Invention of Violence in Nineteenth-Century England', *Journal of Victorian Culture*, 2004, vol. 9, no. 1, pp. 22–42; Drew D. Gray, 'The Regulation of Violence in the Metropolis: The Prosecution of Assault in the Summary Courts, c. 1780–1820', *London Journal*, 2007, vol. 32, no. 1, pp. 75–88; and Drew D. Gray, 'Settling Their Differences: The Nature of Assault and its Prosecution in the City of London in the Late Eighteenth and Early Nineteenth Centuries', in Katherine Watson (ed.), *Assaulting the Past: Violence and Civilization in Historical Context*, Cambridge: Cambridge Scholars Publishing, 2007, pp. 124–40.
18 These offences were not, however, the only ones committed by men, nor only committed by men. The day-to-day business of police courts is explored more fully in the forthcoming study by David G. Barrie and Susan Broomhall, *Police Courts: Crime, Control and Community in Scotland, 1800–1892*, Aldershot: Ashgate, 2012.
19 For statistical breakdowns of the crimes before police courts in Scotland, see 'Fourth Report by Her Majesty's Law Commissioners, Scotland, 1839', pp. 278, 304, 323, 332, 335, 336, 338.
20 *The Police Intelligencer*, 11 April 1832, no. 206, Bailie Crichton, p. 3.
21 Ibid., 24 March 1832, no. 192, Bailie Anderson, p. 1.
22 Ibid., 13 April 1832, no. 208, Sheriff Court, Bailie Crichton, p. 3.
23 Ibid., p. 2.
24 Ibid.
25 For a recent investigation into the experience and impact of Irish migrants in Scotland, see Martin J. Mitchell (ed.), *New Perspectives on the Irish in Scotland*, East Linton: Tuckwell Press, 2009. Still useful is James E. Handley, *The Irish in Modern Scotland, 1798–1845*, Cork: Cork University Press, 1945.
26 Duffie was sentenced to thirty days in the Bridewell for the injuries that were sustained to McGurrachan. *The Aberdeen Journal* (Aberdeen, Scotland), 10 April 1833, no. 4448.
27 *The Police Intelligencer*, 26 September 1831, no. 36, Bailie Morton, p. 1.
28 David G. Barrie, *Police in the Age of Improvement: Police Development and the Civic Tradition in Scotland, 1775–1865*, Cullompton: Willan, 2008, ch. 8.
29 *Police Reports*, 15–22 August 1829, Glasgow Police, Bailie McLellan, p. 61.
30 Ibid., p. 61.
31 Ibid., p. 62.

32 Ibid., 26 August–4 September, Glasgow Police, pp. 91–2 (original emphasis).
33 *The Police Intelligencer*, 20 August 1831, no. 5, Bailie Anderson, p. 4.
34 On changing perceptions of masculinity in the City Guards, see Susan Broomhall and David G. Barrie, 'The Changing of the Guard: Policing and Masculinity in Enlightenment Scotland', *Parergon: Journal of the Australian and New Zealand Association for Medieval and Early Modern Studies* (to be published in 2011, vol. 28, no. 1, pp. 65–90).
35 *The Police Intelligencer*, 31 August 1831, no. 14, Bailie Morton, p. 1.
36 Ibid., 10 and 11 October 1832, Robert Ritchie, p. 2.
37 See Barrie and Broomhall, 'Policing Bodies'.
38 *The Police Intelligencer*, 23 September 1831, no. 34, Bailie Morton, p. 3.
39 Annemarie Hughes, 'The "Non-Criminal Class": Wifebeating in Scotland, c. 1800–1949', *Crime, Histoire & Sociétés/Crime, History & Societies*, 2010, vol. 14, no. 2, pp. 31–54.
40 Ibid., p. 42.
41 Ibid., p. 36.
42 Hughes argues that 'the press embarked on a process of educating and advising victims in ways to reform men and thereby avoid abuse rather than disseminating ideas to men about moral authority and self-restraint'. Ibid., p. 40.
43 Clark, *Struggle for the Breeches*, p. 259.
44 Kilday has shown that the Scottish justiciary prosecuted only a small number of cases for domestic assault in the eighteenth and early nineteenth centuries. Kilday, *Women and Violent Crime*, pp. 87–92.
45 *The Aberdeen Journal* (Aberdeen, Scotland), 5 February 1823, no. 3917.
46 In relation to violence specifically, Nancy Tomes has argued similarly that courtroom testimonies from witnesses provide evidence of the degree of violence that could be tolerated, as well as the limits of acceptable behaviour. N. Tomes, 'A "Torrent of Abuse": Crimes of Violence between Working Class Men and Women in London, 1840–1875', *Journal of Social History*, 1978, vol. 11, no. 3, pp. 328–45 (p. 329).
47 *The Aberdeen Journal*, 5 February 1823.
48 *The Police Intelligencer,* 9 September 1831, no. 22, Bailie Morton, p. 3.
49 Davis, 'A Poor Man's System of Justice?'.
50 *The Police Intelligencer,* 13 April 1832, no. 208, Bailie Crichton, p. 4.
51 Ibid., 4 September 1832, George Small, Esp. Bailis, p. 4.
52 *Police Reports*, 6–23 July, Glasgow Police, p. 22.
53 Criminal Procedure Act 1853, 16 & 17 Vict., c.30. For more on this Act, which applied to England and Wales, see Wiener, 'The Victorian Criminalization of Men'.
54 Under the 1862 Burgh Police (Scotland) Act magistrates were empowered to prosecute assault charges so long as the assault was not to the danger of life, or a lethal weapon had been used to the effusion of blood, or a limb had been broken, or the accused had three previous convictions for the same crime. 25 & 26 Vict., c. 101, 1862.
55 Hughes, 'The "Non-Criminal Class"', p. 44.
56 *The Police Intelligencer*, 27 April 1832, no. 218, Bailie Crichton, p. 3.
57 Ibid.
58 Ibid., 4 October 1832, Robert Ritchie, p. 3.
59 Ibid., 20 August 1831, no. 5, Bailie Anderson, p. 2.
60 Foyster, *Marital Violence*, p. 72.
61 See Tomes, 'A "Torrent of Abuse"' for more details of English domestic violence legislation over the course of the nineteenth century.
62 *The Police Intelligencer*, 23 August 1831, no. 7, Bailie Morton, p. 3.
63 *The Aberdeen Journal* (Aberdeen, Scotland), 22 May 1833, no. 4454.
64 *The Police Intelligencer*, 7 September 1831, no. 20, p. 2.
65 *The Aberdeen Journal* (Aberdeen, Scotland), 12 August 1840, no. 4831.
66 *Police Reports*, 8 August 1829, Glasgow Police, Bailie McLellan, p. 47.

67 Davis, 'A Poor Man's System of Justice?', p. 331.

68 John Tosh, 'Masculinities in an Industrializing Society: Britain, 1800–1914', *Journal of British Studies*, 2005, vol. 44, no. 2, pp. 330–342 (p. 333); and John Tosh, *Manliness and Masculinities in Nineteenth-Century Britain: Essays on Gender, Family and Empire*, Harlow: Pearson Education, 2005.

69 'Statement and Review of a Recent Decision of the Judge of Police in Edinburgh: Authorising his Officers to Make Domiciliary Visits in Private Families, to Stop Dancing' [George Thomson], Edinburgh: Printed for Manners and Miller by John Moir, 1807, ECL, YHV 8198 42289.2.

70 'Letter Explanatory of a Late Judgement in the Court of Police: With a Copy of the Judgement', Edinburgh, John Brown [1807], ECL, YHV 8198 42289.2.

71 'Postscript to Mr Thomson's Statement, in Reply to a Letter Published as "Explanatory of a Late Judgment in the Court of Police"', Edinburgh, James Ballantyne [1807], pp. 2–3.

72 'Report of Two Cases Decided in the Police Court on Thursday, 30th April', p. 3, ECL, YHV 8198 42289.2.

> They need no longer submit to the grievance of having their rest broke in upon, every night in the week, by the intolerable combination of noises resulting from distant fiddling, dancing, carriages rattling, and chairmen swearing in Gaelic, they now know, they have an equally prompt and efficacious remedy. The Police officers are abundantly accessible.

73 *The Police Intelligencer*, 31 March 1832, no. 197, Bailie Anderson, p. 3.

74 Ibid., 1 September 1832, George Small, Esp. Bailis, pp. 2–3.

75 Ibid., 31 March 1832, no. 197, Bailie Anderson, p. 1.

76 Ibid., 27 April 1832, no. 218, Bailie Crichton, p. 3.

77 Ibid., p. 2.

78 *Police Reports*, 15–22 August 1829, Glasgow Police, Bailie McLellan, p. 70.

79 An *actual* act of sex with a child might have gone direct to a higher court.

80 *Police Reports*, 28 August–4 September, Glasgow Police, p. 92.

81 *The Police Intelligencer*, 8 October 1831, no. 45, Bailie Aitchison, p. 2.

82 Ibid., 19 August 1831, no. 4, Bailie Anderson, p. 1.

83 Ibid., 27 October 1831, no. 55, Bailie Aitchison, p. 3.

84 Ibid., 1 November 1831, no. 59, Bailie Aitchison, p. 3.

85 Ibid., 5 April 1832, no. 201, Bailie Crichton, p. 2.

86 Ibid., 20 August 1831, no. 5, Bailie Anderson, p. 1.

87 Ibid., 22 August 1831, no. 6, Bailie Anderson, p. 3.

88 Rowbotham examines the use of 'dialect' for the speech of Irish working-class women to argue that it was an attempt by media to stress the un-British foreignness of such women. J. Rowbotham, 'Criminal Savages? or "Civilizing" the Legal Process', in Rowbotham and Stevenson, *Criminal Conversations*, pp. 91–105 (p. 103).

89 M. J. Wiener, *Reconstructing the Criminal: Culture, Law, and Policy in England, 1830–1914*, Cambridge: Cambridge University Press, 1990, pp. 300–6.

4

BECOMING POLICEMEN IN NINETEENTH-CENTURY ITALY

Police gender culture through the lens of professional manuals

Simona Mori[1]

In this chapter I explore the representation of masculinity as it emerges from professional manuals that were published over the course of the nineteenth century, aimed at Italian policemen. Such publications did not explicitly address gender as an issue, being more strictly concerned with professionally training police officers. As all police personnel were male, the working environment was inclined to be universalized, and gender profiles remained invisible. This was typical of all professional areas involving the exercise of institutional powers. In the absence of any interactions between men and women, the authors of such handbooks overlooked gender as a discourse-orienting category.[2]

Yet specialized literature did articulate forms of masculinity, as its aim was to build a professional profile in line with the needs of both the institutions and the individuals called to embody that profile. Specialized literature performed at least two different tasks: first, it outlined a subset of professionally useful traits drawn from features compatible with contemporary masculine stereotypes; second, it imparted this view of 'being a man' to police personnel, through confrontation with models already embedded within that culture.

Investigating the relationship between professional and masculine identity seems pertinent in regard to the nineteenth century, all the more so as the focus here is not so much the working class, who have already been explored by scholars in these terms, but public and private clerical staff.[3] Indeed, professionalism and masculinity have been deeply intertwined since the advent of bourgeois society.[4] For the average European man of the nineteenth century, they were largely overlapping and mutually influential. Although professional status owed much to masculine ideologies, the ideas themselves were far from being firmly established but rather evolved in response to diverse stimuli, which could be – at times, especially so – of an economic nature.

For the Italian police, our focus here, contemporary reflections about the figure of the policeman produced representations of masculinity that were broadly consistent with the socially accepted norms of gender, yet also prioritized certain values over others.[5] Merged with the professional profile of police personnel, these norms were then projected onto society through the service that these men performed every day, creating a circular process.

In order to reveal notions of gender embedded in these manuals, it is necessary to analyse them in the context of broader cultural frames of gender in the nineteenth-century Western world, developed in most detail by scholarly work focused on Anglo-American history. Italian historiography, which has not generally been particularly concerned with these issues, has made some notable recent progress, but is still far from offering a comprehensive reconstruction of national specificities.[6] The analysis here, then, is a first foray into a field that is just beginning to be explored. Its focus is primarily on civilian police, whose representations have been least studied by scholars. The masculine image of the *carabiniere*, therefore, will be examined only in its relationship to the image of civilian police.[7]

The police culture of the pre-unitarian states

In Italy, the professional figure of the policeman emerged in the second half of the nineteenth century, through a process interwoven with the Risorgimento and the founding of the nation-state, with the emergence of a new constitutional and administrative culture and with the diffusion, within Italian society, of a new bourgeois and propertied mentality.[8] In the early decades of the nineteenth century the literature on the police published in various states of the peninsula consisted on the one hand of texts for quick reference with purely practical aims, and on the other hand of theoretical legal treatises. Manuals in the first group were broadly aimed at the many institutional actors who were in charge of territorial administration, most of whom did not in fact qualify as 'police'. This ambiguity is a reflection of the poor organization and division of tasks that marked the activities of the police in the first half of the century. The first of these texts, translated from French in 1809, presented a series of entries arranged alphabetically, intended to put 'readily before the eyes a number of topics which are in themselves widely different and diverse, and which fall under the category of prompt adjudication and immediate police action'.[9] The focus of the discussion was less the elusive man holding diverse responsibilities than the exceedingly general functions that he embodied. Only the profile of *maires*, who were in charge of public order in communities, was clearly defined: 'like the head of a large family, exerting beneficial, protective and honourable authority'.[10]

In fact, in this first generation of texts, masculinity emerged mostly through the guise of fatherhood, that is, through a metaphor of power commonly deployed in the political culture of absolutism. This was the metaphor of the masculine-fatherly, placed a step below the feminine-motherly that was embedded in the abstract concept of *polizia*, which drew most authors' attention at the time.[11] The use of the feminine gender for institutions was very common. In the Jacobin age, for example, it was made manifest through allegories that adorned the headings of official documents.[12] That the police also was conceived of as a woman is demonstrated by the epigraph to an Italian manual published later in the century. The sentence, drawn from a famous head of the French police, reads: '*La police c'est ma mère/je y tiens à être son enfant*' (The police is my mother, I wish to be its child).[13]

The same female abstract concept prevailed in legal treatises, which despite being concerned with police regulations seemed to obscure the people who were in charge of the services that would require the application of these rules in concrete contexts. If, occasionally, these treatises dwelt upon the qualities required of the police officer, the figure that emerged from their pages was that of the Roman magistrate. These police officers, it was stated, 'are to be constantly on guard against the impulses [of their feeling]: being always as calm and impassive as the law, nothing ought to move them: pain, passion, sensibility, hatred must find the way to their hearts closed'.[14] The mixture 'of wisdom, prudence and enlightenment that constantly needs to be the ornament of the magistrate' even evoked the image of the great emperors of antiquity: Titus, Trajan, Marcus Aurelius, Antoninus Pius and Constantine. References to Roman imagery persisted even after the constitutional riots of 1820–1 and the repressive response that followed. Although some authors tried to render their subject more concrete, the officer that these treatises imagined still remained the tribune, or the *praefectus urbi*.[15] For decades, then, the few allusions that developed a masculine iconography created one that was modelled on classical values and which, although particularly suitable in combining power and the law, remained foreign to everyday experiences and could not therefore be deployed as an effective operational model.[16]

Only in the second half of the 1840s did a realistic portrait of the police officer begin to emerge within the diverse Italian contexts. In the repressive climate of the time, this portrait developed from liberal criticism directed against the police forces of the peninsula's absolutist governments. Such opinions relied heavily on the collective imagination, turning the traditional image of the cop, *lo sbirro*, into the symbol of a despotic and opaque political power, operating in the absence of any guarantees.[17] The debate culminated in the revolutions of 1848, when provisional governments put the reform of the police on the agenda, anticipating the shift to constitutional systems.[18] Within this context, officers in charge of public safety were to be seen ideally as 'honest magistrates, worthy citizens who could be of help to the public; and they should have as their guarantee not so much military bayonets or daggers as the public's trust'.[19] What was required of these men was not simply to fulfil their duties 'through worthy actions', but also to exercise 'the great ministry of educating the people to the new system', indeed, to become 'apostles of the Risorgimento for the masses' and to aspire 'to civil glory by being themselves eminently national'.[20]

The cop–policeman dichotomy, created by this constitutionally oriented literature, put forward a range of models of masculinity. Two of them were placed at the opposite ends of a hypothetical moral list, one embodying the misled police-man and the other projecting a form of secular holiness, while two other figures were forged in the middle ground of politics. Thus, the four models available were the reprobate, the subject of an authoritarian system, the citizen of a nascent democracy and the apostle of the nation.

The apparatus of government was not slow to respond to such allegations, and was committed to improving police forces. Among the zealous officials who put pen to paper to eradicate the prejudice widespread among the public was Raffaele Mozzillo, employed by the Central Bureau of Police of the Kingdom of Naples. Mozzillo was the author of a notable work that tried to parry liberal objections with a detailed analysis of the traits that should characterize the practical activities of the police, if not yet the personnel itself.[21] What emerged from this representa-tion was a profile that was workable both at a professional level and as a code of male behaviour and identity, different from the one that was articulated by patriotic pamphlets.

As a symbol of authority and power, Mozzillo's police certainly had a manly face.[22] According to Mozzillo, any society needed somebody to watch over 'dan-gerous people' and directly employed

> well selected coercive means, avoiding slow and costly judicial proceedings . . . Now the authority which exercises such power, which endeavours to check and render all mischievous attempts harmless, reaches the wicked man wrapped up in his dark plans, chases him and gets hold of him; . . . this authority, this magistrate, this power is termed the Police.[23]

Yet, with respect to its other functions, this power was tempered by a series of attitudes that sat uneasily with those gender values. This stemmed primarily from the auxiliary nature of judiciary police, which restrained the very severity it was supposed to uphold. In the service of criminal justice, it was to be 'benign', 'silent and unobtrusive . . . ever present'. Operating alongside municipal administration, it was to provide 'effective and useful cooperation', because, being 'immediately in touch with all classes', the police would be able to gain 'plenty of varied and useful knowledge, which, being exploited with the same quickness that qualifies every one of its actions, will easily accomplish what to other authorities would be very difficult to obtain'. Overall, therefore, 'its ordinary activity is neither violent nor rigid, it is prompt in facilitating order; a continuous, rapid and yet moderate activity, gaining experience from what happens day to day'.

Thus reduced, this power – although sharing some of the most critical qualities for public action – comprised qualities such as adaptability, omnipresence, discre-tion and moderation to such an extent that it ultimately took on some strongly feminine connotations. Indeed, taken as a whole, the portrait of the police drawn by Mozzillo seemed to evoke that maternal world within which bourgeois men were initially raised before being thrust into the harsh world of their fathers.[24]

The elaboration of this model from within the police continued after the events of 1848, alongside the work of reorganization undertaken by governments in order to improve the effectiveness of their forces.[25] During this period, Bartolomeo Fiani, delegate of police in Pisa (which was then ruled by the grand dukes of Tuscany), published the most comprehensive work on public safety that the pre-unification age had ever seen. He set himself the dual goals of providing a solid theoretical framework and offering practical advice 'which is especially important in that part in which police, abandoned by law, must rely entirely on man's prudence'.[26] It was this necessary discretionary power that drew increasing attention to the men who were working in the police, calling for a more concrete pedagogy. The thorough training of young employees was considered the only viable way to bridge the gap between the 'mission so noble and so generous' entrusted to them and the public's 'antipathy and aversion' to which they were subject.

After discussing the rules, Fiani devoted ample space to the actors. In order to protect society and the state, magistrates in charge of public safety were to be free and strong in prevention, standing in 'as good family men for the indispensable silences of the law'.[27] The trope of paternity recurred in these pages at the core of the representation of the officer of the absolute state. Although the conduct of the officer lay largely beyond the discipline of law, this resemblance to the figure of the father enabled him to exert self-restraint for a good cause. Fiani's work repeatedly returned to what he presented as the key that could prevent the abuse of power: moral restraint and the 'qualities of character' possessed by the police magistrate. These were skills that could be, according to some, 'superhuman' like theological virtues, or, for others, human like the cardinal virtues. Fiani listed them with an eye to Catholic theology: wisdom, righteousness and loyalty, discretion, prudence and moderation, exemplary morality, temperate and courteous manners, patience and calmness of mind, energy and firmness.[28] Within this list, an attitude of self-control seemed to prevail over the assertive aspects of the self. Although scholars have noted that education of the nineteenth-century man oscillated between self-assertion and self-control, the pedagogy aimed at the police laid far more stress on the latter.

The policeman in the national and constitutional state: between the ideal and reality

The transition of Italy (almost in its modern geopolitical entirety) to the constitutional system, after the annexations to Piedmont and the achievement of national unity in 1861, did not stifle these issues. Indeed, the police of the new state stemmed largely from the old pre-unity organizations. This meant that men with an older mentality, who were thus prone to act as *sbirri* rather than as policemen, continued to work under the constitutional systems created by the Savoy.

The organization of 'Public Security' in the Kingdom of Italy became centralized, uniform and more widespread.[29] Everywhere the same type of decentralized officers began to operate in the employ of the General Office of the Ministry of the Interior. From the *appuntato* to the *delegato*, from the *ispettore* to the *questore*, those holding inferior and intermediate ranks multiplied, while a body of guards of Public Security was put in charge of the urban centres. This apparatus endowed with a civil status coexisted on national territory with the army corps of the Royal *Carabinieri*, which had been introduced in Piedmont as early as the 1820s along the lines of the French *gendarmerie*, and was used mainly in rural areas. The two-headed police structure during this period was to permanently influence Italian history. In the liberal age the two forces, despite having similar roles, undertook different tasks and were often positioned as antagonistic, opting for self-representations that were differentiated partly on the basis of oppositional masculine ideals.[30]

How many men were involved in the activities of the police at this time? It was an entirely male world, initially consisting of 25,000 men and then doubling by the beginning of the next century. In total, 70–80 per cent were military individuals (*carabinieri*) and the remainder were civilians (one-third as administrative officers and two-thirds as police officers), in a nation of around 30 million people.[31] There was a critical need to provide the personnel – whether recruited under pre-unity administration or newly employed – with working models consistent with the new order. This urgency gave great impetus to the production of handbooks, moderating speculative ambitions for a more pedagogical vision. This literature would offer some highly articulate representations of masculinity, especially for civilian police, which are the focus of the following section.

The requirements of the good policeman of the unified state varied according to hierarchical position. As stated in a pamphlet published by a former head of the police in 1862, officers and guards were to remain distinct as far as tasks and profiles were concerned: 'let there be but a few good true officers and let there be a sufficient number of not bad agents: the police service will then become more responsive, powerful and energetic'.[32] Senior officers were expected to hold a degree in law, in exchange for a salary that, at least in theory, would allow for respectable relations with the most distinguished urban citizens. This, however, would not relieve officers from the obligation to cultivate contacts with all ranks of society:

> with respect to . . . the other class – the workmen – once he has accepted in his meetings the most important merchants, factory leaders, industrialists, etc., [the police officer] might, indeed should, gain access to those workplaces, among those workers, to study their needs on site and to determine, so to say, what they require, and to prevent them, to prevent strikes.[33]

Here, then, the figures of the head of the police in the province and his direct subordinates came to be characterized by flexibility, by the ability to adjust to circumstances as well as to different geographical and social contexts. As the peninsula had such different local characteristics, it became important to place in the provincial hubs 'men in every respect suitable to the special population centres to which they have been assigned . . . there where everything is particular, it is of the utmost importance that the police officer should meet education with education, culture with culture'.[34] In addition to the manly qualities of dignity, firmness, of 'being the ideal courageous citizen', high-ranking officials were also expected to display 'refinement of mind'.[35] Moving down the hierarchy, priorities changed accordingly. The inspectors of the police station, who were to exercise the conciliatory office in their neighbourhood, were required to show appropriate conduct, displaying 'familiar ways, persuasive, fraternal and not stilted'.[36] Delegates and sub-delegates, in charge of a portion of territory, should 'see and hear everything', like 'sophisticated sentinels' capable of 'treasuring everything', and never 'sparing a kind word, or advice'.[37] In the case of guards, what counted was primarily force of numbers and basic literacy, as the obligation of writing up the minutes was meant to deter them from committing improper acts. There are many feminine features in the versatile profiles mapped out by the author of the booklet; the qualities most emphasized are, once again, adaptability, alertness, constant presence, understanding, humanity, persuasiveness and calmness.

The 'Instructions for Officers of Public Security' issued by Bettino Ricasoli's government in 1867 presented a model in-between two semantic fields: the masculine paradigm typical of the bourgeois age but also a paradigm inspired more by a maternal role.[38] Thus, policemen were encouraged on the one hand to show dignity, self-respect, courage, firmness, impartiality and great care for duty; on the other, they were to 'pry into the needs of the masses, get to know their moral and economic interests, investigate the level of their education, and study their real social conditions'.[39] When establishing relations with citizens, they were supposed to abstain from both 'servile deference' and 'unruly arrogance', and to deal fairly with all, treating the disadvantaged with particular kindness, patience and compassion. At the core of this discourse lay a strong call to emotional involvement, to a feminine 'passion for one's duties', which was listed as the main moral quality of this servant of the state, originating from 'the most generous repository of kindness' in his soul.[40]

In the following decades, the growing tensions in Italian society surfaced again under a new guise: the issue of reform of the police that would enable the police to cope with the exigencies of the industrialized world, at the same time creating efficiency and good press. The key, evident to all, lay once again in recruitment and training, operations that in order to be successful would, however, require more resources than were available. In fact, despite some improvement, the performance of the forces concerned was to remain unsatisfactory throughout the liberal age. Nevertheless, there was an intensified effort for specialized writing, as the number of works published on 'public security' during the period demonstrates.

The best known of these texts was the work of Giovanni Bolis, a senior officer of the Ministry of Interior who would later be appointed as general manager of the police. The title of his work, *The Police and the Dangerous Classes of Society*, is symptomatic of the Second Industrial Revolution climate that was gaining ground in Italy.[41] In line with an established trend, the book began by observing the inadequate character of current employees, 'who for the most part might quite easily be called "misfits"', as another specialist wrote in the same context. For Bolis a turning point could be reached only through an awareness of the high vocation of the police, by acknowledging that the law required the police officer to enter 'a true priesthood' in the service of society.[42] To the range of models available to post-unitary policemen, a kind of Christ-like image was thus enthusiastically added:

> if peace is disturbed in a family, if the labourer is robbed of his earnings, [he finds in the police officer] a protector, a defender . . . who will resolve his quarrels, who will give him justice; the traveller, the foreigner applies to him for support . . . it is . . . [he] who guarantees the weak against the oppressor, who encircles the citizen with care and supervision, and ensures the citizen's life and goods against the violence of the wicked; . . . he warns and recalls to duty the woman whom misery has led astray, and he provides her with asylum and refuge if she has repented; he takes the beggar from the street and ensures him that shelter which public charity has provided; he very often replaces the duties of parents, and he keeps boys from vice . . . If a sudden illness strikes an unhappy traveller on the road, the police officer picks him up lovingly, assists him and provides the necessary care; he follows the citizen in every act of his life, and prevents misfortune in homes if ruin threatens, and he prevents the joys of family from being disturbed by danger . . . Where a fatal disease, the terror of mankind, saddens an entire village, the police officer forgets all danger to himself and willingly offers his service . . . Indeed even if the anger of enemies sometimes covers him with spit and bile, still he forges on in that which the law shows him is his mission. What other field of State Administration has ever given as many martyrs of duty . . . ?[43]

This rhetorical strategy was grafted onto symbolic ground that had already been well prepared by the Risorgimento, which had drawn heavily from the realm of the sacred.[44] It proposed the policeman as a new hero of the nation, attributing to him a mission, a priestly function that emphasized constant self-dedication and sacrifice. This was a prospect that was particularly helpful given the budget of public security; with the low salary levels that were offered to employees, bonuses could not be used for motivation. At the same time the image of the cleric that was cultivated by Bolis's manual perfectly embodied that role of patronage and care that was so crucial to the police while discarding once and for all the paternal metaphor which had been compromised by the authoritarian rhetoric of the preunification age.

With priesthood the images of the policeman and the *carabiniere* appear to converge. The latter saw his features increasingly defined through texts that set his model as somehow separate and prominent among the officers involved in public safety.[45] The corps had stood out in its patriotism demonstrated in the wars of the Risorgimento, and its culture relied on the values of heroism and sacrifice more than the police. The priestly vocation was clearly evident in the obligation of celibacy. In carabineers' self-representation, however, emphasis lay with the state rather than with society, with the salvation of the king and his institutions rather than of the populace. The corps was entirely identified with the values and traditions embodied by the Savoy dynasty. Military status emphasized dedication and obedience, and the hierarchical principle rigidly bound any action. Whereas the police officer was encouraged to create proximity, the carabineer operated on a degree of distance. He was to keep away from civil society and its enticements: 'the use . . . of the modes of bourgeois society is not suitable for him; his completely military character grants him a special status that must be preserved in his every action'. The policeman, on the contrary, was allowed to conceal and camouflage himself for service reasons, to better carry out his duties of investigation and prevention, even to the point of mingling with those whom he must control.[46] The splendid uniform of the carabineer aimed to distinguish him in order to separate him and to excite admiration and reverence, thus imposing a representation of sovereignty centred less on activity than on authority. Civilian police officers also wore a uniform, but for them the uniform was more burden than honour, and allocation of weapons – an instrument reinforcing their masculine identity – cannot be compared to that of their military colleagues.[47] While the *carabiniere* carried a powerful firearm, the *carabine*, which gave him his name, the policeman usually wore a sidearm, the much less impressive sabre. Police manuals were very careful not to emphasize the role of weapons in the police behavioural code; indeed, the literature was highly reticent on this point.

Of these two masculine models, that of the carabineer offered the clearest-cut features, and seemed firmly fixed in a concept of manhood as a disciplined force, directed by a higher source. Compared with this figure, the image of the policeman appeared ever changing, all encompassing, prone to assume feminine features related to the communicative nature of contact, identification and care with which they were associated. The former was decidedly closer to the type of masculinity that has been defined as hegemonic for the bourgeois age, while, in relation to that model, the latter appears in an eccentric and, in many respects, complementary position.[48] In the concept of 'a hierarchy of masculinity', we may conclude that the model of the policeman as drawn from pedagogical literature was positioned significantly lower.[49]

The manuals for police officers that were in circulation in the first decades after unification, therefore, offered a representation of masculinity that was distinguished from that of the cop as well as from that of the military police. It was an image that developed particularly from the preventative tasks that were mainly entrusted to these officers. In the light of this analysis, I turn now to investigate to what extent this representation was supported by the gender discourse of Italian society more broadly at and after this period. One might ask, in other words, whether the Christ-like model that this literature produced was current in the last decades of the century, and whether the idea of sacrifice retained its appeal in the prosaic life of the unitary state. Moreover, were the constitutional and patriotic guises in which police discourses were forged contradicted by later political choices? These choices ranged from the exceptional measures that the Savoy government chose to cope with the problems of public order to the extensive involvement of police in the electoral strategies orchestrated by prefects in provinces.[50]

In this vein, some information can be drawn from memoirs, an area of police writing that became abundant in the late nineteenth century. Several officers and agents ventured into autobiographical narration after leaving the service, including some notorious commissioners from the pre-unification age who were eager to justify themselves to the public. Towards the end of the century, these memoirs tended to undermine the milder interpretations of official sources and offered a realistic picture of the life of the policeman in united Italy, thus producing a kind of counterpoint to the handbooks that have been considered so far.

Autobiographies by no means rejected the sacrificial scheme. On the contrary, they relied heavily on it to emphasize the lack of economic rewards for deserving officers.[51] Devotion to duty, abstaining from any possibility of personal reward, became a form of revenge on the mediocrity of the bureaucracy for the accomplished police officer. This is a destiny that is accepted as inescapable: public safety, 'Marius' wrote at the end of the century, is 'a strong and bitter wine', whose appeal in spite of everything never fades for those who have tasted it.[52] Domenico Cappa, former major of police and author of a lengthy memoir, offered his readers an encounter with a 'cohort of brave and strong performers of their duty'.[53] The parade would serve to show 'how much courage and self-denial, how much sacrifice and heart, how much goodness, often simple and modest, have found an everlasting altar in souls that were clothed in the unfairly vilified and despised uniform of the guards of public security'.[54]

These arguments were important in offering some compensation to policemen for the precarious conditions that marked their life. Because the police officer could not claim the material assets that were key to bourgeois liberal masculinity, the development of an alternative model was useful to him. The Christ-like model was perhaps not equally intense as far as manhood was concerned, but it had the advantage of being well rooted in Italian culture and had moreover enjoyed a renewed emphasis during the Risorgimento, as already mentioned. However, towards the late nineteenth century the ability of this metaphor to represent the self-image of the policeman was slowly fading. Marius himself sanctioned the end of the ascetic model in his work of 1896. He questioned the value of a literary model still so popular, Inspector Javert of Victor Hugo's *Les Miserables*, from which Italian police culture had drawn inspiration:

> Javert's life was held constantly between these two words: keep watch and monitor. He was aware of how useful he was, and how his functions had a religious value: he was a spy, as other people are priests! . . . Alas, Javert is a symbol. Diogenes today would seek him in vain.[55]

Competence, intelligence and science

Although dedication and sacrifice were losing their attraction, competence became increasingly appealing, delineated at first in customary ways as the result of experience gained entirely on the ground, a kind of cunning refined with practice, and then, as we shall see, in more up-to-date ways. Cappa's autobiography bears witness to the practical attitude to competence through the portrait of the main character, himself:

> When you speak about Cappa [says a colleague of the protagonist in the autobiography] you have to take off your hat . . . I was on patrol with him . . . and I knew immediately that he has a keen sense of smell . . . He's a real truffle hound! . . . Only from the walk of a person, without ever having seen or known that person, he can tell you, after having followed him for a moment, what kind of person that is and what he does for a living.[56]

Intelligence, especially if resting on faith, became in this model the real weapon of the police officer drawn in memoirs. For those who were amply gifted with it, intelligence could be regarded as replacing muscles and the regulation pistol:

> I, always confident in a force other than my own, instead of being confident of my strong constitution, instead of arming myself with offensive and defensive weapons, I have hardly ever worn in the day or by night, either alone or accompanied, a weapon of any kind, except my sword . . . when I had to wear the uniform. As I was almost always dressed in civilian clothes, the only weapon in my hands was my traditional umbrella.[57]

Insight, intelligence and acumen became a special source of pride for the men involved in public safety, the distinctive qualities with which the policeman could hope to counter the comparison with the *carabiniere* that was always at stake. The changing conditions of society required appropriate qualities to match new challenges – qualities that the civilian police liked to imagine were in their possession by statute:

> The delinquency of a nation . . . is a complex, dynamic and protean phenomenon. It has a real army organized for different objectives, all competing for the same purpose – which is anti-social, as anti-juridical as you want, but by no means less real and threatening . . . This army with its strategy and its tactics; this illegal state within the legal one, with its traditions and its history, is to be fought by another strong and disciplined army, that wherever and however you may call it, will always be the police.[58]

The growth of social conflict and the emergence of criminality raised an inflammatory topic that had been carefully avoided in the delicate post-Risorgimento period. It was, however, at the core of the important work by Giuseppe Alongi, who evoked the theme in the very title of *Police and Delinquency*, in which they were regarded as two different forces confronting one another. The anti-crime army could not rely on military systems though; the tools that would grant victory in the ongoing war were primarily intellectual. Moreover, their use required a flexibility that the carabineers did not possess. Pondering whether 'police personnel should be military or civilian', Alongi argued that the investigative service specifically required civilians – disciplined agents to be sure, but free in initiative and movement:[59]

> This . . . is ill-suited to the uniform and *ésprit de corps* that belongs to carabineers. And so, while crime, like any other social phenomenon, follows the course of its evolution, changes shape and becomes different, the carabineer remains crystallized within the unbreakable limits of his regulation, made even more rigid by the superiors' instructions, increasingly guided by the one-sidedness of military rigour.[60]

Intellectual qualities stand out, alongside expertise, in late nineteenth-century texts.

So far, as we have seen, the image of the policeman had been remarkably polarized morally. He was either holy or evil, as the midpoint position between these models was quite difficult to sustain, and the process of professionalization of the institution difficult and slow.[61] The first signs of maturation were to be found in the 1880s, the decade in which manuals – to which we now return in the conclusion – finally turned their attention to the issue of expertise and competence.[62] New cultural models shaped this trend, some of them coming from foreign organizations (in particular the British Metropolitan Police), some from the social sciences.[63]

This change of perspective was already noticeable in the work of the prefect of Cremona, Pietro Celli. His manual was published in 1880 with the intention of summarizing, 'like a system, the precepts of the Police, regarded both as a science and an art'.[64] Police personnel would need to gear up to competently perform the activities of observation, prevention, repression and investigation. Moreover, the necessary wealth of skills and knowledge could not be generic, as policing 'requires unity of action, physical strength and material operations, culture and special knowledge that make it almost a technical profession'.[65]

Five years later, Giuseppe Alongi would deem this too timid an assertion, persuaded that the policeman was a technical professional in every respect.[66] The entire work of this competent officer bore witness to its cultural moment, densely interwoven with references to the studies of social scientists, who were referred to as teachers, colleagues and fellow travellers in his acknowledgements. The homage to the scholarly world was so marked that Alongi turned to the words of the famous criminologist Cesare Lombroso to show Italian police the way forward. In order to fight ever more sophisticatedly organized crime, a warring attitude would no longer suffice: 'Lombroso goes further than that, and justly calls for a police that is scientific, not *routinier*, a police that is technical, specialist'.[67]

> So far we . . . have created the police as people used to make war in heroic times: all random, empirically, except for the individual merit in muscle strength and cunning of a few warriors who often determined the victory. We have officials who are – and claim they are – skilled, as Achilles and Odysseus were; however, we have none who, as any officer of any Armed Forces would do (let alone Moltke), will ground their investigation on the scientific evidence offered by studies of statistics and criminal anthropology. We have none who are willing to expand their talent by way of the immense and, what's more, entirely governable forces of science.[68]

With the intention of fully responding to Lombrosian theory, Alongi inaugurated an intertwining of police and science by dedicating one of the six chapters of his monograph to the exposition of the 'Scientific Criteria of Delinquency'.[69] A few years later, as a superintendent, he began publishing a journal of forensic policing in collaboration with the medical doctor and university professor Salvatore Ottolenghi, a disciple of Lombroso.[70] This project, however, failed soon afterwards because of financial difficulties but Alongi would go on to publish a *Manual of Scientific Police* in 1898. The connection between the two worlds was perfected in 1902, when Ottolenghi established the School of Scientific Police in Rome for the sector, which he was to direct for many years.[71]

Through this path a new professional model would come to be embedded in the imagination of the Italian police, a model that suggested in turn a definition of masculinity which was updated to the 'spirit of the time' for intellectually ambitious officials. In the age of positivism, the ideal of the male athlete coexisted alongside that of the male scientist, which was perhaps less widespread but still equally important.[72] Scholars have been only partly concerned with this theme, focusing their attention on tracking the new cult of mass virility, which was physical and competitive, and tied to the first great crisis of bourgeois civilization as well as to the harbingers of nationalism and feminism.[73] However, the scientific and technical specification of intellectual activity was, at that moment in history, a quality of male distinction that enjoyed broad support in the cultured classes. In another way, this was part of a long line that, ever since the Renaissance, had identified being a male in Italy with the mastery of the liberal arts, favouring the curial ideal over the warrior in the conceptual pairing through which the *Ancien Régime* constructed virility.[74]

The figure of the scientist-policeman became rapidly more democratic in application. Alongi's *Handbook of Scientific Police* was intended for an educated audience composed of 'doctors, experts, lawyers, magistrates, public safety officers, students, writers, journalists', as the subtitle lists them, whom he wished to provide with a detailed catalogue of the latest technical and scientific instruments. Nonetheless, Alongi's handbook also suggested a simplified manual aimed at agents, which was to be titled significantly *Science and Duty: A Book for the State Police Agent* and would proffer the same scientist model, devoting ample space to concepts of social and medical science.[75] Therefore, a different representation of masculinity and police emerged at all levels of the hierarchy: a representation focusing less on moral qualities than on mastery over the knowledge provided by the new sciences.

It is also in these circumstances that police culture began to receive more vivid stimuli in terms of gender distinctions. Up to that point, manuals had only occasionally touched on this issue, as has been noted. The feminine became significantly relevant in a page that Alongi devoted to the positive effects of marriage on the professional performance of public security officers, who were not subject to a requirement of celibacy, as in the case of the carabineers, but could marry only with the authorization of their superiors:[76]

> In order to arouse the zeal of men and reinvigorate their discipline, we deem it useful to grant agents more widely than today the possibility to marry, while requiring certain conditions of age, and especially of morality of the bride. What the feeling of family can accomplish in all men, and therefore also in the agent of state police, it is easy to guess. Besides, the Minister of Interior well understood this fact, when writing thus in the instructions preceding the regulation of the guards: 'It was noted that most married agents, who are currently in the corps, are distinguished by their zeal and attachment to the service, which they recognize as the means of subsistence for themselves and their families: that non-married men live isolated for the most part and as foreigners to the city where they are, with no relations or support; that the expenses of the family are compensated by the assistance they receive thence; that in general married men are more sober and more exemplary in their conduct, and are consequently more esteemed by the public' . . . The police officer in England and France is as good a family man as a zealous servant of the government.[77]

The opening of police culture to science also brought about an objective perspective in relation to women. It created a channel through which to incorporate new data on female delinquency, the subject of an extraordinary series of studies encouraged by legislators' renewed attention.[78] The first important text was published in Turin in 1891 under the title *The Criminal Woman and the Prostitute*, co-written by Lombroso and Ottolenghi, and immediately followed by other works.[79] These studies moved from an analysis of the biological differences between men and women to argue for the inferiority of the latter on a scientific basis, identifying in prostitution the most typical symptoms of female delinquency: 'with the prostitute the woman offers an equivalent – and perhaps more widespread – of the born male criminal'.[80] In the regulations for the police, women had until then featured explicitly only in that role, while other behaviours that were detrimental to social safety and order were generally obscured within a

universal masculinity.[81] Now, however, criminology sought the causes of typical
female deviance on a biological and psychological basis, only to discover that they
lay in the recognizable difference between female biology and psychology, and a
masculine norm. The investigation of crime thus involved a general reflection on
gender issues that was recast according to the scientific truths of the day, and in
which even the best trained police personnel could be acculturated and involved.[82]
As a result, police personnel found themselves sharing in some measure the strong
position held by social scientists. As active subjects in the process of developing
new categories of gender, police officers had the opportunity to strengthen male
identity and pride, recognizing themselves as examples of the gender to which the
highest intellectual and creative power was ascribed.[83]

In late nineteenth-century handbooks for the police there was always room
for a chapter on prostitution, but authors' hearts were elsewhere.[84] This relative
lack of attention was certainly related to the growing suspicion that police were
colluding with pimps and prostitutes. But the common opinion that real crime
was masculine was certainly just as influential a factor. Female delinquency was
considered but a pale reflection of male, mainly irrelevant within the overall
economy of prevention and punishment. Lombroso had made it clear in his study
of prostitution:

> if it is true that we had to prove that in mind and body woman is a man
> arrested in his development, the fact that she is far less criminal than he, and
> that she is all the more compassionate than him, can compensate a thousand
> times for her deficiency in the realm of intellect.[85]

Therefore, keeping watch on brothels was regarded as a task that might have been
dutiful but was certainly not profitable for the public image and self-representation
of the Italian police.[86]

It was certainly much more rewarding to focus on the portrait of the real enemy,
the criminal army against whom the forces of public safety were employed in an
ongoing war. The stronger this army appeared, the more the policeman gained in
stature. Former head of police Augusto Bondi was well aware of this when, writing his memoirs, he proved exceedingly generous with the adverse party:

> We are confronted – he wrote – with born criminals, with depraved and
> indomitable perverts, with mad and miserable men, with some overwhelmed
> by the turmoil of evil, with others who have turned crime into a profession,
> and know all the tricks and violence of crime; with all sorts of unruly individuals, by nature, by chance, with the strangest men that the very bottom of
> humanity has ever brought to the surface. It is an ever-continuing struggle
> against this army of enemies of themselves and of others, scattered to the far
> corners of civil community, and often cleverly mingling even with the best
> society.[87]

A chapter of Bondi's book was devoted to his service as public security delegate in Sardinia in 1891. Not by chance does he give great prominence to the meeting he arranged with a famous local bandit, who had been a fugitive for years.[88] The gigantic image of this character occupies centre stage, infusing as much romantic manhood to the figure of the police officer as the bandit himself: 'He and I were at that moment, in his conscience, two loyal ancient knights who had momentarily laid down their arms, but were each fighting for a just cause'.[89]

Notes

1 Translation by Susan Broomhall and Greta Perletti.
2 See, in general, S. Bellassai and M. Malatesta, 'Mascolinità e storia', in S. Bellassai and M. Malatesta (eds), *Genere e mascolinità. Uno sguardo storico*, Roma: Bulzoni, 2000, pp. i–xvi (p. xv); S. Bellassai, *La mascolinità contemporanea*, Roma: Carocci, 2004, p. 29; and more recently M. McCormack, 'Men, "the Public" and Political History', in M. McCormack (ed.), *Public Men: Masculinity and Politics in Modern Britain*, Basingstoke: Palgrave Macmillan, 2007, p. 14.
3 The widespread lack of interest in the public field among historians of masculinity is pointed out by McCormack, 'Introduction', in *Public Men*, p. 3.
4 E. Avdela, 'Work, Gender and History in the 1990s and Beyond', in L. Davidoff, K. McClelland and E. Varikas (eds), *Gender and History: Retrospect and Prospect*, Oxford: Blackwell, 2000, pp. 110–23; J. Tosh, 'Hegemonic Masculinity and the History of Gender', in S. Dudink, K. Hagemann and J. Tosh (eds), *Masculinities in Politics and War: Gendering Modern History*, Manchester: Manchester University Press, 2004, p. 54; A. Rotundo, *American Manhood: Transformations in Masculinity from the Revolution to the Modern Era*, New York: Basic Books, 1993, p. 167; and A. Rauch, *Crise de l'identité masculine 1789–1914*, Paris: Hachette, 2000, p. 113.
5 See a similar approach to the British case in F. Dodsworth, 'Masculinity as Governance: Police, Public Service and the Embodiment of Authority, c. 1700–1850', in McCormack, *Public Men*, pp. 33–53. The complex relation between policing and masculinity is explored in a historical perspective by D. G. Barrie and S. Broomhall, 'Policing Bodies in Urban Scotland, 1780–1850', in S. Broomhall and J. Van Gent (eds), *Governing Masculinities in the Early Modern Period: Regulating Selves and Others*, Aldershot: Ashgate, 2011; I thank the authors for giving me the opportunity to read the text.
6 A recent overview can be found in Bellassai, *La mascolinità*. On nineteenth-century Italian male representation, see especially L. Riall, 'Eroi maschili, virilità e forme della Guerra', in A. M. Banti and P. Ginsborg (eds), *Storia d'Italia. Annali*, 22, *Il Risorgimento*, Torino: Einaudi, 2007, pp. 253–88; S. C. Hughes, *Politics of the Sword: Dueling, Honor, and Masculinity in Modern Italy*, Columbus: Ohio State University Press, 2007; and S. Patriarca, *Italian Vices: Nation and Character from the Risorgimento to the Republic*, Cambridge: Cambridge University Press, 2010, p. 31.
7 On the state of studies on the Italian police, see S. C. Hughes, 'Immaginando una storia della polizia italiana in età liberale', in L. Antonielli (ed.), *La polizia in Italia e in Europa: punto sugli studi e prospettive di ricerca*, Soveria Mannelli: Rubbettino, 2006, pp. 129–40.
8 For an overview see C. Guarnieri, 'L'ordine pubblico e la giustizia penale', in R. Romanelli (ed.), *Storia dello Stato italiano dall'Unità a oggi*, Roma: Donzelli, 1995, pp. 365–405; G. Tosatti, 'La repressione del dissenso politico tra l'età liberale e il fascismo. L'organizzazione della polizia', *Studi Storici*, 1997, vol. 1, pp. 217–55; and M. Bonino, *La polizia italiana nella seconda metà dell'Ottocento. Aspetti culturali e operativi*, Roma: Laurus Robuffo, 2006, pp. 17–87. See also J. A. Davis, *Conflict*

and Control: Law and Order in Nineteenth-Century Italy, London: Macmillan, 1988, pp. 217–41; S. C. Hughes, *Crime, Disorder and the Risorgimento: The Politics of Policing in Bologna*, Cambridge: Cambridge University Press, 1994; M. Broers, 'Policing Piedmont: "The Well Ordered Police State" in the Age of Revolution, 1794–1821', *Criminal Justice History*, 1994, vol. 15, pp. 39–57.

9 *Manuale alfabetico dei* maires, *loro aggiunti e commissari di polizia*, Firenze: Giovacchino Pagani, 1809.

10 Ibid., p. iv.

11 The Italian term for 'police', *polizia*, is feminine.

12 L. Hunt, 'Engraving the Republic: Prints and Propaganda in the French Revolution', *History Today*, 1980, vol. 30, pp. 11–17; and A. M. Banti, *L'onore della nazione. Identità sessuali e violenza nel nazionalismo europeo dal XVIII secolo alla Grande Guerra*, Torino: Einaudi, 2005, pp. 3–32.

13 Giuseppe Alongi, *Manuale di polizia scientifica*, Milano: Sonzogno, 1898, p. 347. The epigraph is drawn from Gustave Macé, *La police parisienne*, 3 vols, Paris: Charpentier, 1885–7.

14 Hautefeuille, *Trattato di procedura criminale, correzionale e di polizia, seguito dall'analisi del codice penale*, 3 vols, Napoli: Simoniana, 1811–13, vol. 1, p. 2.

15 Gaetano Cava, *La polizia. Trattato di Gaetano Cava con de' progetti relativi ad altre attribuzioni proprie della polizia*, Napoli: Marotta e Vanspandoch, 1829, p. 18.

16 On the classical references underlying the representation of the male image between the eighteenth and nineteenth centuries see G. L. Mosse, *The Image of Man: The Creation of Modern Masculinity*, Oxford: Oxford University Press, 1996 [Italian version: *L'immagine dell'uomo. Lo stereotipo maschile nell'epoca moderna*, Torino: Einaudi, 1997], p. 40.

17 S. C. Hughes, 'L'immagine della polizia', in L. Antonielli (ed.), *La polizia in Italia nell'età moderna*, Soveria Mannelli: Rubbettino, 2002, pp. 151–7. Giovanni Bolis, *La polizia e le classi pericolose della società*, Bologna: Zanichelli, 1871, p. 11, describes the cop as the person:

> who could with impunity threaten with handcuffs and prison, who embodied the terror of peaceful citizens, exposed to his arbitrary will and his reprisal, [the person] who flattered power in order to take advantage from it and who instigated the ferocity of power, plotting conspiracies and machinations to his own advantage, so as to be able to vent his base passions more freely.

18 E. Francia, 'Polizia e opinione pubblica in Toscana nel Quarantotto', in P. Macry (ed.), *Quando crolla lo Stato. Studi sull'Italia preunitaria*, Napoli: Liguori, 2003, pp. 141–77.

19 L. Cancrini, *I voti nazionali. Riforma della polizia*, Tipografia dell'Ariosto, 1848, p. 4.

20 Ibid.

21 R. Mozzillo, *Manuale di polizia, ovvero indice ragionato delle leggi, dei reali decreti, delle sovrane risoluzioni e delle massime riguardanti la polizia ordinaria*, 2 vols, Napoli: Tip. Mosca, 1847.

22 Ibid., vol. 1, pp. ix–x.

23 Ibid., vol. 1, p. ix. Subsequent quotations from p. x.

24 Rotundo, *American Manhood*, p. 29ff. For nineteenth-century Italy, see C. Covato, 'Educata ad educare: ruolo materno ed itinerari formativi', in S. Soldani (ed.), *L'educazione delle donne. Scuole e modelli di vita femminile nell'Italia dell'Ottocento*, Milano: Franco Angeli, 1989, pp. 132–3; and M. T. Mori, 'Maschile, femminile: l'identità di genere nei salotti di conversazione', in M. L. Betri and E. Brambilla (eds), *Salotti e ruolo femminile in Italia tra fine Seicento e primo Novecento*, Venice: Marsilio, 2004, pp. 3–18.

25 As well as Davis, *Conflict and Control*; and Hughes, *Crime, Disorder and the Risorgimento*; see G. Santonicini, *Ordine pubblico e polizia nella crisi dello Stato*

pontificio (1848–1850), Milano: Giuffrè, 1981; and S. Mori, 'La polizia fra opinione e amministrazione nel Regno Lombardo-Veneto', *Società e storia*, 2004, vol. 105, pp. 99–141.

26 B. Fiani, *Della polizia considerata come mezzo di preventiva difesa. Trattato teorico-pratico*, Firenze: Tipografia nazionale italiana, 1853–6, p. 4. Subsequent quotations from p. 3. On the importance of this work see M. Sbriccoli, 'Polizia (diritto intermedio)', in *Enciclopedia del Diritto*, Milano: Giuffrè, 1985, vol. XXXIV, p. 119. On the context of the grand dukes see C. Mangio, *La polizia toscana. Organizzazione e criteri d'intervento (1765–1808)*, Milano: Giuffrè, 1988.

27 Fiani, *Della polizia considerata come mezzo di preventiva difesa*, p. 74.

28 Fiani, *Della polizia considerata come mezzo di preventiva difesa*, ch. VII, p. 92.

29 See the data provided for the province of Bologna by Hughes, *Crime, Disorder and the Risorgimento*, pp. 268–72.

30 For an analogy see L. Lopez, 'Commissaires de police et officiers de gendarmerie à la fin du XIXe siècle: pratique professionelles et répresentations', in D. Kalifa and P. Karila-Cohen (eds), *Le commissaire de police au XIXe siècle*, Paris: Publications de la Sorbonne, 2008, pp. 139ff. On Royal *Carabinieri* see G. Oliva, *Storia dei Carabinieri. Immagini e autorappresentazione dell'Arma*, Milano: Leonardo, 1992; C. Emsley, *Gendarmes and the State in Nineteenth-Century Europe*, Oxford: Oxford University Press, 1999, pp. 191–207; and F. Carbone, 'Lineamenti dell'organizzazione di polizia nel Regno di Sardegna: il Corpo dei Carabinieri Reali (1814–1853)', in L. Antonielli (ed.), *Polizia ordine pubblico e crimine tra città e campagna: un confront comparativo*, Soveria Mannelli: Rubbettino, 2010, pp. 97–156.

31 'Quadro, 1863', in C. Astengo and L. Gatti (eds), *Manuale del funzionario di sicurezza pubblica e di polizia giudiziaria*, vol. 1, Milano: Pirola, January 1863, p. 33; G. Alongi, *Polizia e delinquenza in Italia*, Roma: Cecchini, 1887, p. 144; Guarnieri, 'L'ordine pubblico', p. 375; and Oliva, *Storia dei Carabinieri*, p. 78. During Crispi's government there was roughly one policeman for every 500 people and one *carabiniere* for every 150 people. Excluded from these figures are other kinds of guards who were involved in the control of the territory (for example, revenue guard corps, municipal guards, forest rangers).

32 *Degli uffici e funzionarj di pubblica sicurezza. Note di un già questore*, Milano: Tip. Albertari, 1862, p. 18. On the different requirements in terms of masculinity, depending on the hierarchical level of the police officer, although dealing with an earlier context, see Barrie and Broomhall, 'Policing Bodies'.

33 *Degli uffici e funzionarj*, p. 20.

34 Ibid., p. 21.

35 Ibid., p. 22.

36 Ibid., p. 22.

37 Ibid., p. 24.

38 The text, dated 4 April 1867, can be read as an appendix to F. Fiorentino, *Ordine pubblico nell'età giolittiana*, Rome: Carecas, 1978, pp. 129–52.

39 Ibid., p. 130.

40 Ibid., p. 147.

41 Bolis, *La polizia e le classi pericolose della società*. The following citation is from A. Cuniberti, *Malanni e rimedi, ossia il vandalismo campestre prevenuto e represso*, Bologna: Stabilimento tipografico Monti, 1870, p. xi.

42 Bolis, *La polizia*, p. 8.

43 Ibid., p. 8.

44 See especially A. M. Banti, *La nazione del Risorgimento: parentela, santità e onore alle origini dell'Italia unita*, Torino: Einaudi, 2000, pp. 123–8.

45 The most significant work is G. C. Grossardi, *Galateo del Carabiniere*, Torino: Candeletti, 1875 (see the facsimile of the 1879 edition, edited by the Ufficio Pubbliche Relazioni del Comando Generale dell'Arma dei Carabinieri, Roma, 2001). On this

topic see J. Dunnage, 'Les Carabiniers italiens après 1860. Professionnalisme et auto-représentation', in J.-N. Luc (ed.), *Gendarmerie, état et société au XIXe siècle*, Paris: Publications de la Sorbonne, 2002, pp. 411–22.

46   See D. Cappa, *Trentadue anni di servizio nella polizia italiana*, Milano: Dumolard, 1892, p. 107. The quote about the *carabiniere* is taken from Grossardi, *Galateo*, p. 3.

47   On the effect (more intended than real) of the uniform and on the gap between *carabinieri* and police attire see Mozzillo, *Manuale di polizia*, ch. II and Cuniberti, *Malanni e rimedi*, p. 50. About the absence of interest in weapons claimed by the 'good policeman', see, for example, Cappa, *Trentadue anni*, p. 368: 'a weapon carried in one's pocket implies ever-present danger'.

48   R. W. Connell, *Maschilità. Identità e trasformazioni del maschio occidentale*, Milano: Feltrinelli, 1996, p. 70. For criticism of the concept of hegemony as applied to masculinity, see McCormack, 'Men, "the Public" and Political History', p. 17.

49   F. La Cecla, *Modi bruschi. Antropologia del maschio*, Milano: Bruno Mondadori, 2000, p. 33ff. Recent historiography has insisted on the functional changeability of the male models. See, for example, J. Tosh, *A Man's Place: Masculinity and the Middle-Class Home in Victorian England*, New Haven, CT: Yale University Press, 1999; T. L. Broughton and H. Rogers, 'Introduction', in their *Gender and Fatherhood in the Nineteenth Century*, Basingstoke: Palgrave Macmillan, 2007, p. 16; and C. E. Forth, *Masculinity in the Modern West: Gender, Civilization and the Body*, Basingstoke: Palgrave Macmillan, 2008, pp. 29, 67.

50   On the pre-electoral activity of policemen see Marius, *La pubblica sicurezza in Italia*, Milano: Carlo Aliprandi, n.d., pp. 67–75. Marius was a pseudonym. The identity of this frequently quoted author has not yet been ascertained, except for the fact that he was certainly a police officer (see Tosatti, 'La repression', p. 230) and wrote during the 1890s, most probably in 1896. The adoption of special laws for public order was widely debated in the press in the 1870s, and was for the most part harshly criticized. See R. Martucci, *Emergenza e tutela dell'ordine pubblico nell'Italia liberale*, Bologna: Il Mulino, 1980, p. 215; and L. Riall, 'Liberal Policy and the Control of Public Order in Western Sicily, 1860–1862', *The Historical Journal*, 1992, vol. 35, no. 2, pp. 345–68.

51   See, especially, V. Paoletti, *Da Brundisio alle Alpi. Reminiscenze di un ispettore di Sicurezza Pubblica*, Milano: Rechiedei, 1891; and Cappa, *Trentadue anni*. A confirmation comes from Marius, *La pubblica sicurezza*, p. 24 and *passim*.

52   Marius, *La pubblica sicurezza*, p. 39. Alongi makes similar remarks in *Polizia e delinquenza*, p. 46.

53   Cappa, *Trentadue anni*, p. 4. See also the self-portrait in Paoletti, *Da Brundisio alle Alpi*, p. 11.

54   Ibid., p. 4.

55   Marius, *La pubblica sicurezza*, pp. 31ff. On the importance of the figure of Javert see Cappa, *Trentadue anni*, p. 12.

56   Cappa, *Trentadue anni*, p. 274.

57   Ibid., p. 368.

58   Alongi, *Polizia e delinquenza*, p. 39.

59   Ibid., p. 36ff.

60   Ibid., p. 118. Also p. 152.

61   Beside the already mentioned texts see G. Florenzano, *La legge eccezionale e la pubblica sicurezza in Italia*, Napoli: De Angelis, 1875, p. 26.

62   See, especially, Alongi, *Polizia e delinquenza*, pp. 39, 140 and *passim*.

63   On the first aspect see A. Cuniberti, *La polizia di Londra: con note ed osservazioni sulla polizia italiana*, Bologna: Zanichelli, 1872, pp. 32–3, who describes the special agents of the investigative department in London, established in 1862, as 'equipped with some extraordinary skills and great experience . . . truly something special in the field'. See also Alongi, *Polizia e delinquenza*, p. 190.

64 P. Celli, *Della Polizia*, Milano: Tipografia Luigi di Giacomo Pirola, 1880, p. 1.
65 Ibid., p. 19.
66 Alongi, *Polizia e delinquenza*, p. 40.
67 Ibid, p. 39, note 3. The reference is to Cesare Lombroso, *Sull'incremento del delitto in Italia e sui mezzi per arrestarlo*, Torino: Fratelli Bocca, 1879, p. 135.
68 Extract quoted in Alongi, *Polizia e delinquenza*, p. 77 and drawn from an article by Lombroso published in *Archivio di psichiatria e scienze penali ed antropologia criminale*, 1886, vol. VII, p. 611.
69 Alongi, *Polizia e delinquenza*, ch. III, pp. 54ff. On the old-fashioned nature of the manuals of the sector see p. 47. On the cultural climate see S. Montaldo and P. Tappero (eds), *Cesare Lombroso cento anni dopo*, Torino: UTET, 2009; also Davis, *Conflict and control*, pp. 326–38.
70 On this experience see Alongi, *Manuale di polizia scientifica*, p. 174.
71 Salvatore Ottolenghi, *L'insegnamento universitario della polizia giudiziaria scientifica: prolusione*, Torino: Fratelli Bocca, 1897; some brief reference in Tosatti, 'La repressione', pp. 223ff.; also S. Buzzanca, 'La figura di Salvatore Ottolenghi', n.d., available at http://ssai.interno.it/pubblicazioni/instrumenta/16/14_buzzanca.pdf.
72 Mosse, *L'immagine dell'uomo*, pp. 40–55, about the athlete pattern; and L. Benadusi, 'Storia del corpo maschile', in E. Ruspini (ed.), *Uomini e corpi. Una riflessione sui rivestimenti della mascolinità*, Milano: Franco Angeli, 2009, p. 39.
73 See Rotundo, *American Manhood*, p. 222; Mosse, *L'immagine dell'uomo*, pp. 103ff; Rauch, *Crise de l'identité masculine*, p. 254; Hughes, *Politics of the Sword*, pp. 100ff; and Forth, *Masculinity in the Modern West*, pp. 157ff.
74 R. Ago, 'La costruzione dell'identità maschile: una competizione tra uomini', in A. Arru (ed.), *La costruzione dell'identità maschile nell'età moderna e contemporanea*, Roma: Biblink, 2001, p. 21.
75 On the intellectual aspects of the profession of the agent see also A. Bondi, *Memorie di un questore (25 anni nella polizia italiana)*, Milano: Mondaini, 1913, p. 312: 'We are at this point, that the guard is a number and this number needs to be a mind: a little mind, if you wish, but a mind nevertheless'.
76 Alongi, *Polizia e delinquenza*, p. 161.
77 On the topic see Tosh, *A Man's Place*, pp. 53ff.
78 Similarly, J. Harsin, *Policing Prostitution in Nineteenth-Century Paris*, Princeton, NJ: Princeton University Press, 1985, pp. 96ff. On the topic see now M. Gibson, 'Il genere: la donna (delinquente e non)', in Montaldo and Tappero (eds), *Cesare Lombroso*, pp. 155–64.
79 C. Lombroso and S. Ottolenghi, *La donna delinquente e la prostituta: studio*, Torino: Unione tipografico-editrice, 1891; continued by G. Ferrero and C. Lombroso, *La donna delinquente: la prostituta e la donna normale*, Torino: Roux, 1893. The volume came as a sequel to the principal Lombrosian work, *L'uomo delinquente*, Milano: Hoepli, 1876.
80 G. Ferrero and C. Lombroso, *La donna delinquente: la prostituta e la donna normale*, 5th edn, Torino: Fratelli Bocca, 1927, p. 6.
81 *Legge di pubblica sicurezza del Regno d'Italia*, 1865, art. 86.
82 On the relation between norm and deviance in gender analysis see A. McLaren, *Gentiluomini e canaglie. L'identità maschile tra Ottocento e Novecento*, Roma: Carocci, 1999.
83 A comparison between male and female intelligence can be found in Ferrero and Lombroso, *La donna delinquente*, ch. VII, pp. 116–32, where it is concluded, by founding the argument upon Comte, Darwin and Lotze, that 'both when what is required is depth in thought, imagination and when simply the senses or the hands are used, man comes to greater perfection than woman'.
84 The chapter on brothels is hastily dealt with in Marius, *La pubblica sicurezza*, pp. 130ff., while the 'synoptic prospect for the study of the delinquent man' that

is the appendix to Alongi, *Manuale di polizia scientifica*, considers only males. F. Giorio, *Ricordi di questura*, Milano: Artistica, 1882, devotes more space to the topic, although he points out that:

> The sanitary office is repulsive to the majority of employees and guards of the state police. Haggling meat, chasing women, standing in the social decay of the slums is repugnant to every man who has some character and good heart . . . Sanitary policing, as is practised nowadays, is a dishonour to our time.
>
> (p. 167)

85 Ferrero and Lombroso, *La donna delinquente*, p. 6.
86 See, again, Lombroso, *Sull'incremento*, p. 134. Also G. Schmitt, *Fisiologia e costume della prostituzione*, Napoli: Salvatore Romano, 1905, pp. 21ff. and 112.
87 Bondi, *Memorie di un questore*, p. 11.
88 Ibid., pp. 43ff.
89 Ibid., p. 53.

emplotment: there are many other structural ways of pointing to wider or analogous meanings, such as the embodiment of generic conventions.

In police memoirs this is particularly evident in those that do not or do not only follow the case model. Often memoirs focused on types of crime and criminal rather than specific cases, or mixed the two together in a process in which the meaning generated by the text emerges from the combination of the form and the content. This element of the police memoir, the social commentary, draws our attention to a genre that is as important as the detective story for understanding the wider message of many police memoirs: social investigation or urban exploration.

Social investigation as a genre emerged in England with the journalistic work of Charles Dickens and Henry Mayhew in the 1850s and 1860s, most notably with the publication of Mayhew's *London Labour and the London Poor* in 1861–2. Like its later successors, Mayhew's work was driven by a desire not only to draw a readership through sensational detail, but also to expose the dire condition of the poor in England, demonstrating how thin the veneer of Victorian civilization was, and encouraging the wealthy population to turn their attention to bettering the condition of their neighbours. Despite the greater prosperity of the later nineteenth century, social reform remained the basis of this genre as it reached its peak at precisely the same time as the police memoir, in the 1880s and 1890s, with the publication of such well-known titles as Andrew Mearns's *The Bitter Cry of Outcast London* (1883), George Sims's *How the Poor Live* (1883), William Booth's *Into Darkest England* (1890) and Charles Booth's *Life and Labour of the People in London* (1889–1903).[23]

It has been argued that the genre of social investigation constitutes a form of 'auto-ethnography' or anthropology in which the English urban explorers objectified members of their own society as a culture set apart as if they were an alien culture comparable to those encountered in the Americas or Africa, a metaphor dating back at least to Mayhew's *London Labour*.[24] In doing so, the working class and the underclass were rendered alien, objectified by the auto-ethnographer, a participant observer able to pass between worlds, close enough to their subject to know it in detail, but distinct enough to maintain critical distance. This combination of familiarity and distance was illustrated by interspersing detailed descriptions of life in this culture with more detached commentaries on it in the same text. This movement of the text between evocative description and commentary mirrored the ability of the observer to move in and out of the culture being objectified.[25]

This is precisely the role undertaken by many police memoirs, with their detailed descriptions of underworld people and places. For example, there was a constant attempt to illustrate the extent to which it was important for a detective to know the state of crime and criminals in his division in detail, without ever becoming so close to them as to compromise himself.[26] Equally, a central element of the police memoir was the illustration of a world of which the general public had no idea. Fuller made much of how the policeman saw a great deal of variety in life and interacted with all kinds of people.[27] The Rotherhithe in which he began his career in 1881 is described as 'cut off from civilization' owing to its geographic location and the layout of the streets. Because the main street leads nowhere only those who lived there knew of its existence. Most people may have heard of the area 'but its thoroughfares are less familiar to them than to the Scandinavians or the Russians who come there once a year with timber and corn'.[28] He clearly saw the people living there as different in kind: 'the people here – indeed I think it is much the same anywhere below London Bridge – have a different standard of morality. I do not say, everything considered, that they are any worse or any better, but decidedly different.'[29]

It was equally common for memoirs to evoke a world or a way of life that had passed, in large part through the exercise of good policing: another Metropolitan detective Timothy Cavanagh, writing in the 1890s, details how, on his arrival at Stone's End police station in Revel's Row, Borough, in 1855, he discovered that most of 'the Row' consisted largely of brothels. 'What a reflection! Brothels – and known to be such – adjoining a police station. However it was so for many a year, and, as far as I know, they met with no interference'.[30] In general, it is frequent to find the disorderly and occasionally corrupt or violent nature of relations between the police and the policed contrasted with the better, more reasonable condition evident at the time of writing.[31]

A central feature of Victorian social investigation is the comparison of the urban explorer with their colonial counterpart entering a foreign land. Former CID detective inspector John Sweeney perhaps illustrates this most literally in his stories of the East End from the late 1870s to the early twentieth century, in which he describes the 'considerable amount of trouble' caused by the aliens 'who flock in such numbers from the Continent'.[32] He records the extent to which the aliens have 'flooded' the area and largely ousted the native population, not only in the east of the city but also in Soho, which is 'thoroughly a foreign colony'; 'dealing with these people is like dealing with a large rabbit warren'.[33] However, amongst his condemnation, he does admit that:

> in common fairness it must be said that as a class they exhibit many good qualities. They are shrewd and clever; as may be expected, this is particularly true of the Jewish section. They are temperate, and work industriously, their aptitude for labour being considerable.[34]

One of the principal drivers of colonial exploration was, of course, missionary activity, and once again there are close parallels with some configurations of police work. Of course, the link between police work and missionary activity is long established in the literature. For Carolyn Steedman

> the policeman was the target of those organizations that sought to find in the archetype of the respectable working man both the secular counterpart of the missionary (walking daily through hidden haunts), and the guard (protecting the respectable from onslaught).[35]

The police life was aligned with the puritan soul's personal journey to salvation through a life of 'obedience, sobriety and decency', so that '[b]y 1876 it was possible for an officer to speak quite naturally of the police forces of England as "the cloth"'.[36]

For Robert Storch the link between police and missionary activity was that policing formed '[t]he other side of the coin of middle-class voluntaristic moral and social reform'.[37] The police were missionaries in the sense that, like the temperance, educational and recreational reform movements, they sought to shape working-class life into a moral, disciplined form, principally by suppressing traditional working-class recreational and street activities. It was this attempt to introduce an alien form of discipline into working-class communities that generated the resentment and hostility manifest in frequent assaults on policemen in the course of their duty.

However, it is clear from police memoirs that, if one side of the 'missionary' dimension of the police role involves the apparent imposition of middle-class values on some sections of the working class through disciplinary activity, we also need to recognize that the relationship between policing and missionary work had another dimension, providing another set of largely working-class men, policemen, with a way of rendering their social role meaningful. These twin roles of guard and missionary were central to the ways in which policemen sought to give meaning to the years of sacrifice, hard work, public misunderstanding and occasional violence they experienced by relating their role to notions of duty which emphasized the essentially masculine nature of the calling to serve the public in a role that was at once protective and missionary.

Perhaps no work better illustrates this phenomenon than Jerome Caminada's memoirs of his life as head of the detective force in late nineteenth-century Manchester. His recollections focus principally on analysing crimes and criminals in terms of categories of offence and offenders, very much an ethnography of criminal cultures, something carried out for public information as:

> [i]t is a truism that one half of the world does not know how the other half lives. In this great city we have, side by side with enormous wealth and luxury, an inconceivable amount of squalor, misery, degradation, and filthiness of life.[38]

At the same time he defined his role very clearly in moral, missionary terms, seeing his task as releasing the binds that drew the poor into a life of dissipation and vice. His recollections begin 'in the vicious streets around to which my thoughts are at the same time directed, "the wicked never ceased from troubling, nor were the weary ever at rest," for their fitful midnight slumbers gave place, as daylight broke, to the restlessness of evil'.[39] There is a great emphasis on dirt, squalor and sin and the relationship between the physical environment and immorality and the ways in which even those who strove to be virtuous could easily be drawn into vice. In Angel Meadows, 'a district deeply stained with drunkenness, debauchery, crime and vice in every shape – the prevailing callousness of which it was painful to behold . . . that modern Gomorrah – that abscess in the side of a great and wealthy city', he described his role in terms of the rescue of souls from the slide into crime, following a theory of 'criminal progress' as a reversal of the soul's journey to salvation.[40] The present system, which he sought to reform, entrapped men in a life of sin and crime from which he wished to rescue them:

> Alas! Is this dark mantle of sin never to be lifted? Are we to pass by our bruised and wounded brethern Levite-like; or are we to say with the good Samaritan, 'He who has fallen among thieves must be cared for?' Practical treatment will do more for their welfare than all the tracts and pious exhortations that can be given.[41]

Like so many others, Caminada's work was partly a campaign for the comprehension of the public, arguing that a good policeman must possess 'tact, patience and courage', being 'brave enough to face the most formidable ruffian', 'qualities for which, it is to be feared, the majority of the public seldom give him credit'. Accordingly he hoped that '[t]hese stories may tend to illustrate the difficulties and dangers of a policeman's life, and at the same time be the means of arousing the interest and sympathy of the public in favour of a body of men always at its service'.[42] But it was also a campaign against the arguments that conditions of poverty could not be improved, and against the 'self-constituted custodians of the morality of the city', the 'fanatical promoters of social progress, who would put out our pipes, stop our beer, deprive the old woman of her snuff, and who, to keep our criminal propensities in check, would substitute vegetables for beef'. These people were not only excessively puritan, they also had not fully understood the social situation that produced crime.[43]

For Caminada, then, the role of the detective was not to sit and cogitate on the problems of crime like the sleuths of detective fiction, or to provide theoretical solutions to the 'social problem'. Rather, through his detailed knowledge of the 'unknown England' of the criminal underworld and the poorest sections of society, which, like the urban explorer, he was able to enter and leave at will, the policeman was able to intervene in a material and physical way in order to prevent at least some souls from falling into a life of vice and crime. His memoirs stood both as an illustration of the true nature of the social problem, as it was hidden from most respectable observers, and as a testament to the bravery of the police who risked their own well-being by entering this world in order to effect some practical aid to the helpless.

Courage, violence and suffering

In police memoirs considerable effort is expended on descriptions of the criminal underworld and the character types, crimes and modes of life found within it. Clearly much of this is for public entertainment, but it is also, I have argued, central to the more fundamental argument that theoretical reflection on the problem of crime or particular cases was simply a trope of fiction, and that real police work depended upon personal experience of criminals and the world they lived in. Real police work depended upon penetrating the underworld and upon practical and often bodily intervention in criminal life. Only in this way could social improvement be effected.

It is here, in the bodily intervention in the world of crime and the problem of vice, and in the bravery and physical capacity to enter into the most challenging urban environments, that police masculinity overlaps with the ways in which policemen configured their wider social role. Even the figure of the *flâneur*, so central to the tradition of urban spectatorship that characterized social investigation, was generally configured as a fundamentally masculine character, albeit one increasingly competing with other classes and genders in their exploration of the city.[44] However, the *flâneur* was essentially a detached, bourgeois observer; the policeman was a working-class man required to engage physically with a resistant population. Accordingly, it is no surprise that the form of masculinity deployed by policemen in order to enforce a rather different kind of mastery over the city was significantly different from the distant bourgeois *flâneur*. In this section I go on to explore the ways in which policemen wrote about their experience of violence in general, and in particular the extent to which this related to the successful pursuit of their mission.

Turning first to the police newspapers, it is clear that, although the campaign for pension rights and fair conditions of service was probably the dominant element in their pages, another element that was ubiquitous in these publications was the issue of violence against policemen, and it was in relation to this experience of violence that a particular kind of physical police masculinity was defined. These journals were produced and contributed to by rank-and-file officers, and were by no means a tool for expressing the opinions of the police authorities themselves. Accordingly, they might be taken as a good representation of the common experiences of the ordinary policeman.

Almost every issue contains some accounts of violence, be they brief and apparently random, as in the assault on some constables in Marylebone recorded in the *Police Guardian* in February 1875, or the lengthier description the following month of the large riot in Alnwick in which a policeman suffered a fatal heart attack when surrounded by several thousand men and under assault from fists and stones.[45] Violent encounters with soldiers of various kinds seem to have been relatively common, and often quite brutal.[46] Poaching was also a source of potential violence, with one officer recorded as being beaten, kicked and hit with thick sticks when attempting to arrest a group of poachers.[47] Perhaps most common, however, was the general violence meted out to the police by 'roughs' of all kinds. One incident in Birmingham is recorded in which an officer attempts to arrest the ringleaders of a gang of roughs who had killed a dog by pelting it with broken bricks. He had his own skull broken in 'a desperate affray' in which the officers who came to his aid were attacked with missiles and knives.[48] As Archer points out, the use of weapons was often considered 'unmanly' or 'un-English'; however, it is clear that in practice the use of weapons was commonplace, and part of the masculinity required of police was their ability to withstand assault against them, often whilst possessing inferior weapons themselves.[49]

Such incidents were recorded as being depressingly common, with one officer noting that 'in the majority of cases of assaults on Police their assailants are composed principally of the lowest class, who appear to imagine that every defenceless P.C. who crosses their path is to be made a target for their cowardly and brutal assaults'.[50] Unlike the cowardly roughs who ganged up on a relatively defenceless officer patrolling alone, the policeman had to be courageous enough to face gangs of opponents with little support. The officer drew attention to his own experience:

> Not long ago it was my lot to be attacked by a gang of about 50 as blood-thirsty rascals as could be met with in the South of London. I did my best and in the end was kicked all over the road before assistance arrived, and then only after a long struggle we got one of the gang to the station.[51]

This concern with violence was a regular feature of the *Police Review*. Although much of the *Review* was taken up with inquiries about the application of particular laws in particular circumstances, and it included a wide range of features useful to the self-improvement of the police officer, such as an educational column that gave the men samples of arithmetic, paragraphs for dictation practice, spelling, quizzes about laws and so on, it never failed to record instances of violence against the police. For example, in January 1895 a 'savage assault' on a police constable in Portsmouth was recorded, following which it was noted that in large towns the police were always sent into 'the slums' in pairs.[52] In the same issue some officers in Whitechapel were commended for dealing with a man throwing tiles from a roof onto passers by, despite his attempts to attack them.[53] Indeed, every issue included a section 'assaults on police', in this instance detailing not only the above incidents, but also a further attack in Canterbury, three in London, one in Southampton, two in Staffordshire, one in Wolverhampton and an incident in Maidstone, described at length, in which an officer was kicked to the ground by two men who had originally called for his assistance in a dispute with a landlady.[54] Despite their stated intention to kill him, the officer managed to struggle to a nearby house where the owner attempted to shelter him, while the assailants sought to break down the door to continue their attack, before being arrested 'after a tough struggle' by a second officer who arrived to assist the first, who had recovered sufficiently from a brief period of unconsciousness to aid his companion.[55]

All told, eleven assaults on police are recorded in this week's issue of the paper. Although the more sensational events and crimes are accorded more space, the regularity of the appearance of stories of serious violence against the police, and in particular the column on 'assaults on police' present in every issue, indicates that, despite the brevity of the latter, the issue of violence against the police was one of the principal ways in which officers understood the nature of their task and their relationship to the public, on whose behalf they suffered and from who they received little recognition. These records of violence against the police reinforced the perception that a central element of the policeman's role was to face violence and danger on a regular basis.

Given the regularity and often the savagery of these incidents, it is unsurprising that, upon commending Detective Sergeant Partridge on his thirty years of service in September 1895, Sir John Bridge, the magistrate at Bow Street Police Court, felt able to describe 'the great qualification of a useful Police Sergeant' as 'being absolutely without fear', while being possessed of a gentle and mild manner. 'Of course the great qualification of a Police Officer is courage, the next is gentleness, and the utter absence of all swagger'.[56] This combination of courage and temperateness was vital, because it enabled the policeman to face great danger and provocation, while remaining calm enough to deal with the situation in the correct legal manner and without losing his temper and resorting to unnecessary force himself. The *Police Review* was, for example, highly critical of those officers who resorted to violence: 'This habit of Constables striking men is a detestable and abominable practice', and it was frequently compounded by the 'diabolical custom of bringing a counter charge against anyone who threatens to be troublesome in order to shut their mouths and vitiate their testimony'.[57]

It is clear, then, from its ubiquitous presence in the police journals that the experience of public hostility and violence played a significant role in the formation of a sense that the police were a community somewhat apart, if not at times under siege, from the rest of society, and largely misunderstood by them. A central element of police masculinity was the ability to face the 'cowardly' or 'savage' violence of 'roughs', often acting in numbers, with temperateness and courage.

Given the regularity of these events it is unsurprising that their experience of violence and danger also played a central role in attempts by policemen to convey a sense of their role to the public at large through their memoirs. In doing so they indicated not only how much the police officer suffered on behalf of an ungrateful public, but also that their ability to carry out their task successfully depended upon their manly capacity to engage with physical force. Many of these tales are simply stories of the arduous nature of night duty and the common 'first night' story of having to drag an insensible drunk back to the police station.[58] However, many others suffered far more serious hardship on behalf of the public.

Superintendent James Bent's tales are full of horrific assaults on himself and other officers and these assaults seem to have been the focal points around which the trajectory of his career was measured. Bent served in the Manchester division of the Lancashire police, essentially the area comprising the outskirts of Manchester that did not fall into the old city boundary. He served in Pendleton and Longsight before becoming an inspector in Prestwich and eventually commanding the entire

Manchester division from Old Trafford. His reason for recording his memoirs for the public was that his career had been 'an exceedingly eventful one' marked by 'dangers encountered and overcome', which he felt would give an insight into 'the risks, and the inner workings of police life of which the public at large can have little idea'.[59]

In August 1860 Bent attempted to arrest an armed escaped convict in Culceth Brow, Newton Heath. While attempting to drag the convict out of his mother's house by the heels he was repeatedly struck around the head with a cane topped with a lump of lead, 'inflicting a wound from which the blood flowed freely, blinding me entirely'.[60] He was then struck on the head with a poker, partially stunned, and the dog was set on him, before being beaten with a truncheon taken from his fellow officer, upon which he found that 'partial paralysis had set in'.[61] His head had been 'so pummelled that it was a long time before I was able to resume my duties, and even to this day I often feel the effects of the injuries'.[62] Also while stationed in Newton Heath, he heard complaints that his men were being assaulted by the workers of a steelworks in Miles Platting. Bent took as many men as possible and surrounded the steelworks. Upon approaching one of the workers a hammer was swung at him, but missed – 'had he succeeded there is no doubt I should have been killed in an instant' – upon which he attempted to arrest the man.[63] The disturbance brought 'about thirty' men running into the yard, 'all armed with red-hot iron bars which they had drawn from various furnaces. I was struck by them several times, and my grasp of the prisoner was again broken and I fell', following which he was attacked again. 'A fellow caught me on the head, inflicting a severe wound which penetrated to the bone', after which he was beaten repeatedly on the ground, using his hands to fight off the bars which were 'so pliable with the heat that they got entangled with each other'.[64]

Bent found himself promoted to inspector and rewarded for his courage and dedication to his job, but he was unable to work for some time 'and I do not think I have passed a week since without experiencing very severe pain in the head, and occasional attacks of dizziness, things which were quite unknown to me before the assault'.[65] That these accounts are related at all is interesting enough as an example of the way Bent wished to portray his suffering on behalf of the public. However, these accounts are also at pivotal moments in his narrative. The first account above is the first chapter of the book and earned him a reward, and the second is the one that is pivotal in his becoming an inspector. There is a direct correlation between his suffering for his duty and his rise through the service to new heights.

Bent was far from alone in his account of violence towards the police and its role in shaping his career, nor in the more general emphasis on the importance of masculine physicality to success. John Sweeney emphasized the importance of his early athleticism to his later success in the police, detailing his abilities at boxing, running, wrestling, cricket and hockey. One of his cousins had been world record holder for the high jump.[66] As he put it:

[t]he strength and activity which I thus acquired stood me in excellent stead when I became one of the Force. I often had to give chase to someone who was "wanted", and I invariably ran down my quarry; I went through many sharp encounters with roughs, but I never received really severe punishment.[67]

Even in the detective service there was a degree of physical exertion. As Fuller put it, '[d]etectives have rough work to do and must learn betimes to endure harshness, which can only be learned early and in a rough school'.[68] George Greenham, a former chief inspector in the CID who joined the Metropolitan Police in 1869, concurred: 'The next danger that a detective has often to encounter is the possibility of being stabbed, shot, or otherwise assaulted by determined criminals'. He records various incidents of risk, particularly one in which he was almost strangled.[69] For Sweeney, these dangers affected the qualities that a detective needed to possess: 'He must have perseverance, presence of mind and resourcefulness; he cannot be too strong physically; and he should know his London well, that he may not let himself be decoyed into some *cul de sac* and there quietly disposed of.'[70] Even the apparently straightforward work of shadowing suspects was not without its trials:

> this 'shadowing' is not light work. Day or night, rain or shine, the 'shadower' must follow his quarry's every movement. The detective knows that at any moment the man followed may realize himself pursued, and turn on the pursuer with a knife or revolver; the detective does not know when relief may come.[71]

In short, the detective required just as much strength and courage as the beat officer; he too might find himself under attack from unexpected quarters, in numbers or with weapons. Far from sitting in his study and solving crimes in his mind, the real detective needed to be courageous enough to face danger and physically robust enough to be out in all weathers, or to hunt down and capture his often dangerous quarry.

Andrew Lansdowne's memoirs of detective life are unusually devoid of accounts of violence, although there are one or two situations described that involve real danger. However, it is striking that in conclusion he gives his reasons for leaving the force as follows:

> there comes a time in a man's life when dangers of no ordinary kind are not to be faced with the equanimity of youth. It is not because his courage grows old as he ages, but experience cannot be set aside, and where Ignorance will dare and do, merely because it does not know the risk, Knowledge counsels caution and even hesitation. To use an apt quotation, 'Fools rush in where angels fear to tread.'[72]

Clearly the experienced middle-aged man is not able to act with the immediacy of the courageous youth, who is perhaps not quite as courageous as he seems, being slightly insensible of the real scale of the danger involved.

Despite making little reference to the dangers of police work throughout the stories that comprise the book itself, Lansdowne concludes by defining danger as central to policing:

> Do not suppose that I insist upon this point for personal reasons. I should pass it by wholly if it were not for the fact that an account of the life of a police detective would be incomplete without some reference to the dangers of death which beset the calling, and which every detective in the service must be prepared to run.[73]

He goes on to give an account of an attempt to arrest a man for passing stolen cheques, upon which the man draws a revolver and attempts to kill him, only failing because he had forgotten to fill all five chambers of his revolver, and by chance it was the empty chamber that was presented to Lansdowne. There followed a quarter of an hour's physical struggle in which Lansdowne fought for his life, unaided by a fearful public, until a passing coalman came to his aid.[74] For Lansdowne, then, the capacity to face danger and death, and to overcome these dangers in a physical struggle, was fundamental to police work in general, and the ability to be a detective in particular.

These hard lessons remained the norm when Frank Wensley joined the Metropolitan Police in 1887, serving first in Lambeth. Like the contributor to the *Police Review* above, Wensley records that '[m]ost of the inhabitants of my new division considered that they had a natural right to get fighting drunk and knock a policeman about whenever the spirit moved them. Bruises and worse were our routine lot.'[75] His first lesson came in a street off the New Cut, when he intervened in a drunken quarrel and was thrown through the window of a pub for his trouble.[76] His second lesson in the rigours of policing came when he reprimanded a group emerging 'in high spirits' from a boxing saloon for blocking his path: 'They got me down and jumped on me – there were no ethical rules in the Lambeth code for a rough-and-tumble with a policeman. I thought every rib in my body was broken.' He was only rescued because the tallest member of the force happened to be passing and came to his aid. He too was 'pretty badly mauled' before further help arrived. The extent of his injuries was such that Wensley was laid up for four months after this attack.[77]

These events are recorded at the very beginning of Wensley's text, not only because they occurred at the start of his career, but also because they represented a rite of passage for the new policeman, a lesson in the kind of job he had signed up for. The pivotal role that physical engagement with violence played in most police memoirs, and the constant presence of stories and records of violence in the police newspapers, suggest that many officers saw the ability to deploy a physical masculinity as central to their ability to carry out the tasks of policing successfully.

Conclusion

Drawing particularly on the published memoirs of policemen, the principal device by which members of the police sought to present themselves and their worth to the public at large, and supported by statements from trade journals that emphasize similar sentiments in the conversations policemen had with one another, this chapter argues that masculinity played a fundamental role in attempts to configure policing as a meaningful activity. For many policemen it was their masculine physicality that gave them the capacity to negotiate the violent and dangerous streets of the Victorian underworld.

The police memoir functioned in a manner similar to the accounts of social explorers that were so popular at the same time, anatomizing the world of crime and types of criminals as if they were an alien culture, set apart from the rest of civilized society. The wider moral message of these texts, like those of the urban explorers, emphasized the irony that even in the most advanced and civilized nation there were great enclaves of incivility, vice and crime just a stone's throw away from the gleaming wealth of the Victorian metropolis. This underworld was simultaneously completely self-contained, a culture apart, with its own values and patterns entirely distinct from those of civilized society; and yet it was also permeable and seductive, easy to be drawn into, even for those born outside of its influence, but difficult to escape, particularly for those born within its embrace and who had little knowledge of the values and morals of the respectable.[78]

The greatest irony of all was that, being a distinct culture set apart from normal society, the public were largely unaware of its true nature in the ordinary run of their lives; moreover, most of the information they thought they possessed about it was based on the fictional accounts of mystery writers that greatly misrepresented its nature and the best way to deal with it. The police memoir sought to make clear that it was only through the activities of the police that this world could be known, governed and its effects mitigated. This knowledge was not gained through the disengaged gaze of the *flâneur*, nor were crime or social problems solved by thinking about them in a study in the way that social reformers or fictional detectives seemed to deal with the world's ills. Rather, the ability to deal with crime and poverty depended upon the capacity of the police to enter the underworld and engage bodily with criminals, something that depended on their physical masculinity: their courage in the face of danger, their strength and their ability to endure hardship. This was not straightforwardly the 'hard man' toughness of the Victorian 'rough', although policemen needed to be equal to their challenge in order to maintain their authority over the streets. Nor was it simply the more gentlemanly manliness of the 'plucky chap'. Rather, this was a more complex physical masculinity in which the capacity to give and receive violence in a physical encounter was fundamental to the ability to pass through the underworld streets and maintain authority in them, while at the same time enabling the officer to bring respectable values to the outcast and perhaps save some of them from lifelong servitude to vice. It was the capacity of the policeman to endure personal danger and frequent assault with equanimity that enabled him to penetrate the dark and dangerous parts of the city that were foreign territory to the respectable members of society, without descending into brutality himself. Without this steadfastness and physical prowess, the practice of policing, which depended upon detailed personal knowledge of, and to some extent the respect of, the criminal classes, would not be possible.

Notes

1 Most notable are C. Emsley, *Hard Men: The English and Violence since 1750*, London: Hambledon Continuum, 2005; M. J. Wiener, *Men of Blood: Violence, Manliness, and Criminal Justice in Victorian England*, Cambridge: Cambridge University Press, 2004; and J. C. Wood, *Violence and Crime in Nineteenth-Century England: The Shadow of our Refinement*, London: Routledge, 2004.
2 C. Emsley, *The Great British Bobby: A History of British Policing from the Eighteenth Century to the Present*, London: Quercus, 2009, pp. 144–76 (pp. 144–5, 149).
3 Emsley, *Hard Men*, pp. ix, 135 and generally 131–46.
4 Ibid., p. 135. On the working-class nature of police recruits, see H. Shpayer-Makov, 'The Making of a Police Labour Force', *Journal of Social History*, 1990–1, vol. 24, pp. 109–34; H. Shpayer-Makov, *The Making of a Policeman: A Social History of a Labour Force in Metropolitan London, 1829–1914*, Aldershot: Ashgate, 2002; and H. Shpayer-Makov, 'Explaining the Rise and Success of Detective Memoirs in Britain', in C. Emsley and H. Shpayer-Makov (eds), *Police Detectives in History, 1750–1950*, Aldershot: Ashgate, 2006, pp. 103–33 (p. 103).
5 J. E. Archer, ' "Men Behaving Badly"?: Masculinity and the Uses of Violence, 1850–1900', and A. Davies, 'Youth Gangs, Gender and Violence, 1870–1900, in S. D'Cruze (ed.), *Everyday Violence in Britain, 1850–1950: Gender and Class*, London: Longman, 2000, pp. 41–54, 70–85.
6 On which see particularly C. Emsley, *Policing and its Context, 1750–1870*, Basingstoke: Macmillan, 1983; Shpayer-Makov, *Making of a Policeman*; C. Steedman, *Policing the Victorian Community: The Formation of English Provincial Police Forces, 1856–80*, London: Routledge, 1984; and D. Taylor, *Policing the Victorian Town: The Development of the Police in Middlesbrough, c. 1840–1914*, Basingstoke: Palgrave Macmillan, 2002.
7 Shpayer-Makov, *Making of a Policeman*; and Taylor, *Policing the Victorian Town*, pp. 113–15.
8 Emsley, *Policing and its Context*, pp. 82–5.
9 *The Police Review and Parade Gossip: Organ of the British Constabulary*, vol. I, 2 January 1893, p. 1.
10 C. Emsley, *The English Police: A Political and Social History*, 2nd edn, London: Longman, 1996, pp. 99–103.
11 P. Lawrence, ' "Scoundrels and Scallywags and Some Honest Men . . .": Memoirs and the Self-Image of French and English Policemen, c. 1870–1939', in B. Godfrey, C. Emsley and G. Dunstall (eds), *Comparative Histories of Crime*, Cullompton: Willan, 2003, pp. 125–44 (pp. 128, 130, 139–40); and also his ' "Images of Poverty and Crime": Police Memoirs in England and France at the end of the Nineteenth Century', *Crime, Histoire & Sociétés/Crime, History & Societies*, 2000, vol. 4, pp. 63–82.
12 Shpayer-Makov, 'Explaining the Rise', pp. 115, 116.
13 A. Lansdowne, *A Life's Reminiscences of Scotland Yard: In One-and-Twenty Dockets*, London: Leadenhall Press, 1890, p. 2.
14 Shpayer-Makov, 'Explaining the Rise', pp. 104–7.

15 Lawrence, 'Scoundrels', pp. 128, 139–40; Shpayer-Makov, 'Explaining the Rise', p. 117.
16 Lawrence, ' "Scoundrels" '; Shpayer-Makov, 'Explaining the Rise'.
17 For an interesting analysis of the devices of realist fiction, see L. R. Furst, *All is True: The Claims and Strategies of Realist Fiction*, London: Duke University Press, 1995.
18 Lawrence, ' "Scoundrels" ', p. 131.
19 H. White, *The Content of the Form: Narrative Discourse and Historical Representation*, Baltimore: Johns Hopkins University Press, 1987.
20 R. A. Fuller, *Recollections of a Detective*, London: John Long, 1912, p. 17.
21 Lansdowne, *A Life's Reminiscences*, pp. 1–2.
22 H. White, *Tropics of Discourse: Essays in Cultural Criticism*, Baltimore: Johns Hopkins University Press, 1978, pp. 86, 88.
23 See D. Englander and R. O'Day (eds), *Retrieved Riches: Social Investigation in Britain, 1840–1914*, Aldershot: Scolar Press, 1995; and J. R. Walkowitz, *City of Dreadful Delight: Narratives of Sexual Danger in Late Victorian London*, Chicago: Chicago University Press, 1992, pp. 15–39.
24 D. Epstein Nord, 'The Social Explorer as Anthropologist: Victorian Travellers among the Urban Poor', in W. Sharp and L. Wallock (eds), *Visions of the Modern City: Essays in History, Art, and Literature*, Baltimore: Johns Hopkins University Press, 1987, pp. 122–34.
25 J. Buzard, *Disorienting Fiction: The Autoethnographic Work of Nineteenth Century British Novels*, Princeton, NJ: Princeton University Press, 2005, pp. 12–13, 28, 34 and *passim*.
26 See F. P. Wensley, *Detective Days: The Record of Forty-Two Years' Service in the Criminal Investigation Department*, London: Cassell, 1931, pp. 12, 17–18.
27 Fuller, *Recollections*, pp. 15–16.
28 Ibid., pp. 21–2.
29 Ibid., pp. 22–3.
30 T. Cavanagh, *Scotland Yard Past and Present: Experiences of Thirty-Seven Years*, London: Chatto and Windus, 1893, p. 10.
31 See, for example, J. Caminada, *Twenty-Five Years of Detective Life*, vol. 1, Manchester: Heywood, 1895, p. 17.
32 J. Sweeney, *At Scotland Yard: Being the Experiences During Twenty-Seven Years' Service of John Sweeney, Late Detective Inspector, Criminal Investigation Department, New Scotland Yard*, ed. F. Richards, London: Grant Richards, 1904, p. 297.
33 Ibid., pp. 300–7.
34 Ibid., p. 311.
35 Steedman, *Policing*, p. 144.
36 Ibid., pp. 145–6.
37 R. D. Storch, 'The Policeman as Domestic Missionary: Urban Discipline and Popular Culture in Northern England, 1850–1880', *Journal of Social History*, 1975–6, vol. 9, pp. 481–509 (p. 481).
38 Caminada, *Twenty-Five Years*, vol. 2, p. x.
39 Ibid., vol. 1, p. 9.
40 Ibid., vol. 1, p. 12
41 Ibid., vol. 1, p. 20
42 Ibid., vol. 2, Preface.
43 Ibid., vol. 2, pp. xiv–xv, 484, 486 and generally 484–91.
44 J. Rignall, *Realist Fiction and the Strolling Spectator*, London: Routledge, 1992, p. 3; and Walkowitz, *City of Dreadful Delight*, pp. 15–80.
45 *The Police Guardian: A Newspaper Devoted to the Interests of the Police & Constabulary of the United Kingdom & the Colonies*, 26 February 1875, p. 4 and 12 March 1875, p. 6.

46 See, for example, *Police Guardian*, 12 February 1875 and 19 April 1878, p. 5.
47 Ibid., 19 April 1878, p. 3.
48 Ibid., 24 May 1878, p. 3.
49 Archer, '"Men Behaving Badly"', pp. 43–6.
50 *Police Review*, Vol. V, 27 August 1897, p. 411.
51 Ibid., p. 411.
52 *Police Review*, Vol. III, January 1895, p. 6.
53 Ibid., p. 8.
54 Ibid., pp. 11–12.
55 Ibid., p. 11.
56 Ibid., September, p. 427.
57 *Police Review*, Vol. III, April 1895, p. 164.
58 See, for example, Cavanagh, *Scotland Yard*, pp. 28, 30.
59 J. Bent, *Criminal Life: Reminiscences of Forty-Two Years as a Police Officer*, Manchester: Heywood, 1891, p. vii.
60 Ibid., p. 5
61 Ibid., pp. 6, 7
62 Ibid., p. 8
63 Ibid., p. 76
64 Ibid., p. 77
65 Ibid., pp. 79–80.
66 Sweeney, *At Scotland Yard*, pp. 1–2.
67 Ibid., pp. 2–3.
68 Fuller, *Recollections*, p. 18.
69 G. H. Greenham, *Scotland Yard Experiences from the Diary of G. H. Greenham, Late Chief Inspector, Criminal Investigation Dept.*, London: George Routledge, 1904, quotation at p. 68. See also pp. 92–3 and the rather anti-climactic story at pp. 69–74.
70 Sweeney, *At Scotland Yard*, pp. 35–6.
71 Ibid., p. 35.
72 Lansdowne, *A Life's Reminiscences*, p. 183.
73 Ibid., p. 184.
74 Ibid., pp. 186–7.
75 Wensley, *Detective Days*, p. 8.
76 Ibid., p. 2.
77 Ibid., p. 2.
78 Caminada, *Twenty-Five Years*, vol. 1, pp. 12, 18–20.

6

SHEDDING THE UNIFORM AND ACQUIRING A NEW MASCULINE IMAGE

The case of the late-Victorian and Edwardian English police detective

Haia Shpayer-Makov

One of the distinctive aspects of the police labour force in Victorian and Edwardian Britain was its all-male character. No woman in the period under discussion ever became an integral part of either the uniformed or the plain-clothes units. If women were occasionally employed, it was on a temporary basis and in an unofficial capacity, as will be discussed below. On the whole, the imposition of law and order was the preserve of men. Only during the First World War did women start entering the police workforce.[1] Thus, by the sheer absence of women, the modern police network, formed in the middle decades of the nineteenth century, was conceived as a masculine occupation. This state of affairs was the result of a conscious decision on the part of policy makers – all men – who shared the general world view that jobs requiring strength and the use of force were best performed by men.[2] They were, no doubt, also guided by the long-standing notion that the status of occupations and their practitioners rested upon the exclusion of women.[3] Added to the denial of equal opportunity for women was the commonly held paternalist attitude that presumed to protect women from the risks inherent in police work.[4]

The founders of the modern English police (first in London in 1829) and their successors were determined, albeit without acknowledging this explicitly, to build a force that not only would be based on the labour of men, but also would be imbued with and convey distinctly masculine attributes and values. First and foremost, power was central to an occupation designed to enforce law and order in society, and masculinity was consistently equated with power well beyond the gender relationship.[5] Furthermore, intrinsic to the formation of the modern police in Britain specifically was a focus on crime prevention and deterrence rather than on detection. To contemporary policy makers this principle mandated a pronounced male corporality in the form of a continuous presence of uniformed police patrols in the streets. The uniform conferred power and authority on the bearer and served to enhance his standing as representing the patriarchal state. In addition to eliciting deference to the new forces of law and order, the authorities were also anxious to legitimize the policing function and gain widespread acceptance of it.[6] At the same time, they faced deep-seated concerns by the public lest the new police resemble a standing army.[7] They attempted, therefore, to play down the military features of the police. Patrol officers wore a blue (not red) uniform and top hats (from 1864 helmets), and carried no weapons except for a wooden truncheon.[8] However, to project the necessary awe and clout, the officer had to have a physique that communicated the might possessed by the police and underscored their role in society. Police officers were expected to be strong in order to overpower persons if an offence was committed, to convey an image of manliness to deter potential offenders, and to be conspicuous in case help was needed.[9]

To attain these ends, all recruits to the police had to be exceptionally tall, sturdy, healthy, young and capable of sustained physical exertion (in addition to being literate and in possession of a good character reference).[10] 'The physical strength and constitution of each applicant' were in fact more important than the 'standard of educational acquirements'.[11] Once he entered service, his body was constantly subject to correction. In a concentrated period of learning immediately after acceptance, continuing thereafter even as a fully-fledged constable, drill was rigorously imposed as a disciplinary technique both for the body and for the mind and will.[12] The heightened masculinity of the police officer's body thus reinforced the manly features imparted by his uniform.

The surplus of police candidates during the period allowed the authorities to select men whose health and physical qualities were well above those of the average working man.[13] Not surprisingly, their imposing constitution attracted the desired attention.[14] On a visit to London, a former New York police commissioner could not but be highly impressed at the sight of the 'commanding figure of the London policeman, standing serene, potent, and dignified amidst the crush in the congested thoroughfares'.[15] Although for much of the nineteenth century beat officers were also the subject of jokes and ridicule,[16] often focusing on 'the love-making of the policeman, by which he obtains good suppers from credulous cooks, and weighty money-gifts from soft-hearted housemaids',[17] the references to the officers' sexual appeal presented them as virile men.

Moreover, as the century progressed, the 'popular notion that the policeman is the wielder of power' grew stronger, in part as a consequence of the officers' public presence and the authority they conveyed.[18] The author, journalist and social reformer Harriet Martineau, in comparing soldiers and policemen, found that while the soldier resembled 'a machine moved by the voice of his officer . . . the policeman is absolute on his beat'.[19] In her view, 'the crowd opens to make way for the policeman: he commands help from men, and they yield it: he imposes quiet on women, and they stop brawling: he looks at children, and they slink out of sight'.[20] This view was shared by a growing number of people, including those of working-class origin, who were slower to acquiesce to police activities and the newly acquired social status of the police. By the beginning of the new century, the perception that Britain, and London in particular, had a reliable – and perhaps the best – police force in the world was widespread in 'respectable' society.[21] A unifying depiction in the mainstream press was that the policeman met the prime attributes of hegemonic manliness – impressive physique, authority and virility.

To become a detective, a police officer had to shed his uniform. This chapter examines how the transition from policeman to detective affected the officer's manly image. How did police authorities mould and preserve the masculine identity of detectives in the vocation's formative period from the 1840s to the First World War? No less importantly, as 'public affirmation was . . . absolutely central to masculine status',[22] did public discourse accord with the police leadership's objective and perceive detectives as broadly associated with masculinity? The contemporary media illuminate this issue, not only reflecting current popular sentiments but also shaping them. Although police goals and policies dictated the nature of detective work, and hence the detective's persona, the media, too, played a significant role in constructing his identity, as most people had no contact with detectives and learnt about them from the written word.

A large amount of printed matter about detectives was available to the growing literate public of the time. Although detectives remained a small minority in each police department and in the general police body throughout the period, their exploits featured prominently in the press and in fictional works – the prime sites in which the detective image was both moulded and contested. The literary world dedicated considerable, and growing, attention to police detectives, but it was the press, with its insatiable appetite for the topic, that was widely assumed to provide the most authentic descriptions of reality in general and of detectives in particular. Moreover, police detectives, conscious of their reputation and self-image, contributed to the perceptions of themselves through published memoirs. Police journals, too, sketched the life histories of police detectives.[23] These forms of print culture will be discussed in the context of the detectives' notions of their manliness.

Although no single definition of manhood existed in Britain in this period,[24] and perceptions of masculinity were not restricted to one class or another, certain masculine attributes tended to be related to a specific class. It will be argued here that, although most police detectives belonged to the working class and some to the lower middle class, the manly ideals they came to represent transcended class. In addressing the masculine image of an increasingly important figure in the gallery of Victorian and Edwardian stereotypes, this chapter will add to our understanding both of the police detective's image in the period and, more broadly, of the role this image played in society.

A marginal role for women

Almost without exception, police detectives were recruited from the existing pool of uniformed officers throughout the period.[25] This in itself ensured the identification of police detection as a male occupation. In addition to the reasons cited above for barring the uniformed ranks to women, a decisive factor in excluding them from detective work was the premise that 'what a man cannot discover, a woman would have but scant chance of finding out', as stated in an article in the *Saturday Review*, which came to the defence of the police during the unsuccessful pursuit of Jack the Ripper.[26] This perspective, which assumed the inferiority of women when it came not only to physical strength but also to mental ability and social status, rationalized the gendered discrimination. Moreover, if the French philosopher and psychoanalyst Jacques Lacan is correct in defining the detective as 'the agent of patriarchy who enforces the Law-of-the-Father', then women were obviously not the appropriate choice to fulfil this specific policing mission.[27]

Quite a few commentators disagreed with this exclusionary standpoint, and suggestions to see women employed in the ranks of the detective police were voiced from time to time in print.[28] The growing number of fictional female detectives who were featured in novels and stories from the 1860s onwards indicates that the idea was not uncommon, and that some men did not think it unreasonable for women to be competent criminal investigators, both as amateurs and as employees of the police.[29] As early as 1864, Mrs G., the protagonist of *The Female Detective*, affirmed that 'the woman detective has far greater opportunities than a man of intimate watching, and of keeping her eyes upon matters near which a man could not conveniently play the eavesdropper'.[30] In fact, often, such as in the Loveday Brooke stories written by Catherine Louisa Pirkis, the female detective character is more impressive than her male counterparts.[31] At times, for example during the search for Jack the Ripper, some newspapers suggested the recruitment of women ('within due limits') into the detective police as a way of improving the service.[32] Despite implicit as well as explicit recommendations, however, the men in charge remained loyal to their perception that official detection should be male-based.

Notwithstanding the official rules of acceptance into the police, some police tasks required the involvement of women. While women employees conducted searches of female suspects, guarded female prisoners in police stations and cleaned the stations,[33] others were entrusted with avowedly detective duties, namely taking statements from children, female offenders, witnesses and victims of sex offences.[34] These tasks – 'deemed inappropriate or impossible for men to perform' – were an extension of women's traditional engagement in welfare activities, which were mainly concerned with women and children.[35] The detective branch of the Metropolitan Police force was the most enterprising in using the services of women. During the 1880s, in response to an outcry by released women prisoners about the difficulties they encountered in trying 'to earn an honest livelihood and retrace past errors' as a result of conspicuous surveillance by uniformed policemen, the Convict Supervision Office at Scotland Yard appointed three women to monitor these former convicts.[36]

Otherwise, women were employed on an *ad hoc* basis. The assumption was that women were adept at obtaining information without arousing suspicion. In his attempts to expose a quack doctor in Manchester in 1884, Chief Detective Inspector Jerome Caminada of the Manchester City Police (later superintendent) sent two female detectives 'to seek advice from the reverend quack, each of whom pretended to be plagued with different complaints'.[37] Some were asked to pass on information by mingling with thieves; others put on a disguise and went into service as maids.[38] Women were also employed as common informers.[39] William Melville, head of Special Branch (1893–1903), had a woman live in the same house as the anarchist Francis Polti in order to watch him.[40] Her vigilance and reports helped the Branch find incriminating explosive materials in his possession. Women detectives frequented 'the dubious haunts' of foreign anarchists, reported new arrivals and extracted information from them.[41] Women were chosen to fulfil detective tasks not only because they were not identified with the all-male police institution, and therefore could not be easily recognized as acting for the police, but also because they were more suitable for certain missions. A woman was utilized by the police to lay a trap for Thomas Titley, a chemist who was suspected of selling noxious drugs to women in need of an abortion.[42] Women's sex appeal was also expected to be of value for criminal investigation. Beautiful women who 'had the gift of melting men with a look' were of special use for the men of Scotland Yard.[43]

However, although such women were in practice often entrusted with assignments performed by full-time police detectives, they were denied the benefits received by official detectives. Although police authorities acted on the premise – quite uncommon among contemporary employers – that organizational efficiency required a permanent workforce, women's work was not deemed valuable enough for them to have more than a fleeting presence in the detective force. The services of women were sought only occasionally and were generally dispensed with once the mission was completed. The exclusion of women from the permanent male staff meant that they were deprived of regular income and social protection – medical care, sickness pay, old-age pensions and other benefits given to regular police employees. Furthermore, unlike male detectives, women's successes in gathering valuable information that led to a criminal's capture and indictment was rarely made public and rarely earned them special awards.

Apparently, private detective agencies were more willing to provide women with sustained employment.[44] The head of one of the private detective agencies in London even declared that he preferred women to men in the field, and therefore hired only a few men, albeit as managers or superintendents.[45] His staff, he said, consisted mainly of young women (aged twenty to twenty-two) and boys, as they performed their business well and did not get drunk and 'blab' about it. They were probably also paid less than men. Inextricably aligned with the private sphere in the Victorian world view, women were as a matter of course entrusted with cases dealing with 'intricate domestic relations', particularly divorce suits and other matrimonial cases, including family disputes, which absorbed a significant portion of private detection after the passage of various laws that improved women's rights within the family in the latter half of the nineteenth century.[46] Yet women worked in other detection cases too. When a Nottingham textile firm had reason to believe that their new designs had been passed on to a rival house, they commissioned a woman from London to work at the looms and ascertain who the culprit was. In another instance, the inventors of a patent availed themselves of the services of a woman to find out how a rival firm had got hold of a similar product.[47] A London manufacturer assigned a female detective to befriend those of his employees who had access to the company's money in order to report on their lifestyle and social milieu. A Russian woman used her background in situations when it was 'thought that bogus companies are being formed, or that swindling is being carried on over commercial transactions'.[48] Women detectives also dealt with cases of blackmail. They thus worked in a variety of jobs, in fact, the kind of jobs usually performed by male private detectives.

Even so, private investigation firms were not unaffected by the popular notion that detective work required manly virtues. The distinct preponderance of male over female private detectives indicates that the 'stronger sex' was preferred. That this was not the result of a lack of interest on the part of women is clear from the response of no fewer than seventy applicants to an advertisement by a private agency in 1889 seeking 'a lady to undertake some detective work'.[49] Nonetheless, although from the late nineteenth century public service employers, for example the post office and prison service, were increasingly willing to hire women, police detection, and policing generally, continued to be a masculine pursuit.[50] As a result, the profile of a police detective during the Victorian and Edwardian periods was devoid of any overt feminine features. The marginal presence and exposure of women who acted as detectives in the working world reinforced the equation between crime fighting and men and therefore the masculine aura of the occupation.

New clothes, old image

The need to dispense with the police uniform upon becoming a police detective meant that the detective lost the most visible sign of his authority. Indeed, lacking a uniform, he was liable to be verbally abused or physically attacked precisely for carrying out his duties as a police officer, even by law-abiding citizens who, unable to identify him, suspected him of foul play and responded accordingly.[51] Nevertheless, he managed to retain his masculine image and even gain in stature. Notably, the removal of police uniform did not deprive detectives of their manly appearance. As detectives were selected from the uniformed ranks, they were endowed with an above-ordinary physique. Verbal descriptions of police detectives in the press portrayed them as tall, muscular and broad-chested.[52] Visual images, which appeared profusely in illustrated magazines and elsewhere, amplified this message, underlining their bodily vigour and physical prowess.[53] In contemporary thinking, 'manly vigour included energy, virility, strength – all the attributes which equipped a man to place his physical stamp on the world'.[54] The bodily representation of the police detective accordingly signified vitality and the exertion of considerable effort, and the concomitant assurance that police detectives were capable of coping with the harsh physical demands of crime investigation, such as long-term tracking in diverse situations. Significantly, illustrations of police detectives commonly displayed them as actively policing the behaviour of the public, reinforcing the connection between body and social power.[55]

What added to this portrayal of manliness were the many depictions in the press and in the detectives' own memoirs – published mostly from the 1880s onwards – of physical confrontations with offenders or suspects. Usually the detectives were portrayed as being in command of the situation and overcoming the challenge to their authority.[56] At times, they were shown as victims of violence, enduring pain and injury that could leave an indelible mark on them.[57] These accounts, however, in no way damaged their masculinity; in fact, they were presented as empowering experiences, hardening, maturing and teaching them to become more competent in defending themselves. Aggression against their opponents was projected a priori as justified, thus confirming the principle of the monopoly of the state on the use of violence.

Their physical stature did not always work in their favour. Many commentators argued that the efficiency of police detection was actually undermined by their superior height, as perceptive criminals recognised 'the policeman at a glance, through the thin disguise of private clothes' and alerted their friends.[58] Another criticism was that it was difficult, if not impossible, to eliminate the effects of the extensive amount of drill that was required of them as uniformed officers, and the body language they had acquired thereby.[59] The mechanized movements of the body during drill, parade and the beat itself were entrenched in the officers, so that wearing plain clothes or any other attempts to conceal their identity could not erase the signature of uniformed service.[60] Detective Inspector Andrew Lansdowne observed in his memoirs that the common definition of a police detective was one who 'marches along the streets with the measured tread of a bobby, warning all thieves of his approach, and making it clear to every criminal that a detective is near'.[61] Thus, their physique, which displayed attributes essential to law enforcement, could also impair that very same goal. Criticism was voiced both within and outside police discourse, especially when spectacular crimes went unsolved, that the detectives' former service in uniform, although an experience vital to detective work, at the same time conflicted with the essential covertness intrinsic in detection, and hence could obstruct the cause of justice.[62]

Their commanding build nevertheless meant that police detectives exhibited the trait most commonly bound up with masculinity. Moreover, as the century wore on, the focus on their powerful physique tallied with the growing popularity of male physical culture, which measured masculinity by athletic skills and encouraged the promotion of the physical abilities of the elite and the population at large.[63] The police detectives' deportment exuded good health, a topic of interest in the Victorian period.[64] That police detectives projected physical fitness and good health was particularly reassuring in the late nineteenth and early twentieth centuries against a background of rising fears, evoked in part by the poor results of the physical examinations of army recruits during the Boer War, that the nation's collective health was deteriorating.[65] It was presumed that the young generation, enfeebled by city life, would not be able to sustain Britain's military and industrial might or defend colonial holdings. By comparison, the detectives' obvious fitness shone.

Furthermore, in an intellectual climate governed by the belief that 'the health of the body and that of the mind were interdependent' and that 'training up the body assured a robust sort of mind',[66] the detective appeared to combine both. The many accounts in various media formats of detectives engaged in daring exploits and rigorous physical effort only served to underscore their masculinity.[67] They appeared not only fit to fight, but also as brave warriors, willing to take risks and even sacrifice their lives 'to protect the children of the empire from the trespasses of evil-doers'.[68] The texts articulated the impression that police detectives reflected the traditional virtues of a strong military presence applied to meeting challenges in a civilian battlefield that called for decisiveness, courage and endurance.[69] Indeed, accounts by investigative journalists and authors who roamed the streets of slum areas in the company of detectives with the aim of learning and exposing how the poor and downtrodden lived describe their escorts as authority figures, respected and feared by those who needed to be restrained.[70] The visual portraits that police journals attached to life sketches of detectives stressed qualities integral in hegemonic masculinity – self-assurance and self-possession.[71] The officers looked dignified, sober and self-controlled, exemplars of the conviction then that physical exercise helped instil Christian values.[72] Even though detectives were deprived of the powerful impact of uniform, their physical appearance and ability and their manly conduct radiated masculinity from head to toe. In this respect, however, they were not unlike their uniformed counterparts.

Related core values

A value related to masculine culture was ethical behaviour. Yet intrinsic in the work of the police detective was capturing criminals and the need to 'make himself well acquainted with all criminals in his district, with their associates, habits, places of resort, residence, and method of crime'.[73] This made him appear more prone than uniformed officers to dishonesty and shady dealings with the underworld and with people who operated on its margins. Indeed, the strong opposition to the formation of a detective police in the first half of the nineteenth century stemmed partly from such a fear. In time, however, the media – both the press and literature, which initially focused on detectives' potential or actual malpractice – gradually ceased to dwell on their contacts with criminals and informers unless to underscore their clever, and indispensable, ways of defeating crime.[74] Except for the scandal in 1877, which revealed that senior detectives at the central office at Scotland Yard had conspired with swindlers to subvert the cause of justice,[75] the media usually cast detectives as 'unstained in morals, and in honour'.[76] Allegations of corrupt practices and misconduct by police detectives were reported only infrequently in newspapers other than the radical or socialist press. The media thus fully collaborated with the police in affirming the integrity and moral excellence of police detectives and assuring the public that proximity to the seamy side of life did not inevitably lead detectives along a corrupt path.

Police detectives also rid themselves of the tainted association, prevalent in the first half of the nineteenth century, with intrusive continental spies who served despotic governments and spied not only on enemies of the state and criminals but also on innocent and unsuspecting subjects.[77] Although 'Victorian legislators did not regard espionage as an overly serious problem',[78] secrecy in government was viewed with great unease by many sectors of public opinion, who preferred to see themselves and the society in which they lived as open and transparent.[79] This feeling of unease permeated the police leadership as well. As a result, the creation of detective departments inside some urban police forces, and the extension of the Metropolitan Police of London detective service (formed in 1842) from headquarters to the divisions around the city (in 1869), were postponed because of an abhorrence of the 'spy system'.[80] To counter associations with spying and render police detectives more respectable, the police authorities deliberately posited the police detective as relatively visible. In routinely patrolling the streets of their division, and appearing in court as witnesses, they demonstrated that the nature of police detection in Britain was not predominantly surreptitious. After the mid-century, the British media by and large reinforced this message.[81] Neither the press nor the literary world characterized police detectives as clandestine. Moreover, the repeated criticism in the print media that English police detectives worked 'a little too openly', not only in terms of the policeman's distinctive posture but also in executing their duties in the light of day,[82] helped establish their reputation as unthreatening sleuths.[83]

Spying continued to be viewed as a 'dirty business' fit for foreigners as late as the eve of the First World War,[84] but by that time the English police detective had long since ceased being connected with spying, and in any case, perhaps partly as a result of the improved image of police detection, the public had become more tolerant of a certain level of deception to procure incriminating evidence.[85] Disguise was assumed to be inevitable in many instances, but time and again detectives tried to play down its use in their rhetoric, declaring that they only rarely employed such means, possibly because it could have been perceived as blatant deception.[86] The one media format that did emphasize the resort to disguise was fiction, yet there it was presented as a manifestation of special skills and high cognitive faculties that served only to enhance the aura of mystery and romanticism associated with detectives and hence the manly image of their vocation.

Such descriptions – physical strength, self-confidence and honesty – also applied to uniformed policemen. However, detectives, unlike ordinary policemen, were also characterized by brain work – an attribute usually reserved for the middle classes – even though much of their job demanded physical labour. Uniformed officers, too, were expected to be 'intelligent',[87] but detectives were expected to have more than 'the ordinary intelligence'; in fact, to have 'the shrewdest intellects' among police officers.[88] They need not possess scholastic knowledge, but they had to be 'men of intelligence as to the ways of the world, or the manners of the world'.[89] James Monro, assistant commissioner of the Metropolitan Police in charge of the CID (1884–8), and commissioner during 1888–90, detailed the qualities that formed a good detective: 'Acquisition of useful information, observation of character, quiet attention to little things, application of the results of observation, fertility of resource' and 'knowledge of human nature'.[90] Because most police detectives had no more than a basic formal education, police discourse time and again reiterated that their intelligence was inborn.[91] Scotland Yard detectives – stationed at the headquarters of the Metropolitan Police and in charge of solving the most serious crimes, amongst them sensational murders and white-collar transgressions – were 'supposed to be the cleverest in the force' by the police as well as the press.[92] At the peak of the pyramid of clever officers were the men selected to monitor political dissidents and guard royalty and other dignitaries, from 1883 known as the Irish Branch and from 1887 the Special Branch. They were required to possess not only 'great tact and cleverness' but also education and at times a knowledge of languages, and, more than ordinary detectives, to be able to 'pass muster fairly enough in any assembly of gentlemen'.[93]

In effect, police detective work was defined both within and outside police circles more in terms of the mental than the physical demands upon its officers. Because it was bound up with 'special qualifications and highly-developed intelligence', suggestions were periodically made by opinion leaders to recruit detectives not from the uniformed ranks, consisting almost entirely of working-class men, but directly from the educated and professional classes.[94] These suggestions, however, were not generally taken up, and detectives continued to be chosen from amongst constables who were considered 'uncommonly sharp'.[95] A key requirement accounting for the link between detectives and mental work was the extensive reading and writing inherent in their tasks, far exceeding that required in the uniformed ranks. In addition to reporting every move of theirs to their superiors, detectives took notes when collecting evidence and interviewing suspects, documented and narrated the cases they handled, and prepared cases for the prosecution in writing.[96] In fact, police detectives were exceptional in the context of workers from a humble background in terms of the amount of paperwork they were expected to produce. This intimate identification with intelligence and literacy elevated the detectives above other police officers whose masculinity was essentially physically based, and in effect created two types of masculinity within the police service.

The distinctive identity of police detectives was reinforced by special privileges granted by the all-male police management. As these privileges were commonly associated with dominant middle-class notions of masculinity, they enhanced the connection between such notions and police detectives. To attract the 'best intelligence of the police' to join the detective ranks and remain there, detectives were offered better working conditions than the uniformed branch.[97] The police reward structure was premised on the notion that, although officers did not earn high wages, their employment was free of seasonality and economic vicissitudes, and if they were deferential and acquiesced to police rules and regulations they could count on long years of steady employment.[98] Although all policemen were protected against the misfortune of being sustained by charity or the poorhouse – the hallmarks of working-class dependence – most detectives earned more than uniformed officers, enough to conform to the breadwinner ideal and more easily assume the role of the paterfamilias at home.[99] Considered specialists who had been specially selected for their 'conspicuous qualities', they enjoyed a higher status in the police.[100] Uniformed policemen always complained that they failed to get credit when involved in the investigation of crime, and that therefore detectives got many more commendations.[101]

Police detectives also came closer to middle-class codes of masculinity in enjoying a degree of independence in their work. Although all police officers worked in a highly disciplined environment, where they were subject to an 'overdose of regulations and restrictions' and to severe punishment if they did not follow them,[102] within this framework detectives were more autonomous.[103] While the uniformed constable was 'obliged to begin at a particular end, and visit all the parts in prescribed order, so that the sergeant may know where to drop in on him at a given moment', the detective was not attached to a beat and was therefore freer from the scrutiny of superior officers.[104] Additionally, inquiries sometimes took him to unexpected and distant locations, or even abroad (with all expenses paid and generous gratuities at the end in the event of success), where supervision was less possible.[105] Yet over and above the flexibility integral to the job, the demands of investigative work were recognized as necessitating some freedom of action. Even though senior officers were troubled by the lack of continuous supervision over detectives, and made arrangements for them to report routinely about their whereabouts,[106] they took it for granted that the detective should be 'left to himself – to his own ingenuity and to the development of his trained common sense' in detecting crime.[107] As James Monro made clear in referring to the unit at Scotland Yard:

> In no department is the elasticity of police administration more required than in the detective branch; and in no work is the development of individuality more essential than in the performance of detective duties. On such individual development Scotland Yard relies for success in the detection of crime.[108]

Although it cannot be said that the detective 'was beholden to no one', and entirely 'kept his own counsel',[109] he was allowed self-expression and discretion.[110] The prerogatives enjoyed by police detectives evoked jealousy on the part of uniformed officers and generated tension between the two branches. Such tensions pointed to the duality within the police between a working-class model of masculinity and a model that derived much of its substance from middle-class notions of masculinity.

The image of the police detective in the printed media

Detective fiction, proliferating in the Victorian period, systematically endorsed the premise that investigative work demanded intensive mental exertion, yet rejected the assumption governing the mainstream press, especially from the late nineteenth century onwards, that police detectives possessed exceptional mental traits. Although fictional private detectives, epitomized by Sherlock Holmes, embodied qualities that were 'radically gendered as masculine in Victorian culture: observation, rationalism, factuality [and] logic',[111] the bulk of fictional detective texts portrayed police detectives as incompetent, mediocre and lacking the cerebral aptitude necessary to be efficient detectives.[112] To illustrate their perception of the inevitable relationship between successful investigation and reason, the figure of the private detective was invented. Far removed from any contact with reality, he (and sometimes she) was often an upper- or upper-middle-class gentleman, or at the very least a member of the proper middle classes.[113] These figures were singled out as the principal crime investigators in society, whose professional stature often guided police detectives. If the police failed to follow the instructions of the private detective, they were bound to make mistakes and would be unable to decipher the case.

The extent to which this condescending portrait undermined the manly image of police detectives is difficult to assess. After all, 'intellectual abilities were almost always foregrounded as the most striking differences between men and women'[114] (and between uniformed officers and detectives). But it is reasonable to assume that although some readers saw police detection through the prism of fiction writers, notably Arthur Conan Doyle, others did not distinguish between private and public investigators and were influenced by the cerebral figure of the private detective to identify the vocation as a whole with rational thinking.[115]

The press, too, criticized police detectives for inefficiency, especially in response to botched cases or failure to solve well-publicized crimes. Apart from the pioneering days of police detection, this occurred most notably in the first half of the 1880s, which was marked by a tide of Fenian terror, and at the end of the decade, which was overshadowed by the inability to catch Jack the Ripper.[116] Yet although newspapers occasionally (and perceptively) admitted that 'chance not unfrequently [sic] does as much as head', and that mistakes happened, increasingly they viewed police detectives as demonstrating 'professional scrutiny'.[117]

A precursor of this trend was author-journalist Charles Dickens, who as early as the 1850s wrote about police detectives in a highly complimentary tone as impressive both physically and mentally.[118] He perceived them as engaged in 'games of chess', setting 'themselves against every novelty of trickery and dexterity that the combined imagination of all the lawless rascals in England can devise, and to keep pace with every such invention that comes out'.[119] Gradually, as befitting men with a manly mentality, detectives were personified as shunning the manifest expression of emotions or passions – which were linked to the private sphere, the women's realm. As men governed by reason, they were frequently presented as coolly examining 'evidences of depredation', identifying clues and interpreting them, and effecting 'smart captures'.[120] Their principal officers displayed acuity 'in holding and keeping clear the threads of many intricate plots'.[121] All this was done 'with the scent of a blood-hound, and with a perseverance that admits of no comparison, and, in the end, will generally overtake and capture the criminals'.[122] As an article in the Tory *Quarterly Review* asserted, they were never 'found wanting in courage, coolness and readiness for action, when required'.[123] At times, when the efficiency of the detective department was questioned, blame was put on the system of criminal justice for its restrictive policies rather than on individual detectives.[124]

In addition to intellectual energy and superiority of will, the occupation of police detection was identified with other notions of masculinity commonly ascribed to the middle class.[125] Even though police detectives worked within a rigid bureaucracy and depended on their superior officers for the allocation of cases, promotions and rewards, they were widely identified with the trait of individuality. Press reports and even fictional texts delineated them as enterprising and bold, making independent and dispassionate decisions and determining their own steps.[126] Even if this was not the everyday reality of police detectives, the portrayal suited the need of the rising popular press in the late nineteenth and early twentieth centuries for intriguing themes and compelling characters who stood out from the masses. Added to this was support for the forces of law and order. The combination resulted in prominent exposure in the press of detectives in the context of accomplishment.

Quite a few police detectives gained publicity – another privilege generally denied to persons of their class. Their names were routinely mentioned in the press when they were involved in an important investigation or when they gave evidence in court. This publicity did not always work to their advantage, as was seen above. Increasingly, however, while the results of the prevention of crime could not be 'tabulated in figures' nor end up as 'thrilling stories' or 'exciting incidents',[127] when police detectives were effective in resolving a sensational crime they enjoyed 'public applause' and 'the glory of success'.[128] Dealing primarily with crimes that gained extensive press coverage, members of the exclusive coterie at Scotland Yard were most likely to attain an aura of success and even a celebrity status, popularly correlated with manliness. Significantly, the police detective was described as a public servant dedicated to his work, driven by an inner sense of vocation, and discharging his duties in an objective manner. He 'was doing work of enormous value to society' in 'the constant war . . . waged against crime',[129] and thus could be seen to meet the definition of English manhood. The police detective also appeared to possess the attributes of the imperial male, but unlike him his hunting skills were directed not at animals but at law breakers, and his knowledge was not zoological, but, from the beginning of the twentieth century, scientific, largely as a result of the growing use of fingerprinting by police detectives.[130] Similar to imperial explorers who uncovered new facts about distant places, his investigations sought to cast light on dark corners of the domestic scene. Clearly, the figure of the police detective embraced a host of qualities, personifying manly values mainly linked to the business and professional community and the 'respectable' working classes, but also to the image of the ultra-masculine men who contributed to the glory of the empire.

The self-representation of police detectives

This compilation of manly ideals transmitted by the press was even more intensely replicated in detectives' memoirs, which reflected the social identity they fashioned for themselves and for public consumption. Indeed, a pervasive sense of their own masculinity emerges from their self-representations. Detectives projected themselves as strong, intelligent, 'subtle of instinct, patient of endeavour, quick in emergency', enterprising, self-reliant and hardworking, exercising both reason and morality in their work and uniquely capable of both physical and mental effort.[131] The autobiographical texts also communicated a strong sense of professional competence and fulfilment.[132] Moreover, the memoirists aimed at convincing readers that their service had been not only indispensable but also selfless, and that they had committed themselves to serve society as a whole.[133] Accordingly, the memoirs echoed the impression conveyed by the press that detective work was a laudable public service and the police detective a figure imbued with civic responsibility. 'The public have a right to nothing short of [the] . . . best services' from detectives, Detective Inspector Robert Fuller stated in his memoirs.[134] Such pronouncements struck an idealistic and public-spirited note, but were also an indication of the detectives' deep-seated sense of manliness.

   The recurrent structure of the detective memoirs itself testified to the importance of their job for them. Their childhood and youth were only briefly described, whereas accounts of the criminal cases they handled and the criminals they encountered took up the bulk of these texts. The separation of the private from the public sphere in their life was evident in the almost total absence of any mention of their domestic lives while in service. Although most detectives experienced a rise in their standard of living, this was not indicated in their memoirs. They appeared to have allowed no time for leisure or habits of consumption – widely associated with indulgence and lack of hardship[135] – as if 'comfort, pleasure, domestic ties and even life itself were things that had to be sacrificed for the sake of the nation'.[136] The message they sent was that 'manliness had to be earned . . . by mastering the circumstances of life and [that] it lay within the grasp of every man who practiced self-help with single-minded discipline'.[137] Some uniformed officers also published memoirs that were in the same vein, but proportionately detectives published many more such texts. Moreover, fully identified with crime investigation, unlike the uniformed officer, the police sleuth stood out as a romantic hero cloaked in glamour.

Conclusion

To the late Victorian and Edwardian audience, who held that 'what a man did in his working life was an authentic expression of his individuality',[138] the traits identified with police detectives in the press, in their memoirs and in police culture cast them in the mould of manly men. Significantly, their manliness did not relate specifically to their class or origin, but crossed social boundaries. It also transcended the binarism of physicality/rationality, although not the heterosexual gender divide. Indeed, in incorporating some of the glamour of the fictional private detective, together with that of the idealized soldier, explorer and other gallant defenders of empire extolled in adventure and spy fiction, the police detectives' image was coherent from a gender point of view. In fact, the defining characteristic of their public presence was manliness, irrespective of their location in the police hierarchy. As such they represented their vocation as it was conceptualized by the men who shaped it, reflecting the crucial importance of a masculine image. Uniformed work, too, embodied a masculine status, but of a more limited scope and appeal. Not only did uniformed police officers have a lower social standing in the police as well as in society at large, their masculinity remained principally that of the working class. By contrast, the police detectives, although working closely with their uniformed colleagues, appeared more charismatic and versatile, projecting masculine norms most valued by the social elite.

The attractive image of the police detectives no doubt enhanced not only their own status but also that of the police, the legal system, the governing class and the state which they symbolized. Yet it had an even greater, if more subtle, impact on society at large. In the process of image moulding, a new kind of male hero was created, illuminating a 'homosocial' institutional route to self-fulfilment and bourgeois respectability, and, more generally, projecting a role model for the growing number of lower-class men aspiring to upwards mobility and a manly character.[139] The uniformed branch offered this opportunity to its most promising officers only. The detective hero was no superman; he was within reach of men of humble origin. He was no idle gentleman whose success was gained effortlessly or a Sherlock Holmes who was at liberty to decide whether to work or pursue his hobbies, but a responsible citizen who by struggling hard managed to throw off the constraints of his background and attain a position of authority and prestige in his work organization and in society at large.

As powerful figures with the potential to inspire men, police detectives thus underscored popular notions of respectable masculinity in society. In contrast to the enfeebled and jaded clerk, who was, similarly, 'a refugee from the proletariat and a parvenue' yet 'a stigmatized figure who crystallized many of the anxieties about modern society's impact upon male bodies', the police detective was well built and assertive. He was a self-made man who was 'fortunate' to be engaged in a 'calling' suitable for men with 'love of adventure and of excitement' and marked by 'ever-varying changes in the daily duty, in scene and incident, the uncertainty of movement and lack of monotony'.[140] Journalist Alex Innes Shand, writing in 1886, could 'imagine no career indeed so full of emotional interest to a man of mental and physical energy, with a natural talent for the profession'.[141] In embodying the prospect of social mobility and even stardom, the police detective anticipated the democratization of the hero that took place in the inter-war period, when 'working-class characters came to be imbued with more of the attributes associated with manly behaviour'.[142]

Evidently, the police detective was a hero fit for his age. Not only did his build convey bodily qualities that attenuated the worrying symptoms regarding the physical degradation of the young generation and the future of the state and the nation, but this popular hero also provided some sort of answer to growing anxiety in the late nineteenth and early twentieth centuries over the shifting power relationship between men and women in society. Improvements in the legal status of women during the second half of the nineteenth century were beginning to undermine patriarchal power. Women were also entering the white-collar job market in growing numbers, especially in the field of clerical work, which until then was a male preserve.[143] The New Woman seemed to challenge the traditional 'angel in the home' concept.[144] The period was also marked by concerns about manifestations of effeminacy in the ruling classes, allegedly fomented by long years of peace, and resulting in the softening of the English elite, as symbolized, *inter alia*, by the Oscar Wilde affair at the end of the century.[145] Most threatening for many men (and women) was the rise of the women's movement at the end of the century, demanding the vote and other measures that would allow women to play a greater role in society. The dominant reaction, as historian John Tosh pointed out, 'was to reaffirm sexual difference – to define masculinity in terms which made the least possible concession to the feminine'.[146] The figure of the detective was one such response. He was constructed as a suitable agent to stand firm against such tendencies. It is therefore no coincidence that Sherlock Holmes, a private detective, and similar heroes embodying gentlemanly virtues, rose to prominence precisely at that time. The literary world opted to view these private detectives as the epitome of manliness. The press, in its role as a reporter of reality, singled out the official crime investigator as reinforcing distinctions between men and women and sending a reassuring message to the public.

Indeed, the press greatly influenced the masculinization of police detectives. The police had created a specialization within the police service that, although it formed only a very small portion of the entire force, was to a great extent its showpiece. The police thus had a stake in promoting the detectives' image. Newspapers, for their part, were only too willing to promote this manly hero as representing the essence of police work, not only because the press supported law and order, but also because the public's growing fascination with detectives served its own interests as an expanding industry, particularly from the end of the century onwards. If literary texts reflected the unease many middle-class men and women felt at the elevation of police detectives, from an historical perspective, the press played a more responsive role as a harbinger of developments in the second half of the twentieth century when the police detective became one of the most popular figures in all forms of media.

Notes

1 On the entrance of women into the Metropolitan Police of London during and after the First World War, see the memoirs of Lilian Wyles, *A Woman at Scotland Yard*, London: Faber and Faber, 1952, pp. 11–15. Wyles was recruited in 1918 and served until 1949. In 1922 she was the only woman to be appointed to the CID – 'to deal with the child, the girl, and the woman in all cases of sexual offences' – where she met a fair amount of indifference and even hostility (p. 118).
2 'Report of the Committee on the Employment of Women on Police Duties', *Parliamentary Papers* (henceforth *PP*), Cmd 877, 1920, pp. 1091, 1093. The men most influential in determining the rules and regulations of the Metropolitan Police of London were the Home Secretary and senior civil servants. All the other police forces (including the City of London Police) were governed by the local elites. For details, see J. Moylan, *Scotland Yard and the Metropolitan Police*, London: Putnam, 1929, pp. 63, 66.
3 L. Segal, *Slow Motion: Changing Masculinities, Changing Men*, New Brunswick, NJ: Rutgers University Press, 1990, p. 110; and J. Tosh, *Manliness and Masculinities in Nineteenth-Century Britain*, Harlow: Pearson Education, 2005, p. 37.
4 'Report of the Committee on the Employment of Women on Police Duties', p. 1092.
5 Tosh, *Manliness*, p. 20.
6 W. L. Melville Lee, *A History of Police in England*, Montclair: Patterson Smith, 1971 [1901], p. 331; and *The Times*, 27 March 1885, p. 9.
7 A. Wynter, 'The Police and the Thieves', *Quarterly Review*, 1856, vol. 99, pp. 160–200 (p. 163).
8 Moylan, *Scotland Yard and the Metropolitan Police*, pp. 170–2.
9 H. Shpayer-Makov, *The Making of a Policeman*, Aldershot: Ashgate, 2002, pp. 36–7.
10 Ibid., pp. 34, 37.
11 J. Monro, 'The London Police', *North American Review*, 1891, vol. 151, pp. 615–29 (p. 621).
12 R. J. Park, 'Muscles, Symmetry and Action: "Do You Measure Up?" Defining Masculinity in Britain and America from the 1860s to the early 1900s', *International Journal of the History of Sport*, 2007, vol. 26, pp. 1604–1636 (p. 1604); W. J. Gordon, 'The Everyday Life of a Policeman', *Leisure Hour*, 1890, p. 604; and National Archives, HO347/1, 'Departmental Committee on the Metropolitan Police', 1868 (henceforth '1868 Committee'), pp. 19–20.
13 'The Policeman's Diary', *All the Year Round*, 5 January 1889, p. 6; Shpayer-Makov, *Making of a Policeman*, pp. 38–9.
14 'The Policeman's Diary', p. 7.
15 W. McAdoo, 'The London Police from a New York Point of View', *Century Magazine*, September 1909, vol. 128, pp. 649–70, pp. 649–50. See the illustrations on pp. 651 and 665 for typical depictions of the figure of the uniformed officer as conspicuous in the landscape.
16 'The Metropolitan Police and What is Paid for Them', *Chambers's Journal*, 2 July 1864, vol. 41, pp. 423–6, p. 423; 'The Police of London', *Quarterly Review*, July 1870, vol. 129, pp. 87–129, p. 127; and E. H. Glover, *The English Police*, London: Police Chronicle, 1934, p. 40.
17 H. Martineau, 'The Policeman. His Health', *Once a Week*, 2 June 1860, vol. 2, pp. 522–6, p. 522.
18 Ibid. See also 'The Police of London', p. 128; pp. 594–7 of A. Innes Shand, 'The City of London Police', *Blackwood's Magazine*, November 1886, vol. 140, pp. 594–608.

19 Martineau, 'The Policeman. His Health', p. 522.
20 Ibid.
21 McAdoo, 'London Police', pp. 649, 658; and C. Emsley, 'The English Bobby: An Indulgent Tradition', in R. Porter (ed.), *Myths of the English*, Cambridge: Polity Press, 1992, p. 124, quoting the Independent Radical MP John Burns.
22 Tosh, *Manliness*, p. 35
23 Police journals were not necessarily edited by police officers, but they reflected their views and hence were highly popular amongst them.
24 Tosh, *Manliness*, p. 2.
25 C. Warren, 'The Police of the Metropolis', *Murray's Magazine*, November 1888, vol. 4, pp. 577–93, p. 586.
26 See 'The Metropolitan Police', *Saturday Review*, 3 November 1888, p. 522 and H. L. Adam, *C.I.D.*, London: Sampson Low, Marston, 1931, p. 204, in which Inspector Sweeney of the Special Branch candidly declares that he did not employ women in his private inquiry agency, which he opened after he had retired from the Metropolitan Police, because he found 'that a man can do almost anything that a woman can do and do it better'.
27 T. L. Ebert, 'Detecting the Phallus: Authority, Ideology, and the Production of Patriarchal Agents in Detective Fiction', *Rethinking Marxism*, 1992, vol. 5, pp. 6–28 (p. 7). According to Ebert, women detectives 'do not so much challenge patriarchy as act as surrogate agents enforcing its laws' (p. 14).
28 'The Metropolitan Police', *Saturday Review*, p. 522.
29 For studies of female detectives in the fiction of the time, see J. A. Kestner, *Sherlock's Sisters: The British Female Detective, 1864–1913*, Aldershot: Ashgate, 2003; C. T. Kungl, *Creating the Fictional Female Detective: The Sleuth Heroines of British Women Writers, 1890–1940*, Jefferson: McFarland, 2006; and P. Craig and M. Cadogan, *The Lady Investigates*, Oxford: Oxford University Press, 1986, ch. 1.
30 A. Forrester, Jr, *The Female Detective*, London: Ward & Lock, 1864, p. 4.
31 C. L. Pirkis, *The Experiences of Loveday Brooke, Lady Detective*, London: Hutchinson, 1894.
32 'The Metropolitan Police', *Saturday Review*, p. 522; the *Pall Mall Gazette*, too, insinuated that the CID did not benefit from being exclusively male (8 October 1888, p. 3).
33 J. Caminada, *Twenty-Five Years of Detective Life*, London: John Heywood, 1895, vol. 2, p. 57; C. Arrow, *Rogues and Others*, London: Duckworth, 1926, p. 32; *Police Guardian*, 23 March 1895, p. 1; and J. Hanmer, J. Radford and E. A. Stanko, *Women, Policing, and Male Violence: International Perspectives*, London: Routledge, 1989, pp. 15–17. See letter to *The Times* suggesting that a resident matron should be placed in every police court and station to take care of women in custody (reprinted in *Police Review*, 29 October 1897, p. 522).
34 City of Manchester, *Police Instruction Book*, Manchester: John Heywood, 1908, pp. 87–8.
35 Hanmer, Radford and Stanko, *Women, Policing, and Male Violence*, p. 14. The parliamentary committee set up in 1920 to inquire into and report on 'the nature and limits of the assistance which can be given by women in the carrying out of police duties' heard from witnesses that there was scope for policewomen to engage in the detection of crime, particularly in cases involving women and children ('Report of the Committee on the Employment of Women on Police Duties', pp. 1090, 1092). The committee itself reached the conclusion that 'in the investigation of cases of indecent assault upon women or children the services of policewomen may be of great assistance in taking statements from the victim' (p. 1091). The Committee on the Employment of Policewomen, which sat in 1924, heard evidence from the chief constable of Lancashire, in whose force the women were employed almost entirely on detective work, that, although they performed 'exactly the same duties as the men', they indeed concentrated on crimes committed by or against women and children

('Report of the Departmental Committee on the Employment of Policewomen', *PP*, Cmd 2224, 1924, p. 197).

36 *Police Guardian*, 10 August 1889, p. 4. Also see G. Dilnot, *Scotland Yard*, London: Percival Marshall, 1915, pp. 61–2.

37 Caminada, *Twenty-Five Years of Detective Life*, pp. 4, 32.

38 Ibid.

39 C. Tempest Clarkson and J. Hall Richardson, *Police!*, New York: Garland, 1984 [1889], p. 296. Several women worked in the secret department of the Home Office headed by Mr Jenkinson during the 1880s (*Reynolds's News*, 5 May 1895, p. 3). As part of their job of keeping an eye on Irish activists they joined the Irish National League, some of them becoming presidents or secretaries of branches or holding other official positions. To conceal their identity, they presented themselves as city clerks or as tradespeople. According to First Detective Sergeant Patrick McIntyre of Special Branch, they were paid well (ibid.). The department came under attack as a secret service system organized along continental lines, and was disbanded in the late 1880s.

40 *Daily Chronicle*, 16 April 1894, p. 5.

41 P. Latouche, *Anarchy!*, London: Everett, 1908, p. 232.

42 For details, see A. McLaren, *A Prescription for Murder*, Chicago: Chicago University Press, 1993, pp. 107–10.

43 C. Bishop, *From Information Received*, London: Hutchinson, 1932, p. 44.

44 *Police and the Public*, 10 August 1889, p. 4 (quoted from the *St James's Gazette*). Also see the advertisement of Slater's Detective Agency, at the end of Timothy Cavanagh's memoirs, promoting itself as an 'organization of expert Male and Female Assistants of all ages and sizes'. T. Cavanagh, *Scotland Yard: Past and Present*, London: Chatto and Windus, 1893. The advertisement presented the agency as dealing with divorce and other discreet inquiries.

45 'Espionage as a Profession', *Spectator*, 18 February 1893, p. 222.

46 *Police and the Public*, 10 August 1889, p. 4.

47 Ibid., p. 5.

48 Ibid.

49 Ibid., p. 4.

50 In line with police strategy, railway companies also sometimes employed the wives of railway employees as detectives. *Police Guardian*, 26 September 1896, p. 5.

51 *Police Service Advertiser*, 17 February 1866, p. 1.

52 'Royal Commission upon the Duties of the Metropolitan Police', *PP*, 50, 1908, p. 64 (henceforth '1908 Commission'); and *Police Review*, 1 October 1897, p. 474.

53 For examples see *Moonshine*, 17 January 1885, p. 25; *Fun*, 4 March, 1885, p. 90.

54 J. Tosh, 'Gentlemanly Politeness and Manly Simplicity in Victorian England', *Transactions of the Royal Historical Society*, 2002, vol. 12, pp. 455–72 (p. 460).

55 For examples see *Illustrated Police Budget*, 22 June 1895, p. 1; 29 June 1895, p. 1; 5 October 1895, p. 12.

56 A. Lansdowne, *A Life's Reminiscences of Scotland Yard*, New York: Garland, 1984 [1890], pp. 186–7; R. Jervis, *Chronicles of a Victorian Detective*, Runcorn: P. and D. Riley, 1995 [1907], p. 20; and C. E. Leach, *On Top of the Underworld*, London: Sampson Low, Marston, 1933, p. 103.

57 *Manchester Times*, 31 August 1872; *Police Guardian*, 18 January 1878, p. 2; 12 August 1881, p. 3; *Police Review*, 4 December 1893, p. 583; 8 June 1894, p. 271; and H. Brust, *I Guarded Kings*, New York: Hillman-Curl, 1936, p. 66.

58 B. Jerrold and G. Doré, *London: A Pilgrimage*, introduction by P. Ackroyd, London: Anthem Press, 2005 [1872], p. 196. See also National Archives, HO45/9442/66692, 'Report of the Departmental Commission to Inquire into the State, Discipline, and Organisation of the Detective Force of the Metropolitan Police', 1878 (henceforth '1878 Commission'), p. 5; Leach, *On Top of the Underworld*, p. 109; and *Police Review*, 28 December 1894, p. 614, reprinted from *Answers*; '1908 Commission', 51, pp. 251–2.

59 '1868 Committee', pp. 278, 311; and '1878 Commission', pp. 5, 23, 48.

60 '1878 Commission', pp. 75, 259.

61 Lansdowne, *Reminiscences of Scotland Yard*, p. 3. See also 'Our Police System', *Dark Blue*, February 1872, vol. 2, p. 697; '1908 Commission', 51, pp. 250–1; and Warren, 'The Police of the Metropolis', p. 589.

62 M. Laing Meason, 'The French Detective Police', *Macmillan's Magazine*, February 1882, vol. 45, pp. 300–1.

63 B. Haley, *The Healthy Body and Victorian Culture*, Cambridge, MA: Harvard University Press, 1978, pp. 124–37.

64 Ibid., p. 3.

65 G. R. Searle, *The Quest for National Efficiency*, London: Ashfield Press, 1990, pp. 60–1.

66 Haley, *Healthy Body*, pp. 4, 21.

67 *Police Review*, 20 April 1894, p. 187; and C. E. Forth, *Masculinity in the Modern West*, Basingstoke: Palgrave Macmillan, 2008, p. 115.

68 V. Grey, *Stories of Scotland Yard*, London: Everett, 1907, p. 118.

69 *Police Review*, 19 April 1895, p. 187; Tosh, 'Gentlemanly', p. 460

70 See, for example, H. Mayhew, *London Labour and the London Poor*, London: Frank Cass, 1967 [1861–2], vol. 4, pp. 330–4; and Jerrold and Doré, *London*, p. 174.

71 *Police Review*, 4 December 1893, p. 583; 20 April 1894, p. 187; 27 April 1894, p. 199; 22 November 1895, p. 559; and 8 January 1897, p. 19.

72 On the development of ideals of Christian manliness in Victorian Britain, see, for example, N. Vance, *The Sinews of the Spirit*, Cambridge: Cambridge University Press, 1985; J. A. Mangan and J. Walvin (eds), *Manliness and Morality*, Manchester: Manchester University Press, 1987; and Donald Hall (ed.), *Muscular Christianity*, Cambridge: Cambridge University Press, 1994.

73 *Police Instruction Book*, p. 86.

74 H. Shpayer-Makov, 'From Menace to Celebrity: The English Police Detective and the Press, c. 1842–1914', *Historical Research*, 2010, vol. 83, pp. 672–692 (pp. 681–2); and H. Shpayer-Makov, *The Ascent of the Detective: Police Sleuths in Victorian and Edwardian England*, Oxford: Oxford University Press, 2011, ch. 6.

75 For details, see G. Dilnot, *The Trial of the Detectives*, New York: Charles Scribner's, 1928. It was this scandal that precipitated the restructuring of the detective system in the Metropolitan Police in 1878 and the formation of the CID.

76 'Detectives as They Are', *Chambers's Journal*, 9 July 1870, p. 445.

77 *Police Guardian*, 9 August 1878, p. 3, reprinted from the *Globe*.

78 A. Rogers, *Secrecy and Power in the British State*, London: Pluto Press, 1997, p. 18.

79 'The French Detective Police', *Saturday Review*, 11 February 1882, p. 175; and D. Vincent, *The Culture of Secrecy*, Oxford: Oxford University Press, 1998, pp. 50–8.

80 '1868 Committee', p. 15.

81 *Police Guardian,* 12 April 1878, p. 2, reprinted from the *Daily Telegraph*, 9 August 1878, p. 3, reprinted from the *Globe*; *Police Review*, 28 December 1894, p. 614, reprinted from *Answers*.

82 A. Griffiths, *Mysteries of Police and Crime*, London: Cassell, 1899, vol. 1, p. 37; and '1908 Commission', 51, p. 268.

83 McAdoo, 'London Police', p. 670.

84 Rogers, *Secrecy and Power*, p. 22.

85 Shpayer-Makov, 'From Menace to Celebrity', p. 684.

86 Lansdowne, *Reminiscences of Scotland Yard*, p. 3; and R. A. Fuller, *Recollections of a Detective*, London: John Long, 1912, pp. 213–14.

87 'The Police of London', p. 102; and 'London Police Duty', *Leisure Hour*, 26 April 1879, vol. 28, p. 279.

88 'Police Detectives', *Leisure Hour*, 29 October 1857, vol. 6, p. 692; 'The Police of London', p. 98; Shand, 'The City of London Police', p. 606; and '1878 Commission', p. 5.

89 '1878 Commission', p. 14; and 'Detectives as They Are', p. 445.
90 Monro, 'The London Police', p. 626.
91 See, for example, '1878 Commission', pp. 15, 23.
92 'Our Police System', pp. 695, 698. See also National Archives, HO45/11000/223532, letter by Edward Henry to Under-Secretary of State, 13 May 1913.
93 'Our Police System', p. 699. See also *Sun*, 28 September 1897, p. 2.
94 Monro, 'The London Police', p. 626.
95 'Our Police System', p. 694.
96 '1878 Commission', p. 73; Departmental Committee of 1889 Upon Metropolitan Police Superannuation (henceforth '1890 Committee'), *PP*, vol. 59, 1890, pp. 426, 430; *Instruction Book for the Government and Guidance of the Bristol Police Force*, Bristol: J. W. Arrowsmith, 1894, p. 18; Lansdowne, *Reminiscences of Scotland Yard*, p. 12; Arrow, *Rogues and Others*, p. 217; and '1908 Commission', 51, p. 382.
97 '1878 Commission', pp. xv–xvi.
98 Ibid., p. 75. Also see Joanne Klein, *Invisible Men: The Secret Lives of Police Constables in Liverpool, Manchester, and Birmingham, 1900–1939*, Liverpool: Liverpool University Press, 2010, pp. 8, 113.
99 Ibid., p. viii.
100 Desborough Committee on the Police Service, *PP*, vol. 27, 1920, p. 612.
101 Ibid.
102 *Sun,* 27 September 1897, p. 2; Shand, 'The City of London Police', p. 601; and *The Revolution in the Police and the Coming Revolution of the Army and Navy*, London: D. Chatterton, n.d.
103 '1878 Commission', pp. x, 68.
104 'Our Police System', p. 696; and G. Rayleigh Vicars, 'County Police', *Westminster Review*, March 1896, vol. 145, p. 282.
105 '1878 Commission', p. v; and *Police and Public*, 6 July 1889, p. 1.
106 Ibid.; *Police Orders*, 20 December 1904 and 24 December 1907; and *Police Instruction Book*, p. 87.
107 Monro, 'The London Police', pp. 626–7.
108 Ibid. See also C. E. Howard Vincent, *Police Code and Manual of the Criminal Law*, London: Cassell, Petter, Galphin, 1881, p. 105.
109 Tosh, 'Gentlemanly', p. 460.
110 Vincent, *Police Code*, p. 105.
111 J. A. Kestner, *Sherlock's Men*, Aldershot: Ashgate, 1997, p. 2.
112 Shpayer-Makov, *Ascent of the Detective*, ch. 6.
113 Ibid.
114 Forth, *Masculinity in the Modern West*, pp. 143–4.
115 'Our Police System', p. 694.
116 See, for example, 'Our Detective Police', *Chambers's Journal*, 31 May 1884, pp. 337–9.
117 Shand, 'The City of London Police', p. 607.
118 'A Detective Police Party', *Household Words*, 27 July 1850, vol. 1, pp. 409–10. For Dickens's impact, see, for example, 'The London and French Police', *Saturday Review*, 8 July 1882, p. 47.
119 'A Detective Police Party', *Household Words*, 10 August 1850, pp. 459–60.
120 'Police Detectives', pp. 693–4; Shand, 'The City of London Police', p. 607; and *Police and Public*, 24 August 1889, p. 3 and 5 October 1889, p 2.
121 'The Police of London', p. 99; and *Police Review*, 11 May 1894, p. 222, quoting the *Daily Chronicle*.
122 'Police Detectives', pp. 694–5.
123 'The Police of London', p. 99.
124 *The Daily Telegraph*, 7 March 1882, p. 2.
125 M. Roper and J. Tosh (eds), *Manful Assertions: Masculinities in Britain since 1800*, London: Routledge, 1991, p. 17.

126 See, for example, *The Times,* 1 August 1910, p. 7.
127 Monro, 'The London Police', p. 623.
128 'Our Police System', p. 698.
129 'The London and French Police', p. 47.
130 On imperial men as hunters, see J. M. MacKenzie, 'The Imperial Pioneer and Hunter and the British Masculine Stereotype in Late Victorian and Edwardian Times', in Mangan and Walvin, *Manliness and Morality*, pp. 176–98.
131 G. H. Greenham, *Scotland Yard Experiences*, London: George Routledge, 1904, p. 8; T. P. M'Naught, *The Recollections of a Glasgow Detective Officer*, London: Marshall, Hamilton, Kent, 1887, pp. 9–10; M. Moser, *Stories from Scotland Yard*, London: George Routledge and Sons, 1890, pp. 22–5, 31–5; and J. G. Littlechild, *Reminiscences of Chief-Inspector Littlechild*, London: Leadenhall Press, 1894, p. 3.
132 Fuller, *Recollections of a Detective*, pp. 16, 18; and J. Sweeney, *At Scotland Yard*, London: Grant Richards, 1904, p. 348.
133 Fuller, p. 17.
134 Ibid.
135 Forth, *Masculinity in the Modern West*, p. 116
136 Ibid., p. 131.
137 Tosh, 'Gentlemanly', p. 458.
138 Tosh, *Manliness,* p. 37.
139 Forth, *Masculinity in the Modern West*, p. 142.
140 Littlechild, *Reminiscences*, pp. 2–3. See also Lansdowne, *Reminiscences of Scotland Yard*, p. 4.
141 Shand, 'The City of London Police', p. 607.
142 K. Boyd, 'Knowing Your Place: The Tensions of Manliness in Boys' Story Papers, 1918–39', in Roper and Tosh, *Manful Assertions*, p. 145.
143 Tosh, *Manliness*, p. 21
144 Ibid., p. 7.
145 M. Boscagli, *Eye on the Flesh: Fashions of Masculinity in the Early Twentieth Century*, Oxford: Westview Press, 1996, pp. 1, 23.
146 Tosh, *Manliness*, p. 22.

7

'WELL-SET-UP MEN'

Respectable masculinity and police organizational culture in Melbourne 1853–c. 1920

Dean Wilson

The social tumult of the Victorian gold rushes of the 1850s produced two profound and interconnected transformations in policing. The first was the centralization of policing in 1853, placing all police services under the command of a single administrator – the chief commissioner of police – accountable to the Lieutenant-Governor of the Colony. The advent of a centralized policing bureaucracy was contentious and far from inevitable, but it was nevertheless a development with significant ramifications for the future of policing in the colony. Responsibility for policing was removed from local communities and vested in a centralized state. Additionally, centralization facilitated the development of a highly bureaucratized, hierarchical and rule-bound organization in which discipline was a vital principle of governance. The second fundamental reform was the adaptation in Melbourne of the London Metropolitan model of policing. Along with uniforms and the beat system of patrol, the theories informing London policing were translated and redeployed within the colonial context. Through discipline, drill, uniforms and the regular patrol of the beat, the London police constable assumed a powerful symbolic role as the neutral and objective representative of impersonal central authority, idealized as the embodiment of the collective will of the people.[1] This chapter explores how this administrative vision of the respectable, disciplined and deferential policeman was inscribed on the body of the constable through an idealized notion of organizational masculinity. It was a vision that aimed to function both externally and internally – projecting out an idealized civic masculinity intended to promote order and cohesion and projecting internally through the police organization to cement adherence to discipline and regulation. This idealized notion of masculinity was simultaneously symbolic, instructive and disciplinary. Although signifying the rational authority of the state, the police constable was also deployed as an exemplar of virtuous manly conduct who would serve to instruct those policed in the appropriate values and norms of respectability. In addition to these civic functions, police leaders sought to promote an institutional masculinity built upon deference and obedience that would secure internal discipline within the police organization.

The vision of masculinity that emerged was freighted with broader notions of preventative policing and its reformative capacity. The corporeal mobilization of the police constable as a symbol of central authority arose from transformations in thought that had their genesis in continental Europe. The notion of preventative police had its lineage in the arguments of Italian criminal law reformer Cesare Beccaria, and was extended in England and Scotland by late eighteenth-century and early nineteenth-century reformers such as Jeremy Bentham and Patrick Colquhoun. Preventative policing was one facet of a more expansive reform agenda that promoted regular patrolling, predictable detection of offences and rational punishment to dissuade offenders.[2] These ideas were instrumental in the late eighteenth- and early nineteenth-century transition from sporadic, symbolic and brutal punishments. In 1829, with the advent of London's 'new police', this general theorization of criminal justice reform was inscribed on the person of the police constable through a phalanx of rules and regulations that strove to mould the constable into a neutral, objective and highly disciplined agent of state authority.[3]

The corporeal symbolism of the policeman assumed added significance in the tumultuous social climate of gold-rush Melbourne. In the midst of upheaval and chaos, anxious government administrators placed immense faith in public symbols to convey and constitute aspirations of permanent and stable government authority. Many of the city's central cultural institutions – the University of Melbourne, the public library, mechanics' institutes, botanic gardens and the museum – were founded to promote order and a respect for English cultural values among the populace. There was somehow a faith that the transplantation of these institutions from Britain would create order almost of themselves.[4] Police constables, too, were enrolled as symbolic envoys of the aspirations and ideals of colonial authorities seeking to construct a more stable and cohesive society. Of all symbols of state power, the police was arguably the most significant. As Alan Silver has remarked, the policeman represented 'the penetration and continual presence of central political authority throughout daily life'.[5] In Melbourne, the particular colonial inflection of a gold-rush colony gave added impetus to the invention of disciplined, orderly and morally respectable constables. With many believing a total breakdown of order was imminent, the issue of policing attained crucial importance.[6] Although at the centre of the British Empire in London the constable as symbol of impartially and rationally applied authority was primarily engaged to promote acceptance of full-time professional police, in Melbourne the situation differed.[7] In the colonial city, where police forces with varying levels of adherence to metropolitan standards had been in existence for over a decade, the body of the constable was redeployed as a civilizing envoy in a society perceived to be on the brink of collapse.

Governing deportment

The vision of civic masculinity envisaged by police administrators centred on the visual deployment of disciplined and imposing bodies that would signify the regularity of the institution itself. The physical presentation of individual constables was therefore a key concern. Emulating the London Metropolitan model, the requirements for recruitment stipulated the lower age of thirty years (thirty-five if the candidate had previous policing experience) and required that the candidate be 'of strong constitution and free from bodily complaint'.[8] From 1882 entry into the foot police was open only to men who were under thirty years of age, stood at least five feet and nine inches, and were 'smart, active and could read and write well'.[9] The above-average height for the period chosen as a benchmark suggests that the police constable was to symbolically and literally stand tall amongst colonial men.[10] Gait as well as height was considered important, and the candidate was made to stand to attention before the Police Board, and then asked to walk across the floor 'to give the board an opportunity of judging his style, whether he is a sloucher or a smart well-set-up man'.[11] In 1919, the *Police Journal*, circulated to all members of the Police Association, noted approvingly that recent recruits were 'much larger' than previously and constituted 'a better type, both physically and intellectually'.[12] This would suggest that superior physicality not only was desired by police leadership, but also had been internalized by station-level police as an integral attribute of police masculinity. Nevertheless, by the early twentieth century, physical stature was more rigorously enforced than in earlier years, indicating the continued desire of police administrators to fashion a police force of exemplary physical masculinity that marked the power of the police institution. In 1919 new standards for foot constables stipulated both height and age, but also contained new categories of measurement such as a minimum weight of ten stone eight pounds and a minimum expanded chest measurement of thirty-eight inches.[13] As late as 1925 the *Argus* newspaper was extolling the virtues of physical might for policing, with its claim that 'a foot policeman in uniform should by his obvious physical proportions and strength command a respect for his capacity to deal with every situation demanding a physique well above average'.[14]

Although the administrative vision of the ideal constable rested upon physical form, it was also actively produced through an elaborate web of rules and regulations that advanced in complexity throughout the nineteenth century and into the twentieth. Police were to be not only large but also respectable. Rules to govern conduct and demeanour commenced with the Police Regulation Act of 1853, which outlined the moral qualities desired of policemen who were to be 'of good character for honesty, fidelity, and activity'.[15] The broad requirements of the Police Regulation Act were expanded and refined in 1856 with the publication of the *Manual of Police Regulations*. Following the recommendations of a commission of the Legislative Council investigating the state of Melbourne police in 1854, the *Manual* was drafted by Acting Chief Commissioner Charles

MacMahon, a former career military officer and member of the colony's elite, with the assistance of Henry Moors, a police clerk.[16] Alongside an outline of the general duties of a constable, the *Manual* also detailed the desired virtues of the exemplary constable. Constables should 'be extremely cautious in their demeanour, and be sober, orderly and of regular habits'.[17] In 1877 the more extensive and detailed *Regulations for the Guidance of the Constabulary of Victoria* was published.[18] Alongside providing instruction on such diverse matters as treating snakebite and filing a crime report, it further cultivated the official conception of civic masculinity, privileging the impeccable standards of behaviour and presentation desired of the lower ranks.

The *Manual* and *Regulations* represented a codification of both the civic and the respectable vision of masculinity that was to be projected outwards, and the corresponding and overlapping conception of deferential institutional masculinity envisaged for within the police organization. Importantly, both the 1856 and the 1877 publications were intricate guides to conduct and deportment. Handbooks conveyed the administrative vision of the model policeman to the lower ranks through their detailed rules regulating appearance, bearing and personal habits.

The most obvious symbol of the police constable's broader role as an agent of state power was the uniform, which signified his separation from the community. The uniform was a symbolic marker of both civic and institutional conceptions of masculinity. Rendering constables highly visible to the populace, the uniform was a visual cue that would ideally draw attention to desired standards of public male behaviour, which in theory would be exhibited by individual policemen. Internally, the uniform inscribed an institutional masculinity based upon deference to rank and hierarchy. By 1853 the uniforms of the London Metropolitan Police along with the theory of policing they represented were directly grafted on to the Melbourne police.[19] The London uniform was dark blue, a colour chosen specifically as it avoided the military association of red and was thought to be civilian, neutral and sober. The uniform was intended to deter prospective offenders while rendering the policeman identifiable to citizens seeking his aid. Additionally, however, the numbers and letters worn on the policeman's collar made him physically visible and traceable, with his conduct monitored and identity easily ascertained by superior officers.[20] Uniforms therefore marked the individual constable as a servant of the public bound by the strict bureaucratic control inherent to the vision of institutional masculinity sought by police leaders. The distinct blue uniform was also infused with the notion of civic masculinity, being the most visible way in which the constable was mobilized as the representative of benign, coherent and systematically applied state authority. In colonial Melbourne, the uniform also carried additional significance. The blue-coated constable represented the civilizing influence of colonial authority, taming the frontier metropolis as an exemplar of the English values of respectability and rational justice.

Along with the blue uniform, constables were expected to adopt regulated modes of deportment that would convey ideals of rationality, consistency and discipline. Regulations, rulebooks, district orders and drill practice stipulated modes of standing and walking that envisaged the constable as disciplined and dispassionate. Deportment was thus a crucial component of the desired institutional masculinity, one that police leaders hoped would project the image of police authority as rational, consistent and ordered. In 1858, constables were warned against standing 'in a lounging and listless attitude' when addressing members of the public and received a district order that when spoken to by citizens they should 'immediately come to attention and remain in such a position for the time'.[21] By 1877, police regulations informed constables that they must avoid any appearance of 'lounging, loitering or gossiping', and that they were not permitted to enter into any conversation except that directly related to police matters.[22] In 1888, John Barry, a serving senior constable who wrote the *Victorian Police Guide*, reiterated the point, noting that 'nothing . . . seems worse in the eyes of the public than to see a constable lounging about in a lazy slovenly manner, as if it were a burden to him to carry his own weight'.[23] Posture and gait were therefore corporeal elements of a desired institutional masculinity that aimed to project ideals of personal discipline and organizational integrity.

The posture and regulated gait of the constable were complemented by the system of beat patrol, which envisaged individual constables moving at a regular pace through space. The regularity and uniformity of the constable on the beat would be projected out onto the space through which he moved, police authorities hoped, bringing about control over public space through steady surveillance and physical example. Devised by a former officer of the London Metropolitan Police, police beats were introduced to Melbourne in 1854 and divided the city into discrete units to provide round-the-clock surveillance.[24] The regularity of spatial division was to complement the regulated body of the constable. Beats were revised in 1859 including detailed maps of individual beats compiled by Superintendent Freeman, which he claimed 'relate with minuteness the manner in which they should be worked'. Individual beats were timed, the superintendent having noted where every constable would be at ten-minute intervals.[25] By 1888 two miles per hour was assessed as the correct walking pace to observe 'people and places'.[26] The beat system was envisaged as a giant outdoor incarnation of Bentham's panopticon – a massive vision-machine in motion constructed from a multitude of human moving parts. Importantly, the beat system, comprising well-regulated constables, extended symbolic metaphors of the police institution as rational and consistent. The values of an orderly and benign state were to be perpetually reinforced in microcosm through interactions between constable and citizen. This was a mission that extended well beyond the enforcement of the law. The individual constable was a street-level envoy for colonial aspirations to civilization and decorum modelled upon the imperial centre. The constable was to be a model of self-restraint, moral virtue and sobriety that those being policed would hopefully try and emulate.

The shaping of a particular form of normative, middle-class, respectable masculinity that privileged cleanliness, posture and obedience continued to be reinforced in the nineteenth century by a surfeit of minor regulations that sought to regulate the minutiae of the constable's appearance. On parade and in the stationhouse, sub-officers were to check that boots were polished and tunics correctly buttoned, with random inspections to ensure that 'the men are properly and cleanly dressed'.[27] The physical presentation of the sub-officer was intended to have an exemplary function; he was instructed to 'show an example of neatness in his dress and appointments, and of perfect cleanliness in his person'.[28] Fashioning the constable's presentation extended beyond attire and hygiene and even incorporated the regulation of facial hair. Beards and moustaches were to remain short and trimmed, and policemen were not to 'indulge in fancy styles or fashion, nor wear long hair, nor allow the beard to grow of unseemly dimensions'.[29] The prohibition of public smoking further refined the image of the police constable as respectable and clean.[30] Corporeal regulation thus encapsulated notions of both civic and institutional masculinity. The person of the constable symbolically embodied notions of order that evidenced the metropolitan sophistication of the colonial metropolis. Simultaneously, superior officers exercised tight somatic control over the constable which crafted an institutional masculinity distinct from that of other working-class men.

Neutral and respectable men

Although the institutional vision of constabulary masculinity rested upon physical display, it also sought to craft an institutional personality that was neutral, aloof and taciturn. Underpinning this was police authorities' idea that policemen should not be perceived as representing local vested interests, but should be viewed as the physical embodiment of a mystical and benign law ultimately derived from the collective will of the community being policed. Neutrality was enforced through prohibition of political participation, which was thought to shield individual constables from 'extra-legal' influences. The policeman was forbidden to vote and instructed to 'observe strict neutrality in all matters connected with politics'. Such neutrality extended beyond political participation, towards the crafting of a demeanour devoid of opinion, prejudice and emotional display. A constable was to be 'civil and attentive to all persons of every rank and class'.[31] The 1877 *Regulations* again accented the necessity for 'self control and coolness' on the part of constables, who were to carry out their duties with 'forbearance, mildness, urbanity and perfect civility towards all classes'. The fashioning of the constable's demeanour was specifically intended to inspire a 'kindly feeling' towards the police among the public, so that they would be 'respected and looked up to'.[32]

The political neutrality of the police constable was reinforced through the inculcation of specific modes of conduct intended to reinforce authority and respectability. The police constable was to consistently display a 'mild, conciliatory and decorous line of conduct' that conveyed the fairness and benevolence of central authority, repeatedly performed through personal interactions with the public.[33] Regulating exchanges with the public rested on devising rules that sought to project respectability while precluding overly familiar interactions that might fissure the institutional façade. The 1856 *Manual* counselled against indulging in 'idle chatter' while patrolling.[34] Rulebooks and district orders subsequently sought to shape the constable's demeanour as a predictable delivery device for rational conceptions of order. Distant reserve was therefore promoted as the desirable stance in interactions with the public, the constable advised always to be 'guarded as to his demeanour'.[35] In 1859 Chief Commissioner Frederick Standish ordered stronger supervision over men at suburban stations, as 'it is a common habit of theirs to lounge about in a most unwelcoming manner, chatting with civilians and even drinking with them'.[36] The weight that police authorities placed on maintaining distance between civilians and constables is evident in police charge sheets from the period, which are replete with cases of constables being disciplined for the offence of 'gossiping' with civilians.[37] By 1877 police regulations stipulated that constables were not permitted to enter into any conversation with a member of the public unless it related directly to police matters.[38] The detachment of constables from working-class communities served two interconnected purposes in the construction of masculinity. On one level, in theory at least, it enabled the constable to operate as a benevolent figure of paternalistic authority, capable of dispensing rational justice empty of local or class inflection. On another level, it was intended to sequester the constable from those aspects of rough working-class masculinity – intemperance, fecklessness, insubordination – that might undermine organizational discipline and the image of respectability.

As the police leadership aspired to have the civic masculinity of constables admired from afar by those policed, those policemen who formed overly familiar ties within their communities quickly earned the ire of their superiors. In 1880 Sergeant Bell of the North Fitzroy station found himself reprimanded for holding membership at a local bowling club. Superintendent Nicholson thought that there was 'something very wrong where a member of the force can spend so much of his time at a bowling green as Sergeant Bell is represented to do'. Bell was unimpressed with such official interference in what he saw as harmless recreation. As vice-president of the club, Bell retorted with a threat to his superiors that 'after nearly 26 years' faithful service if I cannot take a couple of hours owed a week in outdoor exercise in respectable company I will resign'.[39] Although Bell may have won this small victory, police authorities continued to patrol the boundary between policeman and community with vigour. In 1903, the *Police Gazette* informed members of the police force that it was an 'offence against the discipline of the service' to take part in 'any athletic contest, or any bicycle or horse and foot race, or in any public stage performance' without first gaining the permission of the chief commissioner.[40] Such intensive monitoring of private life was underwritten by an abiding belief in the policeman as a symbol of respectability and morality, and an anxiety that this surface could quickly crack if examined too closely. Isolated from local communities, police increasingly socialized exclusively with one another through such groups as the Police Brass Band, formed in 1891 with the begrudging permission of the chief commissioner.[41]

The desire to inculcate notions of respectability and discipline in individual constables was heightened by the policing situation of gold-rush Melbourne. In the early 1850s, Victoria was a society in flux and new police recruits were drawn from a floating population composed overwhelmingly of newly arrived immigrants. Discipline, rather than police strength, was the crucial issue as Superintendent Sturt suggested when he claimed that 'the difficulty of maintaining efficiency in the Police is not so much from want of men as it is from the little confidence that can be placed in them'.[42] Sturt contrasted this with the era before the discovery of gold, when the police force was composed of those from small households drawn from the local community whose characters were well known to authorities. Despite the trebling of the numerical strength of the police, Sturt remained anxious as he confronted a body of men whose 'habits and characters are but partially known, their places of residence are uncertain, some in public houses, some in board and lodging houses, where their associates may be very questionable characters'.[43] The desire to fashion respectability was thus inextricably intertwined with the privileging of discipline as an organizational strategy in a society of uncertainty. Moreover, the elite masculinity of early police leaders was itself built upon their capacity to control and discipline the bodies of those beneath them in the police hierarchy.

The deployment of discipline and surveillance in the cultivation of an idealized notion of constabulary masculinity was evident in the near-total pervasiveness of the police institution in the lives of its members. Rules and regulations imagined policing as an unremitting occupation that colonized the private world of the constable. This was made abundantly evident in regulation 14 of the 1877 *Regulations*, which informed young constables that they would be 'required to devote their whole time to the police service'. Even when long shifts were over, the constable's obligations to the police service were far from finished. Although married men might return home after their shifts, and single men to the barracks, they were to remain in uniform and be ready to turn out 'when called upon in cases of emergency, such as fire, accidents of any kind, disturbances, & c., or whenever required'.[44] The uniform was removed only to sleep, and even then it was to be kept nearby. For police authorities, such total enmeshment within the institution aided the production of particular forms of masculinity that privileged the desired values of obedience, deference and loyalty, while simultaneously reducing the capacity of contagion from less 'respectable' masculine traits displayed by other working-class men.

Discipline and the surveillance of the constable were also achieved through the spatial segregation of the constable from the community, by way of measures that mirrored geographically the distant and neutral personality prescribed in the rule-books. Married men were required to reside within their districts, and as close as possible to the stations to which they were attached.[45] Although the married man had the small respite of home life, single men faced the pervasive discipline of barracks life. Barracks accommodation had been instituted primarily as a means of maintaining surveillance over constables and more efficiently monitoring and controlling their behaviour. Thus, the members of the Select Committee on Police in 1852 were 'desirous that some incentive should be afforded to men to live in Barracks, feeling assured that due discipline can best be enforced'.[46] Police Superintendent Evelyn Sturt was also a firm believer in the wisdom of housing men in one location to facilitate observation and discipline. Although advocating a continued presence of married men living in private housing and 'having a local interest in the well-being of the City', Sturt favoured a barracks system along military lines that would bring police 'under the immediate control and supervision of their officers'.[47]

Barracks life held to a strictly regimented routine that stressed manual activity and discipline in order to create self-disciplined and obedient constables. Upon waking, the constable spent the first half-hour of the day dressing and folding bedding, sweeping the floors of the room and setting it in order. Gambling and smoking were strictly forbidden, as was entertaining guests. In the evening, police were to retire at 9.30 PM with all fires and lights to be extinguished by 10 PM.[48] For the new recruits sent to Russell Street, Saturday was filled with fatigue work – washing, scrubbing and general renovations around the barracks.[49] The exact time of each man's leaving for and returning from duty were recorded in the reserve occurrence book, as were any irregularities such as constables returning intoxicated.[50] Until 1883, the few leisure hours of the constables were spent drinking beer and swapping stories with comrades in the barracks canteen. However, such homosocial bonding threatened to destabilize the idealized masculinity promoted by police authorities. The tendency of young constables to get 'pretty well on' and incidents such as that of Constable Carter, who assaulted a senior officer after a long drinking session in the canteen, led to its abolition following the Royal Commission's recommendation in 1883.[51] With the beer removed, leisure at the barracks consisted of either a sober game of billiards or some wholesome self-improvement in the police library.[52] Barracks life thus constituted complete enmeshment in the police institution, such that the young recruits absorbed the desired values of discipline, stoicism and obedience to command projected downwards upon the lower ranks from senior officers.

Although the virtues of discipline and obedience were advanced architecturally within the barracks, they were also realized bureaucratically in regulation and rule and the increasingly extensive internal archive that the police organization maintained. The considerable record-keeping capacity of the police bureaucracy assembled not only an archive of the 'criminal class' but also intimate observations, files and records of the infractions of its own members. Record sheets were introduced in 1853, and stimulated an avalanche of internal records of all police members below officer rank. The record was primarily disciplinary; superior officers carefully noted all misdemeanours and infringements against an ever-more elaborate code of rules and regulations. Although sharply criticized by the Royal Commission in 1883, which remarked that record sheets were used by senior officers, particularly station-house sergeants, to 'terrorize the men', the police administration continued to develop its paper-based index of individual constables throughout the nineteenth century.[53] Connected to the archive by the number on his collar, a policeman's obedience to regulation and rule was inscribed on his record by senior officers, who consequently wielded significant power through 'knowledge of the files'.[54]

As the mobilization of sharply presented bodies across space embodying the desired virtues of distance, civility and respectability demonstrates, discipline and obedience were privileged institutional values in the Melbourne police. Unquestioningly obeying the command of superiors was emphasized in regulations which stipulated that the constable was to 'promptly obey' all orders and accept them 'without question or comment'. Regulations relentlessly stressed that discipline and obedience were the bulwark of the police organization. As the 1877 *Regulations* noted, 'discipline . . . is essential to the practical direction, action and efficiency of the force'.[55] The constable was informed that 'it is so important that orders should as a rule be promptly obeyed without demur, that unnecessary or even improper orders, provided they do not involve legal responsibility, should be complied with on the spot'.[56] Regulations sketched a culture of obedience in which officers and sub-officers performed as role models for the virtue of compliance. Indeed, the hierarchy of ranks was imagined as an ascending scale of ever-more virtuous role models who would serve as shining examples for those beneath them. Officers and sub-officers in particular became the locus of the police bureaucracy's fixation with discipline, deferring to their superiors while acting as an 'example of strict and prompt obedience'.[57]

The idealized notion of a controlled organizational masculinity promoted by police authorities was also imparted through the colonization of the constable's private world. Numerous regulations and rules sought to fashion exemplary and morally upright working-class men entirely devoted to the organization. Should the single constable wish to marry, he was required to obtain permission from the officer of his district, who was to ensure through investigation that the marriage would not 'bring discredit on the force'. The restriction on marriage was intended to produce a police force that would echo standards of respectability prescribed by police administrators.[58] In the scant leisure hours available the policeman was not to drink at 'public places of amusement or in public houses'. Men with a trade were forbidden from practising it, and even when a policeman's wife had 'a trade, profession or business' he was obliged to get special permission from his officers before allowing her to work at it. Constables were also forbidden from accumulating debts in the community for fear that this would 'impair their efficiency to discharge their duties'. Despite their low pay, policemen who became insolvent were obliged to resign, although they could later be reinstated, and this appears to have been a frequent occurrence. When Senior Constable Curran resigned, unable to meet the demands of his creditors, his commanding officer noted that his case was 'no worse than others of daily occurrence'.[59] The proscription of some activities co-existed with the promotion of others thought likely to enhance the moral bearing of constables. Religious observance was officially encouraged with officers instructed to ensure that 'particular attention is paid to the proper observance of Sunday'.[60]

Punishment and the limits of discipline

The administrative vision of civic masculinity promoted by the police leadership to be embodied by the respectable, sober, obedient and distant constable was only ever partially realized. However, police administrators deployed a range of formal sanctions to enforce the respectable ideal, removing those who tainted the sobriety and propriety to which the administration aspired. The most common of these formal sanctions were dismissal, demotion and transfer. Those who most patently transgressed the bureaucratic ideal of masculinity were dismissed. The importance of obedience within the police hierarchy rendered violence against an officer the most heinous of offences. The Police Regulation Act 1853 created the specific offence of assaulting a superior officer, which carried the possibility not only of dismissal from the police, but also of a fine of twenty-five pounds and possible imprisonment with hard labour for twelve months.[61] William Everon was instantly dismissed in 1854 when he presented for the night duty parade drunk and assaulted his sub-officer. In the same year, Constable John Reilly was also dismissed after assaulting Sergeant Pewtress, who was disciplining him for being absent from his beat.[62] Such outright resistance to authority appears to have abated, however, and, of the 121 men dismissed between 1859 and 1861, only two cases were for the offence of 'insubordination'.[63] In the 1850s it appears that dismissal was used fairly widely, but it declined as the century progressed. Senior Constable Edward Hall recalled his early years in the police force when 'men were punished for a mere nothing'.[64] Although partially indicating a greater adherence to the institutional rules of the police force amongst the men, this may well indicate greater flexibility amongst police administrators who preferred to use other disciplinary measures. Reduction in rank was another form of punishment that administrators could utilize. Sergeant Monckton, for example, was reduced to the rank of senior constable when he was noticed sitting down in a tobacconist's shop while supposedly on duty.[65] Senior Constable John Ahern was similarly demoted when he was discovered to be drunk in charge of a city beat section in the early hours one morning.[66]

Ahern's case was one of many in which drink was the contributing factor in disciplinary proceedings. Drinking amongst the lower ranks proved a perennial problem for police authorities. In 1854 more than a quarter of the Melbourne City Police appeared before the Magistrates' Court for alcohol-related offences committed while on duty.[67] Of fifty-one dismissals from the police force in 1859, twenty-nine were for alcohol-related offences.[68] For police authorities, the problem appeared endemic, and it specifically undermined the public image of respectability that policemen were supposed to maintain.[69] John Barry's *Police Guide* suggested that the most important quality that a constable could possess was sobriety. The drunken policeman, in Barry's estimation, was 'useless as a member of the force' and 'a shame and a disgrace to his comrades'. The constable who indulged in drink, it was argued, was at the mercy of the publican and any member of the public who observed his weakness. Moreover, drinking on the job rendered arrests for drunkenness hypocritical; it removed the constable's ability to exercise discretion and predisposed him to form unsavoury associations while in hotels, where he was 'liable to meet the very persons who it is desirable he should not be on intimate terms with'. Ultimately it was the damage to the public image of the institution that was most reprehensible. As Barry concluded, 'any person in uniform under the influence of liquor, attracts the notice of the public, and their state is remarked on sooner than one in a similar condition, who is dressed in ordinary attire'.[70]

The drunken policeman was the antithesis of the policeman as moral exemplar. Nevertheless there is evidence that, at the station-house level, the heavy-drinking police culture so well documented in contemporary studies had already taken shape.[71] By the standards that policemen used to judge each other, being a drinker did not necessarily constitute being a bad policeman, and there are cases revealing that heavy drinking was an accepted facet of police life for many constables on the beat. In one such case against a senior constable, Constable O'Callaghan gave evidence that he had met the offending officer in the afternoon and had six glasses of strong liquor before going on duty. The chief commissioner was somewhat dismayed that O'Callaghan had alluded to this in his evidence 'as an ordinary matter not needing explanation or apology', concluding that O'Callaghan was 'already a seasoned toper' who, if he wished to remain in the police force, would 'do well to avoid a continuance of a bad habit which seems dangerously familiar to him at present'.[72] Such cases indicate the limits to which idealized notions of masculinity promoted by police leaders were internalized by the rank and file. Elements of a rougher working-class masculine culture continued to compete with the respectable template promoted from above.

Although much disciplinary energy was expended on attempting to conceal and remove drunken constables, those who formed associations within undesirable communities also experienced the heavy hand of police discipline. In 1857 Constable James Wilson was dismissed from the police for being 'acquainted with disreputable characters' when he was found 'absent from his beat and gossiping with a prostitute in a brothel from 1.35 till 2.10 this morning'.[73] In addition to dismissal, the centralization of policing in 1853 had given police administrators a powerful weapon to sever dubious connections between the police and the community: the ability to transfer constables to any station in the colony. Although some constables sought transfers preferring country duty, for others it functioned as a form of banishment. Consequently, those violating the official codes of respectability, obedience and moral integrity could find themselves rapidly relocated. Constable Cook was transferred to a country station when it was revealed that two of his sons had been convicted of housebreaking, apparently justifying the assumption of his commanding officer that they had 'joined the criminal class'.[74] Punishments thus strove to remove – from the city at least – those failing to reach or transgressing the ideal of the sober, upright and morally unblemished constable. Transferring constables who failed to meet the ideal of civic masculinity to the country indicates the importance of the city as a locus of display for the institutional ideal.[75] Nevertheless, many remained who only partially internalized the exacting model of civic and institutional masculinity. This was hardly surprising, as even the author of the *Victorian Police Guide*, John Barry, conceded in 1888 that to come upon a person possessing all of the qualities prescribed for a police constable 'would be to find a person hitherto unknown'.[76]

Mobilizing respectability

The idealized masculine type of the temperate, aloof and moral constable was sketched by police authorities in rule books and promoted through discipline and drill. Nevertheless, this vision of masculinity began to be reconfigured as ordinary policemen developed a distinct occupational identity, one that absorbed elements of the respectable ideal. Most commonly this was expressed through demands for increased pay that would allow police to distance themselves from their working-class compatriots in other occupations and occupy houses in 'respectable' locations. In 1882, policemen before the Royal Commission continually remarked on the impossibility of maintaining a respectable family life on six shillings sixpence per day. Constable Patrick Bourke pointed out that a policeman in the city could not even afford unrespectable housing in a right of way at such a rate. Police often argued that the respectability so frequently demanded of them by their superiors could be attained only on a higher rate of pay. As Constable Rogerson remarked before the Royal Commission in 1882, the pay was 'too little for a man to keep his family in such a respectable position as a constable ought to be in'.[77] Policemen continually argued that their occupation was far more than simply walking around the street. John Barry, for example, argued in 1882 that policing was a skilled occupation requiring 'education, intelligence, physical strength, sobriety and courteous manner to the public'. For Barry this placed the police well above the average member of the public service, who merely had to 'pass an examination, and go into his office'.[78] The notion of policing as a distinct profession and an emergent sense of policing as a discrete occupation demonstrated that many of the values of civic and institutional masculinity promoted in earlier years by police leaders had to some extent infused the working culture of ordinary policemen.

The increasing emphasis that ordinary policemen placed upon their own respectability was underlined in the deputation sent from the Victorian Police Federation to the Chief Secretary in 1912. Petitioning for an increase in police pay and the restoration of police pensions (which had been discontinued in 1902), the members of the Federation stressed the compromised and peculiar position of the constable in the community. They emphasized that the prerequisites of entry into the police force placed police above the usual requirements of working-class occupations as they had to be of 'good physique, education, energy, intelligence and moral character'. In addition to having more exacting entry requirements than other working-class occupations, constables were confronted with other, sometimes costly, demands to maintain a respectable public image. Location and social status compelled police to pay above-average rents, as they were required to 'live in a respectable locality and not in the slums and must be close to the station'. Such demands were placed on an occupation with a starting wage of seven shillings and sixpence, one shilling and sixpence less than the average pay for an ordinary day labourer.[79] This shows that the vision of masculine respectability had to some extent been absorbed into the occupational identity of ordinary policemen. It is also meant, however, that policemen could collectively mobilize notions of respectability and distance from the wider community to argue for improved conditions. By 1917 the collective occupational identity of policemen was further evidenced with the formation of a Police Association. Successive chief commissioners had strongly resisted any previous attempts by policemen to combine, seeing such efforts as undermining the unquestioning loyalty and deference regarded as vital to the police organization.[80]

Conclusion

Instigated at the height of the Victorian gold-rushes, the administrative dream of police leaders that envisaged the constable as a moral envoy of colonial authority and aspiration was infused with civilizing intent. Aloof, impeccably polite, fair, physically robust, spotlessly clean and tirelessly obedient to his superiors, the model constable was imagined as the builder of an idyllic 'little England' in a far-flung colony besieged by massive social dislocation and a highly mobile and anonymous population. The constable provided a model of virtuous, industrious and deferential manhood imagined as instrumental in cementing a stable society from amidst the chaos. Thus, although the physical regulation and discipline of the constable echoed comparable developments in other jurisdictions, it was propelled by a distinctly colonial rationale.[81] The 1877 *Regulations* described the ideal constable as 'active, energetic, temperate and honest'. Duty was to be carried out 'independently, uprightly, conscientiously, and without fear or favour'.[82] This was an elite ideal of respectable masculinity corporeally inscribed by the police leadership on the police constable, through a process that deployed rules and regulations to mould working-class men into models of respectable middle-class manly virtue. The centrality of this symbolism was to fade in importance over the nineteenth century. Moreover, it was a vision only ever partially realized. The working-class backgrounds of ordinary policemen, rates of pay that placed them on a par with labouring occupations and their proximity to working-class life meant that elements of working-class masculinity continued to infuse policing, something particularly evident in the persistence of hard drinking in the lower ranks.[83] Nevertheless, disciplining and crafting the constable into an idealized representation of institutional and civic masculinity had a significant and enduring influence upon the structure, regulation and occupational identity of policing. Ordinary policemen would eventually, at least partially, absorb these institutionally prescribed values. By the later nineteenth century they mobilized such values of respectability, sobriety and moral integrity to argue for the uniqueness of their occupational identity and remuneration to match the lofty virtues of respectability so often reiterated in handbooks and manuals.

Notes

1 W. Miller, *Cops and Bobbies: Police Authority in London and New York, 1830–1870*, Chicago: Chicago University Press, 1977, pp. 73–96.
2 D. Philips, '"A New Engine of Power and Authority": The Institutionalization of Law Enforcement in England 1780–1830', in V. A. C. Gatrell, B. Lenman and G. Parker (eds), *Crime and the Law: The Social History of Crime in Europe since 1500*, London: Europa, 1980, p. 175; E. Monkkonen, *Police in Urban America, 1860–1920*, Cambridge: Cambridge University Press, 1981, p. 40; and M. Foucault, *Discipline and Punish: The Birth of the Prison*, translated by A. Sheridan, London: Penguin, 1977. For the Scottish case see D. G. Barrie, 'Patrick Colquhoun, the Scottish Enlightenment and Police Reform in Glasgow in the Late Eighteenth Century', *Crime, Histoire & Sociétés/Crime, History & Societies*, 2008, vol. 12, no. 2, pp. 57–79.
3 R. Reiner, *The Politics of the Police*, 2nd edn, London: Harvester Wheatsheaf, 1992, pp. 62–3.
4 D. Goodman, *Goldseeking: Victoria and California in the 1850s*, Sydney: Allen and Unwin, 1994, p. 88; also D. Goodman, 'Fear of Circuses: Founding the National Museum of Victoria', *Continuum*, 1990, vol. 3, no. 1, pp. 18–34; and P. Fox, 'The State Library of Victoria: Science and Civilisation', *Transition*, 1988, vol. 26, pp. 14–26.
5 A. Silver, 'The Demand for Order in Civil Society: A Review of Some Themes in the History of Urban Crime, Police and Riot', in D. Bordua (ed.), *The Police: Six Sociological Essays*, New York: John Wiley, 1967, pp. 12–13.
6 Goodman, *Goldseeking*, p. 77.
7 On the role of the constable in London see W. de Lint, 'Nineteenth-Century Disciplinary Reform and the Prohibition against Talking Policemen', *Policing and Society*, 1999, vol. 9, no. 1, pp. 33–59 (p. 37); see also D. Wilson, 'Traces and Transmissions: Techno-Scientific Symbolism in Early Twentieth-Century Policing', in B. Godfrey and G. Dunstall (eds), *Crime and Empire 1840–1940: Criminal Justice in Local and Global Context*, Cullompton: Willan, 2005, pp. 108–9. On the importance of the colonial context in shaping Australian policing see M. Finnane, *Police and Government: Histories of Policing in Australia*, Melbourne: Oxford University Press, 1994, pp. 13–14.
8 Police Regulation Act 1853, s. 7; and *Manual of Police Regulations for the Guidance of the Constabulary of Victoria, and approved by his Excellency the Governor in Council 22 April 1856*, Melbourne: John Ferres Government Printer, 1856, pp. 9–10.
9 *Victoria Government Gazette*, 12 May 1882, p. 1059; and R. Haldane, *The People's Force: A History of the Victoria Police*, Carlton: Melbourne University Press, 1986, p. 102.
10 Although there is some debate regarding average heights in the colonial period, five feet nine inches was above average; see R. Shlomowitz, 'Did the Mean Height of Australian-Born Men Decline in the Late Nineteenth Century? A Comment', *Economics and Human Biology*, 2007, vol. 5, no. 3, pp. 484–8; and G. Whitewall, S. Nicholas and C. de Souza, 'Height, Health and Economic Growth in Australia, 1860–1940', in R. Steckel and R. Floud (eds), *Health and Welfare During Industrialization*, Chicago: National Bureau of Economic Research, 1997, pp. 379–421.

11 Royal Commission on the Victorian Police Force, 1906, p. 21.
12 *Police Journal*, 1 September 1919, p. 14. On the advent of the *Police Journal* see Haldane, *The People's Force*, pp. 159–60.
13 *Police Journal*, 1 September 1919, p. 14.
14 See *Argus*, 16 March 1925, p. 13; 17 March 1925, p. 10; see also Haldane, *The People's Force*, p. 187.
15 Police Regulation Act 1853, s. 7.
16 Haldane, *The People's Force*, p. 51.
17 *Manual of Police Regulations*, 1856, p. 60.
18 *Regulations for the Guidance of the Constabulary of Victoria*, Melbourne: John Ferres Government Printer, 1877.
19 *Argus*, 3 June 1853, p. 6
20 On the London uniform see Miller, *Cops and Bobbies*, pp. 32–3; see also S. Palmer, *Police and Protest in England and Ireland 1780–1850*, Cambridge: Cambridge University Press, 1988, p. 297. On the introduction of the numbering system in Melbourne see *Argus*, 26 July 1852, p. 5.
21 Public Record Office Victoria, Victoria Public Record Series (hereafter VPRS) 1200/1, 27 October 1858.
22 *Regulations*, 1877, p. 17.
23 J. Barry, *Victorian Police Guide Containing Practical and Legal Instructions for Police Constables*, Sandhurst: J. W. Burrows, 1888, pp. 4–5. Although written independently, 400 copies of Barry's guide were subsequently purchased by the Victoria Police Force and kept in stations around the colony; see Haldane, *The People's Force*, p. 115.
24 On the operation of the beat system generally see D. Wilson, *The Beat: Policing a Victorian City*, Melbourne: Circa Press, 2006, ch. 2.
25 VPRS 937/284, 26 April 1859; see also *Argus*, 17 February 1859, p. 5.
26 Barry, *Victorian Police Guide*, p. 7.
27 *Regulations*, 1877, p. 16.
28 *Regulations*, 1877, p. 15.
29 *Regulations*, 1877, p. 3.
30 *Manual of Police Regulations*, 1856, p. 60.
31 *Manual of Police Regulations*, 1856, p. 63.
32 *Regulations*, 1877, p. 21.
33 *Regulations*, 1877, p. 21.
34 *Manual of Police Regulations*, 1856, p. 60.
35 *Regulations*, 1877, p. 17.
36 VPRS 937/284 (2), January 1859.
37 VPRS 937/284, January 1859.
38 *Regulations*, 1877, p. 17.
39 VPRS 937/303 (3), 24 December 1880.
40 *Victoria Police Gazette*, 19 February 1903, p. 92.
41 Haldane, *The People's Force*, p. 119.
42 VPRS 1189/16 (1), 52/3459, 8 September 1852.
43 VPRS 1189/16 (1), 52/1215, 13 April 1852.
44 *Regulations*, 1877, p. 28.
45 *Regulations*, 1877, p. 27.
46 Select Committee on Police, 1852, 'General Report', p. iv, 'Votes and Proceedings of the Legislative Council', vol. 3, 1852–3.
47 VPRS 1189/16 (1), 52/1215, 13 April 1852.
48 *Regulations*, 1877, pp. 59–61.
49 Royal Commission on the Victorian Police Force, *Victorian Parliamentary Papers*, 1906, p. 131.

50 *Regulations*, 1877, p. 27.
51 Royal Commission on Police, 'The Proceedings of the Commission, minutes, evidence, appendices, etc.', *Victorian Parliamentary Papers*, 1883, p. 26; and Testimony of Constable William Rogerson, p. 43; see also General Report, p. xx.
52 Royal Commission on Police, 1883, p. 25 for the police library. The library began in 1859 when the Russell Street barracks was built and was intended to promote police literacy and self-improvement; see Haldane, *The People's Force*, p. 58. For billiards see Royal Commission on the Victorian Police Force, 1906, p. 132. For the difficulties of barracks life see also VPRS 937/334, K1626, 7 July 1891.
53 Royal Commission on Police, 1883, General Report, p. xix.
54 H. Gerth and C. Wright Mills (eds), *From Max Weber: Essays in Sociology*, London: Routledge and Kegan Paul, 1948, pp. 212–15.
55 *Regulations*, 1877, p. 19.
56 *Regulations*, 1877, p. 20.
57 *Regulations* 1877, p. 20.
58 *Regulations*, 1877, pp. 3, 12.
59 VPRS 937/298, 12 October 1876; for regulations regarding insolvency see Police Regulation Act 1853, ss. 61, 62.
60 *Regulations*, 1877, p. 3.
61 Police Regulation Act 1853, s. 15.
62 VPRS 1189/151, 54/6979, 29 June 1854; 54/6847, 26 June 1854.
63 'Report from the Select Committee on the Police Force', 1863, 'Votes and Proceedings of the Legislative Assembly of Victoria', 1862–3, Appendix C, 'Dismissals for 1859, 1860, 1861', pp. viii–x.
64 Royal Commission on Police, 1883, p. 55.
65 VPRS 937/318 (1), 1 May 1886.
66 Service Record of John Ahern, Victoria Police Historical Unit: 'reduced in rank for being drunk in charge of no. 1 division at 2.20', 8 April 1876.
67 Haldane, *The People's Force*, p. 49.
68 Select Committee on the Police Force, 1863, Appendix C, 'Dismissals for 1859, 1860, 1861', p. viii.
69 M. Finnane, 'Governing the Police', in F. B. Smith (ed.), *Ireland, England and Australia: Essays in Honour of Oliver MacDonagh*, Canberra: Australian National University Press, 1990, p. 216.
70 Barry, *Victorian Police Guide*, pp. 3–4, 8.
71 On police drinking in the contemporary context see R. Reiner, *The Politics of the Police*, 4th edn, Oxford: Oxford University Press, 2010, p. 128.
72 VPRS 937/311, 23 February 1884.
73 VPRS 937/284, 24 February 1857.
74 VPRS 937/319, 11 October 1886.
75 It should be noted, however, that some policemen also requested to be moved to the country, viewing country postings as easier work than policing the city, while those disciplined in the country could be moved to the city where they would be under tighter supervision from superior officers. See Wilson, *The Beat*, p. 25.
76 Barry, *Victorian Police Guide*, p. 3.
77 For comparison with warders and clerks see C. McConville, '1888 – A Policeman's Lot', *Australia 1888*, 1983, no. 11, pp. 78–87 (p. 78).
78 Royal Commission on Police, 1883, p. 61.
79 VPRS 3992/1746, 26 April 1912.
80 For the background to the formation of the Police Association see Haldane, *The People's Force*, pp. 151–9. On police unionism in Australia more generally see Finnane, *Police and Government*, pp. 44–5; and M. Finnane, *When Police Unionise: The Politics of Law and Order in Australia*, Sydney: Sydney Institute of Criminology Press, 2002.

81 For the bodily regulation of police constables in other jurisdictions see de Lint, 'Nineteenth-Century Disciplinary Reform'; W. de Lint, 'Autonomy, Regulation and the Police Beat', *Social and Legal Studies*, 2000, vol. 9, no. 1, pp. 55–83; C. Emsley, *The English Police: A Political and Social History*, 2nd edn, London: Longman, 1996, pp. 214–15; and Miller, *Cops and Bobbies*.
82 *Regulations*, 1877, p. 17.
83 On the backgrounds of recruits to the Victorian police force in the nineteenth century see Wilson, *The Beat*, pp. 10–12.

8

OF TABLOIDS, DETECTIVES AND GENTLEMEN

How depictions of policing helped define American masculinities at the turn of the twentieth century

Guy Reel

Introduction

In the fall of 1893, pretty Edith Marshall decided to plant a kiss on a 'New York copper' who was approaching her because she was 'full enough' – that is, having too much of a good time under the influence of alcohol. She screamed with delight when he approached her, kissed his 'unwilling lips', hugged him and would not let him go. The officer, pictured and identified in the sensationalist tabloid the *National Police Gazette* as 'Policeman Hulse', was forced to arrest her. After a lecture in the Jefferson Market Court, she was discharged – a fortunate outcome for Miss Marshall because misbehaving women of the time were often thrown in jail by overzealous police.

The encounter between the moustachioed Officer Hulse and the lace-booted Edith Marshall, who was showing a bit of calf, was on the cover of the *Police Gazette* on 14 October 1893,[1] and its elements – the attractive woman, skirt in disarray, the bemused policeman, the smirking male onlookers, the beer sign – fitted the *Gazette*'s formula. It had a hint of sexual titillation, a possible crime (albeit minor), a possible scandal, a diversion for the men of the street (the observers as well as the *Gazette* readers) and an officer trying, a bit ineffectively, to control the scene. Added to the *Gazette*'s and other newspapers' coverage of even more sensational subjects such as brutal crimes, brazen showgirls and outrageous scandals, this item rather neatly captures the way that police and policing was often portrayed in the tabloid press of the era. The *Gazette*, as a men's magazine aimed at working- and middle-class men (and sometimes read by sneaky boys), showed police alternately as heroes, bunglers, hypocrites and brave men – a mixed bag, in other words, much like the men who read these accounts. In short, the portrayals of police and policing fitted with the hegemonic masculinities of the day – the cultural norm of dominant males, acting aggressively, asserting manliness, sometimes preying on or being threatened by women, but also flawed, and sometimes weakened, in their responses.

The *Gazette*, a famed men's magazine that flourished in the late nineteenth and early twentieth centuries, was aimed at men who sought some context or diversion in a world that was rapidly challenging assumptions about gender roles and the meanings of masculinity. Its portrayals of crime and police sometimes reinforced the emerging notion of other men – notably fighters and sportsmen – as powerful and manly, in contrast with earlier depictions of agrarian, wiry, 'self-made' men. It also showed some police as aggressive champions of 'right' behaviour (whereas officers who deviated from this through corruption or maliciousness were ridiculed and held in contempt), and its content was designed to sell to a mostly white, working- to middle-class male audience. Although police responses to crime were important in conveying this sense of appropriate masculinity, at other times police were shown as somewhat lost as to what to do about the coming wave of assertive, free-thinking women. Therefore, the *Gazette* and other tabloids and sensational newspapers often treated law enforcement officers with nuance, as vehicles to display many of the same challenges and approaches to masculinities that faced the primarily male readers of these publications.

The *Gazette*'s portrayals of masculinity and policing at the turn of the century will be described here, along with those of another important publication that was influenced by the *Gazette*, Joseph Pulitzer's *World*. Because of its remarkable circulation successes and history-making place alongside William Randolph Hearst's *Journal* of the same era, a series of newspapers from the *World* of 1895–6 (along with copies of the *Gazette* from the late 1800s to early 1900s) was examined for portrayals of police and policing. The *World* was not classified as a tabloid. But its pursuit of yellow journalism, with sensationalism, gossip, big headlines and crime news in abundance, was certainly a mixture of the tabloid methods that became dominant later. In 1895 it spent several days and many column inches touting its circulation numbers, and with good reason. At a daily circulation of more than 580,000, it was one of the most important newspapers of its day. The *Gazette* nearly reached similar numbers in its heyday, usually as a result of closely following prize fighting and its related symbol of manhood, bodybuilding. It was the coverage of crime, criminals and police, however, that gave the *Police Gazette* its name – and its reason for being.

Crime and the sensational details of the actions of criminals have been part of the press from the beginning, and they became particularly important in America as the nineteenth century and the growth of the mass media progressed. Economically there is no mystery why there was, and is, so much news about crime and the attempts to curtail it through law enforcement and public derision (editors often justified their focus on lurid and sensational criminal acts by claiming they were simply trying to help the police and root out criminals). Crime news was covered so heavily because it sold so well. Along with sport and sexual titillation, crime and its policing have long been a key moneymaking component for newspapers young and old. But it is not enough to say that newspapers covered crime because crime coverage sold newspapers; contexts for newspapers' crime coverage must be considered as an interaction between public narrative and private consumption – between medium and audience. This is particularly true when one considers the subjects of crime coverage (criminals and police) and those who snatched up tabloids filled with sensational accounts of dastardly deeds – readers who were mostly white, working-class men, often immigrants, seeking escape, information, excitement, ways to identify 'others', and sometimes reinforcement of their manhood in a rapidly changing world that was producing many conflicting thoughts and images about men, women and their roles in society.

Twenty-three-year-old Benjamin Day, after taking control of *The Sun* in New York in 1833, began regular police court news when he hired George Wisner, at four dollars a week, to write crime items, which regularly dripped with sarcasm and derision. 'Jane Dunn, an incorrigible old vagrant and rum head was ordered to the penitentiary for six months', read one short piece.[2] Such casual characterization went on for decades; police court reports became routine, with the police acting as sidekicks to the unsavoury characters that occupied reporters' often mocking accounts. In almost any copy of a major city newspaper from the end of the 1800s until well into the twentieth century one can find similar items. For example, in the *Daily News*, 5 August 1926, a reporter wrote about the reaction of a patrolman to the sight of a woman who had rolled her stockings down in public when she became overheated. She had done this deed:

> under the gaze of the statue of George Washington in Union Square. George remained cold and frigid. But patrolman Harry Levin grew warm and quick. He removed Miss Rathowitz for performing such an act in public and, after locking her up overnight, brought her sternly into the presences of Magistrate Oberwager in Tombs court yesterday.

The officer noted that she rolled down her stockings and men were watching. The judge frowned and sentenced her to 190 days in the House of the Good Shepherd.[3] The middle-class man reading this item could share in the journalist's wry observations (and enjoy the description of the stimulating disrobing) about the patrolman's 'warm and quick' reaction, the statue's frigidity at the woman's provocations, the judge's sternness – all reflecting different aspects of masculinities. Such sub-texts abound in the portrayals of police of this era – newspapers' stories featuring officers were often the conduits through which men of the era could view the crimes, scandals and nefarious or salacious women who graced their pages.

Sensationalism helped build readership – mostly among men from the lower to middle classes; lavish illustrations allowed for easy interpretation among the illiterate. And nowhere was the sensational more readily found than in crime news, along with 'disasters, sex scandals, and monstrosities', as historian Frank Luther Mott described sensationalism.[4] Crime news was often accompanied in this popular news mixture by items about sports, scandal, the theatre and class, including immigration, all inextricably tied to portrayals of masculinities, hegemonic and otherwise, and effects on white, working-class men. Some of these men were police officers and other kinds of lawmen, and the portrayals of police and policing became part of the same two-penny press that became a dominant mass medium. Police were the foils upon which many of the emerging late nineteenth- and early twentieth-century ideals and debates of masculinity were projected – they mingled with the deviant underclass, which included criminals, sports, loose women, brawlers and drunks. Police became, in a sub-textual way, both barometers and guardians of types of masculinities because they were thrust into the roles often traditionally reserved for men (or at least the ideals for men) – heroes, protectors, crime fighters and solvers, and peacemakers. Their successes and failures in controlling the elements of crime and scandal became the framing device for many of the depictions, and often the police were cast as either heroic working men or incompetent boobs. It is the purpose of this chapter to examine some of these portrayals of the era and to consider their meaning in the context of the portrayals of masculinities at the turn of the century.

Tabloid tales

By most definitions, tabloids succeeded 'yellow journalism', the sensation-filled news-shouting that became part of the vernacular amid the competition between Joseph Pulitzer's *New York World* and William Randolph Hearst's *New York Journal*.[5] But tabloid practices existed long before yellow journalism; the tabloid – 'tablet'-like in size – was a convenient format for titillation and scaremongering, and tabloidism was synonymous with yellow journalism, which told readers:

> This way to the big show! We have a mutilated corpse, a scandal in high life, divorce details that weren't brought out in court, a personal attack on the mayor, lifelike pictures of dead rats, the memoirs of a demented dressmaker, some neatly invented prison horrors, and a general denunciation of everybody who owns more than five hundred dollars! Don't miss it![6]

The coverage of crime news is the exploration of the deviant and, as noted by sociologist Emile Durkheim, it enables society to test its limits of tolerance, define acceptable behaviour, provide diversion from the dullness of day-to-day life and allow separation of deviants as 'others'.[7] Tales of fighting this deviance – through police action, mystery solving or just the right-doings of good men (and occasionally women, boys and girls) – are another side of the same coin and allow newspapers and other media to sometimes depict law enforcers as heroic, bold, scientific and rational. Of course, they could also be corrupt, cowardly or comical – see the *National Police Gazette*, 20 June 1885, for a typical array: an illustration of a 'sweet-scented copper' holding his nightstick aloft and portrayed as having insulted, then assaulted, a respectable married woman; a flattering portrait of Captain John Easton, the commander of the second precinct in Brooklyn; an officer chasing a man who had shot into a crowd of 'Chinamen' on a Sunday after-noon in Chatham Square in Chinatown; and a raid on a poker game at Brighton Beach even while nearby gambling on a horse race continues unmolested.[8]

By showing the good and the bad of policing – the chivalrous and the chauvin-istic, the incompetent and the efficient – newspapers were able to convey many of the normative masculine values of their male readerships. Men were expected to respond to threats from criminals, from women and from other groups, and so were police. Newspapers could easily show these dynamics in accounts and pictures of police taking on the various elements of society – and all the while, they too were flawed, just like the men and women they were policing.

Crime and crime fighting were often inseparable in newspaper accounts, and the actions of police and detectives were sometimes naturally woven into crime stories. In many cases, the police were simply shown as characters in the larger play of the urban drama, but they were important characters with responsibilities to protect men, women and children. As such, newspaper editors showed them as first-line defenders of the moral and righteous as well as frequent protectors of the era's hegemonic masculinities. In the nineteenth century these included the notion of white male dominance, along with aggressive, often violent, attempts to protect it. Sociologist R. W. Connell wrote of a social order in which power and even empire have been gendered. In this construct, the types of hegemonic masculinities and threats to them vary by era as different trends emerge, such as more public definition of homosexuality and the increased economic and political power of women.[9]

Many historians have written of the contexts of nineteenth-century America as influences on transitions in masculinities and male sensibilities. These contexts include the growth of cities, the development of urban culture, immigration, the rise of sport as spectacle, the taming of the West and a vast increase in wealth. A large body of scholarly study concerns itself with the development and perception of masculinities during this era, with the years covering the late nineteenth and early twentieth centuries seen by many historians as a key period, particularly in US men's history. In an influential essay, John Higham in 1970 identified a cult of manliness at the end of the nineteenth century – citing a rejection of the ills of city life and a rise in interest in sports and bodybuilding – and argued that, begin-ning in the 1890s, many American men had an 'urge to be young, masculine, and adventurous' because of a reaction against 'the sheer dullness of an urban indus-trial culture'.[10] Later, social historians Elizabeth Pleck and Joseph Pleck named the years 1861–1919 as the period of the 'strenuous life' for men in America, one of four major periods of men's history in the United States.[11] These periods were accompanied by the increasing ubiquity of the mass media, often focusing on threats to men and new roles for women, the creation and growth of police forces and a growth in men's (and some women's) familiarization with weaponry and arms. LeRoy Lad Panek noted that Samuel Colt developed a pocket or house pistol for easy use in defence in 1871; by the end of the civil war thousands of men (and many women and children) had been familiarized with arms and violence, and firearms became common for domestic use.[12] Along with these factors was a sort of moral panic about the portrayals of sensation and crime in the media. The famed moral crusader and postal inspector Anthony Comstock, in *Traps for the Young* (1883), warned of decaying moral standards as part of a crusade that went on for decades.[13] The *Gazette* claimed that it wanted to root out crime by publicizing it; Comstock wanted to wipe out the potential for criminality at least partly by extinguishing it from the press and eliminating the narratives' consumption by young boys, and he decried the details of crimes being published in 'story papers' such as the *Gazette* and the *Fireside Companion*.[14]

But the police played another important role in journalism, often serving as an anchor for a story. In this way they were part of the city scene. As historian Dan Schiller has noted, crime news 'led to another important development – the growth of a cheap urban culture'. Crimes gave reporters a chance to develop a storytelling style and to make news from villains and heroes. They also enabled the rise of objectivity, Schiller argued, because the initial crime stories were based on police reports and supplemented with great detail – some of it speculation, some of it in the reports themselves.[15]

The seeds for crime reporting based on authorities' activities had been sown in the 1700s when formal organized watch forces began in London 'to suppress the thieves and robbers who too often enjoyed the freedom of the city', and John Fielding (half-brother of novelist Henry Fielding) wrote to Prime Minister Thomas Pelham Holles, the Duke of Newcastle, suggesting a gazette to chronicle their activities. The Bow Street Runners, often called London's first professional police force, had been founded in 1749, and the goal of the gazette was to publish information about wanted criminals. The *Quarterly Pursuit,* later called the *Weekly Extraordinary Pursuit*, began publishing for a general gentlemanly readership; it was later simply known as the *Police Gazette*.[16] That London publication should not be confused with the *National Police Gazette*, which operated out of New York City, although the American version was at least partly based on its English counterpart, and the first issue of the *National Police Gazette* did give it a nod. New York's *Gazette* eventually came to serve as a way for editors to condemn crime (while sensationalizing it greatly), support police (while chronicling their heroics as well as their foibles) and demonstrate the right and wrong actions of men and women. Under the leadership of Richard K. Fox, who took over the *Gazette* in 1876 and had a remarkable run of more than forty years as editor, the *Gazette* developed a fairly predictable formula that cemented its place as a men's magazine. It highlighted the petticoats and ankles of showgirls, the muscles of boxers and bodybuilders and the vile, shocking or heroic activities of all sorts of criminals, from outlaw Western legends (Jesse James was an admirer of the publication) to spurned lovers, from depraved rapists to vigilante racists. It also championed working men and made fun of hypocrisies of the clergy, prohibitionists and others while running reams of columns of advertisements for products promising male virility, sexual power, cures for syphilis and corrections for the 'errors of youth'.[17] As Kevin Mumford noted, because of their sexual content and their overwhelming concern with the facility and strength of male genitalia, the *Gazette*'s advertisements, and thus the intended audiences, were inescapable. Alongside advertisements for 'rubber safes' and 'female illustrations', there were notices addressed to 'Sufferers from Nervous Debility, Youthful Indiscretions, [and] Lost Manhood', promising to restore a 'nerveless condition to one of renewed vigor'.[18]

As its illustrations, ads and editorial content attest, the *Gazette*'s focus on working- and middle-class masculine concerns was unmistakable. It covered the exploits of outlaws and police as a way to fascinate its predominately male readership, and it showed cops, robbers, murderers, rakes and thieves, all alongside its exploitation of masculine activities such as bodybuilding and boxing and the gender-bending exploits of women who challenged men's authority and dominance. *The Gazette* of this era did not always directly make a major play of the activities of the police – its lavish woodcut illustrations were more often concerned with showing crimes, skin or muscle – but there were enough examples of police portrayals in its pages to demonstrate the newspaper's editors' overall view of police and investigators. Usually they were treated as honourable, efficient gentlemen who were doing their best to fight the depravity that abounded all around. For example, in a regular column that featured woodcut portraits of leading citizens all over the country, Marshal Pat Burns of the Des Moines, Iowa, Police Department was pictured in 1887 as seeming 'to have been the only man who ever had the courage to collar the notorious prohibition crank, Frank Pierce . . . and cast him behind the bars and bolts, where he belongs'. It continued: 'Marshal Burns is a fearless, faithful officer who is the terror of crooks and cranks who interfere with the welfare of the good people of Des Moines. He is also a very popular one.'[19]

Law enforcement officials (as with other masculine role models, athletes, bartenders and barbers) were regularly honoured in the *Gazette's* pages, and police were frequently shown bravely restoring order against multiple dangers. In 1887 an unnamed officer was pictured (Figure 8.1) diligently chasing 'A wild Indian in New York', according to the caption, adding, 'Dinnie Mause, a drunken redskin, tries to scalp a Bleecker Street car'.[20] But the portrayals as peace officers sometimes carried a subtext; a picture caption from 1888 – 'Locked them all up. Fall River, Mass[achusetts], police suddenly appear at a swell wedding and pull the whole party in for dancing on Sunday' – implied that police were overstepping their bounds. Portrayals were thus not uniform; in the same issue, police chief John Lockwood of Norwalk, Connecticut, was condemned in an item for tying a prisoner to a wagon and dragging him to jail, but City Marshal Robert Blythe, of Mount Vernon, Ohio, was portrayed as a hero after he had a 'desperate and thrilling encounter with a madman' who had been threatening his family. The marshal, 'without side arms or mace', tried to use calming words, as he had before in such situations, but was slashed with a razor.[21] This item, and others like it, drew a stark

A WILD INDIAN IN NEW YORK.

DINNIE MAUSE, A DRUNKEN REDSKIN, TRIES TO SCALP A BLEECKER STREET CAR.

FIGURE 8.1 An unnamed officer was shown chasing a Native American, identified as a 'wild Indian' and 'drunken redskin', in an 1887 issue of the *National Police Gazette*. The era's portrayals of police masculinities varied widely.

contrast between bold, brave, aggressive and sensible lawmen – the same qualities that the *Gazette* touted as praiseworthy attributes in ordinary men – and those who abused their power, got drunk on the job or harassed women. Thus, by covering the police actions, the publication was supporting its own view of appropriate masculine behaviour.

Very often, police were shown as protectors of the social order – as protectors of the very hegemonic masculine society they inhabited. They might have been peacemakers – albeit aggressive ones, sometimes using nightclubs to crack the heads of rowdies. They were also depicted as scientific investigators (an 1894 front page illustration showed a detective investigating a mysterious death in a New York lawyer's office), fighters for justice (shown as trying to maintain law and order in a series of crimes committed by 'white caps' – Ku Klux Klan members in Georgia) and protectors of women against assault and the public from illegal boxing.[22] In these cases, the police were part of a 'civil' society, another aspect of the masculine-dominated culture that the *Gazette* often praised. In general, in covering the police administration, the *Gazette* did its part to be supportive, for example when it complimented the appointment of an 'admirable public servant', William Murray, to the position of New York police superintendent:

But the city is entitled to as much congratulation as the Superintendent, for in his person it has secured a head for its police force of almost ideal character and efficiency. Superintendent Murray was never a newspaper policeman. He has always avoided notoriety and done his excellent work almost by stealth. He has no political backers. He has never posed theatrically as the champion of the public against crime – a sort of blue-coated St. George, as it were. He is, we believe, a poor man, who lives on his salary, and who has never made a dollar during his period of service beside the money paid him by the city. Not a word has ever been breathed against his private character, and his official honesty is equally beyond reproach. He will make the best Superintendent of Police ever put in that position in New York.[23]

The description of Murray as not a 'newspaper policeman' was telling in that he did not seek publicity, another aspect of a responsible man acting professionally. Officers who simply did their jobs, without scandal or complaint, were lauded. Those who failed were criticized, like all men who failed to do their appropriate duties, as was repeatedly illustrated by the *Gazette*'s condemnation of the deviant.

On the same page, near the piece on Murray, was the typical racism and classism that often accompanied an emphasis (by newspaper editors, moral crusaders and others) on threats to white masculinities. A racist joke ('There is said to be an Indian in Colorado that has not tasted liquor in ten years. It is not stated what cigar store it ornamented') was followed by a long diatribe about 'Chinese coolies, the scum of Asia, the dregs of the vilest, the beastliest, the most inhuman and ungodly race on earth'. Their offence in this case was associating with white women at a picnic, at the expense of white men.[24]

As part of its defence of the white, male-dominated, middle-class order, it was normal for the *Gazette* to portray officers generally favourably, as publisher Fox saw part of the paper's mission as being a crime-fighting organ. An editor (possibly Fox, although the piece was unsigned) noted in 1889 that some argued that the 'publication of criminal dealings has a deleterious effect on the morals of the masses'. He also noted the claim that sensationalizing crimes actually promoted those activities. But, pointing out that other newspapers and magazines were using similar crime-news formulas, he argued that bringing crimes to light helped the good people of the community, including the police, to stand up to criminals.[25]

Another element of the *Gazette*'s crime-fighting formula was its accounts of Western outlaws, both as heroes and as villains. Its tales of the untamed West served as an escape from the mechanized manhood of the city life for readers, who were often either factory workers or the working poor. The rugged individualism and wildness of the West were to be admired, wrote the historian Frederick Jackson Turner, as emphasized by Teddy Roosevelt's reclaiming of the wild.[26] Thus, even though they might have been seen as a threat to the social order, some criminals – the brash Westerners particularly – were lionized as masculine heroes. This fitted in with the story of the United States, Turner argued, as a huge page in history that:

begins with the Indian and the hunter; it goes on to tell of the disintegration of savagery by the entrance of the trader, the pathfinder of civilization; we read the annals of the pastoral stage in ranch life, the exploitation of the soil by the raising of unrotated crops of corn and wheat in sparsely settled farming communities; the intensive culture of the dense farm settlement; and finally the manufacturing organization with city and factory system.[27]

The weekly *Gazette* is most often considered a magazine, and it does not fit one characteristic of the usual definition of tabloid newspapers in that it was not a daily publication. But its methods were tabloid-like and gave rise to the increasing tabloidism that followed. As noted, sensationalism was part of the formula, and New York's *Journal* and *World* under the leadership of Hearst and Pulitzer put more and more emphasis on the antics of criminals, police, showgirls and sportsmen. In a real sense, they followed the *Gazette*'s lead by using these characters as a way to tell the stories of the (mostly) men who read the newspapers. They advocated for tough, disciplined men who were not afraid of violence and who could dispense appropriate justice through either brute force or superior intellect. This was the new self-made man at the turn of the century – the man who could respond to threats to his dominance in an effective, aggressive way.

Police and detectives as popular characters

In the second half of the nineteenth century, police officers and detectives began to write their own accounts of what it meant to fight crime. George S. McWatters wrote *Knots Untied; or Ways and By-Ways in the Hidden Life of an American Detective* in 1873. George Walling wrote *Recollections of a New York Chief of Police* (with a customarily lengthy subtitle) in 1887. These were followed by others, including Alfred Lewis's *Confessions of a Detective* (1906) and Thomas Furlong's *Fifty Years a Detective* (1912). Allan Pinkerton, the famed detective who created the first detective agency in the United States, had seventeen books ghostwritten under his name, telling stories of Pinkerton detectives.[28]

Detectives and their stories were becoming popular during this period because of their ability to capitalize on reason to solve crime, as opposed to the street police who simply fought crime as it came to them. The detective craze – using rationality to crack a case – was just another part of the era's growth of faith in new technologies, the emphasis on science and the desire to treat the world objectively. All of these factors influenced journalism as it tried to make sense of and chronicle the rapidly changing world and what was expected of the men and women who inhabited it. The detectives also served as figures representing appropriate male role models – reasonable, fluid, passionate and strong – the perfect foils for the deviant criminals and corrupt cops. An example of this role was found in *Our Rival, the Rascal: A Faithful Portrayal of the Conflict between the Criminals of this Age and the Defenders of Society – The Police*, by Benjamin P.

Eldridge and William B. Watts, two Boston police officials who recounted their careers as protectors of order. The preface begins:

> As we sit in our office chairs, our rival, the rascal, leers down at us through a thousand masks. He is reckless, gay, demure, stolid, dogged, surly, threatening, desperate. He has the smirk of the confidence man, the furtive glance of the sneak thief, the scowl of the burglar, the menace of the murderer. The moulds of every vice and crime which the world knows are ranged before us in a single group of pictures – the photographs which compose the Rogues' Gallery.[29]

What follows is mostly a recounting of crime and criminals, but the police are also portrayed (sometimes with conceit), and the authors offer what they call a 'just tribute to the ability, zeal, fearlessness and unflagging devotion to duty of our brother officers in the police service and the admirable administration of the boards of direction of our police throughout the country'.[30] Many of the same patterns that emerged in these authors' retellings of their careers were found in newspaper accounts: the contrast between the strong, rational men and the weak, corrupt ones; the praise for competent police administrators; the laudatory tones of congratulation for good police and their work.

During this period, the place of the police in popular culture, as actors, authors and characters in crime stories, was solidified. Near the turn of the century, journalists became writers of detective stories as well as characters in the stories themselves, and in these stories reporters were often portrayed as partners with law enforcement. The journalists, plucky and clever, helped detectives solve crimes. Many stories starred the 'reporter who has formed a relationship with the genius detective', wrote Panek.[31] Reporters thus gained some 'masculine' cachet, and their objective treatment of facts merged nicely with the rational, science-driven methods of the detectives.

Tied to this trend in the early twentieth-century era of sensationalism and urban culture was the growing popularity of the hard-boiled detective, a 'product of the action pulp magazine industry that spread itself across the United States during the 1920s and 1930s'.[32] A magazine called *Black Mask*, founded by H. L. Mencken and George Jean Nathan in 1920, helped create the popular images of the private detective. Soon, 'machine guns, tough guys, .45 automatics, hoodlums, cops and cons blossomed on the covers of the pulps'.[33] The writing, influenced by Dashiell Hammett, a former agent for the Pinkerton firm of detectives, was terse, and the heroes were strong, clear-eyed and mean if necessary. They were often loners, sympathetic but tough, mortally so if need be. These were 'classless, restless men who spoke the language of the street'.[34] These fictions, many based on true crimes, helped lead to a culture of portrayal of angry men fed up with criminals, defending society and women from the deviant; many were law enforcers unto themselves, outside the reins of law. They may have been gallant or violent, in keeping with masculine norms of the era, but the existence of the genre bears testimony to a will for action against a feeling of helplessness. By taking the law into their own hands, they also showed a rejection of a formal police culture founded on strict bonds of discipline.

The focus on police officers in newspapers of this era was much on their ability to fight crime at hand – that is, those crimes of passion or of the streets that could be responded to with some immediacy. In this role the police were the crime fighters while the detectives were the solvers. Each had its own role in the construction of masculinity; the officer may not have been portrayed as being as smart as the detective, but his role in fighting deviances was more likely to be identifiable to the working class.

In 1907, the *World* touted the record of Detective Bureau head James McCafferty by noting in a headline, 'The New Detective Chief Has Solved Many Murder Mysteries.'[35] So the portrayals of the types of law enforcement officers diverged. An officer might wield a club or a gun, or stumble on the job, but there was more opportunity for variety in the portrayals of detectives: the hard-boiled type might well solve problems with fists or weapons, but the logical Sherlock Holmes type was much more likely to use reason. Yet although intelligence and deductive reasoning may have been seen as birthrights of gentlemen in Victorian America and England, thanks in great part to Arthur Conan Doyle, police went about crime fighting in the opposite manner – they figured out who was a criminal, then applied crimes to that person. Approaching crime that way, Panek continued, 'the cops are fit to solve only the most pedestrian of crimes'.[36] He concluded that, in this context, the police often looked thuggish and stupid. In an age when the ideas of Cesare Lombroso, the Italian criminologist who held that some criminality was inherited, enjoyed some popularity, that amounted to an assault on their lower-class manhood.

Panek's study is primarily of detective fiction, but some of these characterizations held over in real-life newspaper accounts. In addition, newspapers brought fictional detective stories directly to American readers. Magazines were important, but publisher S. C. McClure helped to create the idea of the syndication of copy for newspapers, and in 1891 and 1892, having bought the rights to the Sherlock Holmes stories, he sold them for syndication to such publications as the *Baltimore Sun*, the *Boston Sunday Globe*, the *New York Sun*, the *New York World*, the *Times Picayune*, the *Grit* (Pennsylvania) and the *Washington Post*, among many others. So the fictional accounts of Holmes solving crimes appeared along accounts of real-life police sensationalisms, giving the odd feeling to readers of a police force fighting with reason on the one hand and might on the other. 'Side by side with news from the police blotter or the courts . . . newspapers ran stories about Sherlock Holmes and other fictional detectives and commentary about the detective story as a literary form.'[37] As Panek pointed out, the police were not portrayed as competent crime fighters in most Holmes stories; in fact, they were 'boobs'.[38] Also, as noted, reporters got in on the act of crime fighting, again showing reason and logic that eluded the police.

One may only speculate about the effect on readers who saw characters such as Sherlock Holmes or other brilliant detectives in their tabloids and newspapers. It may also be said that a variety of interpretations of portrayals of masculinities are possible in stories about an unmarried detective whose primary confidante is his male friend. But the stories of crime and crime solving became not just stories of crime and law enforcers, but also stories about rationality, heroic myth and the creation of narrative. William Randolph Hearst said, in instructions to his writers and editors: 'Murder stories and other criminal stories are not printed merely because they are criminal, but because of the mystery, or the romance, or the dramatic qualities in them. Therefore, develop the mystery, or the romance, or the dramatic qualities.'[39] These creations spilled into the popular imagination, so a character such as Holmes became a hero, not through brute force but through brute intellect, who was able to give reassurance to rational men in a turbulent time. Stephen Knight wrote: 'a figure like Holmes, who treated all problems individualistically and who founded his power on the very rational systems which had inhumane implications was a particularly welcome reversal of disturbing currents'. He continued:

> He chooses to be a lone agent, but he takes cases, neither a mundane policeman nor a self-gratifying amateur. He is a self-confessed Bohemian, yet he lives in busy professional London, not in a Dupin-like romantic hermitage. He shares his lodgings with Watson, being neither a solitary nor matched by a partner. For all their eccentricity his rooms are cozy, filled with masculine gadgets for comfort.[40]

Thus, often in contrast with the detectives, the police lost masculine 'rank'. They sometimes looked sloppy or thuggish, perhaps rendering them less effective in the eyes of the male readers. That is speculation; what may be more relevant is the construct of society in the overall effect of these messages. Diana Barsham wrote that in these stories the message about masculinities was as much about order and civilization as anything. For Doyle, 'the meaning of masculinity was located in the writing practices and ideological interpolations which compelled masculine bodies to respect the privileged laws of their own representation'.[41] That is certainly in keeping with the messages of editors of tabloids and crime-fighting organs such as the *Police Gazette*, as they used language that sensationalized the deviant, praised the defenders of order and lauded professionalism in crime fighting whenever possible.

When one considers the contemporary portrayals of another kind of (often lawless) lawman, particularly in the *Police Gazette*, one can see this relationship between the wild and the civilized in the sub-text of police and crime stories. The Western hero was a taming influence on nature, but often lawless in society, yet had a sense of justice and was admirable in his rigidity. The detective hero, on the other hand, is a hero of function in an age of reason and reactions to a mechanized world.[42]

Policing the big city: news of the *World*

After the turn of the century, tabloids began to dominate the print media's land-scape, and, with them, focus on the scandalous, the criminal and the attempts by law enforcement to provide protection and keep society civilized sharpened. Aurora Wallace described the tabloids as growing in the 1920s in a 'symbiotic' relationship with the police.[43] Emblematic of this relationship – the tendency of the press to link its fortunes to stories about police and policing – was the cover-age provided by Joseph Pulitzer's *World*. Although in its early years it did not rely on illustrations as much as tabloids did, the *World* was typical of the press of its day as it showed police in various roles, such as that of workingman, buffoon and, very often, hero. In 1896, an attractive quarter-page portrait of moustachioed policeman John Quinn ran above an item describing his heroics in rescuing a man who was trying to commit suicide by drowning. After punching the victim to subdue him, Quinn pulled him to the shore. 'Quinn has saved eight persons from drowning', the article concluded. A day earlier a story ran about a policeman who saved a man from being lynched by an angry mob when an older man killed his young wife in a fit of jealousy.[44] As observed in the analysis of masculinities portrayed in the *Gazette*, we see the heroics of the police in these accounts – hero-ics of ordinary officers.

During this period, most *World* crime stories focused on the criminals, but even a casual reader would pick up on the portrayals of police, who were often named in the stories (frequently with last names only, and many with tell-tale Irish sur-names). Aside from the routine depictions of police answering crimes, there were occasional playful jabs at their incompetence or their annoying habit of overstep-ping their bounds. One depiction (Figure 8.2) shows a rotund officer as the Statue of Liberty. Round was then a very common body shape among police if *World* illustrations are to be believed; these were images of big men who had gone soft and who had overindulged on the public dole. Instead of holding a tablet with the date of the Declaration of Independence, he holds a tablet that reads 'KEEP OFF THE GRASS'. The over-line says 'The Statue of Liberty. (With Amendments to suit the present times in New York)'. This amounted to a ridiculing of the officers as fat, over-reaching boobs, demeaning them as men and professionals. Another depiction was in a feature story about a Chicago policeman, F. Patrick Furlong, who had been advised by his supervisor to shave off his fiery-red whiskers. The department was facing some layoffs, and the inspector told Furlong that he might escape them if he shaved his moustache and sideburns. Others called him 'Farmer Cop' because of them, he told him. Furlong reluctantly went to a barber and had them shaved, but when the layoffs came he was among the fired. Outraged, he threatened a lawsuit. The inspector said that he would try to reinstate him.[45] Again, the clipping of the whiskers might be seen as demeaning to the officer – an almost literal de-masculinization.

The abuse of power by officers is seen in many items, often when they har-assed, insulted or assaulted women. For example, one item told the tale of an

FIGURE 8.2 Image of officers as overweight boobs were common caricatures in the late nineteenth century, as shown in Joseph Pulitzer's *World. The World,* 20 December 1895, p. 6.

officer, Patrick Fitzgibbons, drunk at his post. The piece noted that he had been tried twice before for insulting women and for insubordination and drunkenness. In this case he did not escape punishment, and was to be dismissed from the force.[46] Police abuses also became a hot topic among later tabloids, including the zany New York *Graphic*, which won fame for its 'composographs', a depiction, posed and photographed in the newspaper's art department, of a sensational real-life scene. The *Graphic*, like the *World*, held a particular contempt for the habit of law enforcement of preying on innocent women, as:

> the particular stink that made judges and vice cops most obnoxious arose from the Night Court, where women were framed. Magistrates, lawyers, bondsmen, and cops practiced extortion on women, both on prostitutes and on women guilty of nothing else but being women.[47]

This abuse of power – dominance over women often simply to assert authority – is a key component of hegemonic masculinity. In the press accounts, however, it implies the opposite of strength, because officers are wrongly asserting their power. This, again, amounts to a criticism of them as men.

As in the *Gazette*, the coverage of in-house police organization was a recurring theme, often to illustrate a bloated bureaucracy. On 20 April 1907, the *World* reported on the New York Police Department's stripping inspectors of high rank and salary to put them back into police precincts, and it ran a composite of pictures and illustrations showing the inspectors' heads over small bodies (Figure 8.3). The odd effect was perhaps meant to emphasize that the officers' heads were about to be figuratively lopped off, as indicated by a large illustration two days later showing yet another rotund officer holding a bag labelled 'Easy Money $' as he sadly

FIGURE 8.3 The *World* displayed a technological prowess in this composite illustration/photograph used to emphasize the axing of key police personnel, p. 12.

pondered the shake-up (Figure 8.4).[48] In fact, the *World*'s images of police did not vary much from the late nineteenth century well into the twentieth century. The evolution from the *Gazette*'s portrayals was subtle; although the *Gazette* did question police actions and imply that sometimes they failed to engage the appropriate methods of defending masculinity, the *World* took the portrayals further, often depicting officers as buffoons.

That is not to say, however, that officers were roundly satirized. In many cases portrayals were of police as enforcers and working men; sometimes they were heroes, sometimes they were inept or corrupt. In short, they were a lot like the men who read the newspaper, and they were aware of women's changing roles. The same week of the departmental shake-up saw the *World* publish a pair of stories entitled 'Who Says Women Would Not Make Fine Police?' The stories highlighted how three 'determined' New York women had tackled two thieves

WHERE DO I STAND?

FIGURE 8.4 Editors often wished the days of 'Easy Money' for fat public employees would come to an end. Such portrayals were often used to diminish the manliness of law enforcement officers.

and how another, by herself, had made use of a revolver and dagger to capture a burglar in Brooklyn.[49]

Conclusion: good cops/bad cops – ordinary men

Many researchers, including Gray Cavender, have concluded that portrayals of crime paint a picture of the world that is false, racist and alarming. Paul Kooistra and John S. Mahoney, in an essay called 'The Historical Roots of Tabloid TV Crime', argued that shows such as *America's Most Wanted* (and, one might add, *Cops*) are the natural products of yellow and tabloid journalism.[50] These shows are tightly edited and might be unrealistic, but such treatments attract readers and viewers and shape their perception of police and crime fighting. A similar point can be made about portrayals of police in shows ranging from *Hill Street Blues* to *CSI* and *Law and Order*. In a real sense, the depictions of police and detectives in tabloids, pulps and fiction of the nineteenth and early twentieth centuries predicted many of today's media frames. The crime-fighting hero might be bumbling, genius, eccentric or neurotic, but he was also all too human, and an all-too-ordinary man.

Thus, what most stands out when one examines these portrayals from tabloids and other media of the era is that coverage of crimes might have been sensational and overwrought, but very often the portrayals of police seemed more nuanced than the sensationalist treatment of the crimes and scandals. The *Illustrated Daily News* (now the New York *Daily News*) began in 1919 and made its reputation on pictures, pictures and more pictures; a camera still adorns its masthead. One of its most iconic representations of a police officer was on 25 July 1925, which showed a friendly, well-groomed officer stopping traffic to allow a cat to carry her kittens across the street.[51] It also ran photos and accounts of officers in their normal roles of walking beats or responding to crimes. As discussed, the *Police Gazette*, the *World*, the *Graphic* and other publications also often struck a balance in their coverage of police. So although newspapers seemed driven by crime and its effects to shout ever louder of dangers and deviance, the portrayals of police have seemed far more multifaceted. The officers were simple men, working men, often Irishmen. They worked hard in poor jobs. Some drank, some were corrupt; but often they were good men just doing their jobs and trying to protect the status quo. In other words, these were the men who read the *Gazette* and the *World*. They were men who went to work, and often drank, but who fought fiercely and with pride over what they perceived were their domains – their recreations and their camaraderie, away from women and the home.

This more tempered portrayal of police may in part reflect the responses to turn-of-the-century challenges to masculinities. The changing roles of women, the threats from immigrants and crime, the growing popularity of boxing, football and other sports, the culture of the theatre and showgirls – all of these mediated through a sometimes out-of-control press – deeply affected the men who frequented the saloons, barbershops and sporting rings of the day. The police were there to protect and respond to these factors, in many cases directly. A magazine such as the *Police Gazette* probably reflected the notion of many men that working-class officers, despite their many foibles, were *of* the white male readership. This must have been a comforting notion to the readers of the *Gazette*, whose editorial policies specifically stated that the publication was there to support the police in ridding society of criminal elements. Other newspapers may not have stated it as directly, but it was clear that they, too, very often supported the police. An added romanticization of Western lawmen and brilliant detectives may have made the ordinary officer seem boorish by comparison, but he still held his own, and played his role, on the streets. It was there that he interacted with ordinary citizens, and it was there that he was shown, often in a bad light, but equally often in a good one, carrying out the fight to preserve, protect and defend society under all manner of threats to and redefinitions of what it meant to be a man.

Notes

1 *National Police Gazette*, 14 October 1893, p. 1.
2 J. Stevens, *Sensationalism and the New York Press*, New York: Columbia University Press, 1991, p. 22.
3 Cited in Stevens, *Sensationalism*, p. 126.
4 F. Mott, *American Journalism, a History: 1690–1960*, New York: Macmillan, 1962, p. 442.
5 W. J. Campbell, *Yellow Journalism: Puncturing the Myths, Defining the Legacies*, Westport, CT: Praeger, 2003, p. 7. The term 'yellow journalism' was derived from the adventures of the cartoon character the Yellow Kid that ran in these papers.
6 Frank M. O'Brien, *The Story of the Sun*, New York: Appleton, 1928, p. 418.
7 E. Durkheim, *The Rules of the Sociological Method*, edited by S. Lukes, translated by W. Halls, New York: Free Press, 1982, pp. 50–9.
8 *National Police Gazette*, 20 June 1885, pp. 8, 4, 8 and 9 respectively.
9 R. W. Connell, *Masculinities*, Berkeley: University of California Press, 1995, pp. 225–43.
10 J. Higham, 'The Reorientation of American Culture in the 1890s', in J. Higham (ed.), *Writing American History*, Bloomington: Indiana University Press, 1970, p. 79.
11 E. Pleck and J. Pleck (eds), *The American Man*, Englewood Cliffs, NJ: Prentice-Hall, 1980, p. 6. The other major periods of men's history, according to Pleck and Pleck, were the years of 'agrarian patriarchy' (1630–1820), the 'commercial age' (1820–60) and an era of 'companionate providing' (1920–65). The contemporary era likely is the beginning of a 'new epoch in the history of gender relations', they wrote (p. 6).
12 L. Panek, *Probable Cause: Crime Fiction in America*, Bowling Green, OH: Bowling Green State University Press, 1990, pp. 5–6.
13 See H. Horowitz, *Rereading Sex: Battles over Sexual Knowledge and Suppression in Nineteenth-Century America*, New York: Knopf, 2002
14 Panek, *Probable Cause*, p. 8.
15 D. Schiller, *Objectivity and the News: The Public and the Rise of Commercial Journalism*, Philadelphia, University of Pennsylvania Press, 1981, pp. 68–9.
16 Schiller, *Objectivity and the News*, pp. 96–8.
17 See almost any issue of the *National Police Gazette* from the 1880s into the early twentieth century, for example 28 January 1896, p. 15.
18 K. Mumford, ' "Lost Manhood" Found: Male Sexual Impotence and Victorian Culture in the United States', *Journal of the History of Sexuality*, 1992, vol. 3, no. 1, pp. 33–57.
19 *National Police Gazette*, 1 October 1887, p. 3.

20 *National Police Gazette*, 3 September 1887, p. 4.

21 *National Police Gazette*, 1 September 1888, pp. 5, 2, 3, respectively.

22 *National Police Gazette*, 7 April 1894, p. 1; 12 January 1895, p. 6; and 3 October 1885, p. 9 respectively.

23 *National Police Gazette*, 20 June 1885, p. 2

24 Ibid.

25 *National Police Gazette*, 23 March 1889, p. 2.

26 Cited in J. Pettigrew, *Brutes in Suits: Male Sensibility in America, 1890–1920*, Baltimore: Johns Hopkins University Press, 2007, pp. 28–9.

27 Ibid, p. 29.

28 Panek, *Probable Cause*, pp. 8–9.

29 B. Eldridge and W. Watts, *Our Rival, the Rascal: A Faithful Portrayal of the Conflict between the Criminals of this Age and the Defenders of Society – The Police*, Boston: Pemberton 1897, p. vii. The full text of this book, including portraits of the authors and mugshots of such undesirables as 'English Harry', 'Frisco Slim' and 'Sheeny Si', is available online at Google Books.

30 Eldridge and Watts, *Our Rival, the Rascal*, p. viii.

31 L. Panek, *The Origins of the American Detective Story,* Jefferson, NC: McFarland & Company, 2006, p. 56.

32 W. Ruehlmann, *Saint with a Gun: The Unlawful American Private Eye*, New York: New York University Press, 1974, p. 57.

33 R. Goulart (ed.), *The Hardboiled Dicks: An Anthology of Pulp Detective Fiction from the Pulp Magazines*, Los Angeles: Sherbourne Press, 1965, p. xii.

34 K. Millar, 'The Writer as Detective Hero', *Show*, January 1965, p. 35.

35 *World*, 20 April 1907, p. 2. In another demonstration of a newspaper taking note of threats to white hegemonic masculinities, the item just below McCafferty's hiring, 'Father of Negro's White Wife Goes to Jail', told of a white man being convicted for 'violating public decency' by allowing his daughter to marry the African-American man.

36 Panek, *American Detective Story*, pp. 54–5.

37 Ibid, p. 30. For example, Panek notes on p. 114 that the *New York Times* ran Howard Fielding's 'A Secret of the Heart' in 1896.

38 Panek, *American Detective Story*, p. 43.

39 Quoted in N. Crawford, *The Ethics of Journalism*, New York: Knopf, 1924, p. 231.

40 S. Knight, *Form and Ideology in Crime Fiction*, Bloomington: Indiana University Press, 1980, p. 80.

41 D. Barsham, *Arthur Conan Doyle and the Meaning of Masculinity*, Burlington, VT: Ashgate, 2000, pp. 2–3.

42 See E. Margolies, *Which Way Did He Go? The Private Eye in Dashiell Hammett, Raymond Chandler, Chester Himes, and Ross Macdonald*, New York: Holmes and Meier, 1982.

43 Aurora Wallace, *Newspapers and the Making of Modern America: A History*, Westport, CT: Greenwood Press, 2005, p. 14.

44 'Jealousy Caused It', *World*, 16 June 1896, p. 5; 'Policeman Quinn Rescues His Eighth Man from Drowning', *World*, 17 June 1896, p. 2.

45 'Will Sue for His Whiskers', *World*, 15 December 1895, pp. 1, 47.

46 *World*, 6 December 1895, p. 5.

47 L. Cohen, *The New York* Graphic: *The World's Zaniest Newspaper*, Philadelphia: Chilton Books, 1964, p. 145.

48 *World*, 18 April 1907, p. 8.

49 *World*, 17 April 1907, p. 3.

50 See J. Ferrell and N. Websdale, *Making Trouble: Cultural Constructions of Crime, Deviance, and Control*, New York: Aldine de Gruyter, 1999.

51 L. McGivena, *The* News: *The First Fifty Years of New York's Picture Newspaper*, New York: News Syndicate, 1969, pp. 158–9.

9

QUIET AND DETERMINED SERVANTS AND GUARDIANS

Creating ideal English police officers, 1900–45

Joanne Klein

When a young man joined an English police force, he was issued with an instruction book, an essential guide to his basic duties written by chief constables.[1] These books varied in length and content but they all presented a clear image of the ideal police officer as the epitome of a masculine worker. Armed only with a truncheon, men in uniform upheld the law and protected the innocent. Their presence prevented crime and preserved public order. But this image was more challenging than it might first seem to be. At the centre of the English police ideal were policemen who earned the respect of the public, yet who were capable of being physically dominating when necessary. Men exercised authority over the public but did so by keeping command over themselves. Training new constables required reinforcing positive qualities such as vigilance, intelligence and judgement while discouraging negative traits such as insubordination, drunkenness and violence. The strategy in instruction books was to present the police ideal as a challenge to be won. Although superior officers did not really expect their men to embody every virtue, they strived to teach recruits that good policing depended more on mental and emotional strength than on brute force. This basic image had changed little from when the first Metropolitan Police instruction book was issued in 1829. However, beginning around 1900 and continuing into the 1940s, instruction books started including noble histories of English policing, linking policemen not just to 1829 but to valiant medieval traditions. These gave the classic 1829 image more depth, bolstering it up in response to fundamental shifts in policing. Expanding traffic duties were absorbing ever-increasing police resources and for the first time were bringing policemen into significant contact with potential middle- and upper-class lawbreakers. This ushered in an era of incivility as all parties adjusted to these new relationships. At the same time, the invention of the telephone made calling a policeman more convenient and created a new public habit, especially after the introduction of police call box systems in the 1930s. In response to the rising demands on police time and the new interactions with the public, instruction books began highlighting the constable's honour and duty to service and tracing them back to ancient English customs. The basic 1829 police image remained intact but was given more consequence, insisting that the policeman's role remained constant notwithstanding any transformation in his duties.

Policing in the first decades of the twentieth century was transitioning into its more modern form, in part as a result of how traffic brought the police into contact with all levels of the public and how telephones created new civilian expectations for police attention. During the nineteenth century, the working classes had adjusted to the presence of constables, and by the 1900s their interactions and conflicts had settled into fairly standard routines.[2] Rather than policemen becoming detached from their working-class roots as Mike Brogden has argued,[3] working-class civilians and policemen retained a common cultural context so they could interact on relatively similar terms, as shown in recent studies by Clive Emsley and Haia Shpayer-Makov, as well as in my research on the everyday lives of constables.[4] But with traffic, policemen were now interacting with the middle and upper classes who discovered that they did not necessarily appreciate police attention. They often responded with incivility and indignation when their behaviour was challenged. A higher-class driver confronted for breaking the law by a working-class constable could feel his world had turned upside down; traffic created civilian–police tensions that crossed class lines to a significant degree for the first time.[5] Barbara Weinberger has argued against any tendency to romanticize mid-century policing, but strains on policemen caused by traffic argue against romanticizing even early decades.[6] The 1930s police box and pillar systems later took on a patina of nostalgia, but when created their function was to help fewer policemen cover more beats so that constables could be reassigned to traffic duty. Many constables loathed their cramped conditions and longer beats. The telephones incorporated into them made it easier for both headquarters and the public to contact them, an advantage to efficiency in certain ways but also undermining the constable's powers of discretion. Constables still walked beats but now could be summoned with a phone call; policemen working in new traffic divisions coped with resentful and agitated drivers and pedestrians. In some cities, to ease the men's burden, a handful of policewomen were hired to take over duties linked to children and young women at risk. Yet forces remained uncomfortable with the idea of policewomen and kept them strictly segregated both in their own units and out of the main areas of instructions to recruits. New sections on traffic laws, telephone exchanges and policewomen appeared in instruction books but the basic masculine image of the policeman not only remained intact, but also was reinforced. With policemen now in professional contact with all levels of society, police forces needed to emphasize the qualities of the ideal officer more than ever to their recruits.

Dating back to the earliest decades of modern policing, instruction books were saturated with language painting a picture of the ideal policeman. Perhaps to his surprise, a recruit browsing his book for adjectives found only a handful on his physical traits but dozens on the mental and emotional virtues he needed to demonstrate. The goal here was to overthrow his common working-class preconception that policing was as easy as walking around. He expected that he should be fit, active, healthy, industrious and sober, and that he should be punctual, accurate, efficient and neat and smart in his appearance. But more daunting were the many abstract qualities. He needed to understand that policing was not easy; he had to balance the strength to preserve law and order with the sympathy to earn public support. On the one hand he was to be alert, determined, attentive, vigilant and firm, but he was also to be careful, moderate, quiet, cool and forbearing. He must show intelligence, judgement and discretion, and be kind, cheerful and good-tempered. To earn the respect of the public so necessary to be successful, he himself had to be respectful of the public. He practised courtesy, civility and tact. He was fair, honest and truthful. Because he worked alone much of the time he was independent and impartial, but as part of the force he was co-operative and loyal. Most of all, he needed a sense of humanity, to know that he served the public as well as the law. He did all of this with integrity and dignity. Not surprisingly, between 1900 and 1945, half of all men left the force because they would not or could not work with these daunting expectations. Men left voluntarily after finding the discipline too restrictive or the physical demands too hard, to look for more rewarding work or when hopes for promotion did not come through. Forces weeded out men who did not have the 'character of a policeman', which did not mean that those who remained were paragons, but at least they had the sense not to be caught too often neglecting their duty, drinking on duty or committing disorderly conduct or similar offences.[7] With policemen now interacting more with all classes, convincing recruits to exercise good judgement took on more urgency.

England employed a system of preventative policing and on the first pages of instruction books police forces solved the problem of making this sound manly to recruits by making success the definitive personal challenge. The Metropolitan Police preface stated that 'The protection of life and property, the preservation of public tranquillity, and the absence of crime, will alone prove whether those efforts have been successful.'[8] Crime and disorder meant that policemen had failed. If either became too common, 'there must be reason to suppose that the police are relaxing in their efforts'.[9] Stopping crime was each man's individual duty, not a vague goal: 'It must therefore be your constant endeavour to exercise such vigilance as to render it difficult for any one to commit a crime within that portion of the district which is under your immediate charge.'[10] Recruits read this basic sentence in nearly every preface from 1829 through into the 1970s. But new to the 1900s was a reminder that '*prevention rather than detection was . . . the true aim of a police system*', with Liverpool calling detection easier than prevention and too easily corrupted in 1903, 1911, 1926 and 1944.[11] The need for detection meant that preventative policing had failed to stop the criminals in the first place. Chief constables understood that recruits often joined the force with romantic views of fictional detectives from the *Strand* and best-selling author Edgar Wallace, and that they needed to restore the patrol officer as the foundation of English policing. As detective fiction grew in popularity with its tendency to portray constables as 'P.C. Plod', instruction books responded by building up the constable as the central hero of the police mission.

Chief constables began conjuring up romantic images of the constable to inspire their men regarding both their key role and the qualities they should represent. In the nineteenth century, prefaces told how England founded the new police in 1829 to replace corrupt watchmen of old, and that recruits became part of this modern innovation. In 1903, while still stressing this narrative, Liverpool presented policing as part of a heroic English history of public service both stretching back to medieval times and looking into the future.[12] Liverpool's chronicle proved so effective that it remained in use through the 1940s and was copied by Birkenhead (1926), Wallasey (1929) and Bolton (1934).[13] It inspired the Metropolitan Police to produce their own version in 1912 stretching back to Edward III that was copied by Bristol in 1914 and remained in use into the 1950s. Manchester went a step further in 1923, taking their history back to Saxon times and Edward I's Statute of Winchester.[14] As service duties increased, forces such as Manchester (1908/1923) and Preston (1924) framed the constable's mission in terms of chivalry and honour.[15] After the 1919 Police Act improved conditions of service, the emphasis on policing as a dedicated career grew:

> The police service is a vocation, in the truest sense of the word, and only if a man feels called to it, and is ready and willing to devote time and thought to the nature of his duties, can he hope to give satisfaction to the public and his own conscience.[16]

In 1925, London men were instructed that they 'should help anybody whom he sees in difficulties . . . especially the aged and infirm persons and children'.[17] In one of the more theatrical statements, Wallasey recruits read that:

> Life on earth is one continuous conflict between the forces of good and evil, and, if you set a high ideal of duty and of public service for yourself, you will definitely join the right side, and take a share in the good work of the world by helping others less fortunate than yourself.[18]

Although not overtly calling policemen modern knights, books in the 1920s and 1930s linked police work back to Anglo-Saxon and medieval traditions. Recruits were told that not only were they part of this proud history, but also, as modern policemen, they were 'the handy man of the Constitution', representing 'the disciplined organisation of the civil power'.[19]

Although ideal police qualities remained constant from the nineteenth century, instruction books now spent more time explaining to recruits why these characteristics were important rather than simply stating them. With the 1890 and

1919 Police Acts, forces were gradually attracting a better quality of recruit at the same time that policing was becoming more challenging. Chief constables needed to convince each policeman how important he was to the success of the police mission. Page-long sections detailed the constable's character, ending with a daunting list of attributes. They declared, 'let the Constable be *truthful, fair and civil* to everybody, *obedient* to his superiors, *sober and respectable* both on and off duty, *clean and smart* in his person and habits, [and] *zealous and energetic* in the execution of his duties'.[20] To put their powers of personal discretion in terms that most men could understand, the chief constable of Wallasey wrote in 1929: 'A Constable, so to speak, is in a similar position to a referee at a football match. A referee has to decide whether a player who breaks a rule must be cautioned, ordered off the field, or in more serious cases reported to the Association.'[21] At the same time, men were reminded that they were part of a hierarchy. But chief constables were careful to explain why this was important, and that recruits should remember 'that he who has been accustomed to obey will be considered the best qualified to command'.[22] Liverpool, Birkenhead, Wallasey and Bolton reassured recruits that obedience and masculinity went hand in hand:

> No man need hesitate about submitting himself to discipline, or think that he is doing anything derogatory to his manhood or his self-respect; he is only making himself part of a great human machine, working easily and without friction for the common good.[23]

Instruction books linked strength of character to practical requirements that men give up bad habits which undermined their effectiveness as constables. Although many of these rules were old, instruction books began to give reasons for them and to put them in a more realistic context. For example, regulations had always banned drinking on duty or even the appearance of soliciting drink. Now the message was that real men knew how to hold their drink and were intelligent enough not to compromise the reputation of the force over a beer. This did not require that they be teetotallers off duty. In fact, 'the man who has the strength of mind to drink intoxicants, and yet never drink more than is good for him, is every bit as good as he who abstains altogether'.[24] Regulations against smoking in uniform, either on or off duty, and in favour of a good appearance in uniform generally were now presented more clearly as a way to win public confidence. As Bristol insisted in 1914, 'A slovenly or untidy Police Officer can never be looked upon as efficient.'[25] The outer man projected the character of the inner man. A dirty or untidy constable:

> may be a good man in other ways, but he certainly raises the suspicion that he is not. He offers a bad example to his younger comrades and cannot gain the respect and confidences of those with whom his duties bring him into contact.[26]

Rather than simply being presented as breaking rules, a constable with bad habits could not carry out his duties efficiently, set a poor example for his colleagues and endangered the mission of the force.

A good habit that instruction books hoped to instil in constables was the need to study their duties and apply them intelligently, which grew in significance after the 1919 Police Act increased education standards and put more emphasis on promotion examinations. Recruits were from the working class where a man was expected to earn a decent wage and head his family.[27] So books emphasized that successful policemen earned rewards, including better pay and promotion, equating success with intelligence, knowledge and judgement. Studying brought advancement so that men who did not study were not doing their duty as men. Not only did men need to educate themselves about their duties, they should do so on their own initiative. Instruction books might include many details on their conditions of service and duties but:

> [s]omething must necessarily be left to the intelligence and discretion of individuals, and according to the degree in which they show themselves possessed of these qualities, and to their zeal, activity, and judgment on all occasions, their claim to future promotion and reward will be considered.[28]

The meaning was simple: the best way to gain promotion was to improve their minds. Police forces filled their superior officer positions from the ranks, a big incentive to study for promotional examinations, even more so after 1900 when even chief constables began to be drawn from the police ranks.[29] Men were urged not to be satisfied with simply earning a wage but to plan for their futures, similar to the presentation of policing as being historic but also looking forward.

Despite the straightforward picture of discouraging theft and disorder presented in the basic 1829 image, policemen had picked up odd jobs over the decades since then. Only in the twentieth century, however, did instruction books begin to include this miscellany in their portrayal of the ideal officer, finally recognizing that policing included a confusing variety of responsibilities. This new image was most clearly articulated in the Manchester 1923 guide, which began by listing the new centres of attention and working back to older ones:

> His multifarious duties include, to name only a few, the regulation of traffic, ambulance and first-aid service, the inspection of weights and measures, the taking of precautions against the spread of contagious diseases among animals, the supervision of licensed premises, places of amusement, and common lodging houses, and the relief of vagrants.[30]

Other increasing duties included working with children and assisting with Police-Aided Clothing Associations, founded in the late nineteenth century to help poor children attend school and find work.[31] Chief constables explained that many duties 'may seem to be outside the scope of police duty proper' but insisted that 'anything which helps the very poor and so relieves them from the temptations to crime, anything which helps to take the children of the criminal classes away from evil surroundings and companions' was still 'true police work'.[32] Many of these new responsibilities, such as first aid, caring for needy children and even coping with lost property, could be difficult to categorize as masculine. Tidying up misplaced umbrellas after absent-minded commuters had a distinctly housewifely quality. Instruction books began framing these duties as part of the heroic tradition of English policing, and therefore manly occupations.

Chief constables had to figure out how to accommodate traffic and its related duties into the masculine image of policing as constables now spent an increasing amount of time coping with motor vehicles and the unexpected tasks that traffic produced. Traffic became a messy intersection of old and new. Streets still teemed with horse-drawn vehicles, handcarts and livestock. By the 1890s, bicycles and slippery tramlines added to the confusion.[33] Into this came automobiles, lorries and motor cycles. Great Britain went from 32,000 motor vehicles in 1905, to 363,000 in 1920, and 2,048,000 in 1940.[34] Police forces pulled men from regular beats to maintain order on the roads; even men not assigned to traffic were called on to deal with hurt pedestrians, runaway horses and numerous collisions. Traffic caused unanticipated work. For instance, as more people used public transportation, the police grappled with a mountain of lost items turned in by tram, cab and bus drivers that had to be catalogued, stored and disposed of if unclaimed. In Birmingham, an average of 5,460 items were turned in to the police every year between 1900 and 1918, jumping to 15,900 a year between 1919 and 1929, and soaring to 43,300 a year in the 1930s.[35] Traffic caused a particular strain on the relationship between the police and the public. Drivers, cyclists and pedestrians had to adjust to new speeds, noises and traffic laws, and everyone was learning new rules and regulations. Many civilians found themselves on the receiving end of police attention for the first time, and tempers frayed. The middle and upper classes had been accustomed to viewing policemen as social inferiors, and now had to learn to take orders from traffic constables either as drivers or as pedestrians. If caught for infractions, they did not understand that their excuses were only too familiar to policemen. Women could resent this as much as men, but a man, especially one who could afford a vehicle, could be particularly sensitive to a working-class constable in authority over him. The 1920s and 1930s saw a jump in members of the public charging policemen with behaving in an 'uncivil and impolite manner', including 'shouting and bawling' at drivers and pedestrians who misunderstood traffic signals or broke street regulations.[36] In a special pamphlet issued on traffic duty in 1931, constables were reminded that although 'the Police Officer at times must give orders to the public he must never forget that he is still a public servant. Tact and courtesy are essential.'[37] The growing emphasis on policing as an honourable vocation was one way of fortifying good behaviour as part of its masculine ideal as more men found themselves spending more time patrolling traffic.

The telephone seemed to be a perfect way to get constables where they were needed, especially with more policemen tied up with traffic duty, but instead they added to the stress of the men still on regular beats. The public quickly got into the habit of phoning. Even walking to an official police telephone was simpler than finding a man on the beat. In 1928, Manchester civilians made 1,337 calls for assistance from police boxes and 1,898 from other telephones. In 1929, they made 4,080 police box calls and 7,512 other calls to the police, three and a half times as many calls as the year before.[38] One common reason to call was to demand first aid and ambulances. By 1900, most forces required men to pass the St John Ambulance examination in first aid. Calls for first aid in Liverpool doubled from the 1900s to the 1930s, and tripled in Birmingham.[39] Manchester handled around 3,000 first aid calls a year in the early 1900s, over 10,000 calls for ambulances in 1929 and nearly 20,000 ambulance calls in 1931.[40] The public learned that they could easily summon a policeman not only for emergencies but also for minor matters, creating 'the natural tendency on the part of the public to use the telephone service more and more'.[41] But with men reassigned from walking beats to directing traffic and the men left behind stretched thin to cover more territory, the public grew impatient when neighbourhood constables could not arrive as quickly as they expected. In the 1920s, forces set up telephone exchanges, often with motorcycle policemen to respond to emergency calls. But these men had to be taken from regular beat duty, stretching thin resources already taxed by traffic responsibilities, and soon the volume of calls overwhelmed even this system. Policemen spent less time patrolling and more time reacting to calls for help for broken bones, family disputes or barking dogs. The public complained that calls for police assistance were slow, not recognizing that they were often aggravating the problem, calling the police for trivial matters such as noisy parties or badly parked cars that might have been resolved without police help if the police had not been so easily summoned. A 1929 Royal Commission worried that 'the Police are in danger of being overburdened with duties, whilst their efficiency is simultaneously being impaired by criticism which is often unfair and undeserved'.[42] The solution often became police box and pillar systems, which sounded good in theory. Policemen no longer had to follow set beats but instead signed in at set times. They could be summoned to the box or pillar by a blue flashing light in case of emergency phone calls. In reality, however, the systems were used more to save money than for efficient policing. Policemen were often assigned double beats to free men for traffic duty and the boxes allowed cities to delay repairs to police stations. The boxes isolated men who now paraded directly to their beats rather than parading together at a station. This damaged force morale and more crucially undermined the ability of young policemen to learn from experienced men. So although the telephone could have improved police efficiency, its main impact on the ranks was to add to the strain and incivility already created by traffic duty.[43]

Perhaps the most demanding lesson recruits needed to learn stepping into this tense environment was that effective policing often meant doing less rather than more, not an obviously masculine trait. Although always stressed, this message became even more important now that policemen were dealing with traffic infractions and phone calls. Words like restraint, moderation, sobriety, coolness and forbearance appeared frequently. Books advised against interfering unless needed, against issuing summonses when no one was being bothered, against making arrests when a summons would do and against calling for assistance unless necessary. On the other hand, when action was called for, constables should not hesitate. 'If a Police Officer is called on to act he must do so with promptness, energy, and determination, for, if he wavers or doubts, the offender may escape, or the opportunity to give help may be lost.'[44] The key was discerning where the line was between inaction and action. Even in action, however, constables needed to exercise discretion. Men were told to 'never strike or use the truncheon but in self defence'[45] and 'never ill treat or abuse a prisoner, or use his staff upon him unless it is absolutely unavoidable'.[46] If a truncheon became necessary, men were to aim for muscle rather than bone, and never to aim for the head. Liverpool constables were even warned to 'never hit a woman, an old or infirm man, or a child'.[47] Instead, men should as much as practicable abstain from violence, as that 'will secure for them the approbation and ready assistance of all well-disposed bystanders'.[48] Policemen needed to use physical force as a last resort, and then as little as necessary to be effective. The 1912 Metropolitan Police instruction book put a fresh emphasis on avoiding force, advising that the constable who employed 'conciliatory methods' could usually convince civilians to co-operate, and he 'is a more useful police officer than his comrade relying too much on the assertion of his authority, [who] runs the risk of seeing that authority challenged and possibly, for the time being, overborne'.[49] Men who learned the lesson of restraint became successful policemen, particularly at a time when they were coming into contact with a wider range of society.

Exercising restraint became an especially necessary quality when provoked, which took on new urgency when coping with aggravated drivers, pedestrians, cyclists and phone callers. Although recruits might enter the force thinking of strength as physical power, the police defined strength as self-control, no matter how aggravating duty could be, in order to earn the respect of the public. Although including physical restraint, maintaining a good temper encompassed every kind of forbearance. Instruction books warned constables that they would be constantly exposed to insults, provocations and bad language, which multiplied along with traffic and telephones. But no matter how annoying civilians became, the men must not reply back in kind. The Metropolitan Police regularly reminded its men not to talk in an impatient, abrupt manner to the public.[50] Men were advised to 'avoid altercations, and display command of temper under insult and *gross* provocation'[51] as a 'policeman in a passion is not only ridiculous but useless'.[52] The smarter option was forbearance. 'By the exercise of restraint he will the better be able to execute his duty, besides possessing a strategic advantage over those who revile him.'[53] Even though young constables especially could find it difficult not to respond in kind when challenged, instruction books repeatedly stated that resistance took more strength and was the smarter option. For preventative policing to work, constables needed the public to respect and trust them. Changes in policing made earning this respect that much harder. Suddenly, the middle and upper classes no longer saw policemen as persons they might approach only if requiring directions, but as enforcers of traffic laws they might be breaking. Policemen now had to win over an entire nation of potential offenders. Twentieth-century instruction books made it clear that:

> to merit and retain that confidence must be the earnest endeavour of every policeman. Without it, he is only a big man with a stick, only one against a thousand; with it, he has at his back every citizen worthy of the name.[54]

Nothing should jeopardize this relationship. Constables served the public and had a duty to help anyone who asked as far as it was within their power to do so. This included answering questions and dispensing advice with patience, kindness and courtesy. Chief constables from the 1910s to the 1930s stressed that 'he must look on himself as a servant and guardian of the general public and treat all law-abiding citizens irrespective of their social positions, with unfailing patience and courtesy'.[55] Although this could be interpreted as respecting the humble, it also meant maintaining patience with the higher in status, who could demand just as much forbearance on the part of policemen as any villain.

Given the effort that chief constables put into creating the image of the stalwart policeman, it might at first seem paradoxical that police forces reacted to increasing demands by shifting a select set of duties to women. Yet rather than diluting the masculinity of the force, giving tasks that seemed to fall within the purview of women to female workers relieved the men of these obligations. Police forces first hired women for the practical purpose of looking after female prisoners; 'female searchers' and warders began appearing at police stations in small numbers by the 1880s. She might be the wife or widow of a resident officer or a 'suitable woman residing near the station'.[56] She searched female prisoners for contraband and weapons, kept on eye on drunken and suicidal prisoners, and acted as chaperone when policemen needed to enter the cell. The move towards hiring these 'searchers' came at least in part in response to pressure from social purity movements that it was more seemly for women to attend to women, but also as a step in line with female factory and sanitary inspectors. Hiring women to supervise female prisoners and to handle matters involving children was practical and deflected possible criticism.[57] By the 1900s, most forces called these women 'police matrons'. This had a professional association linked to prisons, hospitals and schools, and strictly separated them into their own female category. Many forces had one station with special cells for women under the supervision of a matron and so female prisoners were taken there. The matron had similar responsibilities to a station sergeant, and might even be his wife. Like searchers and warders, matrons tended to be police wives, widows and similar respectable working-class women. The matron looked after the prisoners' safety and well-being, separated respectable women from 'disreputable women', reported illness to the inspector on duty and accompanied prisoners to and from hospitals, asylums, court and workhouses.[58] Her work was confined to looking after prisoners; she did no patrol work. Nevertheless, employing women at police stations brought them into a decidedly male atmosphere with its colourful language and sometimes violent prisoners. Policemen appreciated being able to hand over the responsibility for female prisoners to a woman but many still felt uncomfortable about employing women in such a rough environment.

Matrons had been successful enough in coping with women and children that, by the 1920s, police forces slowly began to hire policewomen. This had a double advantage for forces that tried it: more feminine duties associated with women and children could be shifted to policewomen, easing the burden of policemen already under strain. During the First World War, women had been able to join organizations such as the Women Police Volunteers, typically patrolling for women at risk in cities, in factories and around military installations. Although their numbers were cut back as soon as the war ended, some forces saw the advantages of having women take over duties appropriate for the female sphere such as patrolling for 'girls in danger' and hunting down truant children.[59] The first policewomen were viewed by their male colleagues as welfare workers rather than police officers, fulfilling the female role of looking after the moral lives of the young. Policewomen remained segregated in special sections, as the research of Philippa Levine and Louise Jackson has demonstrated.[60] However, they were not limited to station work like the matrons. In most forces, such as Birmingham, matrons continued in parallel with policewomen.[61] Their role was:

> the prevention of crime, immorality amongst women and girls, and helping in the reclamation of those living in depravity to honourable and useful lives; also in cases where it becomes necessary, from a Police point of view, to deal with children, and generally assisting the Superintendents of cases of a nature which better could be dealt with by a woman than a man.[62]

When women or children were involved in some incident, policewomen and sometimes matrons could be called in to assist.[63] With great hesitation male superior officers designed special beats for policewomen's interests, fearing that the women could become victims themselves. The 'lady policemen' proved capable of looking after themselves but men remained resistant to women as patrol officers. Typical duties became patrolling for women and children at risk or in danger in the streets, parks and public places, escorting women and children to various institutions, enquiries about missing children and young people, observations and raids likely to involve women and children, and attending court. They assisted 'females in distress' and worked 'among girls who can be removed from evil influences'.[64] Women received the same training as men and in most forces had the same powers of arrest but were encouraged 'to obtain the assistance of a male colleague' either by arranging his presence ahead of time or by summoning him with a whistle or yell in an emergency.[65] Policewomen developed an expertise in matters involving women and children, and Joan Lock's memoir about 1950s London described hunting down truant school children, arresting streetwalkers and escort duty, very much as outlined in official manuals.[66] However, Stella Condor, writing about the same time and place, broke up fights and arrested a bookie, presenting a work life more like that of a male constable even though policewomen worked in units entirely separate from policemen with their own duties. Similarly to Lock, she also carried out duties regarding women and children and worked as a short-hand writer, but her career showed that the barrier between the special duties of policewomen and those of policemen could be artificial at times.[67] Policewomen prided themselves on their ability to avoid confrontation but acknowledged that this often resulted simply from their duties differing from those of policemen.[68] Assigning women to separate sections and duties allowed police forces to preserve their primary masculine image.[69] Inter-war units remained tiny. Birmingham, for example, had only six policewomen in the 1920s, increasing to sixteen by 1937, out of an authorized strength of nearly 1,600 men.[70] In 1939, only 246 police-women existed nationally in England and Wales, 0.4 per cent of the total police establishment.[71] Instruction books more or less ignored the women, adding a page or two on women's sections but not otherwise including them in descriptions of the occupation. Reading the instruction books from the 1920s to the 1950s, when policewomen were beginning to patrol the streets with full powers of arrest and the same training as the men, the women might not exist.

Ironically, the hiring of policewomen perhaps helped chief constables rein-force the dominant masculine ideal by freeing policemen from the many welfare duties that they had taken on before the women were hired. Policewomen might be appearing in uniform and carving out a special niche for themselves within the police force but their numbers remained small. Policemen admitted their useful-ness in taking over social service tasks but women could do this without upsetting traditional notions of gender. Men were typically friendly to their female col-leagues, but remained uncomfortable about women patrolling and worried about them getting hurt, sometimes to the amusement of women who had served during world wars and were quite capable of handling themselves.[72] However, bringing women into the force as fully-fledged patrol officers with the same duties as men would have been too much innovation in a period already burdened with change. Twentieth-century policing was going through huge adjustments in reaction to traffic, telephones and expanding social welfare duties. Instruction books reflected these transformations. New sections appeared on traffic duties, motor divisions, telephone exchanges, first aid, the Police Federation and policewomen. Many forces added new sections on the history of English policing. But rather than change the ideal policeman, they reinforced this identity in the face of change, and left intact the image of the English policeman meeting the challenge of preventa-tive policing rather than by reforming him in any significant ways. On the surface, anyway, the 1829 image lived on into the 1930s and even the 1950s, updated only as a kind of modern police knight with all of his chivalrous qualities. Only after the Second World War were philosophical essays on police ideals gradually edited out of instruction books, replaced by more matter-of-fact manuals and practical binders of policies necessary for post-war recruits.[73]

Notes

1 Local forces often borrowed material from the London Metropolitan Police, Liverpool, Manchester or even smaller forces, either verbatim or paraphrasing. Chief constables usually wrote prefaces and introductions, some writing philosophical essays. So although books shared many characteristics, they also varied from force to force and over time, along with the personalities of the local communities.

2 See J. Klein, *Invisible Men: The Secret Lives of Police Constables in Liverpool, Manchester and Birmingham, 1900–1939*, Liverpool: Liverpool University Press, 2010, ch. 6.

3 M. Brogden, *On the Mersey Beat: Policing Liverpool between the Wars*, Oxford: Oxford University Press, 1991. Barbara Weinberger makes a similar argument in *The Best Police in the World: An Oral History of English Policing*, Aldershot: Scolar Press, 1995. Both relied on interviews of retired police officers, Brogden twenty-four and Weinberger eighty-five. This missed the experiences of half the men, as only about half made it to retirement between 1900 and 1939. Brogden made no use of Liverpool City Police records to balance his interviews, whereas Weinberger did make extensive use of written records.

4 See C. Emsley, 'The Policeman as Worker: A Comparative Study c. 1800–1940', *International Review of Social History*, 2000, vol. 45, pp. 89–110; H. Shpayer-Makov, *The Making of a Policeman: A Social History of a Labour Force in Metropolitan London, 1829–1914*, Aldershot: Ashgate, 2002; and Klein, *Invisible Men*.

5 See C. Emsley, '"Mother, What Did Policemen Do When There Weren't Any Motors?": The Law, the Police and the Regulation of Motor Traffic in England, 1900–1939', *The Historical Journal*, 1993, vol. 36, no. 2, pp. 357–381 (p. 368); and Klein, *Invisible Men*, pp. 169, 190–6.

6 See Weinberger, *Best Police in the World*.

7 These examples come from all the instruction books used for this chapter. They did not change significantly from city to city or over time. See Klein, *Invisible Men* for a study of the reality of police work versus the ideals presented here. For the origins of these qualities before the modern police, see F. Dodsworth, 'Masculinity as Governance: Police, Public Service and the Embodiment of Authority, c. 1700–1850', in M. McCormack (ed.), *Public Men: Masculinity and Politics in Modern Britain*, New York: Palgrave Macmillan, 2007, pp. 33–53.

8 Metropolitan Police, *Instruction Book for the Government and Guidance of the Metropolitan Police Force*, London: Darling, 1900, p. iii.

9 S. Kershaw, Chief Constable, *Regulations and Instructions for the Southport Police Force, and Fire Brigade, By Order of the Watch Committee*, Southport: Lowes, 1893, p. 2.

10 Major G. J. Teevan, Chief Constable (comp.), *Town of Hove Constable's Hand-Book*, Hove: H. Emery, 1894, p. 9.

11 Liverpool City Police, *Instructions, 1903*, Liverpool: C. Tinling, 1903, p. 6, original emphasis. Also included this passage: Liverpool City Police, *Instructions, 1911*, Liverpool: C. Tinling, 1911; *Instructions, 1926*, Liverpool: C. Tinling, 1926; and *Instructions, 1944*, Liverpool: John Gardner, 1944.

12 Liverpool, 1903, pp. 6–9. Also included this passage: Liverpool City Police, *Instructions*, 1911, 1926 and 1944.

13 County Borough of Bolton, *Police Instructions*, Bolton: Blackshaw, Sykes and Morris, 1934; Birkenhead Borough Police, *Instructions*, no title page, c. 1926; and *Wallasey County Borough Police Instruction Book*, no title page, 1929.

14 City of Manchester, *Police Instruction Book*, Manchester: Co-operative Wholesale Society's Printing Works, 1923, p. 11.

15 City of Manchester, *Police Instruction Book*, Manchester: John Heywood, 1908, p. 75; also included this language Manchester, 1923; and County Borough of Preston,

Police Instruction Book, issued by Authority of the Watch Committee, Preston: R. Seed, 1924.

16 Manchester, 1923, p. 16.
17 Metropolitan Police, *Instruction Book for the Guidance of the Metropolitan Police Force*, London: Printed by the Receiver for the Metropolitan Police District, 1925, p. 31.
18 Wallasey, 1929, p. 37. Wallasey is located just west of Liverpool and is now part of the Merseyside Police Authority.
19 Manchester, 1923, p. 12.
20 Liverpool, 1903, p. 24, original emphasis. The 1911, 1926 and 1944 editions included this passage, as well as Birkenhead, 1926, and Wallasey, 1929.
21 Wallasey, 1929, p. 54.
22 Southport, 1893, p. 3.
23 Liverpool, 1903, p. 15. The 1911, 1926 and 1944 editions include this passage, as well as Birkenhead, 1926, Wallasey, 1929, and Bolton, 1934.
24 Liverpool, 1903, p. 23. The 1911, 1926 and 1944 editions include this passage.
25 City of Bristol, *Bristol Police Force Instruction Book, Issued by Authority of the Bristol Watch Committee*, Bristol: Henry Hill, 1914, p. 30.
26 Liverpool, 1926, p. 43. Also in Liverpool, 1944.
27 See J. Gillis, *For Better, For Worse: British Marriages, 1600 to the Present*, Oxford: Oxford University Press, 1985, pp. 251–2; P. Ayers and J. Lambertz, 'Marriage Relations, Money, and Domestic Violence in Working-Class Liverpool, 1919–1939', in J. Lewis (ed.), *Labour and Love: Women's Experiences of Home and Family 1850–1940*, Oxford: Basil Blackwell, 1986, pp. 194–219; and E. Roberts, *A Woman's Place: An Oral History of Working Class Women 1890–1940*, Oxford: Basil Blackwell, 1984.
28 Metropolitan Police, 1900, p. vii. This basic statement appeared in nearly every instruction book.
29 Previously chief constables and assistant chief constables had typically come from the Royal Irish Constabulary, colonial forces and the military, but this began to change around 1900 with notable chief constables rising from the rank of constable, the first being Sir Robert Peacock of the Manchester City Police in 1898.
30 Manchester, 1923, p. 12.
31 See Klein, *Invisible Men*, pp. 216–19.
32 Liverpool, 1903, p. 9. Also Liverpool, 1911, 1926 and 1944 editions, Birkenhead, 1926, and Bolton, 1934.
33 See Emsley, ' "Mother, What Did Policemen Do" ', p. 361.
34 B. R. Mitchell, *European Historical Statistics 1750–1970*, London: Macmillan, 1978, table F4, p. 351, quoted in Emsley, ' "Mother, What Did Policemen Do" ', p. 358.
35 Birmingham City Police, 'Annual Reports', 1900–39.
36 Standing Order 45, 26 November 1929, Bristol Constabulary, 'Standing Orders, revised 1st December 1930', C. G. Maby, Chief Constable, Bristol: Chief Constable's Office, 1930.
37 Manchester City Police, *Supplementary Instruction Book, Extracts from Acts, Regulations and Orders dealing with the Use on the Public Highways of Motor Vehicles, together with General Instructions thereon*, Manchester: Henry Blacklock, 1931, p. 5.
38 Manchester City Police, 'Annual Reports', 1928 and 1929.
39 Liverpool City Police, 'Annual Reports', 1900–39; and Birmingham City Police, 'Annual Reports', 1900–39. Liverpool averaged 770 calls a year, 1900–18; 900 a year, 1919–29; and 1,470 a year 1930–9. Birmingham averaged 1,555 calls a year, 1900–18; 3,190 a year, 1919–29; and 4,525 a year, 1930–9.
40 Manchester City Police, 'Annual Reports', 1902, 1906, 1908, 1911, 1929 and 1931.
41 'Annual Report of HM Inspectors of Constabulary for 1932', *Parliamentary Papers*, 1932–3, (46) xv, 283, p. 6.

42 'Report of the Royal Commission on Police Powers and Procedure', *Parliamentary Papers*, 1928–9, Cmd 3297, vol. IX, 127, p. 82.

43 For more on the breakdown of traditional beat work, see J. Klein, 'Traffic, Telephones and Police Boxes: The Deterioration of Beat Policing in Birmingham, Liverpool and Manchester between the World Wars', in G. Blaney (ed.), *Policing Interwar Europe: Continuity, Change and Crisis, 1918–1940*, London: Palgrave Macmillan, 2007, pp. 215–36.

44 Metropolitan Police, *Instruction Book for the Guidance of the Metropolitan Police Force*, London: Printed by His Majesty's Stationery Office, 1934, p. 3. The 1912 and 1925 editions included this passage. Similar statements appeared in most instruction books.

45 Manchester, 1908, p. 83.

46 Manchester, 1923, p. 14.

47 Liverpool, 1926, p. 46; also 1944 edition.

48 Liverpool, 1893, p. 60.

49 Metropolitan Police, *Instruction Book for the Guidance of the Metropolitan Police Force*, London: Darling, 1912, pp. 6–7. The 1925 and 1934 editions included similar passages.

50 Metropolitan Police, 1900, p. 78. The 1912 edition had similar concerns.

51 Cheshire Constabulary, 'Memorandum', Form 39/A, 1920.

52 Metropolitan Police, 1912, p. 17. The 1925 edition included a similar passage.

53 Lancashire Constabulary Standing Orders, loose-leaf binder, August 1937 order.

54 Liverpool, 1903, p. 8. Also the 1911, 1926 and 1944 editions.

55 Metropolitan Police, 1912, p. 6. The 1925 and 1934 editions included this passage.

56 Bristol, 1914, p. 31.

57 P. Levine, ' "Walking the Streets in a Way No Decent Woman Should": Women Police in World War I', *Journal of Modern History*, 1994, vol. 66, no. 1, pp. 34–78 (pp. 35–9).

58 Manchester, 1908, pp. 87–8. The 1923 edition included basically the same passage. Wallasey, 1929, had a similar description of a matron's duties.

59 See L. Jackson, *Women Police: Gender, Welfare and Surveillance in the Twentieth Century*, Manchester: Manchester University Press, 2006.

60 See Jackson, *Women Police*; and Levine, ' "Walking the Streets in a Way No Decent Woman Should" '.

61 Birmingham City Police, 'Annual Report', 1922, p. 7.

62 City of Bristol, *Bristol Constabulary Supplementary Instruction Book 1939, issued by Authority of the Bristol Watch Committee*, C. G. Maby, OBE, Chief Constable, p. 15.

63 Sir A. Hordern, Chief Constable, *Notes for the Guidance of Members of the Lancashire Constabulary*, Hutton, Preston: Printed and Published at the County Chief Constable's Office, 1947, p. 5.

64 Birmingham City Police, 'Annual Report', 1922, p. 7.

65 Metropolitan Police, *Instruction Book for the Guidance of the Metropolitan Police Force*, London: Printed by the Receiver for the Metropolitan Police District, 1953, ch. 2, paragraph 50.

66 J. Lock, *Lady Policeman*, London: Michael Joseph, 1968.

67 S. Condor, *Woman on the Beat: The True Story of a Policewoman*, London: Robert Hale, 1960.

68 Weinberger, *Best Police in the World*, pp. 99–101.

69 Women's sections were disbanded and policewomen were integrated into the force as regular police constables in 1969.

70 Birmingham City Police, 'Annual Reports', 1920–39.

71 C. Emsley, *The English Police: A Political and Social History*, 2nd edn, New York: Longman, 1996, p. 158. In 1963, just over 3,000 policewomen existed, 3.5 per cent of the total.

72 Both Lock and Condor, for example, described positive relationships with their male colleagues. See also Weinberger, *Best Police in the World*, pp. 93–102.

73 The 1829 image never disappeared entirely, appearing even in massive multi-ring binders such as the *Lancashire Constabulary General Orders and Regulations*, Preston: Hutton, 1972, section 2, p. 1; the *Merseyside Police Authority Manual of General Instructions*, 1986–9, section 2, p. 1; and the *Greater Manchester Police Instruction Book*, 2nd edn, 1983–91, foreword.

10

SCIENCE AND SURVEILLANCE

Masculinity and the New York State Police, 1945–80

Gerda W. Ray

Introduction

'And there is the ugliest, blackest [long pause] Negro gentleman I've ever seen in my life. Boy, when they painted him, they painted him dark', a New York State Police (NYSP) sharpshooter alerted the marksman lying next to him on the cell block roof, their high-power rifles trained on the convicts below in D yard, Attica State Correctional Facility.[1] They had been deployed to retake a maximum-security prison, and they were impatient for the order to begin. If the officer also sounded contemptuous, it may have been because the prisoners were armed only with knives.

The assault embodies one of the central tensions in the history of masculinity in the United States, the confrontation between the armed white man and the black man.[2] Located both within and beyond dichotomized cultural norms of masculinity as the opposite of womanliness, the despised other, white masculinity in the United States has also been deeply defined by the historic dominance of white men over people of colour. The cultural image of armed white men, whether as agents of state power or as vigilantes, attacking men of colour is as familiar as a Western movie or the beating of Rodney King.

In an overwhelming use of force, hundreds of men, led by the NYSP and also including local police, sheriffs' deputies and prison guards, stormed the prison. The state police shot and killed thirty-nine people and wounded more than eighty others. The victorious police and guards exacted immediate, awful revenge, beating and humiliating the bodies that had challenged state authority and, by extension, their authority. The prisoners were stripped naked and made to crawl across the mud in the yard. The 'ringleaders' were marked with chalk and then beaten by a gauntlet of police and guards. Beatings of prisoners by guards continued for weeks. The visceral brutality against the prisoners may well have been

218   Gerda W. Ray

exacerbated by the deaths of ten of the some two dozen correctional officers taken hostage during the assault, and of one who had died of injuries sustained in the initial prisoner takeover. Attica personnel and the state police officers from Troop A lived in the same small towns and rural communities of Wyoming county. Their families shared similar burdens of round-the-clock schedules and tight state budgets; the hostage correction officer Frank Strollo and trooper Anthony Strollo were brothers.[3] The deaths of the Attica officers were felt deeply by the state police, the prison staff and the communities in which they lived.

The NYSP told the public, and the families of the deceased correctional officers, that the hostages had been killed by the prisoners. This initial official explanation reinforced the image of the prisoners as vicious black men who would gratuitously slit the throats of helpless white men. The prisoners, in a desperate bid to hold off the attack, had indeed held some of the hostages in open view around the yard and vowed to kill them if the prison were attacked. When the assault began, however, the prisoners guarding the hostages held discipline and did not harm the officers.

The next day medical forensics revealed that all but one of the ten hostages who had been killed during the assault had been shot by the state police. The tenth died from a correctional officer's bullet. There was more. Three years later, the official state investigation determined that the assault had been premature, badly planned and unnecessary.[4] Prisoner lawsuits alleging civil rights abuses would take a quarter of a century to reach resolution. But when they did, on 16 February 2000, a federal judge confirmed an award of twelve million dollars to the surviving victims of the police assault and their lawyers. Given the number of prisoner plaintiffs and the length of litigation, the award was not large. It was large enough, however, to signal that the classic confrontation of white male police and black men was on new, unmapped terrain.

This chapter is a case study of how shifting conceptions of masculinity helped structure the post-Second World War development of the NYSP. Policing in the United States has historically been characterized as patriarchal power, exercised either on behalf of the state or more immediately on behalf of male householders.[5] Policing was characteristically male – done by men, on behalf of men, and usually imposed on men. When women first sought and eventually won roles in policing, they did so with the argument that women with strong maternal instincts were needed to cope with female offenders.[6] The masculinity of the US police was more, however, than the sex segregation they shared with other occupations such as skilled craftsmen until the 1970s. The police, like the military, are part of the coercive apparatus of the state. Armed and authoritative, they exercised an explicit male monopoly on violence – power that women were forbidden to wield.[7] The personal exercise of power is especially important in US policing because the structure and function of US policing were developed more as social control than as law enforcement.[8]

The earliest pre-revolutionary police forces were slave patrols and town watches.[9] Both bodies strove for the 'good police' of the community. The definition of that 'good police' rested on the patriarchal authority of the white male elite. As city forces were created in the nineteenth century, they functioned in a context in which local political objectives set many law enforcement priorities.[10]

This high level of local elite control and the very low level of orientation towards formal legal norms fostered what Michael Rogin called the 'counter-subversive tradition' in US policing. The counter-subversive tradition, as Rogin and others have traced it, is the persistent conviction of white male elites that the nation faces an existential threat from hostile races and foreign ideas.[11] Richard Slotkin has unpacked the language and practices of the late nineteenth-century Indian Wars to reveal how white male barbarity against the Indians became understood as proof of the white man's superiority of body, technology and government. As if conquest had reduced the Indians to children, the white man's government was to be the father.[12]

In what Rogin called 'political demonology', opponents, whether Indians, communists, Filipinos, immigrant workers or African Americans, are portrayed in political language and popular culture as threats to core US values. Subversives may be technically citizens, but they are not real Americans. An early state police advocate explained that to black and immigrant men:

> liberty has no meaning other than gross license, and [they] gave incredulous laughter to the notion of invisibly guarded law. Looking about them, these men saw no *gendarmerie*, no *carabinieri*, no uniformed patrol upon the road; from which they joyfully drew an invitation to make of the Decalogue a daily sacrifice.[13]

The counter-subversive tradition valorized all white men, but in the north in the twentieth century it placed special demands on police power, deployed both overtly and covertly.

Insisting that the force established a *white* masculine identity from its inception may seem anachronistic or self-evident. According to the census, nearly 98 per cent of the state's residents were white in 1920. The few blacks were heavily concentrated in the largest cities, which the NYSP did not patrol. Proponents of the force did cite the on-going migration of blacks to New York State and the danger to white women of rape by black males. However, the NYSP's whiteness was initially seen in contradistinction not primarily to African Americans, but rather to late nineteenth-century immigrants from southern and eastern Europe – Italians, Poles, Hungarians, Slovaks and others. The dominant white culture, including the largest labour federation, stigmatized the newcomers as uncivilized. Leading sociologists and criminologists buttressed claims of disproportionate immigrant (and black) criminality with elaborately worthless statistical presentations.[14]

The next section of this chapter analyses how the NYSP privileged physical appearance and presentation of masculinity associated with 'Anglo-Saxon' men. The middle section looks at how the language of masculinity reshaped its Cold War priorities and relationship with the Federal Bureau of Investigation (FBI) in the 1940s and 1950s. The final sections focus on how the NYSP's commitment to white masculinity dominated its surveillance and harassment of the Black Muslims in the 1960s and contributed to the bloodshed of Attica.

Masculinities of the Empire State

For the NYSP, an emphasis on a certain style of masculinity and on the conscious exertion of white male authority had been explicit expectations since the first call for its creation. In 1913, an elite organization of US capital, the New York Chamber of Commerce, recommended state police to replace the National Guard (state militia) at strikes. The Chamber was anticipating vastly expanded international trade, and wanted a military free from domestic obligations. At home, the masculine presence demanded of the new police was distinctive. As international financier A. Barton Hepburn explained, 'We need an unseen bayonet . . . a tangible force in evidence to impress, not to overawe, and thus prevent trouble.'[15]

The militia had fostered a 'citizen-soldier' tradition in which men remained citizens even as they served as soldiers.[16] As the nation became a global power, important elites pushed to revise this understanding of male citizenship. Frederic R. Coudert, an international corporate lawyer who had served as an officer in the Spanish–American War and at the Brooklyn streetcar strike of 1895, criticized the inefficient use of male bodies in militia strike work:

> Raw boys who had never been hardened for outdoor life were called upon to sleep in the streets, insufficiently fed and ill clad . . . Seven thousand men, lacking in training or capacity for that kind of service, were called away from their occupations, when one hundred and fifty men, properly drilled and led, could have smashed the backbone of the disorderly element.[17]

One hundred and fifty men doing the work of 7,000 – that was the new dream of industrial engineering. The men of the state police would be paid state agents and always available. They too were citizens, but their policing was to be an occupation, not a voluntary act of citizenship. The new force removed policing from the politics of citizenship and the city to make it an expression of state power.[18]

The force saw itself as 'free of politics' because it was largely immune to influence from the urban immigrant politicians who controlled city police at the precinct level in the largest cities. Rather, political control was manifest at another level. Superintendents were selected by the governor, and were dependent on the state legislature for their budgets.[19] The force developed as an expression of the governor's authority, and tried to address legislators' concerns while avoiding overt patronage. The superintendent, unlike urban police chiefs constrained by civil service protections, could hire, promote, discipline or fire men at will. Accountable to the governor, the superintendent also exercised a significant degree of independence. This hierarchal organization and relative insulation from popular or bureaucratic accountability made possible a higher level of discipline than that characteristic of either militia or city police.

The NYSP's first superintendent, George F. Chandler, insisted that the standard of masculine military self-presentation of the NYSP was to be much stricter than that of either citizen-soldiers or city police. A doctor who also served as a major in the New York National Guard, Chandler was familiar with the militia's reputation for rowdiness and the city police's image as Irish, corrupt and unnecessarily brutal. He organized the force like a special kind of cavalry company. Ranks were designated with military titles, and the men signed enlistment contracts. Training was physically demanding. Police were expected to be able to handle themselves in a fight or a shootout. Only men who could ride were recruited; their training included using horses in crowd control and performing stunts such as jumping horseback through flaming hoops. Visual assertion of patriarchal power might render its full exercise less often necessary.

Chandler sought to win the force's legitimacy with the sceptical rural and small town citizens who had opposed the creation of the state police and continued to block its expansion throughout the 1920s. Outside of large cities, New York State until World War II was overwhelmingly rural, with a white population that was majority Republican. Many people objected to the expense of a state force and considered it unnecessary. To survive regular legislative challenges, the NYSP needed to be respected and perceived as useful by opinion makers in each community. Chandler shaped the early force by personally examining each recruit physically, seeking a 'distinctively American type of man', a man whose self-presentation would win co-operation in areas that had not before been subject to routine policing. He sought the 'Anglo-Saxon' ideal – tall, square jawed, broad shouldered and 'physically perfect'.[20]

In emphasizing the gentlemanly self-control and 'physically perfect' physique of the 'State Troopers', Chandler signalled that the force patrolling rural New York would look like, or at least act like, an idealized version of the 'Anglo-Saxon' male, not the Irish-surnamed men who dominated city policing. As historian Marilyn Johnson and others have analysed, Irish politicians and police in the late nineteenth century made a significant claim on 'whiteness' by organizing effectively to win political power and, with it, the political patronage that controlled city police appointments.[21] The largely Irish police forces won accolades from city elites when they used clubs effectively against strikers, especially Jews, Italians or other southern Europeans. The customary reliance on coercion by poorly trained police, however, too often included using the 'third degree' against middle-class citizens whose anger led to newspaper exposés and, in New York City alone, investigations in 1894 and 1910.

Opponents of state police, both rural and urban, pointed out that rural New York did not have the large Slavic and other immigrant mining communities of neighbouring Pennsylvania, where the first regularly patrolling state police had been established in 1906. The New York Chamber of Commerce and other elites admired the Pennsylvania State Police, but many working people and farmers, and a few middle-class reformers, were appalled at its record of violent strike-breaking. It was recruited from the Pennsylvania National Guard and commanded by Major John C. Groome, an elite Philadelphia merchant and militia officer. Groome had served in Puerto Rico during the Spanish–American war, and there was similarity between the violent tactics employed against civilians in that conflict and those in Pennsylvania.[22] Groome and his force presented a masculine demeanour, but it was the murderous male fury of the Indian Wars rather than the disciplined paternal presence of a modern state.

Critics did not reject the Pennsylvania State Police because it was all male or because it enacted masculinity. They articulated an alternative, oppositional masculinity, claiming what historians have identified as a republican ideology of manly self-respect.[23] They claimed that 'nearly all of the manhood of the workers had been crushed out by the murderous tactics' of the 'Black Cossacks'.[24] They objected to what they saw as violations of the rights of male citizenship, and expressed an often religiously inspired insistence on the dignity of working men.

In Pennsylvania, it had been possible to overcome the critics with inflated claims about the violence of the Slavic men in isolated mining districts. The Republican Party, and in particular the steel industry that owned many of the coal mines, controlled state-level politics in Pennsylvania. In the State of New York there was lively two-party competition, and a diversity of financial, industrial, transportation and agricultural interests to satisfy.[25] A state police force that enraged large numbers of New Yorkers was not likely to survive successive governors and legislatures.

Chandler taught recruits to emulate an ideal version of officer-class masculinity: 'always be a gentleman, courteous, kind, gentle, fair, keep yourself clean and neat, you and your horse equally well groomed, stand erect, put snap and vigor into your movements'.[26] Recruits learned how to be courteous on the telephone and how to respond to press inquiries. Chandler expressed contempt for any trooper who 'makes a noise over the soup, or eats with his knife, or covers his knife and fork with his great big hands, or takes a piece of bread and wipes it all around his plate and mops up everything'.[27]

Strike work rather than table manners posed the greatest test of the force's gentlemanliness. The NYSP's strike work entailed careful political calculations of citizenship and manliness, positioning, in the name of order, an ideology of male power in the service of capital against a variety of assertions of working-class masculinity. Two of the many strikes in which the NYSP was deployed between 1919 and 1923 illustrate conflicts that were at once of masculinity, whiteness and class. In a 1919 brass and copperworkers' strike in Rome, with a workforce of unskilled Italian and skilled native-born men, the NYSP helped to divide the workers along ethnic lines. The Italian strikers and their entire families paraded and played musical instruments. The NYSP rode their horses into the crowds, using their batons freely. Chandler justified the violence by accusing the workers of being foreigners, radicals and involved in 'Black Hand' activities.[28] Shocked by the accusations and quite possibly by the violence, the native-born men returned to work and the strike was broken.

In the Albany streetcar strike of 1922, by contrast, the NYSP took similarly violent action against militant native-born and immigrant women but was unable to break the strike, which enjoyed widespread community support. Chandler found it impossible to stop the women while retaining the force's image of restraint:

> last night women sympathizers endeavored to start a riot. They had sticks and stones, and one woman in particular was armed with a piece of brass gas pipe and she was very vicious. The language of the women was indescribable and when ordered to move on they refused and showed fight.[29]

A reporter was less reticent: 'Crowds of girls going to their work in the North Albany plants jeered the men and in several instances executed derisive gestures. Men and women in various stages of undress appeared at dwelling windows.'[30] Unlike the praise the force received after attacking Italian families and breaking the Rome metalworkers' strike, their actions against the mostly native-born workers, especially women, was condemned as unmanly.

Calling for an investigation, Senator William E. Martin wrote: 'the people of my district . . . call them "Cossacks". They are extremely cruel and apparently have forgotten the first principles of manhood, to take proper care of women and children.'[31] Chandler affirmed that the only effective way for his men to defeat women was with horses, for 'it is hard for any kind of man to fight a woman'. Instead, 'we would send detachments of mounted men . . . on the gallop, where women started to make trouble'.[32] The difficult part was making sure that force was used only, or at least mostly, against the politically powerless.

The self-conscious projection of white masculinity in the NYSP's early years was juxtaposed to immigrant swarthiness and radicalism and not primarily to African-American blackness. Its motivation reflected capital's urgency to discipline militant workers without inciting widespread opposition. The force's imagery was of northern European manhood, idealized in physique, character and expertise. Hierarchal organization under a single superintendent reporting to the governor made possible a force responsive to political change, especially the New Deal legalization of unions, and committed to expanding and developing autonomous expertise in scientific methods and counter-subversion.

The power to watch

Political surveillance work provided the 'unseen' part of financier Barton Hepburn's bayonet. Surveillance is a profound expression of state power. It is true that there is a strong school in Anglo-American political thought that rejects state spying as incompatible with personal liberty, democracy and the free exchange of ideas. As Gregory Kealey has demonstrated for Canada, however, British reluctance did not hold for policing its colonies.[33] In the United States, that reluctance has never been relevant to spying on people of colour, the least powerful of working people, or radicals. The residents of slave cabins did not have any First or Fourth Amendment protections; nor did the mostly white families in the company towns that persisted into the 1930s. The power to spy – to watch, listen and question – has been, in the United States, a characteristic of class-based male-on-male power.

Created in wartime, the NYSP did political surveillance in its first years for US military intelligence. In 1919, the state police participated in the raids, surveillance and dossier building of the Red Scare. Strike deployments in the 1920s were often preceded by discreet plainclothes checks on union organizing and interviews with business and town leaders. In 1935, in deliberate tandem with President Franklin Roosevelt's renaming the FBI and increasing its independence and status, the NYSP's surveillance capacity was expanded and increased in prestige with the formation of its Bureau of Criminal Investigation (BCI). The BCI housed fingerprinting and forensic analysis, and experimented with new police technologies. It attracted some of the best-educated members of the NYSP, and the creation of a BCI unit within each Troop extended its influence.[34] The BCI epitomized the NYSP's claim to important attributes of modern masculinity – technical expertise and professionalism. These knowledge claims in turn justified the elaboration of a counter-subversive unit that could command increased resources to counter a threat whose dimensions were known only to the BCI.

The state police were no longer a sometimes romantic troop of mounted cavalry, but a large bureaucracy in which most men spent over half their time driving. By the 1930s, the 'American type of man' required by the NYSP included descendants of the previously despised southern and eastern European immigrants. Immigration to the United States from Europe had been cut off in the 1920s, and New Deal programmes offered benefits, not available to African Americans, to white working people regardless of ethnicity. New groups were becoming 'white'. Increasingly, the most important meaning of 'white' was 'not black'.[35]

Like all US police forces aspiring to professionalism in the 1940s, the NYSP subscribed to the 'scientific' fact of disproportionate black criminality. In the words of the eminent police scientist Bruce Smith, 'One set of facts seems to be above question – namely, that Negroes contribute more than their share to the mass of people who fall afoul of the criminal law.'[36] For Smith, this conclusion was, by the last (1940) edition of his textbook, hedged with uncertainties about biology and prejudice; for many whites, it was simply true, and linked above all to rape. As Jacquelyn Dowd Hall and others have argued, rape of white women by black men has functioned in US culture most importantly as an offence not against the female victim, but rather against the principle of white patriarchy.[37] Until the 1930s, the image of the Negro rapist had been routinely reinscribed in the north by lurid newspaper reports of lynchings in the south. Verbal reports were supported by triumphant photograph postcards mailed to friends and relatives, typically depicting a hanged, charred or otherwise mutilated black male body.[38]

Even as lynchings started to decline in the 1930s, large numbers of young black men were still being picked up by sheriffs on petty charges and sentenced to hard labour – 'slavery by another name'.[39]

The NYSP remained overwhelmingly white even as the population of New York State included growing numbers of African Americans, Puerto Ricans and others 'not white' in the US census.[40] Within the increasingly national male sub-culture of police and correctional officials, southern and northern police officials agreed on the criminal threat of working-class black males. Other conceptions of black masculinity crowded white imaginations in the inter-war years: from highly sexualized imagery of jazz musicians to implicitly emasculated visions of old Negro men sitting on Harlem stoops. Black men and their communities created and contested black masculinity in expressions of youthful exuberance and sexual flair as well as a myriad of male respectabilities. Craftsmen, teachers, ministers, shopkeepers – all enjoyed respect within black communities. In front of white police, however, each ran the danger of being perceived as no more than a dangerous stereotype.[41] Ascribed criminal tendencies in turn justified defence of residential and school segregation, black exclusion from well-paying jobs, and other entrenched northern practices. Police were aware of the small middle-class Negro neighbourhoods within larger segregated communities, and police officials in many cities met with middle-class ministers and businessmen. As the civil rights movement grew, however, many northern police officials and FBI director J. Edgar Hoover concluded that the only way to account for Negroes demanding rights was communism.[42]

In the 1940s, the twin threats of black criminality and communist subversion came together for the NYSP, as it did for the FBI, in the support by blacks, white liberals, communists and others in the north for the southern civil rights move-ment. Police and important sectors of the population saw communism, and, by the doctrine of 'parallelism', any movements such as civil rights that communists supported, as threatening the nation. The Right targeted teachers and people train-ing to become teachers because they could poison young minds with ideas of racial equality, thence social upheaval and communist subversion. The gravity of the threat required a virile response. Frederic Coudert, chair of the New York's Rapp–Coudert joint legislative committee of 1940–2, explained the hunt for sub-versive teachers as a test of manhood:

> Now if your dog had rabies you wouldn't clap him into jail after he had bitten a number of persons – you'd put a bullet into his head, if you had that kind of iron in your blood. It is going to require brutal treatment to handle these teachers.[43]

The NYSP proved the iron in their blood. The investigation and subsequent Board of Education trials resulted in fifty professors losing their positions at City College of New York. The committee's files, including the entire membership list of the Teachers' Union, were added to the NYSP subversives list and used in subsequent loyalty checks.[44] In 1949 the legislature passed the Feinberg Bill to strengthen barriers to subversives working as teachers. Anticipating additional investigations, legislators who supported the measure sent telegrams they received from opponents of the bill to the state police so the names could be added to the subversives list.[45]

The Feinberg Bill and subsequent civil service legislation tightening the restrictions against radicals greatly expanded the counter-subversive demands on the NYSP.[46] By the mid-1950s, tens of thousands of state employees had to sign security oaths.[47] The NYSP stood as the counter-subversive gatekeeper to New York public employment. The police investigated anyone who indicated previous membership in a suspect organization or was so accused. These investigations included personal interviews with employees, families and neighbours; name checking against electoral registrations and third-party petitions; and forensic handwriting analysis to settle discrepancies.

The BCI developed covert techniques to circumvent possible court challenges from its targets. The Feinberg Bill put the burden of proving political fitness on the teacher, but its procedures were cumbersome. Moreover, the New York State Appellate court had ruled that a person falsely accused of being a communist could sue for libel.[48] These potential stumbling blocks put a premium on discreet state police investigations communicated unofficially to school authorities who would then take action on grounds not visibly political.[49] Support for civil rights justified hounding teachers who were dismissed from one school district, even to remote regions of the state, through the dispersed Troops of the state police.

Without renouncing physical authority and the police's male monopoly on violence, the BCI promoted a new ideal of masculine police power as it professionalized the NYSP's counter-subversive role. Along with its growing forensic capacity, its expanding collection of subversives' names made the BCI more valuable to the FBI and more worthy of FBI help and co-operation. Fighting subversion was important; it was also an opportunity to expand the BCI's size, budget and prestige, allowing it to share the FBI's carefully developed status as the cynosure of scientific, patriarchal policing. However, this status would be challenged as never before.

Masculinity at war

The Second World War profoundly unsettled US racial hierarchies. The war discredited open avowals of racial superiority and brought together white men of different ethnic and class backgrounds, yet exacerbated racial antagonism. The divide widened after the war as veterans' benefits, federal housing policy and rapid suburbanization combined to propel many of the white working class into middle-class home ownership unavailable to black families. Black veterans, many lacking high school diplomas, were unable to take advantage of the GI educational benefits at the same rate as white men. For many white working men in the north, the 1950s meant a rapid pulling away in social status from the increasing numbers of blacks moving north. For black men, the failure of half the 'Double V' campaign (victory at home and victory abroad) was bitter. The war nevertheless had left many black men with new skills, with a greater willingness to migrate and 'more determined to break racial bonds'.[50] This energy helped fuel financial and practical support for the civil rights movement in the 1950s.

Much of the white male police institution reacted differently. US policing is extraordinarily decentralized, so it is quite possible that there were police leaders who urged officers to treat blacks impartially. The profession as a whole, however, was shifting rightward on race.[51] FBI director Hoover, as self-appointed spokesman for professional policing, helped instil the conflation of communism and civil rights. He resisted providing FBI protection to civil rights activists on the grounds that the state had exclusive responsibility for criminal law enforcement. Only brutal murders, including those of two young white New York men, forced FBI intervention. One of its first steps was to contact the BCI for information about the dead men's subversive affiliations.

As the perceived communist threat began to recede in the 1960s, contemporary sociological constructs of black masculinity created a new narrative of excessive black criminality, the 'social emasculation of the Negro father and the resultant matriarchal character of many Negro households'. Black boys, conservatives averred, grew to adulthood without knowing a man 'honest, sober and industrious'. The absence of a strong male presence left black boys vulnerable to the demagoguery of civil rights leaders, who would rather demand welfare and criticize imaginary police brutality than repair their own communities.[52] Earlier images of the black rapist did not so much disappear as become re-imagined as a product of almost female character weakness. Hoover often eschewed any explanation, simply presenting the wildly disproportionate black male arrest rates in the north as confirmation of the black criminality that southerners like himself had always known.

FBI influence on the NYSP increased substantially with the November 1958 election of Republican governor Nelson Rockefeller. An admirer of the FBI and ally of Hoover's, Rockefeller wanted to make conspicuous improvements in the NYSP and build his credentials as a strong law and order politician. In a rush of change, he appointed a twenty-five-year FBI veteran, Arthur Cornelius Jr, as the first superintendent from outside the force, authorized more troopers and higher wages, and in 1963 finally reduced the workweek to forty hours. The 1950s had been a period of dramatically increased NYSP workload and stagnant wages. The lower ranks had lived in barracks and worked 120-hour weeks. With the economy booming, the private sector offered jobs with better pay, and turnover of trained state policemen was high.[53] Rockefeller's upgrades to pay and working conditions enabled state police to join other white workers in middle-class lifestyles. He also pushed budget appropriations for a new central headquarters, new police academy and other major improvements.

The changes of the 1960s also entailed much closer surveillance of black males.[54] FBI surveillance of the Rev. Dr Martin Luther King Jr and the civil rights movement has been well documented. Hoover expended countless resources on identifying the few communists with whom King consulted, and his seeming obsession with King's sexual activities included wiretaps and blackmail attempts. Similarly, the BCI maintained surveillance on civil rights organizations and activists on campuses, and worked assiduously to identify connections, however distant, between civil rights and communist agitation.

The FBI and BCI's efforts to suppress the Nation of Islam (NOI), or Black Muslims as they were more commonly called by outsiders, invoked both familiar and new themes of the counter-subversive imagination. The NOI was an all-black, pacifist religion, started in Detroit during the Depression, eschewing violence and politics. It encouraged members to obey the law, follow dietary rules and avoid drinking, smoking and adultery. It was organized hierarchically, with the father as authority within the home. Elijah Muhammad, the religion's patriarch, taught that whites were devils who had imposed the false religion of Christianity on blacks for enslavement and subordination.[55] NOI instructed blacks to separate from whites to avoid corruption and exploitation.

Within prisons, NOI attracted converts by offering its own rehabilitative programme. Inmates were encouraged to exercise, study and control their anger. Becoming a Muslim meant developing respect within the prison and thereby protection from other prisoners. It was a way to be a man, not just a prisoner. However, for white men whose masculinity was defined as much by supremacy over black men as over women, NOI's claim to be a religion, a profound knowledge claim by black men, was preposterous, offensive. Hoover and many in police and corrections insisted that this claim was a ruse to avoid the draft and demand special privileges, such as Korans and prayer rugs, within prison.

Despite the fact that none of the tenets or practices of NOI encouraged communism or subversion of any kind, Hoover insisted initially that Black Muslims were communists. Briefing President Eisenhower and his Cabinet in 1956 on 'Racial Tension and Civil Rights', he warned of 'the specter of racial intermarriages' and characterized NOI as among the 'organizations presently advancing integration'.[56] Because law enforcement was unable to connect NOI with any threat of crime or subversion, Eisenhower's Attorney General Brownell refused to add the religion to the Attorney's General's subversives list or to initiate Smith Act prosecutions against Black Muslims as Hoover wanted. Undeterred, Hoover persisted in hounding NOI, and the Attorney General did not stop him. The FBI began wiretapping Elijah Muhammad in 1957, and its surveillance of Malcolm X, NOI's leading minister and organizer in the early 1960s, was unrelenting.[57]

Spying on top officials fitted the long-established FBI pattern of working to undermine any influential and independent black male leadership, including sports and entertainment figures.[58] The campaign against NOI, however, went further. The FBI worked with the BCI, and similar officials in New York, Michigan, California and elsewhere, to sustain close surveillance on thousands of rank-and-file Black Muslim men for over a decade.

In 1960, the New York Department of Corrections, Governor's Office and state police formalized an arrangement by which prison officials transmitted, to the police, dossiers on all Black Muslims confined in state prisons.[59] The police opened files on all correspondents with and visitors to Muslims in prison.[60] When Muslim prisoners filed suit for the right to practice their religion, the State Attorney General's office brought the petitions to the NYSP where they were photocopied and added to each inmate's file.[61] The police also kept track of all people who called themselves or were reported by others to be Black Muslims.[62]

NYSP headquarters maintained files on Black Muslims in prison, and when they were released these records were forwarded to the appropriate Troop jurisdiction.[63] Individual Troop BCI units also attempted to identify more adherents by employing paid informers.[64] Information made control possible, and surveillance included interference in Muslims' jobs, parole status and personal relationships.[65] Black Muslims who did appear to be recruiting were subjected to even more intrusive and illegal surveillance.[66] The NYSP shared information about NOI members with law enforcement in other states, broadening the scope of control and enhancing the BCI's reputation and capacity for counter-subversion. The decision to lavish police resources on 'neutralizing' NOI was not a rational decision directed against any actual threat. The NYSP worked with the state Department of Corrections and the FBI to disrupt the NOI vision of manhood – an ideal of self-discipline, self-respect and patriarchal power, tied to aspirations for autonomy from white domination.

From slave patrols to New York state prisons, generations of armed white men had struggled, as they saw it, to defend their masculine power and their women against a darker Other masculinity. If their struggle assisted capital in maintaining control over its labour supply, these policemen were generally not perturbed, even as they struggled to maintain their own masculine family authority. Now, in the Nation of Islam, they confronted a successful organization of black men equally committed to a conservative masculine ideology, while asserting autonomy from the patriarchal control of white men over people of colour. We do not know how much of the police's repressive response was born of habitual assumption of a right to monopolize violence, and how much of uninformed fear. But their growing anxiety, as ever-more imprisoned black men regained, developed and preached their own understandings of manhood, sowed the seeds of the atrocity that was Attica.

Conclusion

The sarcasm of the NYSP sharpshooter's use of 'Negro gentleman' is palpable, its use underscoring the absent epithet and demonstrating the speaker's mastery of new codes of racial dominance. For the prisoners, the new forms of subordination had become intolerable. 'We are men. We are not beasts and we do not intend to be driven or treated as such' declared Elliott 'L. D.' Barkley to the television camera the prisoners had demanded.[67] Conditions at Attica were so bad that the Commissioner of Corrections had already taken notice of inmate complaints and started an investigation. The inmates were wretchedly fed, clothed and housed, yet they were required to work for thirty cents a day, less than one-sixth of New York's 1971 minimum wage. The organized groups within the prison, including the Nation of Islam, had not initiated the rebellion; they were the ones who restored order. Black Muslims guarded the hostages and released eleven officers who had been wounded in the initial rebellion.

Neither Governor Rockefeller nor NYSP superintendent William E. Kirwan went to Attica at any time during the five-day standoff. NYSP officers had been at Attica for two days before the assault was launched, listening to prisoner demands being broadcast on national television and growing anxious about the fate of the hostages. Despite the absence of firearms among the prisoners, the NYSP officers had been ordered to fire, and to attack with men from other forces who were not under NYSP discipline. The stage was set for the 'bloodbath' of which Rockefeller had been warned.

The investigations and prisoner lawsuits following Attica formed part of the burgeoning 'prisoners' movement' of the 1970s. Insisting on the prisoners' humanity, the movement called for genuine rehabilitation and shorter sentences. The prisoners' movement formed common cause with the many campaigns in the 1970s against police brutality and in favour of community control of police.[68] These movements pushed the liberalism of the 1930s to include the nation's expanding black male working class within the full definition of masculinity and of citizenship. They often impugned the masculinity of the police by calling them 'pigs' and ridiculing their unmanly subordination to the state.

Recent literature on the history of masculinity in post-war United States has focused on explaining what the authors see as a crisis of masculinity brought on by anxiety.[69] The sources of anxiety were varied – communism, nuclear annihilation, the increased number of women in the workforce and other perceived challenges to the normative privileges of white, middle-class men and, hence, to the nation. Within the post-war NYSP, masculinity was a claim to authority, coercion and surveillance. Those claims were asserted on behalf of the state, most extensively in the form of automobile patrol, and most intensively in counter-subversive work. Surveillance enabled the police and the FBI to elevate their role as protectors of the nation by selecting their targets and exaggerating their threat. As voices much listened to within the newly resurgent Right, police and police organizations ensured that their demands for masculine authority would be taken seriously.

Notes

1 'A Nation of Law?: 1968–1971', *Eyes on the Prize*, New York: Blackside, 1990; T. Wicker, *A Time to Die*, New York: Quadrangle/New York Times Books, 1995; and P. T. Shelton, *History of the New York State Police, 1917–1987*, Albany: Trooper Foundation of the State of New York, 1987.

2 R. T. Takaki, *Iron Cages: Race and Culture in Nineteenth-Century America*, New York: Alfred A. Knopf, 1979.
3 Shelton, *History*, p. 94.
4 Wicker, *A Time to Die*.
5 M. D. Dubber, *The Police Power: Patriarchy and the Foundations of American Government*, New York: Columbia University Press, 2005; M. D. Dubber and M. Valverde (eds), *Police and the Liberal State*, Stanford, CA: Stanford Law Books, an imprint of Stanford University Press, 2008; and W. J. Novak, *The People's Welfare: Law and Regulation in Nineteenth Century America*, Chapel Hill: University of North Carolina Press, 1996.
6 J. Appier, *Policing Women: The Sexual Politics of Law Enforcement and the LAPD*, Philadelphia: Temple University Press, 1998.
7 F. Dodsworth, 'Masculinity as Governance: Police, Public Service and the Embodiment of Authority, c. 1700–1850', in M. McCormack (ed.), *Public Men: Masculinity and Politics in Modern Britain*, New York: Palgrave Macmillan, 2007.
8 J. Richardson, *The New York Police: Colonial Times to 1901*, New York: Oxford University Press, 1970, pp. 49–50. In parallel fashion, US police history started in social history, not legal history. W. R. Miller, *Cops and Bobbies: Police Authority in New York and London, 1830–1870*, 2nd edn, Columbus: Ohio State University Press, 1999; and S. L. Harring, *Policing a Class Society: The Experience of American Cities, 1865–1915*, New York: Rutgers University Press, 1983.
9 S. E. Hadden, *Slave Patrols: Law and Violence in Virginia and the Carolinas*, Cambridge: Harvard University Press, 2001; and A. L. Higginbotham, Jr, *In the Matter of Color: Race & the American Legal Process: The Colonial Period*, New York; Oxford University Press, 1978. On slave patrols in New York see G. R. Hodges, *Root & Branch: African Americans in New York & East Jersey, 1613–1863*, Chapel Hill: University of North Carolina Press, 1999.
10 A. Steinberg, *The Transformation of Criminal Justice: Philadelphia, 1800–1880*, Chapel Hill: University of North Carolina Press, 1989; Richardson, *New York Police*; and R. Lane, *Policing the City: Boston, 1822–1885*, Cambridge, MA: Harvard University Press, 1967.
11 M. Rogin, *Ronald Reagan, the Movie and Other Episodes in Political Demonology*, Berkeley: University of California Press, 1987.
12 R. Slotkin, *The Fatal Environment: The Myth of the Frontier in the Age of Industrialization, 1880–1890*, New York: Athenaeum, 1985.
13 K. Mayo, *Justice to All: The Story of the Pennsylvania State Police*, introduction by Theodore Roosevelt, New York: G. P. Putnam's Sons, Knickerbocker, 1917, p. 7.
14 R. Fosdick, *American Police Systems*, Montclair, NJ: Patterson Smith, 1969 (orig. 1920), pp. 26–7; B. Smith, *The State Police: Organization and Administration*, New York: Macmillan, 1925; and K. G. Muhammad, *The Condemnation of Blackness: Race, Crime, and the Making of Modern Urban America*, Cambridge, MA: Harvard University Press, 2010.
15 Chamber of Commerce of the State of New York, '*Fifty-sixth Annual Report for the Year 1913/1914*', New York: The Press of the Chamber of Commerce, 1914, p. 122. On the Chamber, see S. Beckert, *The Monied Metropolis: New York City and the Consolidation of the American Bourgeoisie, 1850–1896*, New York: Cambridge University Press, 1993.
16 J. M. Cooper, *The Rise of the National Guard: The Evolution of the American Militia, 1865–1920*, Lincoln: University of Nebraska Press, 1997.
17 *New York Evening Post*, 9 January 1914.
18 D. A. Sklansky, 'Police and Democracy', *Michigan Law Review*, June 2005, vol. 103, pp. 1699–1830.
19 The initial legislation provided for a five-year superintendent's term. After 1927, the superintendent served at the pleasure of the governor.

20 New York State Police, 'Second Annual Report for the Year 1919', Albany: New York State Police, 1920, p. 20.
21 M. S. Johnson, *Street Justice: A History of Police Violence in New York City*, Boston: Beacon Press, 2003; and A. Saxton, *The Rise and Fall of the White Republic: Class Politics and Mass Culture in Nineteenth-Century America*, London: Verso, 1990.
22 P. M. Conti, *The Pennsylvania State Police: A History of Service to the Commonwealth, 1905 to the Present*, Harrisburg, PA: Stackpole Books, 1977, pp. 44–7.
23 A. Baron (ed.), *Work Engendered: Toward a New History of American Labor*, Ithaca, NY: Cornell University Press, 1991.
24 Editorial, *New York Call*, 7 December 1914.
25 R. L. McCormick, *From Realignment to Reform: Political Change in New York State, 1893–1910*, Ithaca, NY: Cornell University Press, 1981; and R. F. Wesser, *A Response to Progressivism: The Democratic Party and New York Politics, 1902–1918*, New York: New York University Press, 1986.
26 G. F. Chandler, *Bulletin*, 1 November 1917.
27 G. F. Chandler, *The Policeman's Art as Taught in the New York State School for Police*, New York: Funk & Wagnall's, 1922, p. 32.
28 *Rome Daily Sentinel*, 15 July 1919. *The New York Times*, 17 July 1919, published a press release from the NYSP.
29 Chandler to W. W. Smith (Secretary to the Governor), TLS, 26 February 1921, File 150–141, N. L. Miller, Governor's Subject and Correspondence Files, New York State Archives, Albany (hereafter Miller Papers).
30 *Albany Times-Union*, 8 February 1921.
31 W. E. Martin to Governor Miller, 24 July 1922, Box 14, File 150–642, Miller Papers.
32 G. F. Chandler, *Dawn Days of the State Police*, Troy, NY: Record Newspapers, 1938, p. 20.
33 G. S. Kealey, 'The Empire Strikes Back: The Nineteenth-Century Origins of the Canadian Secret Service', *Journal of the Canadian Historical Association*, 1999, vol. 10, pp. 3–18.
34 Not until 1961 was the BCI formally charged with 'preventing' violations of the criminal law, and not until 1962 with conducting any 'investigations as may be provided for by law'. These legislative refinements simply codified existing practice. Chapter 687, Laws of New York, 1935; Chapter 216, Executive Law, McKinney's Consolidated Laws of New York, 1982.
35 N. I. Painter, *The History of White People*, New York: W. W. Norton, 2010.
36 B. Smith, *Police Systems in the United States*, New York: Harper, 1940, pp. 62–9.
37 J. D. Hall, '"The Mind That Burns in Each Body": Women, Rape, and Racial Violence', in A. Snitow, C. Stansell and S. Thompson (eds), *Powers of Desire: The Politics of Sexuality*, New York: Monthly Review Press, 1983; and D. Apel, *Imagery of Lynching: Black Men, White Women, and the Mob*, New Brunswick, NJ: Rutgers University Press, 2004.
38 J. Allen, H. Als, Congressman J. Lewis and L. F. Litwack, *Without Sanctuary: Lynching Photography in America*, Santa Fe, NM: Twin Palms, 2004. On twentieth-century changes to federal policy see C. Waldrep, 'National Policing, Lynching, and Constitutional Change', *Journal of Southern History*, 2008, vol. 74, no. 3, pp. 589–626.
39 D. A. Blackmon, *Slavery by Another Name: The Re-enslavement of Black Americans from the Civil War to World War II*, New York: Doubleday, 2008; M. A. Myers, *Race, Labor, and Punishment in the New South*, Columbus: Ohio State University Press, 1998.
40 M. M. Klein, *The Empire State*, Ithaca, NY: Cornell University Press, 2001, p. 629: 'One-quarter of the 3.2 million blacks who left the southern cotton belt in the 1940s and 1950s came to New York State.'
41 P. Hill Collins, *Black Sexual Politics: African Americans, Gender, and the New Racism,* New York: Routledge, 2004.

42 Quoted in K. O'Reilly, *"Racial Matters": The FBI's Secret File on Black America, 1960–1972*, New York: Free Press, 1989, p. 13.
43 *The New York Times*, 3 June 1941.
44 L. H. Chamberlain, *Loyalty and Legislative Action: A Survey of Activity by the New York State Legislature, 1919–1948*, Cornell Studies in Civil Liberty, Ithaca, NY: Cornell University Press, 1951, pp. 68–152. Sixteen years later, a security investigation would read the document 'Information obtained from Rapp-Coudert files at Division Headquarters', Box 26, Case 1522, New York State Police, NonCriminal Investigation Case Files of the Special Services Unit, Bureau of Criminal Investigation, New York State Archives, Albany, NY (hereafter NonCriminal).
45 Feinberg Law – Telegrams (1949), Box 6, Case 156; Box 13, Case 623, NonCriminal.
46 Chapter 3022, Education Law, 'Elimination of Subversive Persons from the Public School System', McKinney's Consolidated Laws of New York, 1982. E. Schrecker, *No Ivory Tower: McCarthyism and the Universities*, New York: Oxford University Press, 1986, pp. 113–14; and Chamberlain, *Loyalty*, pp. 187–202. Sections of the Feinberg Law were declared unconstitutional in 1967.
47 For estimates of the number see D. Caute, *The Great Fear: The Anti-Communist Purge under Truman and Eisenhower*, New York: Simon and Schuster, 1978, pp. 270, 342; and R. M. Fried, *Nightmare in Red: The McCarthy Era in Perspective*, New York: Oxford University Press, 1990, pp. 133–4.
48 Matter of Mencher *v.* Chesney, 297 N.Y. 94. Pamphlet, 'Regents Rules on Subversive Activities', Albany: University of the State of New York Press, 1959, p. 10.
49 At Oswego State Teachers' College, for example, the state police and the school's president co-operated in 1949–50 to keep students supportive of the civil rights movement from becoming teachers. A BCI corporal explained:

> [The college president's] secretary stated that the school had decided to use low marks as a means of getting rid of undesirable students. In the event [name deleted] enters another school, his record will be asked for . . . and the writer will be so advised.
>
> (Memo, R.E. Fogarty to Inspector, District D, 8 July 1949, Box 6, Case 190, Item 3, p. 17B, NonCriminal)

50 M. Sherry, *In the Shadow of War: The United States since the 1930s*, New Haven, CT: Yale University Press, 1995; and Gail Williams O'Brien, *The Color of the Law: Race, Violence, and Justice in the Post-World War II South*, Chapel Hill: University of North Carolina Press, 1999.
51 V. Weaver, 'Frontlash: Race and the Development of Punitive Crime Policy', *Studies in American Political Development*, 2007, vol. 21, no. 1, pp. 230–65.
52 C. E. Rice, 'The Negro Crime Rate: Its Causes and Cure', *Modern Age: A Quarterly Review*, Fall 1966, 343–58, pp. 346, 347.
53 Shelton, *History*, p. 38.
54 H. A. Thompson, 'Why Mass Incarceration Matters: Rethinking Crisis, Decline, and Transformation in Postwar American History', *Journal of American History*, 2010, vol. 97, no. 3, pp. 703–34, explores the 'criminalization of urban space' occasioned by New York's draconian drug laws of the 1970s.
55 C. A. Clegg, *The Life and Times of Elijah Muhammad*, New York: St. Martin's Press, 1997; and C. E. Lincoln, *The Black Muslims in America*, Boston: Beacon Press, 1961.
56 Quoted in O'Reilly, *Racial*, pp. 41, 42.
57 O'Reilly, *Racial*, p. 42.
58 T. Kornweibel, Jr, *Seeing Red: Federal Campaigns against Black Militancy, 1919–1925*, Bloomington: Indiana University Press, 1998; M. Ellis, *Race, War and Surveillance: African Americans and the United State Government During World War I*, Bloomington: Indiana University Press, 2001; D. Garrow, *The FBI and Martin Luther King, Jr. From "Solo" to Memphis*, New York: W. W. Norton, 1981; R. A. Hill, '"The Foremost Radical Among His Race:" Marcus Garvey and the Black Scare,*

1918–1921', *Prologue*, Winter 1984, vol. 16, no. 4, pp. 216–31; and E. J. Tolbert, 'Federal Surveillance of Marcus Garvey and the U.N.I.A.', *Journal of Ethnic Studies*, 1987, vol. 14, no. 4, pp. 25–46.

59 The reports followed a standard format. Richard Woodward, Senior Inspector, New York State Department of Corrections turned over the arrest records and photos to the Albany BCI, who forwarded them to headquarters. Memo, G. W. Craig to Martin F. Dillon, 26 April 1960, Item 105; same, Item 112, Suppl. Report; same, 18 May 1960, Item 137, NonCriminal. Reports were made two or three times monthly and generally included several names.

60 Memos, Craig to Dillon, 17 May 1960, Item 116 and throughout, NonCriminal.

61 Memo, Craig to Dillon, 27 April 1960, Item 114; Letter, G. W. Craig to M. F. Dillon, 17 May 1960, Item 115; and Memo, Craig to Dillon, 17 May 1960, Item 117, NonCriminal.

62 Report, M. D. Nemier to Dillon, 12 April 1960, Item 110, NonCriminal.

63 See, for example, Letters, Dillon to H. J. Sanderson (Troop D), J. W. Russell (Troop A) and R. E. Sweeney (Manhattan), 24 May 1960, NonCriminal.

64 Memo, T. H. Denlea to D. M. McGranaghan, 4 August 1961; McGranaghan to Denlea, 8 August 1961; and Denlea to McGranaghan, 5 October 1961, Box 22, Case 1373, Item 484, NonCriminal.

65 See the ongoing surveillance reports on a Black Muslim who observed the Muslim dietary restrictions: Dillon to H. J. Sanderson, 24 May 1960, Box 19 and following, NonCriminal.

66 The BCI searched a Black Muslim's room surreptitiously and reported the text of a letter he was writing. They checked his mail, his girlfriend's and that of the 'colored families' at his previous address: S.R. Slowey to Sanderson, 31 October 1960, Item 238; 1 December 1960, Item 245; and 7 December 1960, Item 243, NonCriminal.

67 'A Nation of Law?: 1968–1971'.

68 American Friends Service Committee, 'Struggle for Justice: A Report on Crime and Punishment in America, Prepared for the American Friends Service Committee', New York: Hill & Wang, 1971.

69 R. D. Dean, *Imperial Brotherhood: Gender and the Making of Cold War Foreign Policy*, Amherst: University of Massachusetts Press, 2001; D. K. Johnson, *Lavender Scare: The Cold War Persecution of Gays and Lesbians in the Federal Government*, Chicago: University of Chicago Press, 2004; and K. A. Cuordileone, *Manhood and American Political Culture in the Cold War*, New York: Routledge, 2005.

11

MANAGERIAL MASCULINITY

An insight into the twenty-first-century police leader

Marisa Silvestri

Recent years have witnessed a growth of interest in the study and theorization of men and masculinities across a range of academic disciplines. This is particularly evident within the field of criminal justice where the literature on masculinity has emerged as an important area of investigation. This growth in literature has made a valuable contribution to our understanding of masculinity in relation to crime and victimization.[1] Our understanding of masculinity in relation to those professionals working in the criminal justice system more broadly, and those working in the police service more particularly, however, remains noticeably underdeveloped. This is not to say that men working in policing have not been considered by scholars; indeed, men have often been at the centre of both academic and policy enquiries. More usually, such enquiries have tended to focus on the rank-and-file officer and on the negative aspects of a police culture characterized by a 'cult of masculinity'. The police service in England and Wales has been the subject of a number of high-profile and damning reports that have emphasized the damaging effects of such a culture on both male and female police officers and on its interactions with offenders and victims.[2]

This chapter critically questions the dominant focus adopted by criminologists to explore masculinity in the police service. It argues that the 'cult of masculinity' so routinely cited when discussing men in policing provides an overly simplistic and narrow reading of the men and masculinities present in the police organization – there is a range of masculinities operating in the police service. This chapter takes the police leader as its focus of investigation. In referring to the police leader I am mindful of the problematic nature of defining who occupies this position and of the tensions that exist between 'leadership' and 'management'.[3] Despite such tensions, the position adopted here accepts the premise that one of the realities of a hierarchical organization is that there are many forms of leadership that deserve recognition and that the power to lead and manage does not lie exclusively in the hands of chief constables. Rather, leaders and managers, 'mini-chief constables', exist at many levels of the organization.[4] Through a focus on the contemporary police leader, an alternative form of police masculinity – a managerial 'smart macho' masculinity – is identified. This form of masculinity is discussed within the context of substantial organizational reform to policing in England and Wales at the end of the twentieth century. In particular, it focuses on the growth of 'new public management' (NPM) principles, a shift from 'transactional' to 'transformational' leadership styles and an increased emphasis on developing equality initiatives during the 1980s and 1990s.

The analysis is informed by a broad base of research that focuses on women's experiences of working in policing.[5] Although the extent to which such analyses can be extended to writing about men and masculinity remains a matter of debate, given the absence of empirical work on men in policing, it is argued that much can be learned about men through the study of women. More particularly, the analysis of the managerial 'smart macho' police leader draws on some of my earlier work in which I carried out thirty in-depth interviews with senior policewomen over a ten-month period in 1998. The fieldwork was carried out within four police service areas in England and Wales and included officers from chief inspector to chief officer ranks; that is, those belonging to the Association of Chief Police Officers (ACPO).[6] Although focused on their work histories, asking senior policewomen to reflect on their careers over time afforded women an opportunity to talk at length about themselves. Policewomen's service length (ranging from under ten to over thirty years) enabled them to reflect on the gendering effects of such reform processes over time. It was through these 'stories of the self' that women were able to provide rich narratives detailing transitions, punctuations, pauses and turning points in their police careers. What follows is a brief insight into what we already know about police men and masculinity.

Exploring the 'cult of masculinity'

Despite the lack of knowledge on police masculinities, one thing that can be stated with absolute certainty is that men continue to dominate the police service in terms of their number. Recent figures show that men currently form 74 per cent of the overall workforce across the forty-three police services in England and Wales. This percentage increases to 86 per cent when considering those occupying the senior ranks of chief inspector and above.[7] The continued dominance of men and limited access of women officers to high rank and specialist roles has been attributed by many to an organizational culture that is characterized by a strong 'cult of masculinity'.[8] Grounded within heterosexuality where particular notions of masculinity govern, Nigel Fielding argues that its stereotypical values may be read as an almost pure form of 'hegemonic masculinity'. In support of his argument, Fielding asserts that stereotypical values serve to highlight 'aggressive, physical action; a strong sense of competiveness and preoccupation with the imagery of conflict and exaggerated heterosexual orientations, often articulated in terms of misogynistic and patriarchal attitudes towards women'.[9] The role of physicality is central to ideas about 'macho' policing and the 'cult of masculinity' offers an opportunity within which a core aspect of the police role – the willingness and the ability to use force – can be celebrated. The glorification of violence and a crime-fighting mission provide the ideological justifications for the authority that is exercised against fellow citizens, 'for the exercise of coercive authority is not something that just anybody can do, it is traditionally the preserve of real men, who are willing and able to fight'.[10] With the perception that police work involves 'strength, action, danger and male fellowship', the work of policing becomes securely defined as 'men's work'.[11] As Frances Heidensohn notes, 'an elision which is frequently made [is that] *coercion* requires *force* which *implies physique and* hence policing by *men*'.[12] As a result, women's perceived lack of physical presence, of tough physique and, above all, of masculinity have been used over the past century as justification of their unsuitability to the demands of the job.[13]

Although such work has provided much-needed insight into police masculinity it remains limited in scope and focus. There are many men (and some women) working in policing who do not fall within the realms of such an occupational culture. Although it may be true that all officers, both managers and rank-and-file officers alike, share in the idealized world of policing as action filled, exciting, adventurous and dangerous,[14] the extent to which both groups can realistically lay claim to such engagement lies at the heart of this chapter. Numerous studies have emphasized the reality of police work as involving much tedium and paperwork with a lack of physical action, adventure or danger for all officers.[15] This reality is particularly true of senior police officers, who are perhaps the least likely to be called upon to exhibit traditional 'macho' displays of physical strength and prowess in the fight against crime. Unable to draw upon such traditional ideas of police masculinity, the work of police leaders becomes distanced from notions of 'real' police work and in turn of 'real' men.[16] Jennifer Hunt's 1984 study emphasizes the way in which 'management cop' culture is tied to gender in an unequivocally negative way. Hunt argues that rank-and-file officers perceived that high-ranking officers were engaged in:

> 'feminine labor' such as public relations and secretarial work. These 'pencil pushing bureaucrats' were not involved in the 'masculine' physical labor which characterized 'real policework' on the street. High ranking administrators were also viewed as 'inside tit men', 'asskissers' and 'whores' who gained their positions through political patronage rather than through superior performance in the rescue and crime fighting activities associated with 'real police work'.[17]

With senior officers less able to access the tools and scripts of 'physicality' so readily available to rank-and-file officers, one might expect to find less gender discrimination at the top of police organizations. Yet research continues to emphasize that women aspiring to police leadership positions and those women holding police rank experience high levels of social closure, exclusion and gender-based discrimination.[18] Senior policewomen continue to encounter a gendered environment in which a culture of hegemonic masculinity persists, albeit in a different setting and form.

Our knowledge of what this setting and form takes, however, remains woefully inadequate. Where the male police leader does appear in the literature he tends to be subsumed within discussions about the merits of the ideology of internal recruitment or studies that emphasize the military origins of his office.[19] Studies by Robert Reiner and David Wall on police leadership provide in-depth biographical accounts of the lives of senior officers. In his analysis of chief constables in England and Wales, Reiner offers an overview of the office of chief constable through a focus on drawing out chief constables' backgrounds, career patterns, policing philosophies and views on social and political issues.[20] Wall develops this further by providing an invaluable socio-legal history of this criminal justice elite between 1836 and 1996.[21] Although excellent in scope, neither of these studies addresses the issue of gender or masculinity as part of the analysis. More recent commentaries on the police leader have also failed to engage with the issue of gender. Instead they are driven and underpinned by a growing discourse that suggests a 'crisis' in police leadership.[22]

Organizational change and the police leader

The broad philosophy, principles and practices of NPM have heavily influenced the general direction of criminal justice policy and the work of the police service in Britain and across the world since the 1980s.[23] At the same time, the requirement to demonstrate equality, fairness and diversity within policing has also been firmly cemented into public policy with the arrival of the Equalities Act 2006 and the Gender Equality Duty in 2007.[24] Although the various facets of managerialist and equality initiatives and policy have been well documented elsewhere, few studies have acknowledged the gendered impact of such policy. The potential of organizational reform agendas is significant, not only in terms of altering organizational structures, policy and practice, but also in relation to the organizational identities within. Susan Halford, Mike Savage and Anne Witz argue that organizational restructuring is tied up with 'redefining and contesting the sorts of personal *identities* and *qualities* which are seen as desirable or undesirable for organizational members to possess'.[25] An insight into these developments provides important context for analysing the making of the contemporary police leader.

Principles of NPM were set in motion by successive Conservative governments from the 1980s onwards and adapted by the New Labour government in the late 1990s. According to Eugene McLaughlin, John Muncie and Gordon Hughes, NPM encompasses a broad range of features including an increased emphasis on achieving results; the setting of explicit targets and performance indicators to enable auditing of efficiency and effectiveness; the publication of league tables illustrating comparative performance; the identification of core competencies; costing of all activities to ensure value for money; externalization of non-essential responsibilities; the establishment of a purchaser–provider split; the encouragement of interagency co-operation; and the redesignation of clients as 'customers'.[26] For many, the application of NPM principles to policing can be traced to the publication of Home Office Circular 114: 'Manpower, Effectiveness and Efficiency in the Police Service' in 1983. Although preoccupied with fiscal concerns of doing 'more with less' and offering 'value for money', Tom Cockcroft and Iain Beattie emphasize the broader effects of the circular when they state that 'this was undoubtedly a signal to chief constables and police authorities that "outputs", the capacity of the police to deliver quantifiable results, would be of increasing importance in the following years'.[27] The expansion of such managerialist principles during the 1990s signified a powerful attempt to transform the policing paradigm from a narrow conception of the police as a law enforcement agency to a broader conception of the police as a service. Matt Long highlights the emergence of a strong performance culture within the police organization with the introduction of performance indicators, league tables and increased internal and external audit and inspection mechanisms.[28]

Securing greater 'quality of service' for citizens (now customers) also became a central police concern during this time and can be seen in the 1990 Quality of Service initiative. At the heart of this initiative were the findings of the *Operational Policing Review* (1990) and the strategic policy document *Setting the Standards for Policing* (1990) developed by the ACPO.[29] Both emphasized the negative outcomes of driving forward efficiency measures within the police service, reporting that public dissatisfaction with the police stemmed largely from inappropriate and outdated policing styles and poor service delivery. In June 1997, the New Labour government announced the introduction of a new duty for local authorities in order to ensure 'best value' for the public. The requirements of New Labour's 'Best Value' regime, underpinned by the Local Government Act 1999, necessitated that police leaders and managers become more active and interventionist than they had been in the past.[30] Such a change required a shift from 'transactional' to 'transformational' leadership within the police service.[31] It is worth noting here that this shift in leadership style was already well under way in a range of other public sector organizations. There was a strong consensus amongst organizational theorists that the autocratic and 'transactional' style of leadership, which once characterized most organizations and organizational men, was outdated and deficient for long-term development or change, and could even be a liability.[32] Bound up with classic and scientific approaches to management, traditional conceptions of leadership were characterized by highly rigid formalized and hierarchical organizations resembling military hierarchies. The common characteristics of the 'ideal manager' were typically aggression, competitiveness and rationality.[33] In its place, a 'transformational' style has taken ascendancy in organizational circles. Underpinned by the principles of participation, consultation and inclusion, those using such styles share power and information to reinforce open communication and create loyalty. They also encourage others to participate so that they feel that they are part of the organization and enhance individuals' appreciation of the worth of others by giving them praise and recognition. Although there has been little recognition among organizational theorists regarding the gendered nature of such a style, many feminist writers have subsequently pointed to the commonality that clearly exists between transformational approaches to leadership and feminist visions of management and leadership.[34] Feminist visions strive to promote the values of mutuality, interdependence, inclusion, co-operation, nurturance, support, participation, self-determination, empowerment, and personal and collective transformation, and as such are seen to have a high degree of congruence with the transformational approach.[35]

These ideas about leadership style have had a profound impact on the police service and on the identity of the twenty-first-century police leader. Faced with a range of different external and at times conflicting demands and challenges, Milan Pagon notes that 'different times call for different people. Not only has police work changed, so have the public and the communities into which it is separated . . . Police leaders have to change themselves, their organizations and their people.'[36] Indeed, Wall notes that the competencies demanded from a modern police manager are 'almost precisely the opposite of those required by their predecessors a century, or so, ago . . . [Moreover,] the qualities once revered are now reviled.'[37]

Although few studies show tangible evidence of the effects of a transformational leadership style for the police organization, the work of John Dobby, Jane Anscombe and Rachel Tuffin does provide some provisional evidence of the benefits of a transformational approach for improving police performance.[38] Police leaders who displayed transformational behaviours in their study were found to have a wide range of positive effects on their subordinates' attitudes to their work, job satisfaction and commitment to the organization. Iain Densten also emphasizes the potential of a transformational approach with its capacity to 'alter the higher order needs of followers by changing their attitudes, beliefs and values'. He goes on to stress that such behaviours are important to police leaders as they 'can directly influence rank and file officers and any process of change'.[39] In short, the message is clear: those using participatory leadership styles are also more likely to bring about successful long-term change in policing.[40] The police service in England and Wales has responded to the call for such a change in leadership style. The National College of Police Leadership has endorsed the need for transformational leadership throughout the service and a new leadership curriculum taking account of the principles of transformational leadership has been developed for its chief officers. Considerable emphasis has been placed on open management and meaningful consultation with all ranks of officers, with a view to affecting the culture of the organization.

Alongside such changes the police service has faced increasing calls from external agencies to develop greater diversity and equality within its ranks.[41] The publication of Home Office Circular 87/1989, 'Equal Opportunities in the Police Service', marked a significant shift towards equality at a policy level, firmly stating government commitment to the concept of equal opportunities.[42] Since then there have been several important initiatives to promote gender equality, including the launch of the Gender Agenda in 2001 under the auspices of the British Association of Women Police. With a key remit to make gender central to the police agenda, Jennifer Brown notes that this women's network offers perhaps the most likely initiative capable of shifting the paradigm of policing. Through asking the 'woman's question', she argues that:

> the *Gender Agenda* raises consciousness about the long hours culture, includ-
> ing breakfast and twilight meetings. It challenges stereotypical thinking
> and offers alternative practices. Its vision is that of a 'moral' and 'ethical'
> approach which ensures that all staff, regardless of their membership of any
> identifiable category, are neither advantaged nor disadvantaged in pursuing
> their duty or their career.[43]

In sum, the extent of structural reform faced by the police service since the 1980s has been significant. An analysis of the ways in which the police service has responded to such organizational change will enable a more comprehensive engagement with some of the more complex debates concerning leadership, gender, policing and change. Existing theorizations of policing have tended to disregard the centrality of police officers as active participants in the construction and reproduction of cultural knowledge and institutional practices. Greater appreciation of the importance of individuals as active participants is emphasized by Janet Chan's study on organizational reform in Australian policing. She critiques existing conceptualizations of police culture for 'their neglect of the active role played by officers in the reproduction or transformation of culture'.[44] This chapter is guided by the notion that police officers play an active role in the interpretation, accommodation, potential transformation of and resistance to organizational change discourses. Applying a gendered lens to such responses provides a further opportunity to develop our understanding of the ways in which police officers faced with such organizational demands have responded, not only as police leaders but as men.

Responding to organizational change

Histories of policing have demonstrated that bringing about change in the police service is a difficult and often protracted process. The police service has a long tradition of exercising resistance to organizational change initiatives.[45] The move to reconstruct police services as corporate entities more particularly has been resisted vigorously by senior police officers, rank-and-file police and their unions.[46] Indeed, Steven Savage reminds us that the British police service has been the most effective of all public sector organizations in '*resisting* reform *and subverting modernization*'.[47] The police response to the Sheehy Inquiry (1993) provides a good example of such individual and collective resistance.[48] Armed with the task of realizing more efficient and cost-effective management of existing resources, the Sheehy Inquiry posed one of the most radical challenges to the police organization, at both administrative and cultural levels, and went on to make over 200 recommendations.[49] In particular, it called for the simplification and streamlining of the rank structure through a reduction of managerial ranks, together with proposals to introduce new conditions of service for officers, including tenure of post, and fixed-term appointments for new recruits and those promoted to higher ranks as a way to end the 'jobs for life' culture. Sheehy's vision of organizational change for policing was strongly resisted by officers and the campaign against it was vociferous. The proposals led to the biggest mass rally by police officers held at any point since the introduction of the new police in 1829.[50] Following a successful lobbying campaign by the police against the Sheehy and White Paper proposals, McLaughlin and Murji note that the Police and Magistrates' Courts Act 1994 contained less than the full reform package.[51]

Such resistance, albeit in a more subtle form, can also be detected in the police response to develop a transformational style of leadership. Reflecting on the changes brought about by NPM, there is little doubt that contemporary chief constables work in stark contrast to their historical predecessors. To suggest that the police leader has adopted a transformational approach, however, may be somewhat premature. In his research on chief constables in the early 1990s, Robert Reiner identified four 'ideal types' of chief officer: the Baron, the Bobby, the Boss and the Bureaucrat. He describes the Baron as 'paternalistic' with a strong military background and a strong preference for 'hierarchical structure' and 'norms of deference'. The Bobby is described as typically from the working class, lacking educational background; 'in a nutshell, he is the bobby on the beat promoted to the top job'. The Boss shares a 'top-down' approach to leadership with the Baron but with the working-class background of the Bobby. The Bureaucrat combines a 'mastery of modern managerial approaches with the charismatic image of a traditional bobby'. His leadership style is more empowering and democratic than the previous three ideal types and he is very much characteristic of the new generation of senior policemen of the 1980s.[52] Nearly a decade later, Reiner observed that the 'bureaucrat' was fast being replaced by the 'businessman'. Here, Reiner characterized police leaders as 'cynical yuppies who know the performance measures for everything and the meaning of nothing'.[53] Wall also refers to chief constables in the 1990s as professionally trained managers working within a corporate police model.[54] In a study of Canadian policing, Frederick Biro, Peter Campbell, Paul McKenna and Tonita Murray concur by noting that senior police officers have become more like 'executives of other organizations – having to balance competing interest, experiencing multi-layered accountability, being accountable for achieving value for money, politically astute and prepared to manage under scrutiny'.[55]

The extent to which the corporate model of policing has resulted in a transformational leadership style is, however, far from convincing. Research indicates that the police organization continues to cling firmly to a style characterized more by transaction than by transformation and that, in reality, the majority of senior police commanders remain autocrats.[56] Robert Adlam and Peter Villiers note that, despite talking the talk of reform, police leaders fail to 'think strategically and act positively . . . even though they may have mastered the jargon of reform. The leadership of the modern police service, by and large, continues to practice "transactional" leadership'.[57] The lack of transformational leadership styles among police leaders is further emphasized by Crank, who suggests that law enforcement leaders respond directly to their unique environment by trying to control officers, giving direction using transactional approaches.[58] Monique Marks and Jenny Fleming's case study of South African police reform demonstrates well the organizational resistance to move towards more transformational participatory approaches. They argue 'that both management and rank and file police officers hold onto established practices and symbolic representations of "discipline", [which] hinder attempts at developing more participatory management techniques with consequences for broader transformational agendas'.[59]

Such findings force us to reappraise the very possibility of developing a model of transformational leadership within the police organization. The manner in which police officers relate to one another in using their power and authority is inextricably bound by the structural and ideological configuration of the police organization itself. Governed by a strict, linear career path, all officers in Britain begin their careers at the bottom and work their way up through a highly structured series of ranks. Although the overall number of ranks throughout England and Wales has been reduced,[60] policing remains firmly rooted in the idea that authority is distributed according to rank. The police organization remains governed and demarcated by hierarchy and rank at a structural level, with police agencies aiming to produce members who are 'disciplined agents expected to follow orders within an organized bureaucracy with militaristic leanings'.[61] Officers quickly learn the scripts required for their place in the organizational hierarchy. They are inducted early on in their careers into the cultural forms that are both 'hierarchical and status laden'.[62] Rituals and routines serve to ensure that officers 'know their place', with clear 'markers of subordination' in operation.[63] At a more cultural level, officers still undergo a series of rituals that continue to symbolize an association and yearning for lost militarism[64] and in so doing enable the quasi-military culture of police to endure.[65]

In its current form the police service is ill-equipped to integrate a transformational leadership style. The police organization is notorious for its unwillingness to share information, with either internal or external agents, and the significance of rank further compounds this position.[66] Typically, within police organizations, 'decision-making is rarely participative or collegial across rank lines'.[67] Maurice Punch draws heavily on the features of solidarity and secrecy that characterize the culture of policing to explain police corruption, arguing that 'there is a deep dichotomy between the values, styles and vulnerability of lower ranks and senior officers which is characterized by social distance, mutual distrust, and varying levels of manipulation, control and acquiescence'.[68] Developing more participatory forms of working within the police organization threatens the very foundations upon which policing and police identity are built. Police reform agendas have, however, brought about an opportunity for police leaders to reconfigure their roles and in turn reconfigure their identities. Police leaders face a different kind of gendered environment to their non-managerial counterparts. Here, officers are faced with a different kind of masculinity, one in which toughness and strength still prevail but in a context in which 'macho' displays of physicality are less likely. There is much to suggest that, following the organizational restructuring in recent decades, leadership styles in policing today hold much in common with a 'smart macho' culture identified by Su Maddock and Di Parkin.[69] It is within a sphere of corporate pressure and performance that the traits associated with 'managerial' masculinity come to dominate and the 'smart macho' police leader emerges.

The 'smart macho' police leader

I have argued elsewhere that the effects of reform agendas have resulted in a form of male dominance characterized by an increased sense of competitiveness, individualism and presenteeism.[70] Driven and preoccupied with meeting performance indicators and targets, this new management style promotes a form of 'competitive masculinity' amongst its officers that encourages:

> a way of relating to the world wherein everything becomes an object of, and for, control . . . [which] generates and sustains a hierarchy imbued with instrumentalist, careerism, and the language of 'success', emulates competition linked to decisive action, 'productivism' and 'risk taking'.[71]

The negative practices generated by performance cultures and the performance pressure that accompanies it are further emphasized by the HMIC report on police integrity of 1999. It states that:

> the increasingly aggressive and demonstrable performance culture has emerged as a major factor affecting integrity not least because for some years there has been an apparent tendency for some forces to 'trawl the margins' for detections and generally use every means to portray their forces in a good light.[72]

Such sentiment is increasingly being echoed within the police literature.[73] Jennifer Brown and Mike Neville propose that there has been no fundamental change in the old order, which positively valued danger and excitement. Rather, they argue that these were mapped directly onto the 'new' order valuing achievement of performance targets.[74] In this way, Brown suggests that, despite a different emphasis and a different language, 'performance culture has the same underlying principles of competition and the condoning of rule bending and rule breaking in order to achieve targets'. As a result, the cult of masculinity 'slides seamlessly into the performance culture'.[75] The same can be said of police leadership: despite organizational talk of positively valuing a 'transformative' leadership style, the narratives of the senior policewomen I interviewed suggest otherwise.

Findings from interviews with senior policewomen suggest that many of them were drawing on different ways of working not traditionally associated within the police organization, characterized by a more holistic style of leadership. Many described their styles in terms of a transformational approach to leading, as opposed to the transactional approach traditionally associated with men in organizations. In particular, senior policewomen's transformational style of leadership was evidenced in the often rigorous, thoughtful and consultative approach adopted in their decision making when taking account of subordinate staff members as individuals with obligations and lives that extend beyond their jobs. Here, senior women were conscious and active in providing support for officers with family commitments to work more flexibly whenever possible. Such approaches were described by senior women as more effective in achieving good relations with colleagues and also made for a more humane face in enacting the function of social control. One officer, for example, noted her ability to 'lead without leaving a trail of bloodshed like some of my male superiors both past and present'.[76] Although keen to stress that using different ways of working would bring untold benefits to the police organization, senior policewomen noted both practical and symbolic difficulties in employing such empowering and interactive approaches. As the following officer stated:

> On two of the most recent promotion boards I was once asked 'Can you bite?', because it was felt I was too nice. In the other one, I was asked, 'How would you get into someone's face?' Nothing has changed you see, they still want a certain kind of leader, obviously one that can bite and get in your face.[77]

By its very nature, adopting a transformative style by employing more participatory and consultative strategies requires a more time-consuming approach to project work. Senior policewomen often experienced the disapproval of management peers and senior management over the length of time taken to reach decisions. The culture of police management was described as one that requires 'quick decision-making and -makers'; the transformational approach takes too long and is therefore perceived to be ineffective. Senior policewomen's ways of working were regularly challenged on the grounds of being ineffective and they were repeatedly made to feel too sensitive and unable to withstand the rigours and demands required of police leaders. As a result, women experienced difficulty in exerting managerial authority with peers and were often perceived to be the weak and 'soft' link in the managerial chain, as the following narratives demonstrate:

I think people perceive my style as weak, but what it really is, is that I won't take responsibility for others.

Sometimes I am concerned that my seniors think I am being too facilitative, too consultative.

I have been criticized for being too approachable. I do take an interest in the welfare aspects of the job perhaps more keenly than my male colleagues . . . This may prove to my detriment, I may have to 'toughen up' in their eyes.

I am very open, a bit too open really. I am not very good at managing my time. I am too available for people. That is one of my faults.

I think I am perceived to be a bit over-sensitive in their eyes.

They'd say I'm a bit soft, that I wait too long to make harsh decisions . . . I think they have an anticipation that I should be more autocratic, take a harsher approach.

Being perceived as not being 'tough' or 'quick thinking' enough for the demands of management and leadership holds serious consequences for those officers wishing to climb the career ladder, and there is a tacit understanding among those in leadership that using more participatory and consultative approaches does not count towards building a suitable profile for becoming a police leader. Rather, women suggested that what was required and valued was the ability to be 'fierce', 'tough' and show displays of 'ruthlessness and competitiveness'. The transformational style was deemed too 'feminine' in orientation and thus at odds with the more traditional command-and-control style of leadership found in the police organization.

The 'smart macho' police leader is also characterized by a strong sense of high visibility and presenteeism. Joan Acker has emphasized an appreciation of the way in which 'time' is conceptualized and structured within organizations in her theoretical work on gendered organizations. For Acker, organizations are key sites where gender divisions are routinely created, exploited, perpetuated and preserved. In thinking about the ways in which organizations reproduce gendered identities, she suggests that the bureaucratic organization has a 'gendered sub-structure'; that is, the social practices that are generally understood to constitute an 'organization' rest on certain gendered processes and assumptions. In defining this sub-structure, she argues that the spatial and temporal arrangements of work and the rules prescribing workplace behaviour can tell us much about the gendered nature of an organization.[78] Understanding the way in which 'time' is conceptualized within the police service is fundamental to achieving an insight into the mindset of the contemporary 'smart macho' police leader. It is through such an appreciation that the gendered nature of police leadership becomes most apparent, and subtle cultural forms of discrimination manifest themselves.

The narratives of senior policewomen overwhelmingly noted the high degree of predictability of male promotion prospects within the police career trajectory. Senior policewomen emphasized that the police career, the work of policing and by implication the lives of police officers are structured to accommodate a male

chronology of continuous and uninterrupted employment. Furthermore, the ability to visibly work long hours and to be ever present through a 'full-time' and
'uninterrupted' career profile has come to be an indicator not only of stamina but
also of one's organizational commitment and credibility within the police service.
Such findings are further emphasized by Davies and Thomas when they observe
that one of the key features of NPM principles has seen the intensification of a
management culture that promotes 'competitive presenteeism' in which 'organizational commitment is demonstrated through macho endurance tests of working
gruelling hours'.[79] Angela Coyle also makes reference to a 'workaholic "macho"
ethos' taking over in local government management.[80]

The importance of achieving organizational commitment and credibility
through such visibility and presenteeism is particularly evident for those police
officers who are involved in managing the demands of work and family life.
Although arguably this is an issue that affects workers in a range of organizations,
there is something fairly distinctive about the way in which police work is organized that favours the lives of men. Given the extra familial responsibilities that
women often bear together with the organizational 'shift-based' pattern of police
work, senior policewomen emphasized the 'irresolvable conflict' between being
a police officer and being a mother. As one senior woman I interviewed noted:

> there are barriers for women . . . I think at the end of the day a lot of it comes
> down to families. It is the biggest barrier to women and whilst this is apparent
> in all organizations, there is something about policing that doesn't sit well
> with the existence of families; maybe this is masculinity at its worst.

Such a view was echoed by all of the women interviewed, including policewomen
with children, those without and those considering having children.

Although important inroads have been made within the police service with
regard to developing equality initiatives that aim to alter the structural configuration of 'time', including the introduction of part-time and flexible working
arrangements, senior policewomen were sceptical of such developments. Given
the perpetual and rapid state of change within the police organization, senior
policewomen not only stressed their fears about their own abilities to re-engage
with their work but also emphasized their concern about an organization that may
not allow them to return as full and committed participants. As Julie Spence,
former president of the British Association of Policewomen, notes, 'part-time
work continues to be characterized by a mentality that constructs those who
assume flexible forms of working as part-able and part-committed'.[81] Utilizing
alternative working patterns does not count towards the profile of earning or
demonstrating either credibility or commitment. On the contrary, the police
career is one that tends to be defined as at odds with domestic responsibilities.
If police officers choose to limit their working hours or opt to undertake them in
an alternative configuration, they do so in the knowledge that they may also be
limiting their career opportunities. All of the senior policewomen I interviewed

who had engaged with flexible working arrangements felt that their promotion prospects had been adversely affected by doing so. One officer recounted her experience of strategically moving in and out of part-time work in order to secure credibility:

> I did resume full-time working just before my promotions and just after promotions because I knew that no one would want me if I had worked part-time. These were most definitely conscious decisions on my part to do this. The police service is great at coming out with guidelines, good practice and policies to support all these different ways of working but when it comes to the workplace none of them do it; none of them respect part-time working . . . They don't make full use of part-timers; they are useless; they simply pigeonhole them.

Further afield, Kim Adams's work on senior police management in Australia also confirms this picture. Her study points to the way in which the commitment of those officers who engage with family-friendly policies is brought into question, with officers being perceived and constructed as 'not really taking the job seriously'.[82] As men have more access to the resource of time and thus are more likely to be able to comply with and work the long hours that are required for most senior jobs, their ability to 'give time' becomes cemented as one of the most desired management attributes in an increasingly competitive environment.[83]

Concluding thoughts

There is much truth in David Collinson and Jeff Hearn's proposition that managers and leaders have become a key group for the understanding of modern masculinities.[84] The pace of police reform since the 1980s has been unrelenting and it is difficult to provide a definitive commentary on the outcome of such change. This chapter has demonstrated that policy has not easily translated into practice. Rather, those involved in police leadership have held onto established practices and symbolic representations of what it means to be a police leader. Other studies have also pointed to the missed opportunities and unintended consequences of reform agendas. Brown, for example, notes that concepts from 'equal opportunities, new public sector management and police reform have all offered the possibility of a paradigm shift for the police service that could have revolutionized its leadership'.[85] In her evaluation of change, however, she identifies a patchier outcome, noting 'untidy, mixed implementation' that results in some new managerialism and an amalgam of humanistic management and an old quasi-military model.[86] Adlam also emphasizes the ways in which police leaders have sustained other rationalities in their leadership practices when he states that:

> [p]olice leadership is a complex alloyage of various discourses. In consequence, it is neither possible nor accurate to reduce police strategic thinking

and policy formulation to any single 'philosophy' . . . Instead, a number of governmental rationalities co-exist in the practices of police governance.[87]

Given the changes brought about by the principles of NPM – a shift towards a transformational leadership style, together with a greater emphasis on achieving equality – there is no doubt that the police organization has become much more 'business like' in orientation. Police leaders are now well versed in the languages of 'efficiency', 'effectiveness' and 'equality' and share much in common with their non-policing managerial counterparts.[88] The possibility of driving forward the ideals of both a managerialist agenda and an equality reform agenda, however, remains a key concern. Marisa Silvestri and Chris Crowther-Dowey note the tense and uneasy relationship between these two reform agendas and suggest that, despite commitment and compliance to gender equality, such values tend to be marginalized in a climate of increasingly economic and technocratic priorities.[89] Police leaders are working in an ever more 'competitive' environment. The removal of layers of management in the police service combined with the intensification of managerial and professional work has serious implications for the ways in which gender is played out in policing. The police organization is one with fewer senior-ranking officers and, far from creating more opportunities, flatter organizational structures have increased the degree of rivalry and competitiveness between officers over a reduced number of higher-level management jobs. Rather than representing an opportunity for change, organizational restructuring and the principles of NPM appear to have strengthened the predominantly 'male' culture of long working hours and aggressive and competitive behaviour. With the announcement by the Home Office in 2010 of moves that will revolutionize the way in which police leaders are trained, selected and appointed, the climate within which police leaders operate looks set to become even more competitive. Although there is much uncertainty about how the police service will respond to the current reform and modernization agenda, it remains deeply gendered at structural, cultural and individual levels and the traditional male career model remains the normative standard for achieving career progression.

Notes

1 T. Newburn and E. Stanko (eds), *Just Boys Doing the Business: Men, Masculinities and Crime*, London: Routledge, 1994; R. Collier, *Masculinities, Crime and Criminology*, London: Sage, 1998; J. W. Messerschmidt, *Masculinities and Crime: Critique and Reconceptualization of Theory*, Lanham, MD: Rowman & Littlefield, 1993; J. W. Messerschmidt, *Crime as Structured Action: Gender, Race, Class and Crime in the Making*, Thousand Oaks, CA: Sage, 1997; J. W. Messerschmidt, 'Masculinities and Crime', in C. Renzetti, L. Goodstein and S. Miller (eds), *Masculinities, Crime and Criminal Justice*, Los Angeles: Roxbury, 2005; T. Jefferson, 'Subordinating Hegemonic Masculinity', *Theoretical Criminology*, 2002, vol. 6, no. 1, pp. 63–88; and D. Gadd, 'Reading between the Lines: Subjectivity and Men's Violence', *Men and Masculinities*, 2003, vol. 5, no. 4, pp. 429–49.

2 Her Majesty's Inspectorate of Constabulary (hereafter HMIC), 'Equal Opportunities in the Police Service', London: HMSO, 1992; HMIC, 'Thematic Inspection of Equal Opportunities', Edinburgh: Scottish Office, 1993; HMIC, 'Developing Diversity in the Police Service: Equal Opportunities Thematic Inspection Report', London: Home Office, 1996; Laming Report, 'The Victoria Climbie Inquiry Report', London: Department of Health, 2003; and Fawcett Society, 'Engendering Justice: From Policy to Practice', London: Fawcett Society, 2009.

3 M. Long, 'Leadership and Performance Management', in Tim Newburn (ed.), *Handbook of Policing*, Cullompton: Willan, 2003.

4 R. Reiner, *Chief Constables: Bobbies, Bosses or Bureaucrats?* Oxford: Oxford University Press, 1991; J. H. Skolnick and D. Bayley, *The New Blue Line: Police Innovation in Six American Cities*, New York: Free Press, 1986; and J. Foster, 'Two Stations: An Ethnographic Analysis of Policing in the Inner City', in D. Downes (ed.), *Crime and the City*, London: Macmillan, 1989.

5 J. Brown, 'Women Leaders: A Catalyst for Change', in R. Adlam and P. Villiers (eds), *Leadership in the Twenty-First Century: Philosophy, Doctrine and Developments*, Winchester: Waterside Press, 2003; F. Heidensohn, *Sexual Politics and Social Control*, Buckingham: Open University Press, 2000; M. Silvestri, *Women in Charge: Policing, Gender and Leadership*, Cullompton: Willan, 2003; M. Ryan and S. Haslam, 'The Glass Cliff: Evidence that Women are Over-Represented in Precarious Leadership Positions', *British Journal of Management*, 2005, vol. 16, no. 2, pp. 81–90; and L. Westmarland, 'Women Managing in the Police', *Police Research and Management*, 1999, vol. 3, no. 3, 62–79.

6 In presenting policewomen's narratives in this chapter, I make no reference to their names, rank or force areas. My decision to present data in such a way relates directly to the relatively small number and high visibility of senior policewomen; an important condition of conducting the research was the assurance of confidentiality.

7 J. Sigurdsson and A. Dhani, 'Police Service Strength England and Wales', *Home Office Statistical Bulletin* 14/10, London: Home Office, 2010.

8 K. Adams, *Women in Senior Police Management*, Payneham: Australasian Centre for Police Research, 2001; M. E. Burke, *Coming out of the Blue*, London: Cassells, 1993; S. Holdaway, *Inside the British Police*, Oxford: Basil Blackwell, 1983; N. Fielding, *Joining Forces: Police Training, Socialisation and Occupational Competence*, London: Routledge, 1988; R. Reiner, *The Politics of the Police*, 2nd edn, Brighton: Wheatsheaf, 1992; D. J. Smith and J. Gray, 'The Police in Action', in *Police and People in London*, vol. 4, London: Policy Studies Institute, 1983; M. Young, *An Inside Job: Policing and Police Culture in Britain*, Oxford: Clarendon Press; 1991; R. Anderson, J. Brown and E. Campbell, *Aspects of Sex Discrimination within the Police Service in England and Wales*, London: Home Office Police Research Group, 1993; F. Heidensohn, *Women in Control: The Role of Women in Law Enforcement*, Oxford: Oxford University Press, 1992; N. Fielding, 'Cop Canteen Culture', in Newburn and Stanko, *Just Boys Doing the Business*; J. B. L. Chan, *Changing Police Culture: Policing in a Multicultural Society*, Cambridge: Cambridge University Press, 1997; and P. A. J. Waddington, *Policing Citizens*, London: UCL Press, 1999.

9 Fielding, 'Cop Canteen Culture', p. 47.

10 P. A. J. Waddington, 'Police (Canteen) Sub-Culture – An Appreciation', *British Journal of Criminology*, 1999, vol. 39, no. 2, pp. 287–309 (p. 297).

11 E. E. Flynn, 'Women as Criminal Justice Professionals: A Challenge to Change Tradition', in N. H. Rafter and E. Stanko (eds), *Judge, Lawyer, Victim, Thief: Women, Gender Roles and Criminal Justice*, Boston: Northeastern University Press, 1982, p. 327.

12 Heidensohn, *Women in Control*, p. 73 (original emphases).

13 F. Heidensohn, '"We Can Handle It Out Here": Women Officers in Britain and the USA and the Policing of Public Order', *Policing and Society*, 1994, vol. 4, no. 4, pp. 293–303.

14 J. Brown, A. Maidment and R. Bull, 'Appropriate Skill–Task Matching or Gender Bias in Deployment of Male and Female Police Officers?', *Policing and Society*, 1993, vol. 3, pp. 121–36.

15 M. Punch and T. Naylor, 'The Police – A Social Service', *New Society*, 17 May 1973; T. Jones and T. Newburn, *Policing after the Act: Police Governance after the Police and Magistrates' Courts Act 1994*, London: Policy Studies Institute, 1997; M. Hough, 'Organization and Resource Management in the Uniformed Police', in K. Heal, R. Tarling and J. Burrows (eds), *Policing Today*, London: HMSO, 1985; and Waddington, 'Police (Canteen) Sub-Culture'.

16 J. Hunt, 'The Development of Rapport through the Negotiation of Gender in Field Work among Police', *Human Organization*, 1984, vol. 43, no. 4, pp. 283–96; and N. Fielding and J. Fielding, 'A Comparative Minority: Female Recruits to a British Constabulary Force', *Policing and Society*, 1992, vol. 2, pp. 205–18.

17 Hunt, 'The Development of Rapport', p. 288.

18 J. Brown, 'Aspects of Discriminatory Treatment of Women Police Officers Serving in Forces in England and Wales', *British Journal of Criminology*, 1998, vol. 38, no. 2, pp. 265–83; Silvestri, *Women in Charge*; and K. C. Gaston and J. A. Alexander, 'Women in the Police: Factors Influencing Managerial Advancement', *Women in Management Review*, 1997, vol. 12, no. 2, pp. 47–55.

19 T. Critchley, *A History of Police in England and Wales*, London: Constable, 1978; C. Emsley, *The English Police: A Political and Social History*, 2nd edn, Hemel Hempstead: Harvester Wheatsheaf, 1996; and T. Cowper, 'The Myth of the "Military Model" of Leadership in Law Enforcement', *Police Quarterly*, 2000, no. 1, pp. 451–64.

20 Reiner, *Chief Constables*.

21 D. S. Wall, *The Chief Constables of England and Wales: The Socio-Legal History of a Criminal Justice Elite*, Aldershot: Dartmouth and Ashgate, 1998.

22 S. Charman, S. Savage and S. Cope, 'Getting to the Top: Selection and Training for Senior Managers in the Police Service', *Social Policy and Administration*, 1999, vol. 33, no. 3, pp. 281–301; I. Densten, 'Senior Australian Law Enforcement Leadership under Examination', *Policing: An International Journal of Police Strategies and Management*, 1998, vol. 22, no. 1, pp. 45–57; Wall, *The Chief Constables of England and Wales*; Brown, 'Women Leaders'; P. Neyroud and A. Beckley, *Policing, Ethics and Human Rights*, Cullompton: Willan, 2001; Adlam and Villiers, *Leadership in the Twenty-First Century*; J. Alderson, 'Police Leadership', in Adlam and Villiers, *Leadership in the Twenty-First Century*; R. Bunyard, 'Justice, Integrity and Corruption', in Adlam and Villiers, *Leadership in the Twenty-First Century*; N. Richards, 'Strategic Depth', in Adlam and Villiers, *Leadership in the Twenty-First Century*; and P. Quinton and J. Miller, 'Promoting Ethical Policing: Summary Findings of Research on New Misconduct Procedures and Police Corruption', *Home Office Report*, 2003, vol. 12, no. 3.

23 S. Cope, F. Leisham and P. Starie, 'Globalization, New Public Management and the Enabling State: Futures of Police Management', *International Journal of Public Sector Management*, 1997, vol. 10, no. 6, pp. 444–60; M. Vickers and A. Kouzmin, 'New Managerialism and Australian Police Organizations', *International Journal of Public Sector Management*, 2001, vol. 14, no. 1, pp. 7–26.

24 The Gender Equality Duty came into force in April 2007 and requires public authorities to promote equality of opportunity between men and women and eliminate unlawful harassment and discrimination.

25 S. Halford, M. Savage and A. Witz, *Gender, Careers and Organisations*, Basingstoke: Macmillan, 1997, p. 65 (original emphasis)

26 E. McLaughlin, J. Muncie and G. Hughes, 'The Permanent Revolution: New Labour, New Public Management and the Modernization of Criminal Justice', *Criminology and Criminal Justice*, 2001, vol. 1, pp. 301–18.

27 Home Office, 'Manpower, Effectiveness and Efficiency in the Police Service', Circular 114, London: Home Office, 1983; and T. Cockcroft and I. Beattie, 'Shifting

Cultures: Managerialism and the Rise of "Performance" ', *Policing: An International Journal of Police Science and Management*, 2009, vol. 32, no. 3, pp. 527.

28 Long, 'Leadership and Performance Management'.

29 Police Federation Joint Consultative Committee, *Operational Policing Review*, Surbiton: Police Federation, 1990; and Association of Chief Police Officers, *Setting the Standards for Policing: Meeting Community Expectation*, London: ACPO, 1990.

30 Long, 'Leadership and Performance Management'.

31 E. N. Drodge and S. A. Murphy, 'Interrogating Emotions in Police Leadership', *Human Resource Development Review*, 2002, vol. 1, no. 4, pp. 420–38.

32 B. M. Bass and B. Avolio, *Transformational Leadership Developments*, Palo Alto, CA: Consulting Psychologists' Press, 1990; and J. Rosener, 'Ways Women Lead', *Harvard Business Review*, November/December 1990, pp. 119–25.

33 J. White, 'Leading in their Own Ways: Women Chief Executives in Local Government', in C. Itzen and J. Newman (eds), *Gender, Culture and Organisational Change*, London: Routledge, 1995.

34 P. England, 'A Feminist Critique of Rational-Choice Theories: Implications for Sociology', *American Sociologist*, 1989, vol. 20, pp. 14–28; P. Y. Martin, 'Feminist Practice in Organisations: Implications for Management', in E. A. Fagenson (ed.), *Women in Management: Trends, Issues and Challenges in Managerial Diversity*. London: Sage, 1993; Rosener, 'Ways Women Lead'; M. Loden, *Feminine Leadership or How to Succeed in Business without Being One of the Boys*, New York: Times Books, 1985; S. Hegelson, *The Female Advantage*, New York: Doubleday, 1990; and J. Grant, 'Women as Managers: What They Can Offer to Organizations', *Organizational Dynamics*, 1988, vol. 16, no. 3, pp. 56–63.

35 Martin, 'Feminist Practice in Organisations'; and K. Ferguson, *The Feminist Case against Bureaucracy*, Philadelphia: Temple University Press, 1984.

36 M. Pagon, 'The Need for a Paradigm Shift', in Adlam and Villiers, *Leadership in the Twenty-First Century*, p. 167.

37 Wall, *The Chief Constables of England and Wales*, pp. 202–3.

38 J. Dobby, J. Anscombe and R. Tuffin, 'Police Leadership: Expectations and Impact', Home Office Report 20/04, London: Home Office, 2004.

39 Densten, 'Senior Australian Law Enforcement Leadership', p. 46.

40 M. Marks and J. Fleming ' "As Unremarkable as the Air They Breathe?" Reforming Police Management in South Africa', *Current Sociology*, 2004, vol. 52, no. 5, pp. 784–808; J. Casey and M. Mitchell, 'Requirements of Police Managers and Leaders from Sergeant to Commissioner', in Mitchell and Casey (eds), *Police Leadership and Management*, Sydney: Federation Press, 2007; and P. Villiers, 'Philosophy, Doctrine and Leadership', in Adlam and Villiers, *Leadership in the Twenty-First Century*.

41 Fawcett Society, 'Engendering Justice'; Home Office, 'Policing in the 21st Century: Reconnecting Police and the People', Cm 7925, London: Home Office, 2010.

42 Home Office, 'Equal Opportunities in the Police Service', Home Office Circular 87/1989, London: Home Office, 1989.

43 Brown, 'Women Leaders', p. 185.

44 Chan, *Changing Police Culture*, p. 12.

45 Skolnick and Bayley, *The New Blue Line*.

46 D. Bayley, 'It's Accountability, Stupid', in K. Bryett and C. Lewis (eds), *Un-Peeling Tradition: Contemporary Policing*, Centre Australian Public Sector Management, Melbourne: Macmillan Education, 1994; and J. Fleming and G. Lafferty, 'Equality Confounded? New Managerialism, Organizational Restructuring and Women in Australian Police Services', conference paper delivered at Women and Policing Globally Conference, Canberra, Australia, 20–23 October 2002.

47 S. Savage, 'Tackling Tradition: Reform and Modernization of the British Police', *Contemporary Politics*, 2003, vol. 9, no. 2, pp. 171–84 (p. 171) (original emphasis).

48 P. Sheehy, *Inquiry into Police Responsibilities and Rewards*, London: Home Office, 1993.

49 E. McLaughlin and K. Murji, 'The Future Lasts a Long Time: Public Policework and the Managerialist Paradox', in P. Francis, P. Davies and V. Jupp (eds), *Policing Futures: The Police, Law Enforcement and the Twenty-First Century*, London: Macmillan, 1997; R. Morgan and T. Newburn, *The Future of Policing*, Oxford: Clarendon Press, 1997; and P. Rawlings, *Crime and Power: A History of Criminal Justice 1688–1998*, London: Longman, 1999.
50 Morgan and Newburn, *The Future of Policing*.
51 McLaughlin and Murji, 'The Future Lasts a Long Time'.
52 Reiner, *Chief Constables*, pp. 306–9.
53 R. Reiner, 'Copping a Plea', in S. Holdaway and P. Rock (eds) *Thinking about Criminology*, London: UCL Press, 1998.
54 Wall, *The Chief Constables of England and Wales*.
55 F. Biro, P. Campbell, P. McKenna and T. Murray, 'Police Executives under Pressure', Police Futures Group: Ottawa, 2001, cited by Mitchell and Casey, *Police Leadership and Management*, p. 13.
56 Villiers, 'Philosophy, Doctrine and Leadership'.
57 Adlam and Villiers, *Leadership in the Twenty-First Century*, p. xi.
58 J. P. Crank, *Understanding Police Culture*, Cincinnati: Anderson, 1998.
59 Marks and Fleming ' "As Unremarkable as the Air They Breathe" ', p. 785.
60 Before the Sheehy Inquiry, the police service's organizational structure was characterized by nine ranks. Since making its recommendations, the Police and Magistrates' Courts Act 1994 went on to compact the rank structure by reducing the overall number to seven ranks.
61 T. Jefferson, *The Case against Paramilitary Policing*, Milton Keynes: Open University Press, 1990, p. 62; Waddington, *Policing Citizens*.
62 R. Adlam, 'Governmental Rationalities in Police Leadership: An Essay Exploring Some of the "Deep Structure" in Police Leadership Praxis', *Policing and Society*, 2002, vol. 12, no. 1, pp. 15–36 (p. 29).
63 M. Silvestri, *Women in Charge: Policing, Gender and Leadership*, Cullompton: Willan Publishing, 2003, p. 158.
64 Villiers, 'Philosophy, Doctrine and Leadership'; R. Panzeralla, 'Leadership Myths and Realities,' in Adlam and Villiers, *Leadership in the Twenty-First Century*; and Wall, *The Chief Constables of England and Wales*.
65 Adlam, 'Governmental Rationalities in Police Leadership'.
66 A. Reige, 'Three-Dozen Knowledge-Sharing Barriers Managers Must Consider', *Journal of Knowledge Management*, 2005, vol. 9, no. 3, pp. 18–35.
67 Bayley, 'It's Accountability, Stupid', p. 61.
68 M. Punch, *Conduct Unbecoming: The Social Construction of Police Deviance and Control*, London: Tavistock, 1985, p. 183.
69 S. Maddock and D. Parkin, 'Gender Cultures', *Women in Management Review*, 1993, vol. 8, no. 2, pp. 3–9.
70 Silvestri, *Women in Charge*.
71 D. Kerfoot and D. Knights, 'Management, Masculinity and Manipulation: From Paternalism to Corporate Strategy in Financial Services in Britain', *Journal of Management Studies*, 1993, vol. 30, no. 4, pp. 659–677 (p. 677).
72 HMIC, 'Police Integrity: Securing and Maintaining Public Confidence', London: Home Office, 1999, p. 19.
73 J. Miller, 'Police Corruption in England and Wales: An Assessment of Current Evidence', Home Office Report 11/03, London: Home Office, 2003; A. J. P. Butler, 'Managing the Future: A Chief Constable's View', in F. Leisham, B. Loveday and S. Savage, *Core Issues in Policing*, Essex: Longman Group, 2000; M. Fitzgerald and M. Hough, 'Policing for London', London: Home Office, 2002; and Cockcroft and Beattie, 'Shifting Cultures'.
74 J. Brown and E. Neville, 'Arrest Rate as a Measure of Policemen and Women's Productivity and Competence', *Police Journal*, 1996, vol. 69, pp. 299–307.

75 Brown, 'Women Leaders', p. 183.

76 M. Silvestri, *Women in Charge: Policing, Gender and Leadership*, Cullompton: Willan Publishing, 2003, p. 127.

77 Silvestri, Women in Charge, p. 131.

78 J. Acker, 'Hierarchies, Jobs, Bodies: A Theory of Gendered Organizations', *Gender and Society*, 1990, vol. 4, no. 2, pp. 139–58; J. Acker, 'Gendering Organisational Theory', in A. Mills and P. Tancred (eds), *Gendering Organisational Analysis*, London: Sage, 1992.

79 A. Davies and R. Thomas, 'Gendering Resistance in the Public Services', in R. Thomas, A. Mills and J. Helms Mills (eds), *Identity Politics at Work: Resisting Gender, Gendering Resistance*, London: Routledge, 2004, p. 24.

80 A. Coyle, *Women and Organisational Change*, Manchester: Equal Opportunities Commission, 1995, p. 48.

81 Cited in C. Jenkins, 'Gender Just', *Police Review*, 2000, vol. 108, p. 23.

82 Adams, *Women in Senior Police Management*.

83 S. Rutherford, 'Are You Going Home Already?: The Long Hours Culture, Women Mangers and Patriarchal Closure', *Time and Society*, 2001, vol. 10, nos 2/3, pp. 259–76; and R. W. Connell and J. Wood, 'Globalization and Business Masculinities', *Men and Masculinities*, 2005, vol. 7, no. 4, pp. 347–64.

84 D. Collinson and J. Hearn, *Men as Managers, Managers as Men: Critical Perspectives on Men, Masculinities and Managements*, London: Sage, 1996.

85 Brown, 'Women Leaders', p. 176.

86 Ibid., p. 182.

87 Adlam, 'Governmental Rationalities in Police Leadership', p. 32.

88 I. Blair, 'Leadership that Learns', in Adlam and Villiers, *Leadership in the Twenty-First Century*.

89 M. Silvestri and C. Crowther-Dowey, *Gender and Crime*, London: Sage, 2008.

BIBLIOGRAPHY

Manuscripts

Archives nationales, Paris: Y9508, Y11037, Y11267A, Y11949, Y12597, Y12830, Y13163, Y13377, Y13728, Y13764, Y14484, Y15114A, Y15114B, Y15117, Y15402.

Bibliothèque de l'Arsenal, Paris: MSS 10975, 11028, 11040, 11131, 11286, 11751.

Bibliothèque municipale, Orléans: MS 1422.

Bibliothèque nationale de France, Paris: Ld4 3207, 'Paroisse St-Médard de Paris. Prestation de serment par le clergé de cette paroisse, le Dimanche 9 janvier 1791'.

Cambridge University Library, Cambridge: MS Doc. 3971, records of the parish of St Peter's, Cambridge.

Lancashire Constabulary Standing Orders, loose-leaf binders, 1930s.

London Metropolitan Archives, London: ACC/1264/001, 'Disposition of the Patroles in and about London during the Late Riots, Beginning of June 1780'.

National Archives, London: HO45/9442/66692, 'Report of the Departmental Commission to inquire into the State, Discipline, and Organisation of the Detective Force of the Metropolitan Police', 1878; HO45/11000/223532, letter, Edward Henry to Under-Secretary of State, 13 May 1913; HO347/1, Departmental Committee on the Metropolitan Police, 1868.

New York State Archives, Albany, United States: N. L. Miller, Governor's Subject and Correspondence Files; New York State Police, NonCriminal Investigation Case Files of the Special Services Unit, Bureau of Criminal Investigation.

Northamptonshire Record Office, Northampton: Capell Brooke, vol. 162, 'The Order Book of Captian Supple'.

Public Record Office Victoria, North Melbourne: Victoria Public Record Series (VPRS) 937/284, 937/298, 937/303, 937/311, 937/318, 937/319, 937/334, 1189/151, 1189/16, 1200/1, 3992/1746.

Victoria Police Historical Unit, Melbourne: Service Record of John Ahern.

Printed primary sources

The Aberdeen Journal (Aberdeen, Scotland), 5 February 1823, issue 3917.

Adam, H. L. (1931) *C.I.D.*, London: Sampson Low, Marston.

Albany Times-Union.

All the Year Round.

Alongi, G. (1887) *Polizia e delinquenza in Italia*, Rome: Cecchini.

Alongi, G. (1898) *Manuale di polizia scientifica*, Milan: Sonzogno.

'Annual Report of HM Inspectors of Constabulary for 1932', *Parliamentary Papers*, 1932–3, (46) xv, 283.

Answers.

Argus (Melbourne).

Arrow, C. (1926) *Rogues and Others*, London: Duckworth.

Astengo, C. and L. Gatti (eds) (January 1863) *Manuale del funzionario di sicurezza pubblica e di polizia giudiziaria*, vol. 1, Milan: Pirola.

Barry, J. (1888) *Victorian Police Guide Containing Practical and Legal Instructions for Police Constables*, Sandhurst: J. W. Burrows.

Bent, J. (1891) *Criminal Life: Reminiscences of Forty-Two Years as a Police Officer*, Manchester: Heywood.

Birkenhead Borough Police, *Instructions*, c. 1926.

Birmingham City Police (1900–39) 'Annual Reports'.

Bishop, C. (1932) *From Information Received*, London: Hutchinson.

Blackwood's Magazine.

Blizard, W. (1785) *Desultory Reflections on Police: With an Essay on the Means of Preventing Crimes and Amending Criminals*, London.

Bolis, G. (1871) *La polizia e le classi pericolose della società*, Bologna: Zanichelli.

Bondi, A. (1913) *Memorie di un questore (25 anni nella polizia italiana)*, Milan: Mondaini.

Bristol Constabulary (1930) 'Standing Orders, revised 1st December 1930', C.G. Maby, Chief Constable, Bristol: Chief Constable's Office.

Brownlie, J., Writer (1829) *Police Reports of Causes tried Before the Justices of the Peace, and the Glasgow, Gorbals, and Calton Police Courts, From 18th July, till 3rd October*, Glasgow, J. Aitken, held in Mitchell Library, Glasgow, G/364.1.

Brust, H. (1936) *I Guarded Kings*, New York: Hillman-Curl.

Bulletin.

Caminada, J. (1895) *Twenty-Five Years of Detective Life*, vol. 1, Manchester: Heywood.

Campbell, W. J. (2003) *Yellow Journalism: Puncturing the Myths, Defining the Legacies*, Westport, CT: Praeger.

Cancrini, L. (1848) *I voti nazionali. Riforma della polizia*, Tipografia dell'Ariosto.

Cappa, D. (1892) *Trentadue anni di servizio nella polizia italiana*, Milan: Dumolard.

Cava, G. (1829) *La polizia. Trattato di Gaetano Cava con de' progetti relativi ad altre attribuzioni proprie della polizia*, Naples.

Cavanagh, T. (1893) *Scotland Yard Past and Present: Experiences of Thirty-Seven Years*, London: Chatto and Windus.

Century Magazine.

Chamber of Commerce of the State of New York State (1914) 'Fifty-sixth Annual Report for the Year 1913/1914', New York.

Chambers's Journal.

Chandler, G. F. (1922) *The Policeman's Art as Taught in the New York State School for Police*, New York: Funk & Wagnall's.

Chandler, G. F. (1938) *Dawn Days of the State Police*, Troy, NY: Record Newspapers.

Cheshire Constabulary (1920) 'Memorandum', Form 39/A.

City of Bristol (1914) *Bristol Police Force Instruction Book, issued by Authority of the Bristol Watch Committee*, Bristol: Henry Hill.

City of Bristol (1939) *Bristol Constabulary Supplementary Instruction Book 1939, issued by Authority of the Bristol Watch Committee*, C.G. Maby, OBE, Chief Constable.

City of Manchester (1908) *Police Instruction Book*, Manchester: John Heywood.

City of Manchester (1923) *Police Instruction Book*, Manchester: Co-operative Wholesale Society's Printing Works.

Condor, S. (1960) *Woman on the Beat: The True Story of a Policewoman*, London: Robert Hale.

County Borough of Bolton (1934) *Police Instructions*, Bolton: Blackshaw, Sykes and Morris.

County Borough of Preston (1924) *Police Instruction Book, issued by Authority of the Watch Committee*, Preston: R. Seed.

Crawford, N. (1924) *The Ethics of Journalism*, New York: Knopf.

Cuniberti, A. (1870) *Malanni e rimedi, ossia il vandalismo campestre prevenuto e represso*, Bologna.

Cuniberti, A. (1872) *La polizia di Londra: con note ed osservazioni sulla polizia italiana*, Bologna: Zanichelli.

Daily Chronicle.

The Daily Telegraph.

Dark Blue.

Degli uffici e funzionarj di pubblica sicurezza. Note di un già questore, Milan: Tip. Albertari, 1862.

Delamare, N. (1705–38) *Traité de la police*, 4 vols, Paris: Michel Brunet.

Departmental Committee of 1889 Upon Metropolitan Police Superannuation, *Parliamentary Papers*, vol. 59, 1890.

Desborough Committee on the Police Service, *Parlimentary Papers*, vol. 27, 1920.

Des Essarts, N. T. (1786–9) *Dictionnaire universel de la police*, 7 vols, Paris.

Dilnot, G. (1915) *Scotland Yard*, London: Percival Marshall.

Domat, J. (1713) *Les Lois civiles dans leur ordre naturel*, Paris.

Edinburgh Advertiser.

Eldridge, B. and Watts, W. (1897) *Our Rival, the Rascal: A Faithful Portrayal of the Conflict between the Criminals of this Age and the Defenders of Society – The Police*, Boston: Pemberton.

Ferrero, G. and C. Lombroso (1893) *La donna delinquente: la prostituta e la donna normale*, Turin: Roux (5th edn, Turin: Fratelli Bocca, 1927).

Fiani, B. (1853–6) *Della polizia considerata come mezzo di preventiva difesa. Trattato teorico-pratico*, Florence: Tipografia nazionale italiana.

Florenzano, G. (1875) *La legge eccezionale e la pubblica sicurezza in Italia*, Naples: De Angelis.

Forrester, A., Jr (1864) *The Female Detective*, London.

Fosdick, R. (1969 [1920]) *American Police Systems*, Montclair, NJ: Patterson Smith.

'Fourth Report by Her Majesty's Law Commissioners, Scotland, 1839', *British Parliamentary Papers*, 1840 [241].

Frederick II (1777) *Essay on Forms of Government*, in I. Kramnick (ed.), *The Portable Enlightenment Reader*, New York: Penguin, 1995.

Fuller, R. A. (1912) *Recollections of a Detective*, London: John Long.

Fun.

Giorio, F. (1882) *Ricordi di questura*, Milan: Artistica.

The Globe.

Gordon, W. J. (1890) 'The Everyday Life of a Policeman', *Leisure Hour*, p. 604

Goulart, R. (ed.) (1965) *The Hardboiled Dicks: An Anthology of Pulp Detective Fiction from the Pulp Magazines*, Los Angeles: Sherbourne Press.

Greenham, G. H. (1904) *Scotland Yard Experiences from the Diary of G. H. Greenham Late Chief Inspector, Criminal Investigation Dept.*, London: George Routledge.

Grey, V. (1907) *Stories of Scotland Yard*, London: Everett.

Griffiths, A. (1899) *Mysteries of Police and Crime*, vol. 1, London: Cassell.

Grossardi, G. C. (1875) *Galateo del Carabiniere*, Turin (facsimile edited by the Ufficio Pubbliche Relazioni del Comando Generale dell'Arma dei Carabinieri, Rome, 2001).

Hanway, J. (1780) *The Citizen's Monitor: Shewing the Necessity of a Salutary Police*, London.

Hanway, J. (1785) *The Defects of Police the Cause of Immorality, and the Continual Robberies Committed, Particularly in and about the Metropolis*, London.

Hautefeuille (1811–13) *Trattato di procedura criminale, correzionale e di polizia, seguito dall'analisi del codice penale*, 3 vols, Naples: Simoniana.

Hayter, T. (ed.) (1988) *An Eighteenth-Century Secretary at War: The Papers of William, Viscount Barrington*, London: Bodley Head.

Her Majesty's Inspectorate of Constabulary (1992) 'Equal Opportunities in the Police Service', London: HMSO.

Her Majesty's Inspectorate of Constabulary (1993) 'Thematic Inspection of Equal Opportunities', Edinburgh: Scottish Office.

Her Majesty's Inspectorate of Constabulary (1996) 'Developing Diversity in the Police Service: Equal Opportunities Thematic Inspection Report', London: Home Office.

Her Majesty's Inspectorate of Constabulary (1999) 'Police Integrity: Securing and Maintaining Public Confidence', London: Home Office.

Home Office (1983) 'Manpower, Effectiveness and Efficiency in the Police Service', Circular 114, London: Home Office.

Home Office (1989) 'Equal Opportunities in the Police Service', Circular 87/1989, London: Home Office, 1989.

Home Office (2010) 'Policing in the 21st Century: Reconnecting Police and the People', Cm 7925, London: Home Office.

Hordern, A., Sir, Chief Constable (1947) *Notes for the Guidance of Members of the Lancashire Constabulary*, Hutton, Preston: Printed and Published at the County Chief Constable's Office.

Household Words.

Howard Vincent, C. E. (1881) *Police Code and Manual of the Criminal Law*, London: Cassell, Patter, Galphin.

Illustrated Police Budget.

Instruction Book for the Government and Guidance of the Bristol Police Force, Bristol: J. W. Arrowsmith, 1894.

Jerrold, B. and Doré, G. (2005 [1872]) *London: A Pilgrimage*, introduction by P. Ackroyd, London: Anthem Press.

Jervis, R. (1995 [1907]) *Chronicles of a Victorian Detective*, Runcorn: P. and D. Riley.

Jones, W. (1782) *An Inquiry into the Legal Mode of Suppressing Riots. With a Constitutional Plan of Future Defence*, London.

Kershaw, S., Chief Constable (1893) *Regulations and Instructions for the Southport Police Force, and Fire Brigade, By Order of the Watch Committee*, Southport: Lowes.

Kramnick, I. (ed.) (1995) *The Portable Enlightenment Reader*, New York: Penguin.

Laming Report (2003) 'The Victoria Climbie Inquiry Report', London: Department of Health.

Lansdowne, A. (1984 [1890]) *A Life's Reminiscences of Scotland Yard: In One-and-Twenty Dockets*, London: Leadenhall Press.

Latouche, P. (1908) *Anarchy!*, London: Everett.

Leach, C. E. (1933) *On Top of the Underworld*, London: Sampson Low, Marston.

Leisure Hour.

'Letter Explanatory of a Late Judgement in the Court of Police: With a Copy of the Judgement', Edinburgh, John Brown, [1807], Edinburgh Central Library (ECL), YHV 8198 42289.2.

Littlechild, J. G. (1894) *Reminiscences of Chief-Inspector Littlechild*, London: Leadenhall Press.

Liverpool City Police (1900–39) 'Annual Reports'.

Liverpool City Police (1903) *Instructions, 1903*, Liverpool: C. Tinling.

Liverpool City Police (1911) *Instructions, 1911*, Liverpool: C. Tinling.

Liverpool City Police (1926) *Instructions, 1926*, Liverpool: C. Tinling.

Liverpool City Police (1944) *Instructions, 1944*, Liverpool: John Gardner.

Lock, J. (1968) *Lady Policeman*, London: Michael Joseph.

Lombroso, C. (1876) *L'uomo delinquente*, Milan: Hoepli.

Lombroso, C. (1879) *Sull'incremento del delitto in Italia e sui mezzi per arrestarlo*, Turin: Fratelli Bocca.

Lombroso, C. and Ottolenghi, S. (1891) *La donna delinquente e la prostituta: studio*, Turin: Unione tipografico-editrice.

Macé, G. (1885–7) *La police parisienne*, 3 vols, Paris: Charpentier.

McKinney's Consolidated Laws of New York, 1982.

Macmillan's Magazine.

M'Naught, T. P. (1887) *The Recollections of a Glasgow Detective Officer*, London: Marshall, Hamilton, Kent.

Manchester City Police (1900–13, 1927–39) 'Annual Reports'.

Manchester City Police (1931) *Supplementary Instruction Book. Extracts from Acts, Regulations and Orders dealing with the Use on the Public Highways of Motor Vehicles, together with General Instructions thereon*, Manchester: Henry Blacklock.

Manchester Times.

Manual of Police Regulations for the Guidance of the Constabulary of Victoria, and approved by his Excellency the Governor in Council 22 April 1856, Melbourne: John Ferres Government Printer, 1856.

Manuale alfabetico dei maires, *loro aggiunti e commissari di polizia*, Florence: Giovacchino Pagani, 1809.

Manuel, P., *La police de Paris dévoilée, par l'un des administrateurs de 1789*, Paris, Year II.

Marius (n.d.) *La pubblica sicurezza in Italia*, Milan: Carlo Aliprandi.

Mayhew, H. (1967 [1861–2]) *London Labour and the London Poor*, vol. 4, London: Frank Cass.

Mayo, K. (1917) *Justice to All: The Story of the Pennsylvania State Police*, introduction by Theodore Roosevelt, New York: G. P. Putnam's Sons, Knickerbocker.

Melville Lee, W. L. (1971 [1901]) *A History of Police in England*, Montclair: Patterson Smith.

Mercier, L.-S. (1782–8) *Tableau de Paris*, nouvelle édition, 12 vols, Amsterdam.

Metropolitan Police (1829) *Instructions to the Force*, London: J. Hartnell.

Metropolitan Police (1900) *Instruction Book for the Government and Guidance of the Metropolitan Police Force*, London: Darling.

Metropolitan Police (1912) *Instruction Book for the Guidance of the Metropolitan Police Force*, London: Darling.

Metropolitan Police (1925) *Instruction Book for the Guidance of the Metropolitan Police Force*, London: Printed by the Receiver for the Metropolitan Police District.

Metropolitan Police (1934) *Instruction Book for the Guidance of the Metropolitan Police Force*, London: Printed by His Majesty's Stationery Office.

Metropolitan Police (1953) *Instruction Book for the Guidance of the Metropolitan Police Force*, London: Printed by the Receiver for the Metropolitan Police District.

Mirabeau, H.-G. Riqueti, comte de (1782) *Des lettres de cachet et des prisons d'état*, Hamburg.

Mirabeau, V. Riqueti, marquis de (1757) *L'Ami des hommes*, Avignon.

Monro, J. (1891) 'The London Police', *North American Review*, vol. 151, p. 615–29.

Montesquieu, C.-L. de Secondat, baron de (1748) *De l'esprit des lois*.

Moonshine.

Mozzillo, R. (1847) *Manuale di polizia, ovvero indice ragionato delle leggi, dei reali decreti, delle sovrane risoluzioni e delle massime riguardanti la polizia ordinaria*, 2 vols, Naples: Tip. Mosca.

Murray's Magazine.

National Police Gazette.

New York Call.

New York Evening Post.

The New York Times.

New York State Police (1920) 'Second Annual Report for the Year 1919', Albany.

Once a Week.

Ottolenghi, S. (1897) *L'insegnamento universitario della polizia giudiziaria scientifica: prolusione*, Turin: Fratelli Bocca.

Pall Mall Gazette.

Paoletti, V. (1891) *Da Brundisio alle Alpi. Reminiscenze di un ispettore di Sicurezza Pubblica*, Milan.

Pirkis, C. L. (1894) *The Experiences of Loveday Brooke, Lady Detective*, London: Hutchinson.

Police and the Public.

The Police Guardian: A Newspaper Devoted to the Interests of the Police & Constabulary of the United Kingdom & the Colonies.

The Police Intelligencer, or Life in Edinburgh, printed by Forbes and Kay, Kitchen's Court, 171 Cowgate, Edinburgh, 1831–1832, held in Edinburgh Central Library (E.C.L.), YHV 8198 42900.

Police Journal (Victoria).

Police Orders.

Police Regulation Act 1853 (Victoria).

'Police Reports of Cases Tried before the Justices of Peace, and the Glasgow, Gorbals and Calton Police Courts, from 18th July, till 3rd October' (Glasgow, 1829), Mitchell Library, Glasgow, G/364.1, and Edinburgh Central Library (E.C.L.), YHV 8198 42900 (Edinburgh, 1831–32).

The Police Review and Parade Gossip: Organ of the British Constabulary.

Police Service Advertiser.

Porter, A. (2011) 'Police Could Use Water Cannon to Disperse Rioters, Theresa May Says', *The Daily Telegraph*, 18 January 2011.

'Postscript to Mr Thomson's Statement, in Reply to a Letter Published as "Explanatory of a Late Judgment in the Court of Police"', Edinburgh, James Ballantyne [1807].

Quarterly Review.

Regents Rules on Subversive Activities, Albany: University of the State of New York Press, 1959.

Regulations for the Guidance of the Constabulary of Victoria, Melbourne: John Ferres Government Printer, 1877.

'Report of the Committee on the Employment of Women on Police Duties', *Parliamentary Papers*, Cmd 877, 1920.

'Report of the Departmental Committee on the Employment of Policewomen', *Parliamentary Papers*, Cmd 2224, 1924.

'Report of the Royal Commission on Police Powers and Procedure', *Parliamentary Papers*, Cmd 3297, vol. IX, 1928–9.

'Report of Two Cases decided in the Police Court on Thursday, 30th April', p. 3, ECL, YHV 8198 42289.2.

The Revolution in the Police and the Coming Revolution of the Army and Navy, London: D. Chatterton, n.d.

Reynolds's News.

Robinet, J.-B. R. (1777–83) *Dictionnaire universel des sciences morale, économique, politique et diplomatique; ou Bibliotheque de l'homme-d'état et du citoyen*, 30 vols, London: Les libraires associés.

Rome Daily Sentinel.

'Royal Commission upon the Duties of the Metropolitan Police', *Parliamentary Papers*, 1908, vol. 50.

Sackville, C. (1752) *A Treatise Concerning the Militia*, Dublin.

St James's Gazette.

Saturday Review.

Schmitt, G. (1905) *Fisiologia e costume della prostituzione*, Naples: Salvatore Romano.

Sharp, G. (1781) *Tracts Concerning the Ancient and Only True Legal Means of National Defence, by a Free Militia*, London.

Smith, B. (1925) *The State Police: Organization and Administration*, New York: Macmillan.

Smith, B. (1940) *Police Systems in the United States*, New York: Harper.

The Spectator.

'Statement and Review of a Recent Decision of the Judge of Police in Edinburgh: Authorising his Officers to Make Domiciliary Visits in Private Families, to Stop Dancing' [George Thomson], Edinburgh: Printed for Manners and Miller by John Moir, 1807, ECL, YHV 8198 42289.2.

Sun.

Sweeney, J. (1904) *At Scotland Yard: Being the Experiences During Twenty-Seven Years' Service of John Sweeney, Late Detective Inspector, Criminal Investigation Department, New Scotland Yard*, edited by F. Richards, London: Grant Richards.

Tempest Clarkson, C. and Hall Richardson, J. (1984 [1889]) *Police!*, New York: Garland.

The Times.

Turner, B. (1782) *A Plan for Rendering the Militia of London Useful and Respectable, and for Raising an Effective and Well-Regulated Watch, Without Subjecting the Citizens to Additional Taxes or the Interposition of Parliament*, London.

de Vattel, E. (1758) *Le droit des gens ou Principes de la loi naturelle appliqués à la conduite et aux affaires des nations et des souverains*, 2 vols, London.

Victoria Government Gazette.

Victoria Police Gazette.

Victorian Parliamentary Papers, Melbourne, 1883, 1906.

Votes and Proceedings of the Legislative Council (Victoria), vol. 3, 1852–3.

Wallasey County Borough Police Instruction Book, 1929.

Wensley, F. P. (1931) *Detective Days: The Record of Forty-Two Years' Service in the Criminal Investigation Department*, London: Cassell.

Westminster Review.

World.

Wyles, L. (1952) *A Woman at Scotland Yard: Reflections on the Struggles and Achievements of Thirty Years in the Metropolitan Police*, London: Faber and Faber.

Wynter, A. (1856) 'The Police and Thieves', *Quarterly Review*, vol. XCIX, pp. 160–200.

Film

'A Nation of Law?: 1968–1971', *Eyes on the Prize*, New York: Blackside, 1990.

Secondary sources

Acker, J. (1990) 'Hierarchies, Jobs, Bodies: A Theory of Gendered Organizations', *Gender and Society*, vol. 4, no. 2, pp. 139–58.

Acker, J. (1992) 'Gendering Organisational Theory', in A. Mills and P. Tancred (eds), *Gendering Organisational Analysis*, London: Sage.

Adams, K. (2001) *Women in Senior Police Management*, Payneham: Australasian Centre for Police Research.

Adlam, R. (2002) 'Governmental Rationalities in Police Leadership: An Essay Exploring Some of the "Deep Structure" in Police Leadership Praxis', *Policing and Society*, vol. 12, no.1, pp. 15–36.

Adlam, R. and Villiers, P. (eds) (2003) *Leadership in the Twenty-First Century: Philosophy, Doctrine and Developments*, Winchester: Waterside Press.

Ago, R. (2001) 'La costruzione dell'identità maschile: una competizione tra uomini', in A. Arru (ed.), *La costruzione dell'identità maschile nell'età moderna e contemporanea*, Rome: Biblink.

Alderson, J. (2003) 'Police Leadership', in R. Adlam and P. Villiers (eds), *Leadership in the Twenty-First Century: Philosophy, Doctrine and Developments*, Winchester: Waterside Press.

Allen, J., Als, H., Lewis, Congressman J. and Litwack, L. F. (2004) *Without Sanctuary: Lynching Photography in America*, Santa Fe: Twin Palms.

Allen, M. S. (1925) *The Pioneer Policewoman*, London: Chatto & Windus.

Anderson, R., Brown, J. and Campbell, E. (1993) *Aspects of Sex Discrimination within the Police Service in England and Wales*, London: Home Office Police Research Group.

Apel, D. (2004) *Imagery of Lynching: Black Men, White Women, and the Mob*, New Brunswick, NJ: Rutgers University Press.

Appier, J. (1998) *Policing Women: The Sexual Politics of Law Enforcement and the LAPD*, Philadelphia: Temple University Press.

Archer, J. E. (2000) ' "Men Behaving Badly"?: Masculinity and the Uses of Violence, 1850–1900', in S. D'Cruze (ed.), *Everyday Violence in Britain, 1850–1950: Gender and Class*, London: Longman.

Ascoli, D. (1979) *The Queen's Peace: The Origins and Development of the Metropolitan Police, 1829–1979*, London: D. Hamilton.

Avdela, E. (2000) 'Work, Gender and History in the 1990s and Beyond', in L. Davidoff, K. McClelland and E. Varikas (eds), *Gender and History: Retrospect and Prospect*, Oxford: Blackwell.

Ayers, P. and Lambertz, J. (1986) 'Marriage Relations, Money, and Domestic Violence in Working-Class Liverpool, 1919–1939', in Jane Lewis (ed.), *Labour and Love: Women's Experiences of Home and Family 1850–1940*, Oxford: Basil Blackwell.

Balkin, J. (1988) 'Why Policemen Don't Like Policewomen', *Journal of Police Science and Administration*, vol. 16, no. 1, pp. 29–38.

Banti, A. M. (2000) *La nazione del Risorgimento: parentela, santità e onore alle origini dell'Italia unita*, Turin: Einaudi.

Banti, A. M. (2005) *L'onore della nazione. Identità sessuali e violenza nel nazionalismo europeo dal XVIII secolo alla Grande Guerra*, Turin: Einaudi.

Barker-Benfield, G. J. (1992) *The Culture of Sensibility: Sex and Society in Eighteenth-Century Britain*, Chicago: Chicago University Press.

Baron, A. (ed.) (1991) *Work Engendered: Toward a New History of American Labor*, Ithaca, NY: Cornell University Press.

Barrie, D. G. (2008a) *Police in the Age of Improvement: Police Development and the Civic Tradition in Scotland, 1775–1865*, Cullompton: Willan.

Barrie, D. G. (2008b) 'Patrick Colquhoun, the Scottish Enlightenment and Police Reform in Glasgow in the Late Eighteenth Century', *Crime, Histoire & Sociétés/Crime, History & Societies*, vol. 12, no. 2, pp. 57–79.

Barrie, D. G. (2010a) 'A Typology of British Police: Locating the Scottish Municipal Police Model in its British Context, 1800–1835', *British Journal of Criminology*, vol. 50, no. 2, pp. 259–77.

Barrie, D. G. (2010b) 'Police in Civil Society: Police, Enlightenment and Civic Virtue in Scotland, 1780–1833', *Urban History*, vol. 37, no. 1, pp. 45–65.

Barrie, D. G. (2012) 'Anglicisation and Autonomy: Scottish Policing, Governance and the State, 1833 to 1885', *Law and History Review* (to be published in vol. 30).

Barrie, D. G. and Broomhall, S. (2011) 'Policing Bodies in Urban Scotland, 1780–1850', in S. Broomhall and J. Van Gent (eds), *Governing Masculinities in the Early Modern Period: Regulating Selves and Others*, Aldershot: Ashgate.

Barsham, D. (2000) *Arthur Conan Doyle and the Meaning of Masculinity*, Burlington, VT: Ashgate.

Bass, B. M. and Avolio, B. (1990) *Transformational Leadership Developments*, Palo Alto, CA: Consulting Psychologists' Press.

Bates, T. R. (1975) 'Gramsci and the Theory of Hegemony', *Journal of the History of Ideas*, vol. 36, no. 2, pp. 351–66.

Bayley, D. H. (1985) *Patterns of Policing: A Comparative International Analysis*, New Brunswick, NJ: Rutgers University Press.

Bayley, D. H. (1994) 'It's Accountability, Stupid', in K. Bryett and C. Lewis (eds), *Un-Peeling Tradition: Contemporary Policing*, Centre Australian Public Sector Management, Melbourne: Macmillan Education.

Beattie, J. M. (2001) *Policing and Punishment in London, 1660–1750: Urban Crime and the Limits of Terror*, Oxford: Oxford University Press.

Beattie, J. M. (2006) 'Early Detection: The Bow Street Runners in Late Eighteenth-Century London', in Clive Emsley and Haia Shpayer-Makov (eds), *Police Detectives in History, 1750–1950*, Aldershot: Ashgate.

Beattie, J. M. (2007) 'Garrow and the Detectives: Lawyers and Policemen at the Old Bailey in the Late Eighteenth Century', *Crime, Histoire & Sociétés/Crime, History & Societies*, vol. 11, no. 2, pp. 2–23.

Beattie, J. M. (forthcoming) *The First English Detectives: The Bow Street Runners and the Policing of London, 1750–1840*, Oxford: Oxford University Press.

Beckert, S. (1993) *The Monied Metropolis: New York City and the Consolidation of the American Bourgeoisie, 1850–1896*, New York: Cambridge University Press.

Bell, D. A. (1994) *Lawyers and Citizens: The Making of a Political Elite in Old Regime France*, New York: Oxford University Press.

Bellassai, S. (2004) *La mascolinità contemporanea*, Rome: Carocci.

Bellassai, S. and Malatesta, M. (2000) 'Mascolinità e storia', in S. Bellassai and M. Malatesta (eds), *Genere e mascolinità. Uno sguardo storico*, Rome: Bulzoni.

Benadusi, L. (2009) 'Storia del corpo maschile', in E. Ruspini (ed.), *Uomini e corpi. Una riflessione sui rivestimenti della mascolinità*, Milan: Franco Angeli.

Berliere, J.-M. (1996) *Le monde des polices en France*, Brussels: Complexe.

Berlière, J.-M. (2008) 'Du magistrat de quartier au policier spécialisé: Pierre Chénon, *commissaire* du quartier du Louvre (1751–1791)', in J.-M. Berlière, C. Denys, D. Kalifa and V. Milliot (eds), *Métiers de police. Être policier en Europe, XVIIIe–XXe siècle*, Rennes: Presses universitaires de Rennes.

Biro, F., Campbell, P., McKenna, P. and Murray, T. (2001) *Police Executives under Pressure*, Ottawa: Police Futures Group.

Bittner, E. (1990) *Aspects of Police Work*, Boston: North Eastern University Press.

Blackmon, D. A. (2008) *Slavery by Another Name: The Re-enslavement of Black Americans from the Civil War to World War II*, New York: Doubleday.

Blair, I. (2003) 'Leadership that Learns', in R. Adlam and P. Villiers (eds), *Leadership in the Twenty-First Century: Philosophy, Doctrine and Developments*, Winchester: Waterside Press.

Bonino, M. (2006) *La polizia italiana nella seconda metà dell'Ottocento. Aspetti culturali e operativi*, Rome: Laurus Robuffo.

Boscagli, M. (1996) *Eye on the Flesh: Fashions of Masculinity in the Early Twentieth Century*, Oxford: Westview Press.

Boyd, K. (1991) 'Knowing Your Place: The Tensions of Manliness in Boys' Story Papers, 1918–39', in M. Roper and J. Tosh (eds), *Manful Assertions: Masculinities in Britain since 1800*, London: Routledge.

Braddick, M. (2000) *State Formation in Early Modern England c. 1550–1700*, Cambridge: Cambridge University Press.

Brockliss, L. and Jones, C. (1997) *The Medical World of Early Modern France*, Oxford: Oxford University Press.

Brodeur, J.-P. (1994) 'Police et Coercition', *Revue Francaise de Sociologie*, vol. 35, pp. 457–85.

Broers, M. (1994) 'Policing Piedmont: "The Well Ordered Police State" in the Age of Revolution, 1794–1821', *Criminal Justice History*, vol. 15, pp. 39–57.

Brogden, M. (1982) *The Police: Autonomy and Consent*, London: Academic Press.

Brogden, M. (1991) *On the Mersey Beat: Policing Liverpool between the Wars*, Oxford: Oxford University Press.

Broomhall, S. and Barrie, D. G. (2011) 'Changing of the Guard: Governance, Policing, Masculinity and Class in the Porteous Affair and Walter Scott's *Heart of Midlothian*', *Parergon*, vol. 28, no. 1, pp. 65–90.

Broomhall, S. and Van Gent, J. (eds) (2011) *Governing Masculinities in the Early Modern Period: Regulating Selves and Others*, Aldershot: Ashgate.

Broughton, T. L. and Rogers, H. (2007) 'Introduction', in *Gender and Fatherhood in the Nineteenth Century*, Basingstoke: Palgrave Macmillan.

Brown, H. G. (2006) 'Tips, Traps and Tropes: Catching Thieves in Post-Revolutionary Paris', in Clive Emsley and Haia Shpayer-Makov (eds), *Police Detectives in History, 1750–1950*, Aldershot: Ashgate.

Brown, J. (1998a) 'Women in Policing: A Comparative Research Perspective', *International Journal of the Sociology of Law*, vol. 25, pp. 1–19.

Brown, J. (1998b) 'Aspects of Discriminatory Treatment of Women Police Officers Serving in Forces in England and Wales', *British Journal of Criminology*, vol. 38, no. 2, pp. 265–83.

Brown, J. (2003) 'Women Leaders: A Catalyst for Change', in R. Adlam and P. Villiers (eds), *Leadership in the Twenty-First Century: Philosophy, Doctrine and Developments*, Winchester: Waterside Press.

Brown, J. and Heidensohn, F. (2000) *Gender and Policing: Comparative Perspectives*, Houndmills: Macmillan.

Brown, J. and Neville, E. (1996) 'Arrest Rate as a Measure of Policemen and Women's Productivity and Competence', *Police Journal*, vol. 69, pp. 299–307.

Brown, J., Maidment, A. and Bull, R. (1993) 'Appropriate Skill–Task Matching or Gender Bias in Deployment of Male and Female Police Officers?', *Policing and Society*, vol. 3, pp. 121–36.

Bryman, A. (1986) *Leadership and Organisations*, London: Routledge & Kegan Paul.

Bunyard, R. (2003) 'Justice, Integrity and Corruption', in R. Adlam and P. Villiers (eds), *Leadership in the Twenty-First Century: Philosophy, Doctrine and Developments*, Winchester: Waterside Press.

Burke, M. E. (1993) *Coming out of the Blue*, London: Cassells.

Butler, A. J. P. (2000) 'Managing the Future: A Chief Constable's View', in F. Leisham, B. Loveday and S. Savage, *Core Issues in Policing*, Essex: Longman Group.

Buzard, J. (2005) *Disorienting Fiction: The Autoethnographic Work of Nineteenth Century British Novels*, Princeton, NJ: Princeton University Press.

Buzzanca, S. (n.d.) 'La figura di Salvatore Ottolenghi', available at http://ssai.interno.it/pubblicazioni/instrumenta/16/14_buzzanca.pdf.

Cain, M. (ed.) (1989) *Growing Up Good: Policing the Behaviour of Girls in Europe*, London: Sage.

Canepa, G. (1985) 'Criminologia e antropologia criminale. Origini e sviluppo storico', in U. Levra (ed.), *La scienza e la colpa. Crimini, criminali, criminologi: un volto dell'Ottocento*, Milan: Electa.

Carbone, F. (2010) 'Lineamenti dell'organizzazione di polizia nel Regno di Sardegna: il Corpo dei Carabinieri Reali (1814–1853)', in L. Antonielli (ed.), *Polizia ordine pubblico e crimine tra città e campagna: un confront comparativo*, Soveria Mannelli: Rubbettino.

Carlen, P. and Jefferson, T. (eds) (1996) 'Special Issue: Masculinities and Crime', *British Journal of Criminology*, vol. 33, no. 6.

Carrier, J. (1988) *The Campaign for the Employment of Women as Police Officers*, Aldershot: Ashgate.

Carter, P. (2001) *Men and the Emergence of Polite Society, Britain 1660–1800*, London: Longman.

Carter Wood, J. (2004) 'A Useful Savagery: The Invention of Violence in Nineteenth-Century England', *Journal of Victorian Culture*, vol. 9, no. 1, pp. 22–42.

Casey, J. and Mitchell, M. (2007) 'Requirements of Police Managers and Leaders from Sergeant to Commissioner', in M. Mitchell and J. Casey (eds), *Police Leadership and Management*, Sydney: Federation Press.

de Castro, J. P. (1926) *The Gordon Riots*, London: Oxford University Press.

Caute, D. (1978) *The Great Fear: The Anti-Communist Purge under Truman and Eisenhower*, New York: Simon and Schuster.

Chagniot, J. (1973) 'Le guet et la garde de Paris à la fin de l'ancien régime', *Revue d'histoire moderne et contemporaine*, vol. 20, pp. 58–71.

Chagniot, J. (1985) *Paris et l'armée au XVIIIe siècle*, Paris: Economica.

Chamberlain, L. H. (1951) *Loyalty and Legislative Action: A Survey of Activity by the New York State Legislature, 1919–1948*, Cornell Studies in Civil Liberty, Ithaca, NY: Cornell University Press.

Chan, J. B. L. (1997) *Changing Police Culture: Policing in a Multicultural Society*, Cambridge: Cambridge University Press.

Charman, S., Savage S. and Cope, S. (1999) 'Getting to the Top: Selection and Training for Senior Managers in the Police Service', *Social Policy and Administration*, vol. 33, no. 3, pp. 281–301.

Chassaigne, M. (1906) *La Lieutenance générale de police de Paris*, Paris: A. Rousseau.

Chassaigne, P. (2005) *Ville et Violence: Tensions et conflits dans la Grande-Bretagne victorienne (1840–1914)*, Paris: Presses de l'Université Paris-Sorbonne.

Chisick, H. (1981) *The Limits of Reform in the Enlightenment: Attitudes towards the Education of the Lower Classes in France*, Princeton: Princeton University Press.

Clapson, M. and Emsley, C. (2002) 'Street, Beat and Respectability: The Culture and Self-Image of the Late Victorian and Edwardian Urban Policeman', in Louis A. Knafla (ed.), *Policing and War in Europe*. Criminal Justice History, vol. 16, Westport, CT: Greenwood Press.

Clark, A. (1995) *The Struggle for the Breeches: Gender and the Making of the British Working Class*, Berkeley: University of California Press.

Clegg, C. A. (1997) *The Life and Times of Elijah Muhammad*, New York: St. Martin's Press.

Cockcroft, T. and Beattie, I. (2009) 'Shifting Cultures: Managerialism and the Rise of "Performance"', *Policing: An International Journal of Police Science and Management*, vol. 32, no. 3, pp. 526–40.

Cohen, D. (2010) *La Nature du peuple. Les formes de l'imaginaire social (XVIIIe–XXIe siècles)*, Paris: Champ Vallon.

Cohen, E. (1993) *Talk on the Wilde Side: Towards a Genealogy of a Discourse of Male Sexualities*, London: Routledge.

Cohen, L. (1964) *The New York Graphic: The World's Zaniest Newspaper*, Philadelphia: Chilton Books.

Colley, L. (1993) '"What Is to Be Expected of the People?" Civic Virtue and the Common Man in England, 1700–1760', in G. Schochet (ed.), *Politics, Politeness and Patriotism*, Washington: Folger Institute.

Collier, R. (1995) *Masculinities, Law and the Family*, London: Routledge.

Collier, R. (1998) *Masculinities, Crime and Criminology*, London: Sage.

Collinson, D. and Hearn, J. (1996) *Men as Managers, Managers as Men: Critical Perspectives on Men, Masculinities and Managements*, London: Sage.

Connell, R. W. (1995) *Masculinities*, Berkeley: University of California Press, 1995 (and as *Maschilità. Identità e trasformazioni del maschio occidentale*, Milan: Feltrinelli, 1996).

Connell, R. W. and Wood, J. (2005) 'Globalization and Business Masculinities', *Men and Masculinities*, vol. 7, no. 4, pp. 347–64.

Conti, P. M. (1977) *The Pennsylvania State Police: A History of Service to the Commonwealth, 1905 to the Present*, Harrisburg: Stackpole Books.

Cooper, J. M. (1997) *The Rise of the National Guard: The Evolution of the American Militia, 1865–1920*, Lincoln: University of Nebraska Press.

Cope, S., Leisham, F. and Starie, P. (1997) 'Globalization, New Public Management and the Enabling State: Futures of Police Management', *International Journal of Public Sector Management*, vol. 10, no. 6, pp. 444–60.

Corfe, T. (2004) *Riot: The Hexham Militia Riot, 1761*, Hexham: Hexham Community Partnership.

Cosandey, F. and Descimon, R. (2002) *L'absolutisme en France. Histoire et historiographie*, Paris: Le Seuil.

Covato, C. (1989) 'Educata ad educare: ruolo materno ed itinerari formativi', in S. Soldani (ed.), *L'educazione delle donne. Scuole e modelli di vita femminile nell'Italia dell'Ottocento*, Milan: Franco Angeli.

Cowper, T. (2000) 'The Myth of the "Military Model" of Leadership in Law Enforcement', *Police Quarterly*, no. 1, pp. 451–64.

Coyle, A. (1995) *Women and Organisational Change*, Manchester: Equal Opportunities Commission.

Cox, D. (2010) *A Certain Share of Low Cunning: A History of the Bow Street Runners, 1792–1839*, Cullompton: Willan.

Craig, P. and Cadogan, M. (1986) *The Lady Investigates*, Oxford: Oxford University Press.

Crank, J. P. (1998) *Understanding Police Culture*, Cincinnati: Anderson.

Crehan, K. A. F. (2002) *Gramsci, Culture and Anthropology*, Berkeley: University of California Press.

Critchley, T. A. (1967) *A History of Police in England and Wales*, London: Constable (2nd edn 1978).

Crowther, M. A. (1999) 'Crime, Prosecution and Mercy: English Influence and Scottish Practice in the Early Nineteenth Century' in S. J. Connolly (ed.), *Kingdoms United? Great Britain and Ireland since 1500: Integration and Diversity*, Dublin: Four Courts Press.

Cuordileone, K. A. (2005) *Manhood and American Political Culture in the Cold War*, New York: Routledge.

Curtis, L. P. (2001) *Jack the Ripper and the London Press*, New Haven, CT: Yale University Press, 2001.

Daley, H. (1987) *This Small Cloud: A Personal Memoir*, London: Weidenfeld and Nicolson.

Davies, A. (1998a) 'Street Gangs, Crime and Policing in Glasgow during the 1930s: The Case of the Beehive Boys', *Social History*, vol. 23, no. 3, pp. 251–67.

Davies, A. (1998b) 'Youth Gangs, Masculinity and Violence in Late Victorian Manchester and Salford', *Journal of Social History*, vol. 32, no. 2, pp. 349–69.

Davies, A. (1999) ' "These Viragoes are No Less Cruel than the Lads": Young Women, Gangs and Violence in Late Victorian Manchester and Salford', *British Journal of Criminology*, vol. 39, no. 1, pp. 72–89.

Davies, A. (2000a) 'Sectarian Violence and Police Violence in Glasgow during the 1930s', in R. Bessel and C. Emsley (eds), *Patterns of Provocation*, Oxford: Berghahn Books.

Davies, A. (2000b) 'Youth Gangs, Gender and Violence, 1870–1900', in S. D'Cruze (ed.), *Everyday Violence in Britain, 1850–1950: Gender and Class*, London: Longman.

Davies, A. (2008) *The Gangs of Manchester*, Preston: Milo Books.

Davies, A. (2011) 'Youth Gangs and Late Victorian Society', in Barry Goldson (ed.), *Youth in Crisis? 'Gangs', Territoriality and Violence*, Basingstoke: Routledge.

Davies, A. and Thomas, R. (2004) 'Gendering Resistance in the Public Services', in R. Thomas, A. Mills and J. Helms Mills (eds), *Identity Politics at Work: Resisting Gender, Gendering Resistance*, London: Routledge.

Davis, J. A. (1988) *Conflict and Control: Law and Order in Nineteenth-Century Italy*, London: Macmillan.

Davis, J. S. (1984) 'A Poor Man's System of Justice? The London Police Courts in the Second Half of the Nineteenth Century', *The Historical Journal*, vol. 27, no. 2, pp. 309–35.

D'Cruze, S. (1998) *Crimes of Outrage: Sex, Violence and Victorian Working Women*, London: UCL Press.

Dean, M. (1999) *Governmentality: Power and Rule in Modern Society*, London: Sage.

Dean, R. D. (2001) *Imperial Brotherhood: Gender and the Making of Cold War Foreign Policy*, Amherst: University of Massachusetts Press.

Densten, I. (1998) 'Senior Australian Law Enforcement Leadership under Examination', *Policing: An International Journal of Police Strategies and Management*, vol. 22, no. 1, pp. 45–57.

Denys, C. (2010) 'The Development of Police Forces in Urban Europe in the Eighteenth Century', *Journal of Urban History*, vol. 36, no. 3, pp. 332–44.

Denys, C., Marin, B. and Milliot, V. (eds) (2009) *Réformer la police. Les mémoires policiers en Europe au XVIIIe siècle*, Rennes: Presses universitaires de Rennes.

Dilnot, G. (1928) *The Trial of the Detectives*, New York: Charles Scribner's.

Dobby, J., Anscombe, J. and Tuffin, R. (2004) 'Police Leadership: Expectations and Impact', Home Office Report 20/04. London: Home Office.

Dodsworth, F. (2004) ' "Civic" Police and the Condition of Liberty: The Rationality of Governance in Eighteenth-Century England', *Social History*, vol. 29, no. 2, pp. 199–216.

Dodsworth, F. (2007a) 'Masculinity as Governance: Police, Public Service and the Embodiment of Authority, c. 1700–1800', in M. McCormack (ed.), *Public Men: Masculinity and Politics in Modern Britain*, Basingstoke: Palgrave Macmillan.

Dodsworth, F. (2007b) 'Police and the Prevention of Crime: Commerce, Temptation and the Corruption of the Body Politic, from Fielding to Colquhoun', *British Journal of Criminology*, vol. 47, pp. 439–54.

Dodsworth, F. (2008) 'The Idea of Police in Eighteenth-Century England: Discipline, Reformation, Superintendance, c. 1780–1800', *Journal of the History of Ideas*, vol. 69, no. 4, pp. 583–605.

Donnelly, D. (2005) 'Policing the Scottish Community', in Daniel Donnelly and Kenneth Scott (eds), *Policing Scotland*, Cullompton: Willan.

Douglas, R. M. (1999) *Feminist Freikorps: The British Voluntary Women Police, 1914–1940*, London: Praeger.

Drodge, E. N. and Murphy, S. A. (2002) 'Interrogating Emotions in Police Leadership', *Human Resource Development Review*, vol. 1, no. 4, pp. 420–38.

Dubber, M. D. (2005) *The Police Power: Patriarchy and the Foundations of American Government*, New York: Columbia University Press.

Dubber, M. D. and Valverde, M. (eds) (2008) *Police and the Liberal State*, Stanford, CA: Stanford Law Books, an imprint of Stanford University Press.

Duffin, A. T. (2010) *History in Blue: 160 Years of Women Police, Sheriffs, Detectives, and State Troopers*, Workingham: Kaplan.

Duncan, C. (1981) 'Fallen Fathers: Images of Authority in Pre-Revolutionary French Art', *Art History*, vol. 4, pp. 186–202.

Dunnage, J. (2002) 'Les Carabiniers italiens après 1860. Professionnalisme et auto-représentation', in J.-N. Luc (ed.), *Gendarmerie, état et société au XIXe siècle*, Paris: Publications de la Sorbonne.

Dunstall, G. (2006) 'Local "Demons" in New Zealand Policing, c. 1900–55', in Clive Emsley and Haia Shpayer-Makov (eds), *Police Detectives in History, 1750–1950*, Aldershot: Ashgate.

Durkheim, E. (1982) *The Rules of the Sociological Method*, edited by S. Lukes, translated by W. Halls, New York: Free Press.

Dyonet, N. (2005) 'Le commissaire Delamare et son Traité de la police (1639–1723)', in C. Dolan (ed.), *Entre justice et justiciables. Les auxiliaires de la justice du Moyen Âge au XXe siècle*, Québec: Presses de l'Université Laval.

Ebert, T. L. (1992) 'Detecting the Phallus: Authority, Ideology, and the Production of Patriarchal Agents in Detective Fiction', *Rethinking Marxism*, vol. 5, no. 3, pp. 6–28.

Eisenberg, A. (2009) *A Different Shade of Blue: How Women Changed the Face of Police Work*, Lake Forrest, CA: Behler.

Ellis, M. (2001) *Race, War and Surveillance: African Americans and the United State Government during World War I*, Bloomington: Indiana University Press.

Emsley, C. (1983) *Policing and its Context, 1750–1870*, Basingstoke: Macmillan.

Emsley, C. (1984) 'Arms and the Victorian Policeman', *History Today*, vol. 34, no. 11, pp. 37–42.

Emsley, C. (1985) ' "The Thump of Wood on a Swede Turnip": Police Violence in Nineteenth-Century England', *Criminal Justice History*, vol. 6, pp. 125–49.

Emsley, C. (1991) *The English Police: A Political and Social History*, Hemel Hempstead: Harvester, 1991 (2nd edn, London: Longman, 1996).

Emsley, C. (1992) 'The English Bobby: An Indulgent Tradition', in R. Porter (ed.), *Myths of the English*, Cambridge: Polity Press.

Emsley, C. (1993) ' "Mother, What Did Policemen Do When There Weren't Any Motors?": The Law, the Police and the Regulation of Motor Traffic in England, 1900–1939', *The Historical Journal*, vol. 36, no. 2, pp. 357–81.

Emsley, C. (1996) *Crime and Society in England, 1750–1900*, 2nd edn, London: Longman.

Emsley, C. (1999a) *Gendarmes and the State in Nineteenth-Century Europe*, Oxford: Oxford University Press.

Emsley, C. (1999b) 'A Typology of Nineteenth-Century Police', *Crime, Histoire & Sociétés/Crime, History & Societies*, vol. 3, pp. 29–44.

Emsley, C. (2000) 'The Policeman as a Worker: A Comparative Survey, c. 1800–1940', *International Review of Social History*, vol. 45, no. 1, pp. 89–110.

Emsley, C. (2005a) *The English and Violence since 1750*, London: Hambledon Continuum.

Emsley, C. (2005b) *Hard Men: The English and Violence since 1750*, London: Hambledon Continuum.

Emsley, C. (2006a) *The English Police: A Political and Social History*, London: Longman.

Emsley, C. (2006b) 'From Ex-Con to Expert: The Police Detective in Nineteenth-Century France', in Clive Emsley and Haia Shpayer-Makov (eds), *Police Detectives in History, 1750–1950*, Aldershot: Ashgate.

Emsley, C. (2007) *Crime, Police, & Penal Policy: European Experiences 1750–1940*, Oxford: Oxford University Press.

Emsley, C. (2009) *The Great British Bobby: A History of British Policing from the 18th Century to the Present*, London: Quercus.

Emsley, C. and Clapson, M. (1994) 'Recruiting the English Policeman, c. 1840–1940', *Policing and Society*, vol. 3, pp. 269–86.

Emsley, C. and Weinberger, B. (1991) *Policing Western Europe: Politics, Professionalism and Public Order 1850–1940*, London: Greenwood.

England, P. (1989) 'A Feminist Critique of Rational-Choice Theories: Implications for Sociology', *American Sociologist*, vol. 20, pp. 14–28.

Englander, D. and O'Day, R. (eds) (1995) *Retrieved Riches: Social Investigation in Britain, 1840–1914*, Aldershot: Scolar Press.

Epstein Nord, D. (1987) 'The Social Explorer as Anthropologist: Victorian Travellers among the Urban Poor', in W. Sharp and L. Wallock (eds), *Visions of the Modern City: Essays in History, Art, and Literature*, Baltimore: Johns Hopkins University Press.

Ewen, S. (2006) 'Managing Police Constables and Firefighters: Uniformed Public Services in English Cities, c. 1870–1930', *International Review of Social History*, vol. 51, pp. 41–57.

Farge, A. and Foucault, M. (1982) *Le désordre des familles. Lettres de cachet des Archives de Bastille*, Paris: Gallimard Julliard.

Farmer, L. (1997) *Criminal Law, Tradition and Legal Order: Crime and the Genius of Scots Law, 1747 to the Present*, Cambridge: Cambridge University Press.

Fawcett Society (2009) *Engendering Justice: From Policy to Practice*, London: Fawcett Society.

Ferguson, K. (1984) *The Feminist Case against Bureaucracy*, Philadelphia: Temple University Press.

Ferrell, J. and Websdale, N. (1999) *Making Trouble: Cultural Constructions of Crime, Deviance, and Control*, New York: Aldine de Gruyter.

Fielding, N. (1988) *Joining Forces: Police Training, Socialisation and Occupational Competence*, London: Routledge.

Fielding, N. (1994) 'Cop Canteen Culture', in T. Newburn and E. Stanko (eds), *Just Boys Doing the Business: Men, Masculinities and Crime*, London: Routledge.

Fielding, N. and Fielding, J. (1992) 'A Comparative Minority: Female Recruits to a British Constabulary Force', *Policing and Society*, vol. 2, pp. 205–18.

Finnane, M. (ed) (1987) *Policing in Australia: Historical Perspectives*, Kensington: New South Wales University Press.

Finnane, M. (1990) 'Governing the Police', in F. B. Smith (ed.), *Ireland, England and Australia: Essays in Honour of Oliver MacDonagh*, Canberra: Australian National University Press.

Finnane, M. (1994) *Police and Government: Histories of Policing in Australia*, Oxford: Oxford University Press.

Finnane, M. (2002) *When Police Unionise: The Politics of Law and Order in Australia*, Sydney: Sydney Institute of Criminology Press.

Finnane, M. (2005) 'A "New Police" in Australia', in Tim Newman (ed.), *Policing: Key Readings*, Cullompton: Willan.

Fiorentino, F. (1978) *Ordine pubblico nell'eta giolittiana*. Rome: Carecas.

Fitzgerald, M. and Hough, M. (2002) 'Policing for London', London: Home Office.

Fleming, J. and Lafferty, G. (2002) 'Equality Confounded? New Managerialism, Organizational Restructuring and Women in Australian Police Services', conference paper delivered at Women and Policing Globally Conference, Canberra, Australia, 20–23 October 2002.

Flynn, E. E. (1982) 'Women as Criminal Justice Professionals: A Challenge to Change Tradition', in N. H. Rafter and E. Stanko (eds), *Judge, Lawyer, Victim, Thief: Women, Gender Roles and Criminal Justice*, Boston: Northeastern University Press.

Forth, C. E. (2008) *Masculinity in the Modern West: Gender, Civilization and the Body*, Basingstoke: Palgrave Macmillan.

Foster, J. (1989) 'Two Stations: An Ethnographic Analysis of Policing in the Inner City', in D. Downes (ed.), *Crime and the City*, London: Macmillan.

Foster, J. (2003) 'Police Cultures', in Tim Newburn (ed.), *Handbook of Policing*, Cullompton: Willan.

Foucault, M. (1977) *Discipline and Punish: The Birth of the Prison*, translated by A. Sheridan, London: Penguin.

Foucault, M. (1996) 'Governmentality', translated by Rosi Braidotti and revised by Colin Gordon, in Graham Burchell, Colin Gordon and Peter Miller (eds), *The Foucault Effect: Studies in Governmentality*, Chicago: Chicago University Press.

Fox, P. (1988) 'The State Library of Victoria: Science and Civilisation', *Transition*, vol. 26, pp. 14–26.

Foyster, E. (1999) *Manhood in Early Modern England: Honour, Sex, and Marriage*, New York: Longman.

Foyster, E. (2005) *Marital Violence: An English Family History, 1660–1857*, Cambridge: Cambridge University Press.

Francia, E. (2003) 'Polizia e opinione pubblica in Toscana nel Quarantotto', in P. Macry (ed.), *Quando crolla lo Stato. Studi sull'Italia preunitaria*, Naples: Liguori.

Fried, R. M. (1990) *Nightmare in Red: The McCarthy Era in Perspective*, New York: Oxford University Press.

Fuchs, R. G. (2009) 'Magistrates and Mothers, Paternity and Property in Nineteenth-Century French Courts', *Crime, Histoire & Sociétés/Crime, History & Societies*, vol. 13, no. 2, pp. 13–26.

Furst, L. R. (1995) *All is True: The Claims and Strategies of Realist Fiction*, London: Duke University Press.

Gadd, D. (2003) 'Reading Between the Lines: Subjectivity and Men's Violence', *Men and Masculinities*, vol. 5, no. 4, pp. 429–49.

Garrioch, D. (1986) *Neighbourhood and Community*, Cambridge: Cambridge University Press.

Garrioch, D. (1992) 'The Police of Paris as Enlightened Social Reformers', *Eighteenth-Century Life*, vol. 16, pp. 43–59.

Garrioch, D. (1994) 'The People of Paris and their Police in the Eighteenth Century: Reflections on the Introduction of a "Modern" Police Force', *European History Quarterly*, vol. 24, pp. 511–35.

Garrow, D. (1981) *The FBI and Martin Luther King, Jr. from 'Solo' to Memphis*, New York: W. W. Norton.

Gaston, K. C. and Alexander, J. A. (1997) 'Women in the Police: Factors Influencing Managerial Advancement', *Women in Management Review*, vol. 12, no. 2, pp. 47–55.

Gates, P. (2004a) 'Always a Partner in Crime: Black Masculinity in the Hollywood Detective Film', *Journal of Popular Film and Television*, vol. 32, no. 1, pp. 20–9.

Gates, P. (2004b) 'Detectives', in Michael S. Kimmel and Amy Aronson (eds), *Men and Masculinities: A Social, Cultural and Historical Encyclopaedia*, vol. 1, California: ABC-CLIO.

Gates, P. (2006) *Detecting Men: Masculinity and the Hollywood Detective Film*, New York: State University of New York Press.

Gatrell, V. A. C. (1980) 'The Decline of Theft and Violence in Victorian and Edwardian England', in V. A. C. Gatrell, B. Lenman and G. Parker (eds), *Crime and the Law: The Social History of Crime in Western Europe since 1500,* London: Europa.

Gatrell, V. A. C. (1990) Crime, Authority and the Policeman-State', in F. M. L. Thompson (ed.), *The Cambridge Social History*, vol. 3, Cambridge: Cambridge University Press.

Gazier, A. (1878) 'La police de Paris en 1770. Mémoire inédit composé par ordre de G. de Sartine sur la demande de Marie-Thérèse', *Mémoires de la Société de l'Histoire de Paris et de l'Ile-de-France*, vol. 5, pp. 1–131.

Gelfand, T. (1980) *Professionalizing Modern Medicine: Paris Surgeons and Medical Science and Institutions in the Eighteenth Century*, Westport, CT: Greenwood Press.

Gerth, H. and Wright Mills, C. (eds) (1948) *From Max Weber: Essays in Sociology*, London: Routledge and Kegan Paul.

Ghoul, F. E. (1995) *La police parisienne dans la seconde moitié du XVIIIe siècle (1760–1785)*, 2 vols, Tunis: Université de Tunis.

Gillis, J. (1985) *For Better, for Worse: British Marriages, 1600 to the Present*, Oxford: Oxford University Press.

Glover, E. H. (1934) *The English Police*, London: Police Chronicle.

Godfrey, B., Farrall, S. and Karstedt, S. (2005) 'Explaining Gendered Sentencing Patterns for Violent Men and Women in the Late Victorian and Edwardian Period', *British Journal of Criminology*, vol. 45, no. 5, pp. 696–720.

Gold, M. E. (1999) *Top Cops: Profiles of Women in Command*, Chicago: Brittany.

Goodman, D. (1990) 'Fear of Circuses: Founding the National Museum of Victoria', *Continuum*, vol. 3, no. 1, pp. 18–34.

Goodman, D. (1994) *Goldseeking: Victoria and California in the 1850s*, Sydney: Allen and Unwin.

Gramsci, A. (1992) *Prison Notebooks*, vol. 1, with Joseph A. Buttigieg, New York: Columbia University Press.

Grant, J. (1988) 'Women as Managers: What They Can Offer to Organizations', *Organizational Dynamics*, vol. 16, no. 3, pp. 56–63.

Gray, D. D. (2007a) 'The Regulation of Violence in the Metropolis: The Prosecution of Assault in the Summary Courts, c. 1780–1820', *London Journal*, vol. 32, no. 1, pp. 75–88.

Gray, D. D. (2007b) 'Settling Their Differences: The Nature of Assault and its Prosecution in the City of London in the Late Eighteenth and Early Nineteenth Centuries', in Katherine Watson (ed.), *Assaulting the Past: Violence and Civilization in Historical Context*, Cambridge: Cambridge Scholars.

Gray, D. D. (2008) 'The People's Courts? Summary Justice and Social Relations in the City of London, c. 1760–1800', *Family and Community History*, vol. 11, no. 1, pp. 7–15.

Gray, D. D. (2009) *Crime, Prosecution and Social Relations: The Summary Courts of the City of London in the Late Eighteenth Century*, Basingstoke: Palgrave.

Guarnieri, C. (1995) 'L'ordine pubblico e la giustizia penale', in R. Romanelli (ed.), *Storia dello Stato italiano dall'Unità a oggi*, Rome: Donzelli.

Guarnieri, P. (2009) 'Men Committing Female Crime: Infanticide, Family and Honour in Italy, 1890–1981', *Crime, Histoire & Sociétés/Crime, History & Societies*, vol. 13, no. 3, pp. 41–54.

Hadden, S. E. (2001) *Slave Patrols: Law and Violence in Virginia and the Carolinas*, Cambridge, MA: Harvard University Press.

Haldane, R. (1986) *The People's Force: A History of the Victoria Police*, Carlton: Melbourne University Press.

Haley, B. (1978) *The Healthy Body and Victorian Culture*, Cambridge, MA: Harvard University Press.

Halford, S., Savage, M. and Witz, A. (1997) *Gender, Careers and Organisations*, Basingstoke: Macmillan.

Hall, D. (ed.) (1994) *Muscular Christianity*, Cambridge: Cambridge University Press.

Hall, J. D. (1983) ' "The Mind that Burns in Each Body": Women, Rape, and Racial Violence', in A. Snitow, C. Stansell and S. Thompson (eds) *Powers of Desire: The Politics of Sexuality*, New York: Monthly Review Press.

Handley, J. E. (1945) *The Irish in Modern Scotland, 1798–1845*, Cork: Cork University Press.

Hanmer, J., Radford, J. and Stanko, E. A. (1989) *Women, Policing, and Male Violence: International Perspectives*, London: Routledge.

Harring, S. L. (1983) *Policing a Class Society: The Experience of American Cities, 1865–1915*, New York: Rutgers University Press.

Harris, A. (2004) *Policing the City: Crime and Legal Authority in London, 1780–1840*, Columbus: Ohio State University Press.

Harsin, J. (1985) *Policing Prostitution in Nineteenth-Century Paris*, Princeton, NJ: Princeton University Press.

Hay, D. (1989) 'Using the Criminal Law, 1750–1850: Policing, Private Prosecution, and the State', in D. Hay and F. Snyder (eds), *Policing and Prosecution in Britain, 1750–1850*, Oxford: Clarendon Press.

Hayter, T. (1978) *The Army and the Crowd in Mid-Georgian England*, Basingstoke: Macmillan.

Hearn, J. and Collinson, D. L. (1994) 'Theorizing Unities and Differences between Men and between Masculinities', in Harry Brod and Michael Kaufman (eds), *Theorizing Masculinities*, Thousand Oaks, CA: Sage.

Hegelson, S. (1990) *The Female Advantage*, New York: Doubleday.

Heidensohn, F. (1992) *Women in Control: The Role of Women in Law Enforcement*, Oxford: Clarendon Press.

Heidensohn, F. (1994) ' "We Can Handle It Out Here": Women Officers in Britain and the USA and the Policing of Public Order', *Policing and Society*, 1994, vol. 4, no. 4, pp. 293–303.

Heidensohn, F. (2000) *Sexual Politics and Social Control*, Buckingham: Open University Press.

Heidensohn, F. (2003) 'Gender and Policing', in Tim Newburn (ed.), *Handbook of Policing*, Cullompton: Willan.

Henry, H. M. (1968) *Police Control of the Slave in South Carolina*, New York: Negro University Press.

Hibbert, C. (1958) *King Mob: The Story of George Gordon and the Riots of 1780*, London: Longman.

Higginbotham Jr, A. L. (1978) *In the Matter of Color: Race & the American Legal Process: The Colonial Period*, New York; Oxford University Press.

Higham, J. (1970) 'The Reorientation of American Culture in the 1890s', in J. Higham (ed.), *Writing American History*, Bloomington: Indiana University Press.

Hill, R. A. (Winter 1984) ' "The Foremost Radical Among His Race:" Marcus Garvey and the Black Scare, 1918–1921', *Prologue*, vol. 16, no. 4, 216–31.

Hill Collins, P. (2004) *Black Sexual Politics: African Americans, Gender, and the New Racism*, New York: Routledge.

Hitchcock, T. and Cohen, M. (eds) (1999) *English Masculinities, 1660–1800*, London: Longman.

Hodges, G. R. (1999) *Root & Branch: African Americans in New York & East Jersey, 1613–1863*, Chapel Hill: University of North Carolina Press.

Holdaway, S. (1983) *Inside the British Police*, Oxford: Basil Blackwell.

Horowitz, H. (2002) *Rereading Sex: Battles over Sexual Knowledge and Suppression in Nineteenth-Century America*, New York: Knopf.

Hough, M. (1985) 'Organization and Resource Management in the Uniformed Police', in K. Heal, R. Tarling and J. Burrows (eds), *Policing Today*, London: HMSO.

Hughes, A. (2010) 'The "Non-Criminal Class": Wifebeating in Scotland, c.1800–1949', *Crime, Histoire & Sociétés/Crime, History & Societies*, vol. 14, no. 2, pp. 31–54.

Hughes, S. C. (1994) *Crime, Disorder and the Risorgimento: The Politics of Policing in Bologna*, Cambridge: Cambridge University Press.

Hughes, S. C. (2002) 'L'immagine della polizia', in L. Antonielli (ed.), *La polizia in Italia nell'età moderna*, Soveria Mannelli: Rubbettino.

Hughes, S. C. (2006) 'Immaginando una storia della polizia italiana in età liberale', in L. Antonielli (ed.), *La polizia in Italia e in Europa: punto sugli studi e prospettive di ricerca*, Soveria Mannelli: Rubbettino.

Hughes, S. C. (2007) *Politics of the Sword: Dueling, Honor, and Masculinity in Modern Italy*, Columbus: Ohio State University Press.

Hunt, J. (1984) 'The Development of Rapport through the Negotiation of Gender in Field Work among Police', *Human Organization*, vol. 43, no. 4, pp. 283–96.

Hunt, L. (1980) 'Engraving the Republic: Prints and Propaganda in the French Revolution', *History Today*, vol. 30, pp. 11–17.

Hunt, L. (1992) *The Family Romance of the French Revolution*, Berkeley: University of California Press.

Jackson, L. A. (2003a) 'The Unusual Case of "Mrs Sherlock": Memoir, Identity and the "Real" Woman Private Detective in Twentieth-Century Britain', *Gender & History*, vol. 15, no. 1, pp. 108–34.

Jackson, L. A. (2003b) 'Care or Control? The Metropolitan Police and Child Welfare, 1919–1969', *The Historical Journal*, vol. 46, no. 3, pp. 623–48.

Jackson, L. A. (2006) *Women Police: Gender, Welfare and Surveillance in the Twentieth Century*, Manchester: Manchester University Press.

Jefferson, T. (1990) *The Case against Paramilitary Policing*, Milton Keynes: Open University Press.

Jefferson, T. (2002) 'Subordinating Hegemonic Masculinity', *Theoretical Criminology*, vol. 6, no. 1, pp. 63–88.

Jenkins, C. (2000) 'Gender Just', *Police Review*, vol. 108, available at http://www.janes.com/.

Johnson, D. K. (2004) *Lavender Scare: The Cold War Persecution of Gays and Lesbians in the Federal Government*, Chicago: University of Chicago Press.

Johnson, M. S. (2003) *Street Justice: A History of Police Violence in New York City*, Boston: Beacon Press.

Jones, T. and Newburn, T. (1997) *Policing after the Act: Police Governance after the Police and Magistrates' Courts Act 1994*, London: Policy Studies Institute.

Kaiser, C. (1982) 'Les cours souveraines au XVIe siècle: morale et Contre-Réforme', *Annales: ESC*, vol. 37, pp. 15–31.

Kaplan, S. L. (1981) 'Note sur les *commissaires* de police de Paris au XVIIIe siècle', *Revue d'histoire moderne et contemporaine*, vol. 28, pp. 669–86.

Kaplan, S. L. (1996) *The Bakers of Paris and the Bread Question, 1700–1775*, Durham, NC: Duke University Press.

Kaplan, S. L. and Milliot, V. (2009) 'La police de Paris, une "révolution permanente"? Du *commissaire* Lemaire au lieutenant de police Lenoir, les tribulations du *Mémoire sur l'administration de la police* (1770–1792)', in C. Denys, B. Marin and V. Milliot (eds), *Réformer la police. Les mémoires policiers en Europe au XVIIIe siècle*, Rennes: Presses universitaires de Rennes.

Kealey, G. S. (1999) 'The Empire Strikes Back: The Nineteenth-Century Origins of the Canadian Secret Service', *Journal of the Canadian Historical Association*, vol. 10, pp. 3–18.

Kelly, G. A. (1979) 'The Political Thought of Lamoignon de Malesherbes', *Political Theory*, vol. 7, pp. 485–508.

Kerfoot, D. and Knights, D. (1993) 'Management, Masculinity and Manipulation: From Paternalism to Corporate Strategy in Financial Services in Britain', *Journal of Management Studies*, vol. 30, no. 4, pp. 659–77.

Kestner, J. A. (1997) *Sherlock's Men*, Aldershot: Ashgate.

Kestner, J. A. (2003) *Sherlock's Sisters: The British Female Detective, 1864–1913*, Aldershot: Ashgate.

Kilday, A.-M. (2007) *Women and Violent Crime in Enlightenment Scotland*, Woodbridge: Boydell Press.

Kilday, A.-M. (2010) 'Desperate Measures or Cruel Intensions: Infanticide in Britain', in Anne-Marie Kilday and David Nash (eds), *Histories of Crime: Britain 1600–2000*, Basingstoke: Palgrave Macmillan.

King, P. (1998) 'The Rise of Juvenile Delinquency in England 1780–1840: Changing Patterns of Perception and Prosecution', *Past and Present*, no. 160, pp. 116–66.

King, P. (2004) 'The Summary Courts and Social Relations in Eighteenth-Century England', *Past and Present*, vol. 183, no. 1, pp. 125–72.

King, P. (2007) 'Newspaper Reporting and Attitudes to Crime and Justice in Late-Eighteenth and Early-Nineteenth-Century London', *Continuity and Change*, vol. 1, pp. 73–112.

Klein, J. (2007) 'Traffic, Telephones and Police Boxes: The Deterioration of Beat Policing in Birmingham, Liverpool and Manchester between the World Wars', in G. Blaney (ed.), *Policing Interwar Europe: Continuity, Change and Crisis, 1918–1940*, London: Palgrave Macmillan.

Klein, J. (2010) *Invisible Men: The Secret Lives of Police Constables in Liverpool, Manchester and Birmingham, 1900–1939*, Liverpool: Liverpool University Press.

Klein, M. M. (2001) *The Empire State*, Ithaca, NY: Cornell University Press.

Knight, S. (1980) *Form and Ideology in Crime Fiction*, Bloomington: Indiana University Press.

Kornweibel Jr, T. (1998) *Seeing Red: Federal Campaigns against Black Militancy, 1919–1925*, Bloomington: Indiana University Press.

Kungl, C. T. (2006) *Creating the Fictional Female Detective: The Sleuth Heroines of British Women Writers, 1890–1940*, Jefferson: McFarland.

La Cecla, F. (2000) *Modi bruschi. Antropologia del maschio*, Milan: Bruno Mondadori.

Lane, R. (1967) *Policing the City: Boston, 1822–1885*, Cambridge, MA: Harvard University Press.

Langford, P. (1991) *Public Life and the Propertied Englishman 1689–1798*, Oxford: Oxford University Press.

Lawrence, P. (2000) ' "Images of Poverty and Crime": Police Memoirs in England and France at the End of the Nineteenth Century', *Crime, Histoire & Sociétés/Crime, History & Society*, vol. 4, pp. 63–82.

Lawrence, P. (2003) ' "Scoundrels and Scallywags and Some Honest Men . . .": Memoirs and the Self-Image of French and English Policemen, c. 1870–1939', in B. Godfrey, C. Emsley and G. Dunstall (eds), *Comparative Histories of Crime*, Cullompton: Willan.

Lears, T. J. J. (1985) 'The Concept of Cultural Hegemony: Problems and Possibilities', *The American Historical Review*, vol. 90, no. 3, pp. 567–93.

Lee, C. (2003) *Murder and the Reasonable Man: Passion and Fear in the Criminal Courtroom*, New York: New York University Press.

Leishman, F. and Mason, P. (2003) *Policing and the Media: Facts, Fictions and Factions*, Cullompton: Willan.

Lemke, T. (2002) 'Foucault, Governmentality, and Critique', *Rethinking Marxism*, vol. 14, no. 3, pp. 49–64.

Lemmings, D. and Walker, C. (eds) (2009) *Moral Panics, the Media and the Law in Early Modern England*, Basingstoke: Palgrave Macmillan.

Levine, P. (1994) ' "Walking the Streets in a Way No Decent Woman Should": Women Police in World War I', *Journal of Modern History*, vol. 66, no. 1, pp. 34–78.

Lock, J. (1979) *The British Policewoman: Her Story*, London: Hale.

Long, M. (2003) 'Leadership and Performance Management', in Tim Newburn (ed.), *Handbook of Policing*, Cullompton: Willan.

Lincoln, C. E. (1961) *The Black Muslims in America*, Boston: Beacon Press.

de Lint, W. (1999) 'Nineteenth-Century Disciplinary Reform and the Prohibition against Talking Policemen', *Policing and Society*, vol. 9, no. 1, pp. 33–59.

de Lint, W. (2000) 'Autonomy, Regulation and the Police Beat', *Social and Legal Studies*, vol. 9, no. 1, pp. 55–83.

Loden, M. (1985) *Feminine Leadership or How to Succeed in Business without Being One of the Boys*, New York: Times Books.

Long, M. (2003) 'Leadership and Performance Management', in Tim Newburn (ed.), *Handbook of Policing*, Cullompton: Willan.

Lopez, L. (2008) 'Commissaires de police et officiers de gendarmerie à la fin du XIXe siècle: pratique professionelles et répresentations', in D. Kalifa and P. Karila-Cohen (eds.), *Le commissaire de police au XIXe siècle*, Paris: Publications de la Sorbonne.

McConville, C. (1983) '1888 – A Policeman's Lot', *Australia 1888*, no. 11, pp. 78–87.

McCormack, M. (2005) *The Independent Man: Citizenship and Gender Politics in Georgian England*, Manchester: Manchester University Press.

McCormack, M. (2006) 'Citizenship, Nationhood and Masculinity in the Affair of the Hanoverian Soldier, 1756', *The Historical Journal*, vol. 49, no. 4, pp. 971–93.

McCormack, M. (2007a) 'The New Militia: War, Politics and Gender in 1750s Britain', *Gender and History*, vol. 19, no. 3, pp. 483–500.

McCormack, M. (2007b) 'Men, "the Public" and Political History', in M. McCormack (ed.), *Public Men: Masculinity and Politics in Modern Britain*, Basingstoke: Palgrave Macmillan.

McCormack, M. (ed.) (2007c) *Public Men: Masculinity and Politics in Modern Britain*, Basingstoke: Palgrave Macmillan.

McCormick, R. L. (1981) *From Realignment to Reform: Political Change in New York State, 1893–1910*, Ithaca, NY: Cornell University Press.

McGivena, L. (1969) *The News: The First Fifty Years of New York's Picture Newspaper*, New York: News Syndicate.

MacKenzie, J. M. (1987) 'The Imperial Pioneer and Hunter and the British Masculine Stereotype in Late Victorian and Edwardian Times', in J. A. Mangan and J. Walvin (eds), *Manliness and Morality*, Manchester: Manchester University Press.

McLaren, A. (1993) *A Prescription for Murder*, Chicago: Chicago University Press.

McLaren, A. (1997) *The Trials of Masculinities: Policing Sexual Boundaries, 1870–1930*, Chicago: University of Chicago Press.

McLaren, A. (1999) *Gentiluomini e canaglie. L'identità maschile tra Ottocento e Novecento*, Rome: Carocci, 1999.

McLaughlin, E. and Murji, K. (1997) 'The Future Lasts a Long Time: Public Policework and the Managerialist Paradox', in P. Francis, P. Davies and V. Jupp (eds), *Policing Futures: The Police, Law Enforcement and the Twenty-First Century*, London: Macmillan.

McLaughlin, E., Muncie, J. and Hughes, G. (2001) 'The Permanent Revolution: New Labour, New Public Management and the Modernization of Criminal Justice', *Criminology and Criminal Justice*, vol. 1, pp. 301–18.

Maddock, S. and Parkin, D. (1993) 'Gender Cultures: Women's Choices and Strategies at Work', *Women in Management Review*, vol. 8, no. 2, pp. 3–9.

Maguire, M., Morgan, R. and Reiner, R. (2007) *Media Made Criminality: The Representation of Crime in the Mass Media*, Oxford: Oxford University Press.

Mahood, L. (1994) 'The "Vicious" Girl and the "Street-Corner" Boy: Sexuality and the Gendered Delinquent in the Scottish Child-Saving Movement, 1850–1940', *Journal of the History of Sexuality*, vol. 4, pp. 549–78.

Malin, B. J. (2010) 'Viral Manhood: Niche Marketing, Hard-Boiled Detectives and the Economics of Masculinity', *Media Culture Society*, vol. 32, pp. 373–90.

Mangan, J. A. and Walvin, J. (eds) (1987) *Manliness and Morality*, Manchester: Manchester University Press.

Mangio, C. (1988) *La polizia toscana. Organizzazione e criteri d'intervento (1765–1808)*, Milan: Giuffrè.

Margairaz, D. (2005) 'L'invention du "service public": entre "changement matériel" et "contrainte de nommer"', *Revue d'histoire moderne et contemporaine*, vol. 52, no. 3, pp. 10–32.

Margolies, E. (1982) *Which Way Did He Go? The Private Eye in Dashiell Hammett, Raymond Chandler, Chester Himes, and Ross Macdonald*, New York: Holmes and Meier.

Markoff, J. (1989) 'Images du roi au début de la Révolution', in M. Vovelle (ed.), *L'image de la Révolution française*, Paris: Pergamon.

Marks, M. and Fleming, J. (2004) ' "As Unremarkable as the Air they Breathe?" Reforming Police Management in South Africa', *Current Sociology*, vol. 52, no. 5, pp. 784–808.

Martin, P. Y. (1993) 'Feminist Practice in Organisations: Implications for Management', in E. A. Fagenson (ed.), *Women in Management: Trends, Issues and Challenges in Managerial Diversity*, London: Sage.

Martin, S. E. (1980) *Breaking and Entering*, Berkley: University of California Press.

Martucci, R. (1980) *Emergenza e tutela dell'ordine pubblico nell'Italia liberale*, Bologna: Il Mulino.

Merrick, J. (1991a) 'Patriarchalism and Constitutionalism in Eighteenth-Century Parlementary Discourse', *Studies in Eighteenth Century Culture*, vol. 20, pp. 317–30.

Merrick, J. (1991b) 'Politics on Pedestals: Royal Monuments in Eighteenth-Century France', *French History*, vol. 5, pp. 234–64.

Merrick, J. (1993) 'Fathers and Kings: Patriarchalism and Absolutism in Eighteenth-Century French Politics', *Studies on Voltaire and the Eighteenth Century*, vol. 308, pp. 234–64.

Merrick, J. (1997) 'Sodomitical Inclinations in Early Eighteenth-Century Paris', *Eighteenth-Century Studies*, vol. 30, pp. 289–95.

Messerschmidt, J. W. (1993) *Masculinities and Crime: Critique and Reconceptualization of Theory*, Lanham, MD: Rowman & Littlefield.

Messerschmidt, J. W. (1997) *Crime as Structured Action: Gender, Race, Class and Crime in the Making*, Thousand Oaks, CA: Sage.

Messerschmidt, J. W. (2005) 'Masculinities and Crime', in C. Renzetti, L. Goodstein and S. Miller (eds), *Masculinities, Crime and Criminal Justice*, Los Angeles: Roxbury.

Millar, K. (1965) 'The Writer as Detective Hero', *Show*, January 1965, p. 35.

Miller, J. (2003) 'Police Corruption in England and Wales: An Assessment of Current Evidence', Home Office Report 11/03, London: Home Office.

Miller, S. L., Forest, K. B. and Jurik, N. C. (2003) 'Diversity in Blue: Lesbian and Gay Police Officers in a Masculine Occupation', *Men and Masculinities*, vol. 5, no. 4, pp. 355–85.

Miller, W. (1977) *Cops and Bobbies: Police Authority in London and New York, 1830–1870*, Chicago: Chicago University Press (2nd edn, Columbus: Ohio State University Press, 1999).

Milliot, V. (2003) 'Jean-Charles-Pierre Lenoir (1732–1807), lieutenant-général de police de Paris (1774–1785): ses "mémoires" et une idée de la police des Lumières', *Mélanges de l'École française de Rome, Italie et Méditerranée*, vol. 115, pp. 777–806.

Milliot, V. (2005a) 'Le métier de *commissaire*: bon juge et "mauvais" policier? (Paris, XVIIIe siècle)', in C. Dolan (ed.), *Entre justice et justiciables. Les auxiliaires de la justice du Moyen Âge au XXe siècle*, Québec: Presses de l'Université Laval.

Milliot, V. (2005b) 'Qu'est-ce qu'une police éclairée? La police "amélioratrice" selon Jean-Charles Pierre Lenoir, lieutenant-général à Paris (1775–1785)', *Dix-huitième siècle*, vol. 37, pp. 117–30.

Milliot, V. (2006) 'Écrire pour policer: les "mémoires" policiers, 1750–1850', in V. Milliot (ed.), *Les Mémoires policiers, 1750–1850. Écritures et pratiques policières du Siècle des Lumières au Second Empire*, Rennes: Presses universitaires de Rennes.

Mitchell, B. R. (1978) *European Historical Statistics 1750–1970*, London: Macmillan.

Mitchell, M. J. (ed.) (2009) *New Perspectives on the Irish in Scotland*, East Linton: Tuckwell Press.

Moi, T. (2001) *What Is a Woman? And Other Essays*, Oxford: Oxford University Press.

Monkkonen, E. H. (1981) *Police in Urban America, 1860–1920*, Cambridge: Cambridge University Press.

Morgan, R. and Newburn, T. (1997) *The Future of Policing*, Oxford: Clarendon Press.

Mori, M. T. (2004) 'Maschile, femminile: l'identità di genere nei salotti di conversazione', in M. L. Betri and E. Brambilla (eds), *Salotti e ruolo femminile in Italia tra fine Seicento e primo Novecento*, Venice: Marsilio.

Mori, S. (2004) 'La polizia fra opinione e amministrazione nel Regno Lombardo-Veneto', *Società e storia*, vol. 105, pp. 99–141.

Morris, R. M. (2001) 'Lies, Damned Lies and Criminal Statistics: Reinterpreting the Criminal Statistics in England and Wales', *Crime, Histoire & Sociétés/Crime, History & Societies*, vol. 5, no. 1, pp. 111–27.

Mosse, G. L. (1996) *The Image of Man: The Creation of Modern Masculinity*, Oxford: Oxford University Press, 1996 [Italian version: *L'immagine dell'uomo. Lo stereotipo maschile nell'epoca moderna*, Torino: Einaudi, 1997].

Mott, F. (1962) *American Journalism, a History: 1690–1960*, New York: Macmillan.

Moylan, J. (1929) *Scotland Yard and the Metropolitan Police*, London: Putnam.

Muhammad, K. G. (2010) *The Condemnation of Blackness: Race, Crime, and the Making of Modern Urban America*, Cambridge: Harvard University Press.

Mumford, K. (1992) ' "Lost Manhood" Found: Male Sexual Impotence and Victorian Culture in the United States', *Journal of the History of Sexuality*, vol. 3, no. 1, pp. 33–57.

Murphy, P. V. (1976) 'The Development of Urban Police', *Current History*, vol. 70, pp. 245–8.

Myers, M. A. (1998) *Race, Labour, and Punishment in the New South*, Columbus: Ohio State University Press.

Napoli, P. (2003) *Naissance de la police moderne*, Paris: La Découverte.

Neal, D. (2002) 'Suits Make the Man: Masculinity in Two English Law Courts, c. 1500', *Canadian Journal of History/Annales canadiennes d'histoire*, vol. XXXVII, pp. 1–22.

Newburn, T. and Stanko, E. (eds) (1994) *Just Boys Doing the Business: Men, Masculinities and Crime*, London: Routledge.

Neyroud, P. and Beckley, A. (2001) *Policing, Ethics and Human Rights*, Cullompton: Willan.

Nord, D. E. (1987) 'The Social Explorer as Anthropologist: Victorian Travellers among the Urban Poor', in W. Sharp and L. Wallock (eds), *Visions of the Modern City: Essays in History, Art, and Literature*, Baltimore: Johns Hopkins University Press.

North, J. S. (ed.) (1989) *The Waterloo Directory of Scottish Newspapers and Periodicals, 1800–1900*, 2 vols, Waterloo, ON: North Waterloo Academic Press.

Novak, W. J. (1996) *The People's Welfare: Law and Regulation in Nineteenth Century America*, Chapel Hill: University of North Carolina Press.

Oates, J. (2006) 'Responses in the North of England to the Jacobite Rebellion of 1715', *Northern History*, vol. 43, no. 1, pp. 77–95.

O'Brien, F. M. (1928) *The Story of the Sun*, New York: Appleton.

Oliva, G. (1992) *Storia dei Carabinieri. Immagini e autorappresentazione dell'Arma*, Milan: Leonardo.

O'Reilly, K. (1989) *"Racial Matters" the FBI's Secret File on Black America, 1960–1972*, New York: Free Press.

Pagon, M. (2003) 'The Need for a Paradigm Shift', in R. Adlam and P. Villiers (eds), *Leadership in the Twenty-First Century: Philosophy, Doctrine and Developments*, Winchester: Waterside Press.

Painter, N. I. (2010) *The History of White People*, New York: W. W. Norton.

Paley, R. (1989a) ' "An Imperfect, Inadequate and Wretched System"? Policing London before Peel', *Criminal Justice History*, vol. 10, pp. 95–130.

Paley, R. (1989b) 'Thief-Takers in London in the Age of the McDaniel Gang, c. 1745–54', in Douglas Hay and Francis Snyder (eds), *Policing and Prosecution in Britain, 1750–1850*, Oxford: Oxford University Press.

Palk, D. (2006) *Gender, Crime and Judicial Discretion, 1780–1830*, Woodbridge: Boydell Press.

Palmer, S. (1988) *Police and Protest in England and Ireland 1780–1850*, Cambridge: Cambridge University Press.

Panek, L. (1990) *Probable Cause: Crime Fiction in America*, Bowling Green, OH: Bowling Green State University Press.

Panzeralla, R. (2003) 'Leadership Myths and Realities', in R. Adlam and P. Villiers (eds), *Leadership in the Twenty-First Century: Philosophy, Doctrine and Developments*, Winchester: Waterside Press.

Park, R. J. (2007) 'Muscles, Symmetry and Action: "Do You Measure Up?" Defining Masculinity in Britain and America from the 1860s to the Early 1900s', *International Journal of the History of Sport*, vol. 26, pp. 365–95.

Pateman, C. (1989) *The Disorder of Women: Democracy, Feminism and Political Theory*, Cambridge: Cambridge University Press.

Patriarca, S. (2010) *Italian Vices: Nation and Character from the Risorgimento to the Republic*, Cambridge: Cambridge University Press.

Petrow, S. (1994) *Policing Morals: The Metropolitan Police and the Home Office 1870–1914*, Oxford: Clarendon Press.

Petrow, S. (2005) 'The English Model? Policing in Late Nineteenth Century Tasmania', in B. S. Godfrey and G. Dunstall (eds), *Crime and Empire 1840–1940: Criminal Justice in Local and Global Context*, Cullompton: Willan.

Pettigrew, J. (2007) *Brutes in Suits: Male Sensibility in America, 1890–1920*, Baltimore: Johns Hopkins University Press.

Peveri, P. (2006) 'Les *Principes généraux* du major de Bar ou la police illuminée, 1772', in V. Milliot (ed.), *Les Mémoires policiers, 1750–1850. Écritures et pratiques policières du Siècle des Lumières au Second Empire*, Rennes: Presses universitaires de Rennes.

Philips, D. (1980) ' "A New Engine of Power and Authority": The Institutionalization of Law-Enforcement in England 1780–1830', in V. Gatrell, B. Lenman and G. Parker (eds), *Crime and the Law: The Social History of Crime in Western Europe since 1500*, London: Europa.

Philips, D. and Storch, R. D. (1999) *Policing Provincial England, 1829–56: The Politics of Reform*, London: Leicester University Press.

Piasenza, P. (1990) *Polizia e città. Strategie d'ordine, conflitti e rivolte a Parigi tra sei e settecento*, Bologna: Il Mulino.

Piasenza, P. (1993) 'Opinion publique, identité des institutions, "absolutisme". Le problème de la légalité à Paris entre le XVIIe et le XVIIIe siècle', *Revue historique*, vol. 290, pp. 97–142.

Pleck, E. and Pleck, J. (eds) (1980) *The American Man*, Englewood Cliffs, NJ: Prentice-Hall.

Prest, J. (1990) *Liberty and Locality: Parliament, Permissive Legislation, and Ratepayers' Democracies in the Nineteenth Century*, Oxford: Clarendon Press.

Prokos, A. and Padavic, I. (2002) ' "There Oughtta Be a Law against Bitches": Masculinity Lessons in Police Academy Training', *Gender, Work and Organization*, vol. 9, pp. 439–59.

Punch, M. (1985) *Conduct Unbecoming: The Social Construction of Police Deviance and Control*, London: Tavistock.

Punch, M. and Naylor, T. (1973) 'The Police – A Social Service', *New Society*, 17 May 1973.

Quétel, C. (1981) *De par le Roy. Essai sur les lettres de cachet*, Paris: Privat.

Quinton, P. and Miller, J. (2003) 'Promoting Ethical Policing: Summary Findings of Research on New Misconduct Procedures and Police Corruption', *Home Office Report*, vol. 12, no. 3.

Radzinowicz, L. (1968) *A History of the English Criminal Law and Its Administration from 1750*, vols 3 and 4, London: Stevens.

Rauch, A. (2000) *Crise de l'identité masculine 1789–1914*, Paris: Hachette.

Rauch, C. F. and Behling, O. (1984) 'Functionalism: Basis for an Alternative Approach to the Study of Leadership', in J. G. Hunt (ed.), *Leaders and Managers: International Perspectives on Managerial Behaviour and Leadership*, New York: Pergamon.

Rawlings, P. (1995) 'The View of Policing: A History', *Policing and Society*, vol. 5, pp. 129–49.

Rawlings, P. (1999) *Crime and Power: A History of Criminal Justice 1688–1998*, London: Longman.

Ray, G. W. (1995) 'Cossack to Trooper: Manliness, Police Reform, and the State', *Journal of Social History*, vol. 28, no. 3, pp. 565–86.

Reid, K. (2007) *Gender, Crime and Empire: Convicts, Settlers and the State in Early Colonial Australia*, Manchester: Manchester University Press.

Reige, A. (2005) 'Three-Dozen Knowledge-Sharing Barriers Managers Must Consider', *Journal of Knowledge Management*, vol. 9, no. 3, pp. 18–35.

Reiner, R. (1985) 'Keystone to Kojak: The Hollywood Cop', in Philip Davies and Brian Neve (eds), *Cinema, Politics, and Society in America*, paperback reprint, 2nd edn, Manchester: Manchester University Press.

Reiner, R. (1991) *Chief Constables: Bobbies, Bosses or Bureaucrats?* Oxford: Oxford University Press.

Reiner, R. (1992) *The Politics of the Police*, 2nd edn, Hemel Hempstead: Harvester Wheatsheaf (3rd edn, Oxford: Oxford University Press, 2000; 4th edn, Oxford: Oxford University Press, 2010).

Reiner, R. (1994) 'The Dialectics of Dixon: The Changing Image of the TV Cop', in M. Stephens and S. Becker (eds), *Police Force, Police Service: Care and Control in Britain*, London, Macmillan.

Reiner, R. (1998) 'Copping a Plea', in S. Holdaway and P. Rock (eds), *Thinking about Criminology*, London: UCL Press.

Reiner, R. (2003) 'Media, Crime, Law and Order', *Scottish Journal of Criminal Justice Studies*, vol. 12, pp. 5–21.

Reiner, R. and Newburn, T. (2003) *Policing and the Media*, Cullompton: Willan.

Reinke, H. (1991) ' "Armed as if for War": The State, the Military and the Professionalism of the Prussian Police in Imperial Germany', in C. Emsley and B. Weinberger (eds), *Policing Western Europe: Politics, Professionalism and Public Order 1850–1940*, London: Greenwood.

Reith, C. (1943) *British Police and the Democratic Ideal*, Oxford: Oxford University Press.

Reynolds, E. (1998) *Before the Bobbies: The Night Watch and Police Reform in Metropolitan London 1720–1830*, Basingstoke: Macmillan.

Reynolds, E. (2002) 'Sir John Fielding, Sir Charles Whitworth and the Westminster Night Watch Act, 1770–1775', in L. Knaffa (ed.), *Policing and War in Europe*, Greenwood: London.

Riall, L. (1992) 'Liberal Policy and the Control of Public Order in Western Sicily, 1860–1862', *The Historical Journal*, vol. 35, no. 2, pp. 345–68.

Riall, L. (2007) 'Eroi maschili, virilità e forme della Guerra', in A. M. Banti and P. Ginsborg (eds), *Storia d'Italia. Annali*, 22, *Il Risorgimento*, Turin: Einaudi.

Rice, C. E. (Fall 1966) 'The Negro Crime Rate: Its Causes and Cure', *Modern Age: A Quarterly Review*, pp. 343–58.

Richards, N. (2003) 'Strategic Depth', in R. Adlam and P. Villiers (eds), *Leadership in the Twenty-First Century: Philosophy, Doctrine and Developments*, Winchester: Waterside Press.

Richardson, J. (1970) *The New York Police: Colonial Times to 1901*, New York: Oxford University Press.

Rignall, J. (1992) *Realist Fiction and the Strolling Spectator*, London: Routledge.

Roberts, E. (1984) *A Woman's Place: An Oral History of Working Class Women 1890–1940*, Oxford: Basil Blackwell.

Roche, D. (1998) *France in the Enlightenment*, Cambridge, MA: Harvard University Press (first published Paris, 1993).

Rogers, A. (1997) *Secrecy and Power in the British State*, London: Pluto Press.

Rogin, M. (1987) *Ronald Reagan, the Movie and Other Episodes in Political Demonology*, Berkeley: University of California Press.

Roper, M. and Tosh, J. (eds) (1991) *Manful Assertions: Masculinities in Britain since 1800*, London: Routledge.

Rosener, J. (1990) 'Ways Women Lead', *Harvard Business Review*, November/December, pp. 119–25.

Rotundo, A. (1993) *American Manhood: Transformations in Masculinity from the Revolution to the Modern Era*, New York: Basic Books.

Rowbotham, J. (2005) 'Criminal Savages? or "Civilizing" the Legal Process', in J. Rowbotham and K. Stevenson (eds), *Criminal Conversations: Victorian Crimes, Social Panic, and Moral Outrage*, Columbus: Ohio State University Press.

Rowbotham, J. and Stevenson, K. (eds) (2003) *Behaving Badly: Social Panic and Moral Outrage – Victorian and Modern Parallels*, Aldershot: Ashgate.

Rowbotham, J. and Stevenson, K. (eds) (2005) *Criminal Conversations: Victorian Crimes, Social Panic, and Moral Outrage*, Columbus: Ohio State University Press.

Ruehlmann, W. (1974) *Saint with a Gun: The Unlawful American Private Eye*, New York: New York University Press.

Rutherford, S. (2001) 'Are You Going Home Already?: The Long Hours Culture, Women Mangers and Patriarchal Closure', *Time and Society*, vol. 10, nos 2/3, pp. 259–76.

Ryan, M. and Haslam, S. (2005) 'The Glass Cliff: Evidence that Women are Over-Represented in Precarious Leadership Positions', *British Journal of Management*, vol. 16, no. 2, pp. 81–90.

Santonicini, G. (1981) *Ordine pubblico e polizia nella crisi dello Stato pontificio (1848–1850)*, Milan: Giuffrè.

Savage, S. (2003) 'Tackling Tradition: Reform and Modernization of the British Police', *Contemporary Politics*, vol. 9, pp. 171–84.

Saxton, A. (1990) *The Rise and Fall of the White Republic: Class Politics and Mass Culture in Nineteenth-century America*, London: Verso.

Sbriccoli, M. (1985) 'Polizia (diritto intermedio)', in *Enciclopedia del Diritto*, vol. XXXIV.

Schiller, D. (1981) *Objectivity and the News: The Public and the Rise of Commercial Journalism*, Philadelphia: University of Pennsylvania Press.

Schrecker, E. (1986) *No Ivory Tower: McCarthyism and the Universities*, New York: Oxford University Press.

Schultz, D. M. (1995) *From Social Worker to Crime Fighter: Women in United States Municipal Policing*, Westport, CT: Praeger.

Searle, G. R. (1990) *The Quest for National Efficiency*, London: Ashfield Press.

Segal, L. (1990) *Slow Motion: Changing Masculinities, Changing Men*, New Brunswick, NJ: Rutgers University Press.

Shelton, P. T. (1987) *History of the New York State Police, 1917–1987*, Albany: Trooper Foundation of the State of New York.

Sherry, M. (1995) *In the Shadow of War: The United States since the 1930s*, New Haven, CT: Yale University Press.

Shlomowitz, R. (2007) 'Did the Mean Height of Australian-Born Men Decline in the Late Nineteenth Century? A Comment', *Economics and Human Biology*, vol. 5, no. 3, pp. 484–8.

Shoemaker, R. B. (1998) *Gender in English Society 1650–1850: The Emergence of Separate Spheres*, London: Longman.

Shoemaker, R. B. (2001) 'Male Honour and the Decline of Public Violence in Eighteenth-Century London', *Social History*, vol. 26, no. 2, pp. 190–208.

Shoemaker, R. B. (2002) 'The Taming of the Duel: Masculinity, Honour and Ritual Violence in London, 1660–1800', *The Historical Journal*, vol. 45, no. 3, pp. 525–45.

Shoemaker, R. B. (2009) 'Print Culture and the Creation of Public Knowledge about Crime in Eighteenth-Century London', in Paul Knepper, Jonathan Doak and Joanna Shapland (eds), *Urban Crime Prevention, Surveillance and Restorative Justice: Effects of Social Technologies*, Boca Raton, FL: CRC Press.

Shore, H. (1999) *Artful Dodgers: Youth and Crime in Early Nineteenth-Century London*, Woodbridge: Boydell Press.

Shore, H. (2003) '"Inventing" the Juvenile Delinquent in Nineteenth-Century Europe', in Barry Godfrey, Clive Emsley and Graeme Dunstall (eds), *Comparative Histories of Crime*, Cullompton: Willan.

Shpayer-Makov, H. (1990) 'The Making of a Police Labour Force', *Journal of Social History*, vol. 24, pp. 109–34.

Shpayer-Makov, H. (2002) *The Making of a Policeman: A Social History of a Labour Force in Metropolitan London, 1829–1914*, Aldershot: Ashgate.

Shpayer-Makov, H. (2004) 'Becoming a Police Detective in Victorian and Edwardian London,' *Policing and Society*, vol. 14, no. 3, pp. 250–68.

Shpayer-Makov, H. (2006) 'Explaining the Rise and Success of Detective Memoirs in Britain', in C. Emsley and H. Shpayer-Makov (eds), *Police Detectives in History, 1750–1950*, Aldershot: Ashgate.

Shpayer-Makov, H. (2009) 'Journalists and Police Detectives in Victorian and Edwardian England: An Uneasy Reciprocal Relationship', *Journal of Social History*, vol. 42, no. 4, pp. 963–87.

Shpayer-Makov, H. (2010) 'From Menace to Celebrity: The English Police Detective and the Press, c. 1842–1914', *Historical Research*, vol. 83, no. 222, pp. 672–92.

Shpayer-Makov, H. (2011) *The Ascent of the Detective: Police Sleuths in Victorian and Edwardian England*, Oxford: Oxford University Press.

Sigurdsson, J. and Dhani, A. (2010) 'Police Service Strength England and Wales', *Home Office Statistical Bulletin* 14/10, London: Home Office.

Silver, A. (1967) 'The Demand for Order in Civil Society: A Review of Some Themes in the History of Urban Crime, Police and Riot', in D. Bordua (ed.), *The Police: Six Sociological Essays*, New York: John Wiley.

Silvestri, M. (2003) *Women in Charge: Policing, Gender and Leadership*, Cullompton: Willan.

Silvestri, M. and Crowther-Dowey, C. (2008) *Gender and Crime*, London: Sage.

Sklansky, D. A. (June 2005) 'Police and Democracy', *Michigan Law Review*, vol. 103, pp. 1699–1830.

Skolnick, J. (1966) *Justice without Trial*, New York: Wiley.

Skolnick, J. H. and Bayley, D. (1986) *The New Blue Line: Police Innovation in Six American Cities*, New York: Free Press.

Slotkin, R. (1985) *The Fatal Environment: The Myth of the Frontier in the Age of Industrialization, 1880–1890*, New York: Athenaeum.

Smith, D. J. and Gray, J. (1983) 'The Police in Action', in *Police and People in London*, vol. 4, London: Policy Studies Institute.

Steedman, C. (1984) *Policing the Victorian Community: The Formation of English Provincial Police Forces, 1856–80*, London: Routledge.

Steinberg, A. (1989) *The Transformation of Criminal Justice: Philadelphia, 1800–1880*, Chapel Hill: University of North Carolina Press.

Stevens, J. (1991) *Sensationalism and the New York Press*, New York: Columbia University Press.

Storch, R. D. (1975) ' "The Plague of Blue Locusts": Police Reform and Popular Resistance in Northern England, 1840–57', *International Review of Social History*, vol. XX, pp. 61–90.

Storch, R. D. (1975–6) 'The Policeman as Domestic Missionary: Urban Discipline and Popular Culture in Northern England, 1850–1880', *Journal of Social History*, vol. 9, pp. 481–509.

Storch, R. D. (1989) 'Policing Rural Southern England before the Police: Opinion and Practice, 1830–56', in D. Hay and F. Snyder (eds), *Policing and Prosecution in Britain, 1750–1850*, Oxford: Clarendon Press.

'Struggle for Justice: A Report on Crime and Punishment in America, prepared for the American Friends Service Committee', New York: Hill & Wang, 1971.

Styles, J. (1987) 'The Emergence of Police: Explaining Police Reform in Eighteenth-Century and Nineteenth-Century England', *British Journal of Criminology*, vol. 27, no. 1, pp. 18–21.

Takaki, R. T. (1979) *Iron Cages: Race and Culture in Nineteenth-Century America*, New York: Alfred A. Knopf.

Taylor, D. (1991) 'The Standard of Living of Career Policemen in Victorian England: The Evidence of a Provincial Borough Force', *Criminal Justice History*, vol. 12, pp. 107–31.

Taylor, D. (1997) *The New Police in Nineteenth-Century England: Crime, Conflict and Control*, Manchester: Manchester University Press.

Taylor, D. (2002) *Policing the Victorian Town: The Development of the Police in Middlesbrough, c. 1840–1914*, Basingstoke: Palgrave Macmillan.

Taylor, D. (2005) 'Beyond the Bounds of Respectable Society: The "Dangerous Classes" in Victorian and Edwardian England', in Judith Rowbotham and Kim Stevenson (eds), *Criminal Conversations: Victorian Crimes, Social Panic, and Moral Outrage*, Columbus: Ohio State University Press.

Taylor, D. (2010) *Hooligans, Harlots, and Hangmen: Crime and Punishment in Victorian Britain*, Santa Barbara, CA: Praeger.

Taylor, H. (1998) 'The Politics of the Rising Crime Statistics of England and Wales, 1914–1960', *Crime, Histoire & Sociétés/Crime, History & Societies*, vol. 2, no. 1, pp. 5–28.

Teevan, G. J., Major, Chief Constable (comp.) (1894) *Town of Hove Constable's Hand-Book*, Hove: H. Emery.

Thompson, H. A. (2010) 'Why Mass Incarceration Matters: Rethinking Crisis, Decline, and Transformation in Postwar American History', *Journal of American History*, vol. 97, no. 3, pp. 703–34.

Tilley, N. (2003) 'Community Policing, Problem-Orientated Policing and Intelligence-Led Policing', in Tim Newburn (ed.), *Handbook of Policing*, Cullompton: Willan.

Toch, H. (1976) *Peacekeeping, Police, Prison and Violence*, Lexington, MA: Lexington Books.

Tolbert, E. J. (1987) 'Federal Surveillance of Marcus Garvey and the U.N.I.A.', *Journal of Ethnic Studies*, vol. 14, no. 4, pp. 25–46.

Tomes, N. (1978) 'A "Torrent of Abuse": Crimes of Violence between Working Class Men and Women in London, 1840–1875', *Journal of Social History*, vol. 11, no. 3, pp. 328–45.

Tosatti, G. (1997) 'La repressione del dissenso politico tra l'età liberale e il fascismo. L'organizzazione della polizia', *Studi Storici*, vol. 1, pp. 217–55.

Tosh, J. (1999) *A Man's Place: Masculinity and the Middle-Class Home in Victorian England*, New Haven, CT: Yale University Press.

Tosh, J. (2002) 'Gentlemanly Politeness and Manly Simplicity in Victorian England', *Transactions of the Royal Historical Society*, vol. 12, pp. 455–72.

Tosh, J. (2004) 'Hegemonic Masculinity and the History of Gender', in S. Dudink, K. Hagemann and J. Tosh (eds), *Masculinities in Politics and War: Gendering Modern History*, Manchester: Manchester University Press.

Tosh, J. (2005a) 'Masculinities in an Industrializing Society: Britain, 1800–1914', *Journal of British Studies*, vol. 44, no. 2, pp. 33–42.

Tosh, J. (2005b) *Manliness and Masculinities in Nineteenth-Century Britain*, Harlow: Pearson Education.

Travers, M. (2010) *Understanding Law and Society*, New York, Routledge.

Vance, N. (1985) *The Sinews of the Spirit*, Cambridge: Cambridge University Press.

Vickers, M. and Kouzmin, A. (2001) 'New Managerialism and Australian Police Organizations', *International Journal of Public Sector Management*, vol. 14, no. 1, pp. 7–26.

Vila, A. C. (2007) 'Elite Masculinities in Eighteenth-Century France', in C. E. Forth and B. Taithe (eds), *French Masculinities: History, Culture and Politics*, Basingstoke: Palgrave Macmillan.

Villiers, P. (2003) 'Philosophy, Doctrine and Leadership', in R. Adlam and P. Villiers (eds), *Leadership in the Twenty-First Century: Philosophy, Doctrine and Developments*, Winchester: Waterside Press.

Vincent, D. (1998) *The Culture of Secrecy*, Oxford: Oxford University Press.

Waddington, P. A. J. (1999a) 'Police (Canteen) Sub-Culture – An Appreciation', *British Journal of Criminology*, vol. 39, no. 2, pp. 287–309.

Waddington, P. A. J. (1999b) *Policing Citizens*, London: UCL Press.

Waldrep, C. (2008) 'National Policing, Lynching, and Constitutional Change', *Journal of Southern History*, vol. 74, no. 3, pp. 589–626.

Walklate, S. (2004) *Gender, Crime, and Criminal Justice*, Cullompton: Willan.

Walkowitz, J. R. (1992) *City of Dreadful Delight: Narratives of Sexual Danger in Late Victorian London*, Chicago: University of Chicago Press.

Wall, D. S. (1998) *The Chief Constables of England and Wales: The Socio-Legal History of a Criminal Justice Elite*, Aldershot: Dartmouth and Ashgate.

Wallace, A. (2005) *Newspapers and the Making of Modern America: A History*, Westport, CT: Greenwood Press.

Wardman, R. C. and Allison, T. (2004) *To Protect and Serve: A History of Police in America*, Englewood Cliffs, NJ: Prentice Hall.

Watson, D. (2005) *Race and the Houston Police Department, 1930–1990: A Change did Come*, Texas: Texas and A&M University Press

Weaver, V. (2007) 'Frontlash: Race and the Development of Punitive Crime Policy', *Studies in American Political Development*, vol. 21, no. 1, pp. 230–65.

Weber, M. (1964) *The Theory of Social and Economic Organisation*, edited and introduced by Talcott Parsons, London: Collier-Macmillan.

Weinberger, B. (1991a) 'Are the Police Professionals? An Historical Account of the British Police Institution', in C. Emsley and B. Weinberger (eds), *Policing Western Europe: Politics, Professionalism and Public Order 1850–1940*, London: Greenwood.

Weinberger, B. (1995) *The Best Police in the World: An Oral History of English Policing*, Aldershot: Scolar Press.

Weinberger, B. (1999) 'A Policewife's Life Is Not a Happy One: Police Wives in the 1930s and 1940s', *Oral History*, vol. 21, pp. 46–53.

Wells, S. K. and Alt, B. L. (1995) *Police Women: Life with the Badge*, Westport, CT: Praeger.

Wesser, R. F. (1986) *A Response to Progressivism: The Democratic Party and New York Politics, 1902–1918*, New York: New York University Press.

Western, J. R. (1965) *The English Militia in the Eighteenth Century: The Story of a Political Issue, 1660–1802*, London: Routledge.

Westmarland, L. (1999) 'Women Managing in the Police', *Police Research and Management*, vol. 3, no. 3, pp. 62–79.

Westmarland, L. (2002) *Gender and Policing: Sex, Power and Police Culture*, Cullompton: Willan.

White, H. (1978) *Tropics of Discourse: Essays in Cultural Criticism*, Baltimore: Johns Hopkins University Press.

White, H. (1987) *The Content of the Form: Narrative Discourse and Historical Representation*, Baltimore: Johns Hopkins University Press.

White, J. (1995) 'Leading in Their Own Ways: Women Chief Executives in Local Government', in C. Itzen and J. Newman (eds), *Gender, Culture and Organisational Change*, London: Routledge.

Whitewall, G., Nicholas, S. and de Souza, C. (1997) 'Height, Health and Economic Growth in Australia, 1860–1940', in R. Steckel and R. Floud (eds), *Health and Welfare During Industrialization*, Chicago: National Bureau of Economic Research.

Wicker, T. (1995) *A Time to Die*, New York: Quadrangle/New York Times Books.

Wiener, J. H. (1969) *The War of the Unstamped: The Movement to Repeal the British Newspaper Tax, 1830–1836*, Ithaca, NY: Cornell University Press.

Wiener, M. J. (1990) *Reconstructing the Criminal: Culture, Law, and Policy in England, 1830–1914*, Cambridge: Cambridge University Press.

Wiener, M. J. (1998) 'The Victorian Criminalization of Men', in P. Spierenburg (ed.), *Men and Violence: Gender, Honor and Rituals in Modern Europe and America*, Columbus: Ohio State University Press.

Wiener, M. J. (2004) *Men of Blood: Violence, Manliness, and Criminal Justice in Victorian England*, Cambridge: Cambridge University Press.

Wiener, M. J. (2007) 'Convicted Murderers and the Victorian Press: Condemnation vs. Sympathy', *Crimes and Misdemeanours*, vol. 1, no. 2, pp. 110–25.

Wiesner, E. (1991) '*Wandervogels* and Women: Journeymen's Concepts of Masculinity on Early Modern Germany', *Journal of Social History*, vol. 24, no. 4, pp. 767–82.

Williams, A. (1979) *The Police of Paris, 1718–1789*, Baton Rouge: Louisiana State University Press.

Williams, C. A. (2000) 'Counting Crimes or Counting People: Some Implications of Mid-Nineteenth-Century British Police Returns', *Crime, Histoire & Sociétés/Crime, History & Societies*, vol. 4, no. 2, pp. 77–93.

Williams, H. and Murphy, P. V. (1990) 'The Evolving Strategy of Policing: A Minority View', *Perspectives on Policing*, vol. 13, pp. 1–16.

Williams, P. and Dickinson, J. (1993) 'The Relationship between Newspaper Crime Reporting and Crime', *British Journal of Criminology*, vol. 33, pp. 33–56.

Williams O'Brien, G. (1999) *The Color of the Law: Race, Violence, and Justice in the Post-World War II South*, Chapel Hill: University of North Carolina Press.

Wilson, D. (2005) 'Traces and Transmissions: Techno-Scientific Symbolism in Early Twentieth-Century Policing', in B. Godfrey and G. Dunstall (eds), *Crime and Empire 1840–1940: Criminal Justice in Local and Global Context*, Cullompton: Willan.

Wilson, D. (2006) *The Beat: Policing a Victorian City*, Melbourne: Circa Press.

Wilson, D. and Finnane, M. (2006) 'From Sleuths to Technicians? Changing Images of the Detective in Victoria', in Clive Emsley and Haia Shpayer-Makov (eds), *Police Detectives in History, 1750–1950*, Aldershot: Ashgate.

Wilson, K. (1995) *The Sense of the People: Politics, Culture and Imperialism in England, 1715–1785*, Cambridge: Cambridge University Press.

Wood, J. C. (2004) *Violence and Crime in Nineteenth-Century England: The Shadow of Our Refinement*, London: Routledge.

Woollacott, A. (1994) *On Her Their Lives Depend: Munitions Workers in the Great War*, Berkeley: University of California Press.

Young, M. (1991) *An Inside Job: Policing and Police Culture in Britain*, Oxford: Clarendon Press.

INDEX